THE FENIAN CHIEF

The Fenian Chief

A biography of James Stephens

DESMOND RYAN

With an introductory memoir by
Patrick Lynch

UNIVERSITY OF MIAMI PRESS
Coral Gables, Florida

ACKNOWLEDGMENTS

THE writer wishes to express his thanks to the Deputy Keeper, Public Records Office, Northern Ireland, for permission to quote from James Stephens's American Diary; to Mr T. P. O'Neill, and the Staff of the National Library for valuable help and advice; to the Trustees of the National Library of Ireland for permission to use and quote from the Stephens Papers there. He is also indebted to Mr William O'Brien, Dublin, Mr Brian O'Higgins, Dublin, and to Brother W. J. Allen, the O'Connell Schools, Richmond Street, Dublin, for the loan and use of rare books and documents, and to Messrs Walter McGrath and James Hurley, Cork, for detailed and first-hand accounts of the Fenian movement in the South based on their own research into original sources. In Kilkenny City, Mrs Margaret Phelan, Secretary of the Kilkenny Archaeological Society, Miss May Sparkes, Father Clohessy, St Kieran's College, Father Murphy, St Mary's Cathedral, were especially helpful and encouraging in the search for records of Stephens's early life and associations there.   D.R.

While the work was being prepared for the press those charged with its revisal were the recipients of kind assistance from a number of persons and institutions. The National Library of Ireland was once more invariably ready with its assistance; we would particularly like to mention Mr Patrick Henchy, the Director, and Mr Alf Mac Lochlainn, Keeper of Printed Books. Mention should also be made of the courtesy shown by the officials of the British Museum Reading Room, and of the King's College Library, University of Aberdeen. The editor's task was made easier through the loan of some critical volumes by Professor R. Dudley Edwards. The completion of the biographical notes was only made possible by the assistance of the editor's friend, Captain Basil Peterson, to whom we should all like to express our gratitude; a critical footnote was also supplied through his researches. The editor was also aided by source-material and comment thereon provided by Mr Aindreas Ó Gallchoir, of Telefís Éireann; and his debt to Mrs Ann Gordon, Secretary to the History Department of the University of Aberdeen, is very great for many reasons. Mrs Mary MacErlean, sister of the editor, was of major assistance both in the correction of proofs and in the onerous task of preparing the index.   O.D.E.

EDITORIAL NOTE

DESMOND Ryan left the present work in a completed and revised state at the time of his death, but further work on the text was necessitated by two factors. It was characteristic of his generosity of spirit that the author assumed a far wider acquaintance with the facts of Irish history on the part of his readers than is likely to be the case, and therefore for the convenience of persons not fully conversant with the background to Stephens's life, a selection of biographical notes has been prepared to follow the main text. The principal characters who appear in this volume are accounted for in the notes, with the exceptions of those too well known to require description (such as Gladstone), those whose *curricula vitae*, so far as they are known, have received full treatment in the text (such as Stephens himself, Jane Stephens, or, on a lower level, 'Pagan' O'Leary), and those too obscure to identify in a note of any value or too peripheral to justify inclusion. Where possible, descriptions have been taken bodily from Desmond Ryan's writings, and any elegance or distinction of style or comment may safely be attributed to him. In addition, occasional notes have been added to the author's to illustrate points which might be obscure to the general reader: such footnotes are clearly distinguished from Desmond Ryan's by being printed in square brackets and followed in all cases by the initials 'O.D.E.'

The other editorial alteration called for arose from the natural revisions which would normally be made by the author in the process of seeing his volume through the press. Citations were clarified, and standardized, occasional sentences were split in the interest of clarity, typographical errors were remedied, and so forth. The letter from Hollywood to Smith O'Brien seemed worthy of inclusion in slightly greater detail: as Desmond Ryan had been the first person to perceive the significance of Hollywood, it was felt that this decision would have met with his approval. The introductory chapter was in need of some revision, and it was therefore recast by Mr Patrick Lynch. The remainder of the text, and the notes, were dealt with by Mr Owen Dudley Edwards, and the final responsibility for editorial decisions taken rests with Mr Dudley Edwards; the proofs have been passed by Mrs Sarah Ryan and Mr Lynch. A cross-check was made on printed quotations which served largely to confirm the author's reliability; most manuscript sources have not been checked, but there seems little reason to doubt their accuracy.

O.D.E.

BIBLIOGRAPHY AND SOURCES

THE main sources have been indicated in the footnotes, in particular the Stephens Papers (N.L.I. MS nos. 10491, 10492) and the American Diary (P.R.O., Northern Ireland). The files of the *Irishman*, Dublin; the Luby Papers, the Larcom Papers on Fenianism and other manuscript material, National Library of Ireland; the Fenian documents quoted in the text from the appendices to Joseph Denieffe's *Recollections of the Irish Revolutionary Brotherhood* (hereinafter cited as 'Denieffe'); the wealth of first-hand material in the two volumes of *Devoy's Post Bag*, edited by William O'Brien and the writer; the invaluable letters and documents from the O'Mahony Papers given in Father William D'Arcy's *The Fenian Movement in the United States, 1858–1886* (hereinafter cited as 'D'Arcy'); O'Donovan Rossa's *Recollections* and his *Prison Life*; and the contemporary British official reports of the Fenian trials.

The reader who desires a general sketch of Fenianism and its leaders will find the following useful, apart from those mentioned above, and in the text and footnotes:

New Ireland, by A. M. Sullivan, 1877.

Recollections of an Irish National Journalist, Richard Pigott (London, 1882). This book was described by John O'Leary as one of the best histories of Fenianism.

The Phoenix Flame. A Study of Fenianism and John Devoy, by Desmond Ryan. (London, 1937).

Recollections of an Irish Rebel, by John Devoy (New York, 1929) (hereinafter cited as 'Devoy').

The Secret History of the Fenian Conspiracy, by John Rutherford (London 1877) (hereinafter cited as 'Rutherford').

The Irish in Britain, by John Denvir (London, 1892). Chapters XXIII–XXVII.

A History of Ireland Under the Union, P. S. O'Hegarty (London, 1952). Chapters XXXII–XXXVIII.

The Fenian Movement, by F. L. Crilly (London, 1908–9).

Wolfe Tone Annual, 1958, *What was the I.R.B.? Who Were the Fenians?* Brian O'Higgins (Dublin).

Fenian Memories, by Dr Mark Ryan (Dublin, 1945).

There is a very full bibliography on many aspects of the Fenian movement in *The Fenian Movement in the United States* above mentioned. Many bibliographical and biographical notes are given in the two volumes of *Devoy's Post Bag* (Dublin, 1948–53) (hereinafter cited by title only).—D.R.

Since the author's death, two most valuable scholarly works have appeared, the first illuminating Young Ireland and the background to the 1948 insurrection, the latter transforming our knowledge of Fenianism in the U.S.A. in the period after Stephens's fall. These are:

Kevin B. Nowlan, *The Politics of Repeal* (London, 1965).

Thomas N. Brown, *Irish-American Nationalism 1870–1890* (Philadelphia, 1966).

To the other works of major value on Fenianism may be added John O'Leary, *Recollections of Fenians and Fenianism* (London, 1896), hereinafter cited as 'O'Leary'.—O.D.E.

Introduction

by PATRICK LYNCH

DESMOND RYAN was born on 27 August 1893 in Dulwich, London, where he was educated by the Christian Brothers. He came to Ireland in 1906 when his father, William P. Ryan, was made editor of *The Irish Peasant*, a provincial paper which, under his direction, became a brilliant instrument of Irish-Ireland propaganda. According to Piaras Beaslai, it was eagerly read by Gaelic Leaguers in every part of Ireland and not even *An Claidheamh Soluis*, the official Gaelic League journal, edited by Patrick Pearse, could compete with it in popularity. When it was condemned by Cardinal Logue, the family moved from Navan to Dublin, where publication was temporarily resumed with William P. Ryan as proprietor as well as editor. The immediate issue on which the Church and the *Peasant* clashed was the proposal that clerical school managers should be assisted by committees of lay parishioners.

There is little doubt that William P. Ryan had a formative part in his son's life as had his uncle, Thomas Boyd, and the writer, Pádraic Ó Conaire, who was a close friend of the family. It was his father, however, who first aroused the boy's enthusiasm for the Irish language and stirred his youthful imagination by his own personal battles to create a national consciousness. It was his library that first introduced Desmond to other literatures and to new and challenging speculations. In a diary, written in 1917, he was to say about his father:

'I stood by my father when he fought for intellectual freedom in Ireland, sacrificing his worldly advancement, fighting with his telling qualities of moral courage and pride in work against travesties of religion and patriotism, holding up moral courage and an admiration for all the parties who work for Ireland's good, championing relentlessly unpopular causes. I have to smile quietly to myself at certain critics of his. He is in exile, but he has peace of mind and has done enduring work. He may not know, but his memory has often upheld me. In Richmond Barracks [after the surrender of Easter Week] a prisoner handed me a piece of cheese "seo duit a mhic Liam P. Ui Riain" he said. The incident lingered in my mind later as I was being marched off between two rows of soldiers. "Ah", I murmured, "like Pa! I can't be too bad. They had to throw me out".'

In 1908 Patrick Pearse opened St Enda's School and Desmond Ryan was one of his first pupils. Here, to quote his own words, he 'went mad' about the Irish language and Irish studies. His fellow pupils in St Enda's were remarkable and varied; they were of all ages and included many whose parents had been prominently and, often, controversially associated with the revival of the Irish language. Of the teachers, Pearse, as headmaster, was, of course, the dominant and decisive influence, though Denis Gwynn recalls that Thomas MacDonagh left an impression on the boys of being able to handle really difficult situations with a lighter, more amusing and more flexible approach.

Desmond Ryan finished his formal education in University College, Dublin, and graduated in the National University in Autumn 1916. In 1913 during the great lock-out in Dublin he had written in support of the workers in James Larkin's paper. He had also been teaching in St Enda's and acting as secretary to Pearse. He had fought in the General Post Office during the Easter Rising. It is doubtful if any colleague was more closely acquainted with Pearse; certainly none was better equipped to become Pearse's interpreter for posterity.

After the surrender in Easter Week he was interned in succession in Stafford Jail, Wormwood Scrubs and Frongoch for three months for his part in the Rising. When released, he sat for his degree examinations in University College, Dublin, and became a reporter on the *Freeman's Journal*. As an admirer of Michael Collins, one of Collins's few socialist admirers, he had supported the Treaty. Disillusioned, however, by the Civil War and reacting against the anti-de Valera policies of the *Freeman*, he returned to London where he spent the next seventeen years reflecting, reading and writing. All his life he was a student and retained the methods of the student. The width of his reading was immense, and he read with diligence and care, usually making notes and cross references. His memory for what he had read always remained clear and accurate. He was thorough and indefatigable in his research and slow and unhurried in his writing. His works range from autobiography and biography to history.

In the years immediately after the Rising he had written of Pearse and St Enda's under the tremendous emotional impact of all that had gone before. Then followed his first book on Connolly, published in 1924 after he had returned to England. He was just thirty years of age and his growing absorption in Connolly's writings and in their significance for oppressed peoples everywhere began to direct his vision towards wider horizons. But only gradually did this new movement express itself in his writing; his next five books still dealt with various aspects of Irish nationalism—*The Invisible Army*, *Remembering Sion*, *Unique Dictator*, *The Phoenix Flame* and *The Sword of Light*. When he finally came home to Ireland in 1939 he began the most fruitful and mature phase of his life's work. First, there was his splendid edition of James Connolly's *Collected Works* in three volumes, and then, with William O'Brien, the great edition of [*John*] *Devoy's Post Bag* in two volumes, a unique contribution to the history of Fenianism.

A *tour de force* was *The Rising*, which is probably the best book written on 1916. Here he assembled all the facts and, as the greatest surviving authority among those who had been closely acquainted with Pearse's life and death, he was in a unique position to write this enduring and dramatic chapter of Irish history. Nowhere else does he better display his concern for truth and his acute sense of history. Indeed, this may be regarded as a book for which his whole life since 1916 had been a preparation; it represents his scholarship at its ripest and the maturity of his judgement on people and events which he knew from personal experience or about which he had read more than any other contemporary historian.

The particular quality of Desmond Ryan's best work, vividly reflected in *The Rising*, owes much to the leisurely conditions in which he was able to do it. After his marriage in August 1933 to Sarah Hartley, a Yorkshire girl, he and she shared a loving companionship in their domestic life which created the necessary setting for a writer of Desmond Ryan's temperament and interests. They lived quietly. With her he was able to support those prolonged researches into nineteenth-century Irish studies, which mean so much to those who love Ireland's past, but which, until recently, appealed to only the most adventurous publishers. He was a most generous man, particularly of his time as students and researchers from all parts of the world have such reason to know. It was his wife who protected him from the more unreasonable demands that friends and visiting scholars alike were so often tempted to make on one who gave so freely and who so liked to give.

It was my good fortune to have enjoyed Desmond Ryan's friendship during the last twenty-five years of his life. I first met him during the winter of 1940 when he accepted an invitation to speak at a meeting of a cultural organization called An Craobh Ruadh founded by Dr Roger McHugh and the late Dr Patrick McCartan, and of which I had been Honorary Secretary. Desmond Ryan had returned to Ireland in 1939 and was editing *The Torch* in Dublin. At the meeting he read a paper on the Irish cultural heritage. The text does not survive, but I recall that he championed the cause of Irish neutrality in the Second World War by asserting the distinctive contribution that Ireland could make to civilization as a repository of the European cultural values which found intellectual expression in the Irish Republican tradition.

Much of what Desmond Ryan wrote treated some aspect of this theme. He was a citizen of the world who loved Ireland. He had no doubt of Ireland's debt to other countries, other civilizations and other cultures; he believed that an intelligent and exalted Irish patriotism could assimilate these influences and nourish itself on them. He had a deep love of all Irish studies and of the Irish language in particular, but he was critical of exaggerated attitudes and positions in support of any cause. He looked on life with a certain ironic scepticism which made him slow to pass final judgements. With his unsurpassed knowledge of nineteenth-century Irish secret societies and conspiracies, he knew the mistakes that the leading figures in these movements had often made in judging one another. All this had taught him how prone people can be in extreme situations to reach conclusions from insufficient evidence about motives and actions.

If one force more than another played the determining part in shaping his character it was the Fenian tradition; and it is entirely appropriate that his last book should be a biography of a great Fenian, James Stephens. His father and Pearse were in different ways products of that tradition. He was to be the first historian to establish the individual characteristics of the Fenian leaders, to show them as human beings rather than as legendary figures of fantasy. His candour and honesty spared neither people nor causes. He was gentle in manner but always was strong-willed. His mind was an open, fair and questioning one. He was unreceptive to all dogma, but inflexible in defending his own convictions. He displayed an absolute concern for truth, irrespective of the consequences. He was the very model of an honest man, always prepared to revise his opinions and change positions if new evidence warranted it. He could see merit, if it existed, in things he disliked, and I have never known anyone more disposed to seeing the good qualities in those whom he criticized, while still retaining his right to criticize them. I do not think he ever wholly disliked a single person as an individual; but there were many whose statements, opinions or actions he censured. Humbug and hypocrisy, above all, he detested.

Desmond Ryan, more than anyone else, was responsible for the acceptance by posterity of Pearse as the leader of the 1916 Rising. This he had sought to do from the publication of his book *The Man Called Pearse*, written in 1919 to *The Rising* in which, in 1948, he attributes Pearse's ascendency mainly to his oratorical skill, to his 'mastery of language, his sincerity, his personality, his fire' as the prophet of ultimate revolution. It was a remarkably successful transfiguration. In July 1914 Pearse had had no knowledge of the preparation for the Howth gun-running; two years later he was the undisputed leader of a secret movement and the recognized architect of the revolution, the starting of which had been one of his principal ambitions.

Desmond Ryan had the satisfaction of living to see Pearse's place established as the leader of the Rising. An extraordinarily close relationship undoubtedly existed between the two men, and Pearse's influence on Ryan was unmistakably great. He never found fault with Pearse, but I can remember him often sweeping aside some piece of uncritical adulation of Pearse by a reference to his own words, written in 1919, in *The Man Called Pearse*—'Pearse never was a legend, he was a man'. Ryan did not like the uncritical worship of Pearse and the idealization of war or revolution that was sometimes linked with it. He particularly resented well-meaning admirers of himself who, consciously or otherwise, would deprive him of his personal identity by sentimentally associating him with their own private impressions of Pearse.

His friends often regretted that he had never written a full biography of Pearse. He would agree that Le Roux's book, which he had translated, was in many respects inadequate and inaccurate. Piaras Beaslai, Cathal O'Shannon and others were sorry that in translating it he had associated himself with the allegation of the kidnapping of James Connolly by the Irish Volunteers in January 1916, a story which they believed to be absurd. His own account of Connolly's disappearance in *The Rising* is factual, and in his characteristic way he reaches no conclusion, though he does retain the chapter-heading 'The Kidnapping of Connolly'. Whenever I asked him why he had not done a complete biography of Pearse, he would reply with more firmness than sharpness 'I have said all I want to say about Pearse'.

An aspect of Pearse of which he often spoke was his sense of humour—a quality which he regretted had become submerged under an excess of ponderous piety about the man. In the summer of 1915 he and Pearse had been on a cycling holiday in Connemara. They visited the Leenane Hotel whose loyal owner was very proud of the honoured part the hotel had played in the royal visit of 1903. Desmond used to recall the glint in Pearse's eye as he admired in the hallway the framed pictures from the *Illustrated London News* of 1903 of the visit of King Edward VII and Queen Alexandra to Leenane in that year. According to Desmond, the picture, (which is still there) that amused Pearse most was a reproduction of His Majesty's carriage being hauled by willing hands from the jetty where the royal party had disembarked to the hotel. The caption of the picture described the 'Connemara cavalry' welcoming their King. This insisting on human qualities and on the ironies of history, was to become a recurring note in what Desmond Ryan wrote about the leading figures of Irish nationalism. It was not that his approach was anti-heroic; rather was it to resist the tendency to apologize for patriots if anything in their lives seemed to make them more human or less perfect for the heroic mould in which false sentiment insisted on placing them.

I can only speculate as to why Desmond Ryan refrained from writing the full biography of Pearse for which he was so well equipped. His personal attachment to the man may have prevented his applying to him biographical methods which might have revealed much that he would have regarded as irrelevant to the short and glorious story of the man who became the leader of the Rising. It was one thing to strip the Pearse legend of fable; but, for Desmond Ryan, Pearse had earned his unique place in history not because he was a poet or friend or a schoolmaster. He had achieved his apotheosis in Easter 1916; and that was all that mattered. That, perhaps, is why Desmond Ryan had said all that he wanted to say about Pearse. Yet, on reflection, I am not so sure. He was too good a historian to regard any part of a man's life as irrelevant to its main purpose. He was too intelligent to accept the facile view that a man should be remembered merely because historical necessity had selected him to play a decisive and indispensable role.

I have no doubt whatever that Desmond Ryan's association with Pearse and his part in the Easter Rising strongly influenced his subsequent attitudes. In Easter Week 'he endured', wrote his friend Francis MacManus, 'a vital epiphany, and anything he would say or do afterwards would be under its potent influence. He could not write except under the power of this revelation'. I believe, however, that, as the years passed, Ryan found himself increasingly in sympathy with James Connolly and engrossed by what he regarded as the perennial relevance

2

of Connolly's intellectual legacy to contemporary Ireland and, above all, to the world at large.

The Desmond Ryan that I knew was at once a patriot, a socialist and an internationalist. He disliked narrow nationalism, especially the familiar Irish varieties, as much as he did colonialism or imperialism. His enthusiasm for mere nationalism had been chilled by the Civil War. It is more directly within our own power, he used to say, to correct the excesses of nationalism. His socialism, like his nationalism, was undogmatic. He had read more widely than anyone I had known the writings of Marxism, Syndicalism and reform Socialism. His socialism derived largely, but not exclusively, from Connolly and, like Connolly, he was impatient of those who insisted that to be a socialist implied the acceptance of quite unrelated attitudes or practices as well. There may be a good case for atheism or free love, he would say, but one does not necessarily have to profess the one or practise the other because one was a socialist. The solemnities of much socialist sermonizing he used to pillory. He found useful correctives to such pomposity in the vision of Engels riding to the foxhunt or Hyndman in top hat at Hyde Park Corner urging the revolution of the proletariat. It is little wonder then that he was so fascinated by the personality and character of Michael Bakunin and I believe that he rather rejoiced that the great anarchist had been there to torment the also great Marx. His wonderful sense of comedy was aroused by the bourgeois virtues of Marx's wife, whom he greatly admired, and of her stern disapproval of the relationship between her husband's colleague Engels and Mary Burns, the Manchester mill-girl and Irish Fenian.

I have said that Desmond Ryan was a citizen of the world. In this he was in the tradition of Tom Paine and Wolfe Tone. Like them, his internationalism was not doctrinaire. He hated racialism in all its forms and would quote Edmund Burke on the folly of indicting an entire state or people. There are always dissenters, he would say, and they win in the end if their cause is good enough. I remember his recollection of the Irish-American father seeking to have his son enrolled in St Enda's: 'What do you teach them?' he asked, and Pearse replied by quoting the motto of the Fianna—purity in our hearts, truth on our lips and strength in our arms. 'I know, I know' said Pearse's impatient American visitor, 'but do you teach them to hate England?' In reply, Pearse gently spoke of the glories of English literature and explained that a purpose of education was to teach people how to understand and love, not to hate. The boy became a pupil at St Enda's. He made bombs with Desmond Ryan in the cellars before Easter Week and took part in the Rising.

No one so concerned, as Desmond Ryan was, with the central significance of truth in human relations could have ignored ultimate values and religious beliefs, yet one finds little evidence of any such preoccupation in his work. I had very many discussions with him about religions and religious convictions, yet it has surprised some of his readers that he had largely ignored religion in his accounts of people who must have been significantly influenced by it. This may seem a remarkable omission, particularly in Ryan's study of the Fenian, James Stephens; it would seem difficult to discuss Fenianism without considering the part played by the Catholic Church. There is a general awareness, of course, of the relations between Fenianism and the Church, but no effort is made to examine the religious and moral conflicts involved. Nor does Ryan consider the influence of Fenianism on many contemporary Catholics and on their descendants. Fenianism may now be a matter of history, but there may be young Irish men and women whose religious attitudes and, perhaps, beliefs—apart entirely from their practice—owe more to the atavistic traditions of Fenianism than to their own informed judgements.

In the Wolfe Tone tradition, he felt more deeply about the common name of Irishman than of a man's specific religious beliefs. He was, I know, acutely critical of very many aspects of institutional and pre-Johannine Catholicism. Yet, one felt that it was more in sorrow than anger that he reviewed political Catholicism in Ireland from Young Ireland to our own day. I remember his interest when I told him that my father had come from Templederry, Co. Tipperary, the parish in which the politically radical Father Kenyon, the friend of the Young Irelanders, had served. Ryan greatly admired Father Kenyon. He regretted the tendency of religious, while professing eternal verities, to identify themselves with social or economic systems, which he regarded as transient. He resented the sweeping condemnation of Marxist Communism by churchmen who failed to see, as he believed, that, economically, the Marxist vision was probably nearer that of Christ than was that of the capitalist system, with its exaggerated emphasis on the profit motive as the determining urge of economic action and the bourgeois society in which he saw merit judged by material achievement. It was a matter of great satisfaction and pleasure for him that his cousin, Reverend Dr John A. Ryan, Professor of Political Economy in the Catholic University of Washington, should have been one of the first Catholic intellectuals to support President Roosevelt's New Deal and also to have been, almost a half-century before Pope John, author of a study *The Church and Interest-Taking* in which he made a sympathetic effort to relate the views of the Catholic Church to those of Karl Marx on the nature of money and capital. I have no doubt that his cousin influenced his views on churchmen and social issues.

Although out of sympathy with institutionalism and conformity he would never make a fuss about his personal position. He was too courteous in manner, too delicate in feeling to strike attitudes which might unnecessarily offend. But when occasion called for it he could be firm and uncompromising. Usually, however, his blend of gentleness and conviction made any explicit assertion of individuality unnecessary.

He was, I think, an unusually happy man with fundamentally a sombre, even pessimistic vision of human existence. When others complained of the ups and downs of life he accepted them as part of his philosophy; he once told me that he enjoyed listening to the complaints of cranks because it helped to settle his own peace of mind.

In the years 1943 to 1956 he and his wife lived near Swords, Co. Dublin, where they ran a poultry farm of five-and-a-half acres. These were unusually happy days. He was in the full vigour of his health and from boyhood he had always liked the country. He got much satisfaction defending his seventy apple trees from the local boys. He was busy at this time on the vast enterprise of the Devoy correspondence, and this brought him into Dublin to the National Library at least once a week and to indulge his favourite recreation—bookshop prowling.

He had very many friends, but he was not a gregarious man. He would talk for hours in a teashop or in the seclusion of his own home, usually very late at night, of the people he had known and the books he had read. His conversation was witty, amusing and learned; he was an excellent mimic; he could illustrate a point by immediately reaching for the appropriate book among the thousands on his shelves. The least informed of his listeners was accorded the same sympathetic attention as the most learned. He made a lasting impression on the student, especially the research student, by the extent of his knowledge, by the rigour and discipline of his own research methodology, and by his appreciation of technical perfection in the work of other historians.

Desmond Ryan most effectively expressed the essential features of his own character and personality in his response to challenges, which were sometimes of his own creation and sometimes not. He reacted against what he regarded as political Catholicism, middle-class prejudices, uncritical worship of Pearse and sentimental nationalism. Yet, being such a fair-minded man, he was always prepared to see the merits in what he opposed and revise his opinions about people and events. He had long wished to write a complete history of the Invincibles and the terrorism of the eighteen-eighties, but feared that it might have been impossible. He little thought at the time that he would come to this task by writing a life of James Stephens in which he would reveal the great Fenian as someone very different from the sinister and somewhat discredited figure who had emerged from the accounts of most of his own contemporaries.

Desmond Ryan's rejection of conventional attitudes was reflected in the clause of his will which directed that 'no formal services or ceremonies of any kind shall be conducted or performed in connection with my funeral'. As a final gesture to assert the individuality of his personality he directed that his remains 'be cremated at the nearest or most convenient crematorium'. He died in Baggot Street Hospital, Dublin, on 23 December 1964 and his remains were cremated in Belfast on 28 December 1964 after the recitation of the Beatitudes. Two days before he died he finished a review of Rev. Professor F. X. Martin's book on the Howth Gun-running and the Kilcool Gun-running in 1914. He had been granted his wish that his brain would survive till the end.

In this, his last book, Desmond Ryan has written the first full biography of James Stephens, Chief Organizer and Head Centre of the Irish Republican Brotherhood, leader and founder of the Fenian movement. In his lifetime Stephens's fame as a revolutionary had spread through Europe and America; his name was associated with the names of Mazzini, Blanqui and Marx. Today, even in Ireland, he is often confused with James Stephens, the poet, novelist and contemporary of Yeats. Sixty years and more, after his death, Stephens, the Fenian chief, remains strangely forgotten for a man of remarkable revolutionary achievements and historic significance. He has been given a grave, a monument, a few ballads; and that is all, except perfunctory mention in the footnotes to history.

James Stephens was born in Kilkenny in 1824 and died in Dublin on 29 March 1901. At the time of his birth the insurrection of 1798 and the Union with Great Britain of 1801 were events of recent memory and, in his case, of family memory because one at least of his own mother's family had fought in the insurrection. His boyhood was dominated by the Liberator, Daniel O'Connell, and the mass movement which won Catholic Emancipation. O'Connell had focussed the eyes of Europe on the Irish cause just as Stephens was to arouse for the Fenian movement the attention of America some thirty years later. Stephens's youth and early manhood were influenced by the decline and fall of O'Connell's Repeal movement and deeply stirred by the rise of Young Ireland in the forties. Above all, he was excited and stimulated by the teachings of the Young Ireland organ, the *Nation* under Thomas Davis, Charles Gavan Duffy, and John Blake Dillon. The call, to which his life's work was the answer, came to Stephens during the great Famine of 1845–47 which half-depopulated the country, and in the futile insurrection of 1848 in which he took part and from which he learnt much about the requirements of successful conspiracy. After that—with the exception of the nine most fruitful years of his life, spent in Ireland 1856 to 1865—he lived in exile in France and America until his return to Ireland in 1891.

The sojourn in France, especially the years from the defeat of the European revolutions of 1848 to the establishment of the Second Empire after Louis Napoleon's *Coup d'Etat* in 1851, was lived in close association with his fellow-exile and future partner in the Fenian leadership, John O'Mahony, dreamer, Irish scholar, tribal chieftain, and democrat. In Paris they met many of the exiled leaders of European national revolutions and acquired a schooling in secret conspiracy. Stephens became a friend of the Italian revolutionary veteran, General Pepe, and taught him English in exchange for lessons in Italian. Like other leaders of the continental revolutionary societies, Stephens and O'Mahony enrolled, almost certainly, in Blanqui's secret organization and in others of the numerous republican and socialist clubs in Paris, partly from genuine sympathy, partly to learn about organized conspiracy. Their membership of these clubs continued until they were disbanded after the *Coup d'Etat* of 1851. Stephens and O'Mahony fought on the republican side against Louis Napoleon in that year.

John O'Leary and Thomas Clarke Luby, future Fenian leaders and life-long associates of the two men, participants like them in the 1848 insurrection, and leaders also in the Fintan Lalor-Philip Grey secret society of that time—considered by John Devoy as the real forerunner of the Irish Republican Brotherhood—did not favour their Parisian activities. Luby thought Fintan Lalor and Philip Grey had left an efficient enough model for secret organization although he visited France in 1851, just before the exploits of his two friends at the Paris barricades. Luby's object was to join the French Foreign Legion to learn infantry tactics, but he found recruiting had been temporarily suspended.

Small groups of Irish insurgents inspired by Grey and Lalor survived the collapse of 1848 and Luby remained in touch with them. In 1854, after two years in Australia, he returned to Ireland to start a revolutionary movement and a newspaper. Two other powerful secret organizations in Ireland, the agrarian Ribbon Society and the Orange Order remained for a time quite uninfluenced by nationalist secret organizations.

Eventually, however, Stephens's organizers won over the Ribbon Society and with their non-sectarian and republican principles, seem also to have penetrated the Orange Order. John O'Leary, indeed, claimed it was easier to make a Fenian of an Orangemen than of a Ribbonman!

The main outcome of the exertions, dreams and disappointments of James Stephens and John O'Mahony in their Parisian exile is told in some detail in this book. It is the story of the rise and fall of the Irish Republican and Fenian Brotherhood in Ireland and the United States.

The founding of the Fenian movement in its first phase is Stephens's outstanding work. There were, of course, many other great Irish movements in his lifetime, the parliamentary agitations led by Isaac Butt, Parnell, Dillon, Redmond, the land struggles in the Tenant Right League of the fifties, and Davitt's more formidable Land League of the seventies and eighties. But Stephens's life work was spent in none of these, although it influenced them all. His one concentrated task and creation was the Fenian movement in Ireland and America. It was the tragedy of his career that in 1865 after seven brilliant years of organization and leadership he came within an inch of launching a revolution, possibly a successful one. In any event, it would have been an upheaval so formidable that the political and social agonies of Ireland might have been shortened. This chance Stephens lost, possibly through his own excessive arrogance and self-esteem, possibly through circumstances outside Ireland and beyond the control of any leader. Two years later, in 1867, he was deposed as Fenian leader because he refused to sanction the forlorn uprising of that year. Thereafter Stephens lived an obscure and often starving exile in Paris in spite of several determined efforts to recover his lost supremacy.

A panel on the Celtic cross over his grave in Glasnevin cemetery reads, 'A day, an hour of virtuous liberty is worth a whole eternity in bondage'. It is a worthy epitaph for the leader who, next to O'Connell and Parnell in nineteenth-century Ireland, built a mass movement that made itself universally known, and whose objectives were eventually achieved, at least for part of Ireland.

The history of Fenianism itself has largely been written, yet until now its principal figure for all his hours of virtuous liberty has had a half-a-century of semi-oblivion. His story, so far as it has been written at all, has been the work of his enemies, honourable and dishonourable alike. In the last years of his own life Desmond Ryan acquired the material for this biography partly in some of Stephens's own papers, and in those of his closest colleagues, Luby, O'Donovan Rossa, O'Mahony, John Devoy, General Millen and Joseph Denieffe.

In this book, based on these sources, James Stephens appears for the first time as he saw himself, and as his closest intimates and fellow-revolutionaries saw him.

When the *Fenian Chief* was being prepared for posthumous publication Mrs Sarah Ryan selected, as editor of the manuscript, Mr Owen Dudley Edwards, a young lecturer in the Department of History of Aberdeen University. Desmond Ryan had high regard for Owen as a friend and greatly admired him as an historian. It would have pleased the author of the *Fenian Chief* that this young editor should have completed the study of James Stephens in a postscript so much in character with the subject of the biography.

PATRICK LYNCH
DUBLIN   *November 1967*

1 *The Silent Student*

JAMES STEPHENS was born at Lilac Cottage, Blackmill Street, Kilkenny in 1824. No record of his birth or baptism has been discovered in the records of the Protestant and Catholic churches in the city so far searched. His parents, John and Anne Stephens, were both Catholics. Stephens and his sister Anne acted as sponsors to their cousin, Joseph Casey, at his baptism in April 1846 at St Mary's Cathedral, Kilkenny. In August 1838 an entry in the records of St Kieran's College confirms the contemporary reference in *Speeches from the Dock* that he attended a Catholic seminary. The entry—a single one—shows that Stephens spent at least one quarter there as a day pupil in his fourteenth year.

His father, John Stephens, was for many years an auctioneer's and bookseller's clerk to William Douglas Jackson of Rose Inn Street. According to a statement in Stephens's American diary, he seems to have owned several cottages. Apart from the reference in the pamphlet, *An Eyewitness: Arrest and Escape of James Stephens*, (New York, 1866), that Stephens's mother was 'of a family of reduced circumstances but of the highest respectability', very little is known of her. Her name occurs on Stephens's marriage certificate in 1863. Stephens himself mentions her briefly once in his autobiographical writings, and it is possible he had no memory of her.

Yet Stephens was a most erratic chronicler, and tended to omit important facts. His father, sister, his maternal cousins the Caseys, his uncle, Patrick Casey, and some other relatives appear only briefly in the same writings. The Caseys were small shopkeepers, one of them, according to one local account, in the hardware business.

Stephens was to spend much of his second exile in Paris in

the late sixties with his four Casey cousins—Andrew, James, Joseph, Patrick, and their mother who had emigrated to France after Joseph Casey's trial and acquittal on charges of suspected Fenian activities in England in 1867. Joseph Casey was held in Clerkenwell prison during the explosion directed at the rescue of the Fenian prisoners there. His brother, Patrick, was implicated in the plot and escaped to Paris. During the Franco-Prussian war, the four Casey brothers fought on the French side. Andrew Casey was severely wounded and received the Legion of Honour. Joseph Casey made his way into literature, not only as a printer and revolutionary journalist of sorts himself, but through the verbal scarification of Michael Davitt in the *Fall of Feudalism*, and through his friendship with James Joyce who used him more sympathetically as the original of the old Fenian exile, Kevin Egan, in *Ulysses*.

The main sources for the early life of James Stephens are his own vague autobiographical recollections with a few meagre and scattered hints elsewhere. Accounts from the Fenian side and from hostile sources are thin and often inaccurate. Local tradition in Kilkenny is slightly more helpful although it, too, is remarkably scant.

This lack of clear information about his boyhood family background, of the influences that moulded his character and convictions, of some twenty odd years of his life, is the most tantalizing obstacle for his biographers. Nearly every phase of his life has now to be recovered line by line from old journals and the private papers of his colleagues, but the first phase is the most obscure of all.

The only certainty in these twenty years is that Stephens was a silent and aloof student, concentrated outwardly on his work as a civil engineer; that he obtained a post in a Kilkenny office in his twentieth year for the work then in progress on the construction of the Limerick and Waterford Railway; that he was an omnivorous reader and even then possessed by the thirst for knowledge which was characteristic of him all his life, and so evident in the lists of his reading and studies which have survived; that he declined to affiliate to any political organization, and distrusted the pacific Repealers of the O'Connell school and the Young Ireland Confederate clubmen of the forties almost equally; and that yet, from some unexplained influence in his twenties, he was already a revolutionary in spirit. The one man he mentions as influencing him politically on the eve of Forty-eight is Dr Robert Cane, one-time Mayor of Kilkenny, a moderate Young Irelander and cultural propagandist. The story that Stephens went to Dublin for some years, worked as a civil engineer and surveyor there, and became active in the Young Ireland clubs as a writer and speaker, though given by both the hostile Rutherford and the Fenian historian John Savage, is not consistent with Stephens's own account of his early years. Rutherford's belief that Stephens was educated as a Protestant and that 'many of his blood and name were Orangemen' arose from confusion with other Kilkenny families of the same name, and from some ambiguous words of Stephens himself in his memoirs of 1848.

In these recollections, published in the Dublin *Irishman* in the eighties, Stephens vaguely sets down that patriotic sentiments were instilled into him from childhood, that later associations and a desire to advance himself in his profession in which he was absorbed for several years, although not interfering with his love of country, prevented him from taking the part in politics he might otherwise have taken. Even more definitely than any such evasive generalities, he declares that 'my younger associates were all more or less of the Orange type', so much so that Stephens in some quarters had the reputation of being a loyalist. Indeed, he adds that a loyalist shopkeeper in Tipperary assured some suspicious policemen who questioned her about a visit of Stephens and some companions to her shop in Cashel, 'Mr Stephens is as loyal a man as ever drew breath, and would rather drown himself than bring into my house any but devoted subjects of Queen Victoria'.

Such at all events is Stephens's story of one of his ruses to throw the police off his trail when he suddenly added secret drillings to railway construction and midnight oil. As the famine-racked Ireland of the forties hurried towards insurrection, the flame of Young Ireland caught James Stephens, as at the same time it caught so many of his ablest future lieutenants. The outward impulse came in all cases from the

decay of the Repeal movement, from the *Nation* newspaper
with its rousing appeal to the pride and glories of the past, its
indictment of social and political ills, its war on sectarian
differences, its revivification of the memory of Tone and the
United Irishmen who had dreamed and fought for an Irish
republic barely fifty years before. Or the impulse came, too,
from the even more militant incitements of John Mitchel and
Fintan Lalor, and their final appeal to harness the land
question to the political struggle. Yet most potently the impulse
was directed and hardened by the social chaos and grim
uprooting of the Great Famine in the mid-forties, and fanned
to white-heat by the revolutions that swept over Europe from
the Paris barricades of February 1848.

From then onwards the Young Ireland flame burned
brightest. John O'Leary, whose sceptical mind had been
fired to life-long rebellion by a spark from the *Nation*, explained
later, that the 'balmy air of constitutionalism', O'Connellism
and its pacific Repeal Association, died away under the shock
of famine and a headlong flight of thousands into exile to
escape hunger and typhus. With the European revolution came
the emergence of an insurrectionary party in the Young
Ireland ranks. John Mitchel, Ulster man with a pen like a
razor, fired to revolt by the *Nation* and Carlyle alike, made a
bold bid in his fiery organ, the *United Irishman*, to provoke a
spontaneous uprising. After a historic trial, Mitchel was
sentenced to fourteen years' transportation and was hurriedly
sent overseas. It was touch and go that Mitchel did not succeed
in sparking off insurrection before he went. Reluctantly, and
with difficulty, the Dublin leaders held back their followers in
the Confederate Young Ireland Clubs from storming Newgate
prison in an attempt to rescue Mitchel.

Even Michael Doheny, the most sanguine of the leaders,
glumly opposed the project, only to wonder for the rest of his
life whether it was not then that the Young Ireland cause had
been really lost. Yet he found the arguments against action
then most cogent: arms were too few; the supply of food in the
capital and country until the harvest inadequate; such an
armed outbreak would precipitate insurrection not among the
sturdy masses who had flocked to O'Connell's monster gather-

ings, but among a multitude decimated by three years of starvation; the Government had uncontrolled power over the import of grain, even if the insurgents seized and distributed all the cattle in the country. Yet Doheny and the more militant leaders knew that a trial of strength between themselves and the Government was inevitable, and that it was a race between Young Ireland and the Government. During most of the year, O'Leary reflected later, 'our minds were in a state of constant ferment and our bodies ever active rushing about from one club or meeting to another; and sometimes in marching and drilling and the like'.

More and more, since the death of O'Connell and the break of the Young Irelanders with the Repeal Association, the titular leadership of Young Ireland had passed to William Smith O'Brien, conservative Protestant landowner, who had passed, stage by stage, as a member of the House of Commons for twenty years, from ultra-loyalism to O'Connell's Repeal Association, to Young Ireland, and at last, under the pressure of events, to leadership of an insurrection he had not planned, never desired, and which was thrust on him by circumstances.

The Confederates were watched in his native city with a somewhat critical sympathy by James Stephens. He had, indeed, given his word to Dr Robert Cane, the principal Confederate leader in Kilkenny, that he would answer any serious call. But he still believed that Young Ireland was right in its aims and wrong in its methods. Even then he seems to have believed in secret organization, helped possibly by a study of such books as Louis Blanc's *Dix Ans*,[1] the progress of events in France, and the old example of the United Irishmen, a living memory in his mother's family.

'Even if I had played an active role in the public arena' he wrote in the *Irishman* in 1882, 'earlier than '48 I could not have conscientiously expressed my belief in the efficacy of the Repeal agitation, for I thought it too much of a windbag, and too little of the real thing. When, however, the Irish Confederation was

---

[1]Louis Blanc, *Revolution francaise, histoire de dix ans* (Brussels, 1843–44), was first translated anonymously as *The History of Ten Years* 1830–40 (London 1844, 1845). A long review of the latter, by T. Devin Reilly, was published in the *Nation*. Reilly's two volumes of the original edition are in the Christian Brothers' O'Connell Schools' Library, Dublin.

started I found it of sterner stuff and held kindly thoughts
towards the Confederates of my own native city, Kilkenny. I
remember listening to a few speeches of Meagher, which raised
high hopes at the period for the cause; but as time slipped by,
I did not see—at least in my own immediate neighbourhood—
any preparations being entered upon for the final and only
issue between the two countries. I heard many rhetorical
efforts but beheld little real work!'

From the summer of 1848 it became clear that grave events,
the very crisis of the Young Ireland movement, were at hand.
Early in July the Government suppressed the organs of all
wings of the movement, the official *Nation*, and the two open
advocates of insurrection, the *Irish Felon* and the *Irish Tribune*
as well as arresting the editors and members of their staffs.
Meagher, Doheny and other prominent leaders were also
arrested and released on bail, pending trial.

William Smith O'Brien had left Dublin for a brief stay in
Wexford after consultations with the Confederate leaders who
were then making hurried preparations for action which
Gavan Duffy considered three months too late, and of which
they informed O'Brien in general terms after the event. A
Council of Five had been appointed after Mitchel's arrest and
transportation, and given extraordinary powers to act in an
emergency. Popular excitement and sentiment, as expressed
in demonstrations, were in favour of revolt.

As this situation developed, James Stephens and a group of
his more intimate friends drilled quietly at the traditional
centre for seditious and secret activities in Kilkenny, from
1798 onwards down in fact to 1916, Moll Mackey's Hill, near
the very spot from which Cromwell's cannon had battered
Kilkenny Castle two hundred years before. There were pike
exercises and formation instructions for squares against
cavalry, with scouts duly posted to give warning of the approach
of the police. There were many alarms and retreats to quieter
spots where the drilling was resumed.

Then at the end of July, the Government struck again, and
in a manner that left its enemies little choice between surrender
and resistance. And it was at that moment that James Stephens
stepped into history.

2 From the Tholsel to Ballingarry

WHEN the House of Commons, on 22 July 1848, voted the suspension of the Habeas Corpus Act in Ireland it spread confusion in the hesitating and divided councils of Young Ireland and forestalled the plans, such as they were, for an outbreak after the harvest had been gathered in autumn. Yet, in spite of the short term advantage to the Government of exploding an insurrection in its own time and breaking Young Ireland, it had launched unwittingly one of its most formidable enemies since Tone on his revolutionary career.

And three days later James Stephens to his own surprise realised that fact. On the news of the proclamation he prepared to fulfil his promise to Dr Robert Cane; it was the crisis, and, if the Irish Confederation meant business, he was at its service unreservedly. The issue of warrants for O'Brien and other leaders was almost at once announced. Already town after town was proclaimed. Dublin, Drogheda, Cork, Waterford had been named as areas where arms must be surrendered, and then came the turn of Kilkenny, that ancient seat of the famous Confederation three hundred years before, the indomitable city which by hard fighting had wrung honourable terms from Cromwell himself, with the admission that it had cost him more men than in all his strife, terror and slaughter at Drogheda.

A meeting of the Confederate Clubs was summoned in the Tholsel of Kilkenny with its high clock-tower and jutting arcade, a storied and venerable building of many uses from town hall to market house, a fitting platform for historic decisions. Stephens accepted the invitation to attend this meeting called for Tuesday, 25 July. On the eve of the meeting, however, he still refused to join the Confederation.

3

His resolution remained the same: he would help to drill the clubs, he would fight in any possible insurrection, but he would waste no time on gatherings with too many glowing speeches and too little effective work. Neither Dr Cane nor the local Confederate leaders had any doubt where he would be or how he would act if danger came. Outwardly, he kept up the pose of aloof civil engineer and absorbed student, although by then he was certainly under suspicion, and rumours had been afloat about warrants for himself and some of his closer friends.

In the two days before the meeting events moved fast and the city was tense with feeling and filled with rumours. Kilkenny, at that moment in fact, was considered to be a key position in the hasty preparations of the Dublin leaders who, after a brief discussion, left the capital and hurried to the country to rally it for the now inevitable clash. Thomas Francis Meagher and John Blake Dillon immediately after the news of suspension of Habeas Corpus agreed that Kilkenny should be the centre and starting place for the insurrection. They made an urgent journey to Co. Wexford to urge this on William Smith O'Brien who was staying with a friend in Ballinakeale near Enniscorthy. A warning had also reached them that a special warrant for O'Brien's arrest was in Dublin Castle. Before they left Dublin there had been no opportunity to hold a full meeting of even the Council of Five empowered to act in an emergency. One, Richard O'Gorman, had already left on an organizing tour of the Clubs in Clare and Limerick, another, Devin Reilly, could not be contacted in time. Dillon and Meagher met the remaining member of the Council, Thomas D'Arcy McGee, in company with a leading Dublin Confederate, P. J. Smyth, in O'Gorman's warehouse. They were all of the same mind on policy and action. McGee left at once for Scotland in an attempt to raise recruits, arms and ammunition among the Confederate Clubs there, and to organize a landing in the west of Ireland, if possible, by a seizure of ships on the Clyde. The failure of this bold mission, initiated by a direct invitation from the Confederates in Scotland, was not due to McGee, who raised recruits, money and arms, and even won over, with Confederate help, the captain and crew of an Irish steamer.

Meagher and Dillon had an uninterrupted journey by coach to Enniscorthy. As they waited in the early hours of a chilly morning in a hotel Meagher took the last number of the suppressed *Irish Felon* from his pocket, and read to Dillon the famous defiant call to arms by Fintan Lalor which stated clearly the hard choice forced on Young Ireland:

'An enemy is able to force the necessity of either fighting or failing . . . Let us fight in September if we may—but sooner if we must. Meanwhile, however, remember this—that somewhere, and somehow, and by somebody, a beginning must be made. Who strikes the first blow for Ireland? Who draws the first blood for Ireland? Who wins a wreath that will be green for ever?'

The defiant writer was already on his way to Tipperary where, after a fruitless effort to put his words into action, he was soon behind the bars of Nenagh jail. Yet of Fintan Lalor and his message more was to be heard.

After a brief tour of Co. Wexford with O'Brien, who agreed that the time had come to make a stand, they reached Kilkenny where they interviewed Dr Cane in his house in William Street. He told them frankly that unless they could bring in strong reinforcements from outside no worthwhile stand could be made in the city. There were less than six hundred effective fighting men in the Kilkenny Clubs, in spite of more enthusiastic paper numbers which had led Meagher to expect some five thousand armed Confederates. And what effective force there was possessed few guns, and even a raid on the city gunshops would yield little. Moreover, the British garrison was a thousand strong in infantry, with two troops of cavalry and some light artillery, all lodged behind solidly fortified walls in their headquarters. With great reluctance Meagher and Dillon accepted the statement of affairs made by Dr Cane and other Confederate leaders. After discussion, Dillon's offer to lead an attack himself with five hundred armed men was dropped as impracticable, and Meagher's offer to dash to Waterford and rush back a hundred armed men by car to supplement Dillon's bold scheme, dismissed as inadequate. Gavan Duffy's comment on this accepted the admission of hard facts as inevitable, yet added that at that moment 'the first chance of success—that subtle electric force whose influence evades arithmetic—vanished away'.

After further discussion it was decided that O'Brien, Dillon and Meagher should go to Co. Tipperary, and summon the people of Carrick, Clonmel and Cashel to arms, and return, if possible, to Kilkenny with armed reinforcements, throw up barricades, and proclaim the Republic to the country. O'Brien did not oppose these plans, although he made it clear that he believed hostilities should be avoided unless provoked by the attempted arrest of the leaders.[1]

While these debates proceeded large crowds gathered in William Street and filled it from end to end as the news of the arrival of the Confederate leaders spread. O'Brien was loudly cheered when he came out and spoke from the balcony of the Citizens' Club House some distance away. He told the people he had come to share with them the perils of a righteous war, and urged the Clubmen to arm themselves. There was a roar: 'We'll die for you!'

Early on the following morning, Monday 24 July, O'Brien and Stephens met for the first time. O'Brien had left Meagher and Dillon to a final consultation with the presidents and officers of the Clubs, and went in search of the Eighty-Two Club in Patrick Street. He could not find the house at once, and while in a shop to which a sudden shower of rain drove him for shelter he began to study a large map of Ireland he always carried with him on his tours. Stephens, who had dashed for the same refuge, recognized him from press portraits and soon introduced himself. He directed O'Brien to the Club, and answered several questions about the topography of the county. With some pride, Stephens added that he had been a student of the map from boyhood and from his travels in his professional capacity knew Leinster perfectly, and no small portion of Munster. O'Brien checked with Stephens's aid the

[1]O'Brien's own defence of his plans and actions, which he prepared for his trial and suppressed to avoid incriminating others, is given for the first time in Denis Gwynn, *Young Ireland and 1848* (Cork 1949), Ch. 20. The account in the text is based on Arthur Griffith ed., *Meagher of the Sword* (Dublin 1916) pp. 173–234; Charles Gavan Duffy, *Four Years of Irish History* (London 1883), being Vol. II of his *Young Ireland. A fragment of Irish History 1840–1850* (London 1880), and Stephens's 'Recollections of '48', *Irishman*, February 4–June 10, 1882.

distance between Kilkenny and various points. They were not to meet again until the insurrection, brief and catastrophic, flashed up some days later. One question obsessed Stephens: Would O'Brien give the signal for action at last?

On Tuesday evening, 25 July, the Kilkenny Confederates held an enthusiastic demonstration under the chairmanship of Dr Robert Cane in the Tholsel. In the hope that Carrick might be the rallying centre for revolt, O'Brien and his companions had left for that town on Monday night. During the Tholsel proceedings a rumour spread through the city, late in the evening, that a detective had arrived with a warrant for the arrest of O'Brien. This story did not reach the assembled Confederates, and became known to a few of them only as the orators finished and the excited crowds made for their homes.

Stephens, in his '48 recollections already mentioned, was convinced by the Tholsel demonstration 'at a glance that agitation had gone its full tether and that the era of action was on the point of commencing'. There is possibly a touch of exaggeration in his picture of 'the fire-laden eyes whenever the national wrongs were discanted on by an orator from the platform'. He explains that his friends pressed him so hard to speak that he consented to appear on the platform and make his maiden speech, 'uniquely for the purpose of giving some words of advice'.

Afterwards he was given to understand that this speech was received 'with rapturous applause', but of that he had no memory whatever, and of nothing but a gathering 'lit up with eager hope' and 'studded with note-taking peelers, sullen and dogged representatives of alienism'.

The speech itself was sharp and to the point:

'Friends, you are called upon by a proclamation of the British Executive to surrender such arms as you may have in your possession, and you are threatened with all the pains and penalties of the law from retaining them after to-morrow's sunset. Now, my deliberate advice to you is this. Treasure your arms as you would the apples of your eyes, and bury them safely in the hope of a happy resurrection'.

Here Stephens first sounded the flamboyant defiance to be repeated throughout all his speeches and manifestoes in the future. It was soon to be followed by very impetuous action. He had taken once and for ever the first step on his lifelong and tortuous path. In his memory of that moment, he felt that he had been seized by some overmastering power that spoke and acted through him, regardless of his conscious will.

After the meeting, Stephens, his father, and a number of friends who had been at the Tholsel, went to a private and informal party at the Victoria Hotel. His father's sympathies were, in general, with the Young Irelanders. Yet that night Stephens saw clearly that John Stephens had not really grasped how serious the crisis was, how near to turmoil, bloodshed, and tragedy, or, that it would involve death, perhaps, outlawry, prison, exile, maybe, and most certainly conflict, for Stephens himself. The shock of all that was indeed to shorten his father's life. A Confederate Clubman, John Grace by name, rushed wildly into the room, beside himself with rage at the rumour that there was a detective at the Rose Inn with a warrant for the arrest of William Smith O'Brien.

One present, a Mr Kavanagh, immediately proposed in indignation that three or four armed men should raid the inn and seize the warrant by force. There was a startled silence. No one spoke. Then Stephens, still in an exalted mood, heard his own voice second the proposal, and call on Kavanagh to follow him at once. He went over to where his father was sitting and grasped both his hands, 'It was a solemn moment of deep emotion for me, but he little dreamt of the tempestuous future that was before me . . . I had seen my father for the last time on earth . . . Soft lie the turf over his ashes where they repose in the City of St Canice'.

Telling Kavanagh to collect revolvers or what arms he could, Stephens paid a short and last visit to his home. He went noiselessly into the house, 'a silence of the dead reigned through it. The one occupant was my only and surviving sister, Anne. She was plunged in a heavy slumber, and not wishing to awaken her, I provided myself with a dagger, and penetrated back into the night. As it was with my father, so also was it with my sister. She, too, passed away shortly afterwards, and that night was the last I laid eyes upon her. She was ever kind and gentle to me, and her memory shall be with me as long as I live, peace be to her soul!'

Armed with revolvers, Stephens and Kavanagh visited the Rose Inn, and found there a big, black-haired, scowling man, their very ideal of what a police agent should be, and challenged him peremptorily. Dourly and with emphasis, he denied that he was a spy. On the contrary, he was a Confederate envoy from Dublin with dispatches, by name Patrick O'Donohue, whose one desire on earth was to deliver those dispatches to O'Brien. Kavanagh grew more and more confused as he fumbled through the papers handed to him, and cried out that there was no doubt that they were a warrant for O'Brien's arrest.

O'Donohue's explanation was in fact the true one. He was a prominent Dublin Club leader, whose over-cautious inquiries in Kilkenny about O'Brien had started the rumours that he was a spy. Stephens very soon believed him, but did not say so. He, too, very much wanted to meet O'Brien and learn whether there was to be an insurrection or not, and here was the very chance. Loftily he waved aside the papers, and declared that as they were addressed to O'Brien it would be most improper for him to read them. He spoke to O'Donohue sternly:

'You want to meet O'Brien? Good! He is in Thurles, twelve miles distant. We'll get a car and drive you there. If we are mistaken, you'll forgive our zeal in the same cause. But if you attempt to escape on the way, we'll shoot you on the spot'.

P. J. Smyth, who had been very busy in Dublin since his parting with Dillon, Meagher and McGee at the brief session of the Council of Five, was waiting for a train at Thurles as O'Donohue and his captors drove up. He had travelled down for a conference with O'Brien, and was on his way back.

'Look here, Smyth!' roared O'Donohue, releasing all his pent-up fury in a tremendous shout, 'these demned rascals take me for a spy, and hold me a prisoner!'

Smyth, highly amused, at once cleared O'Donohue's character, and told them of his talk with O'Brien that morning. Carrick had turned out to be an impossible centre for an insurrection, in spite of the spirit of the rank and file Confederates

there, some three thousand in number, armed mainly with
pikes, and about three hundred rifles and muskets. The sudden
arrival in the neighbourhood of infantry, dragoons, police and
artillery, however, intimidated the local leaders who persuaded
O'Brien that any attempt to hold Carrick would be drowned
in blood. Again the tragic and mocking pilgrimage in quest of
a centre was resumed when O'Brien announced that Cashel
should be occupied and that they must proceed there for the
final call to the country.

Meagher's narrative of the arrival of the Young Ireland
leaders at Carrick, and the tumultuous welcome of the populace
there is a famous and unforgettable record, even if the music
of his rhetoric muffled even harsher facts: 'It was a revolution
if we had accepted it',—and of the talking, inconsequent,
divided local Club leaders, each with 'a plan of action, isolated
from, and in the end, hostile to and contradictory to all the
rest'.

Dillon believed that Carrick should have been held and
saved by the backing of the Tipperary and Waterford Confederates. Gavan Duffy regarded this rejection as the definite
defeat of any chance of effective action, 'had Carrick been
seized, it is probable that three counties would have risen
within forty-eight hours; and that preparations for a rising
would have begun over three provinces'.

On the road to Carrick, indeed, there had been one warning
also described with peculiar vividness by Meagher in his
narrative. John O'Mahony, farmer, scholar, Confederate Club
leader, met O'Brien's party, coming full speed towards them
on a powerful black horse, 'he threw himself from his saddle . . .
and hastened to greet us . . . a true leader . . . we became
sensible in his presence of no emotions, save those of joyous
confidence . . . strange it is, the influence of a man of fine and
soldierly appearance, flinging himself into a revolutionary
movement, has upon the feelings of the utmost stranger'.

This man was to strike the last blow in the Young Ireland
struggle. James Stephens and he had not yet met but they were
to be lifelong friends and comrades.

O'Mahony almost fired the tragic pilgrims to action: 'He
represented to us that the country all about Carrick on towards

Clonmel, and along the Suir on the Tipperary side, was thoroughly alive, and ready to take the field at once'. After their departure from Carrick, he arrived with reinforcements, found his hopes for Carrick rejected by the leaders, and sent his men away again. All his life he protested that the Carrick decision was the gravest mistake of the rising, although he also believed that all could have been saved even after Ballingarry by a retreat of the leaders to his camp in the valley of the Suir.

Yet the story of the check at Carrick, as related by P. J. Smyth at Thurles to Stephens and his companions, did not alarm or dishearten them because Smyth himself had not understood its real significance. On the contrary, the Carrick episode was a mere mention of an unimportant item, enthusiastically submerged by many highly-coloured tales and rumours of fictitious O'Brienite successes and exuberant anticipations that at Cashel the Green Flag was even then flying over the headquarters of a provisional government. Stephens's account of all this is somewhat coloured by his later dislike of Smyth as an 'Aspirationist', yet it is clear Smyth spoke in good faith from what he knew of O'Brien's plans and mood as he left, and the discussions at which he had been present.

Moreover, Smyth's instructions pointed to imminent action. O'Brien had ordered him to return to Dublin, make arrangements for the destruction of the rails at Thurles and in the Dublin suburbs, and take charge of the Clubs in Co. Meath to create a diversion there. Stephens and O'Donohue agreed at once to take charge of tearing up the railway track at Thurles, and later passed the word to the local Confederates, who destroyed portions of the Great Southern and Western Railway line near the town. They proceeded on their way in high spirits.

When, however, Stephens, Kavanagh and O'Donohue at length reached Cashel, they found no green flags, no insurgent army, no provisional government, nothing but deserted streets as in some city of the dead. It was only with great difficulty that they found O'Brien. He told them that all hope of action in Cashel must be abandoned. He, however, was determined to go on with the hopeless quest.

Kavanagh, on the contrary, argued with them all that after

so many disappointments and refusals of support, the struggle must be given up, the odds against any action were too great, and he could commit himself no longer to such a desperate venture. Then and thirty years later, Stephens admitted these arguments were sound and honest, and that Kavanagh left for Kilkenny, in distress and with a heavy heart. Stephens and O'Donohue told O'Brien that they would follow him to the end. Stephens was appointed aide-de-camp on the spot. 'When they expected', wrote Doheny later, 'that every man would make a fortress for them in his very heart, they were almost abandoned, but their resolution remained unchanged'.

They journeyed to Killenaule where O'Brien met a warm reception from barely two hundred men who flocked out to meet him with bouquets and addresses of welcome. Yet the contemporary witness, Father P. Fitzgerald, in his pamphlet *Personal Recollections of the Rising at Ballingarry*, drily hints that this meeting was hardly 'with any improvement in the way of organization or any effective addition to his strength'.

From Killenaule O'Brien's party went on to Mullinahone where some thousands greeted them with every appearance of readiness for a revolution on the spot. O'Brien regarded them as material for a formidable guerrilla army, but sadly recorded that men, ardent for action in the evening, listened to the clergy overnight, and lapsed into inaction in the morning.[2]

Yet the accounts cited by Duffy, McManus, Father Fitzgerald and Stephens indicate that more material pressures than the warnings and exhortations of the clergy disintegrated and dispersed O'Brien's supporters, there and elsewhere.

One sidelight is given in Father Fitzgerald's pamphlet:

'Those who went to meet him [O'Brien] at Mullinahone, remained the whole day in the streets without food or shelter. Some bread was distributed to them at his expense, and they were told that in future they would have to procure provisions for themselves, as he had no means of doing so, and did not mean to offer violence to any one's person or property. This announcement gave a death-blow to the entire movement. These poor fellows returned home late in the evening faint with hunger,

[2]Gwynn, *Young Ireland and 1848*, p. 233.

resolved not to expose themselves a second time to such privations.'[3]

Stephens in his recollections of that time discusses O'Brien's faults as a revolutionary leader, and contents himself with the gentle criticism that O'Brien was 'over-sensitive' in the use of methods by which such warfare should be carried out. He then argues that commandeering and confiscation are legitimate in general after a revolutionary body with popular backing has issued a formal and warning proclamation. In theory, O'Brien never disputed that.

One passage in the undelivered speech at his trial before mentioned showed that, although reluctantly, and as a last resort, O'Brien agreed that 'forced contributions' in a revolution would be 'ultimately necessary' with eventual compensation from national resources. In the meantime he dreamed of finding bodies of men 'sufficiently independent in their circumstances to be able to maintain themselves for a short time on their own resources'. All this, it would seem, applied to O'Brien's ideal revolution whose success would be crowned by a provisional government, not alone of participants, but of others 'prepared to acquiesce in its results', and 'subdue and control anarchical tendencies'. His judgment on the actual event flashed out in the double-edged ironic sentence: 'I am compelled to admit that our escapade—it does not deserve the name of an insurrection—was in a supreme degree contemptible as a result of a great national movement in which many an idle boast and many a futile menace had been employed'.

Whatever O'Brien's theories he turned down most definitely any practical suggestions for commandeering made by Dillon, Doheny and others. Even when, according to the *Annual Register*, 1848, summary of his trial, he served a formal requisition on the Commons Colliery, material for barricades alone was removed while some fifty pounds of blasting powder were left intact. Eight years later when Stephens and he debated the issue, it was evident that O'Brien's distrust of popular

[3]Quoted, Duffy, *Four Years . . .* p. 662 footnote. McManus in his narrative given in the same source mentions buying up bread on several occasions after Mullinahone, pp. 664, 682. For Stephens's criticisms, see his 'Recollections of '48' *Irishman*, 4 March, 1882.

revolt was the over-riding consideration. John Mitchel, who regarded O'Brien with the same respect and admiration as Stephens did, wrote in humorous exasperation in June 1859 to a friend that O'Brien had visited him in Paris, that he venerated O'Brien, but that in a revolution 'patriotic citizens could do nothing less than hang him, though with much reluctance'.[4]

Charles J. Kickham, one of the future outstanding Fenian leaders, was in Mullinahone when he heard of the progress of O'Brien through the county, and he set to work on the manufacture of pikes. This work was in full swing in a forge when a young farmer rushed in with the news that O'Brien and Dillon were outside and looking for him. Kickham went out to meet them, and James Stephens, for the first time. Before midnight Kickham's messengers had gathered some 6,000 men armed with fowling pieces, impromptu pikes and pitchforks, into Mullinahone where they drilled and paraded all that night along the streets and roads leading to the town.[5]

Through all the ebb and flow of the popular emotions, O'Brien appeared to Kickham as a man moving through a dream.

At Mullinahone Stephens took part in the semi-comedy of the capture of the police barracks on Wednesday, 26 July. O'Brien informed him that the presence of the police in the town might damp the spirits of the people. His plan was to take the barracks by a sudden swoop when the garrison was off its guard.

O'Brien, Stephens and O'Donohue, armed with revolvers, walked into the barracks. A constable—who Stephens learned afterwards was really half-dying with consumption—fainted. O'Brien went straight into the main room, covered the sergeant with his revolver, calling on him to surrender and hand over the building, the garrison and all arms. Stephens and O'Donohoe rounded up four more constables, and kept an eye on the semi-comatose casualty.

The chief constable, however, had not raised the white flag

[4]William Dillon, *Life of John Mitchel* (London 1888) Vol. 2 p. 130.
[5]Kickham's account, given to Gavan Duffy, is quoted in full, *Four Years...* pp. 659–62.

yet. He fenced adroitly with O'Brien's demand, and suggested in the most friendly manner that, after all, six armed men would be disgraced and their careers ruined if they surrendered to only three men. The faces of the police must be saved. He and his men were in the fullest agreement with the popular cause. Could not Mr O'Brien retire and return with an overwhelming force?

Stephens had some misgivings when he saw that O'Brien was really moved by the chief constable's plausible and persistent appeal. He said nothing but he thought O'Brien should hold what he had taken. Yet even Stephens was astounded at the outcome. O'Brien said he would retire and return in fifteen minutes with a force that would remove all the chief constable's honourable scruples. O'Brien would never allow himself to inflict unnecessary suffering and disgrace on any true Irishman whatever his uniform.

The three raiders retired and then at the end of the fifteen minutes, O'Brien marched on the barracks in force, he saw the chief constable and four others making away through the back door, arms, ammunition and all, as fast as they could leg it over the countryside to the nearest police barracks at Cashel. All that they left behind them was the scared constable who was only then recovering consciousness. The trick infuriated O'Brien, and he sternly ordered the poor man to be held in such strict custody that Stephens's heart was moved to sincere pity for a peeler for the first and last time in his life. Yet the aroused O'Brien gave him high hopes. O'Brien seemed inclined 'to the martial energy of a Washington combined with the unbending justice of a Rhadamanthus'. Alas! duly recorded Stephens, this was only a temporary severity, O'Brien 'had not moved an inch permanently outside the old groove'.

A Carrick Confederate leader who visited Mullinahone that day was dismayed by this episode. He had come with promises of support in men and arms and felt O'Brien had allowed himself to be cheated. No such feeling weighed down the buoyant and militant Stephens as he remarked the delight and heard the laughter of all Mullinahone as the barracks was duly taken over. He knew, too, that O'Brien had secured one objective, and the main one; the evacuation of the barracks, like similar flights of the police from other barracks in the district, facilitated the preparations for revolt. O'Brien's own private memorandum confirms the story as given by Stephens. It also shows that O'Brien still hoped against hope for aid by simultaneous risings elsewhere. He had sent appeals to Dublin and other places throughout the country directing a general rising. Was it not clear that sections of the police had a certain sympathy with the popular cause, and most certainly no keen desire to fight it?

This sympathy, passive enough, Stephens had already remarked among the Irish soldiers. Meagher, sensing such sympathy, had gone so far as to get a crowd in Callan to cheer the Royal Irish Hussars, 'who listened with deep interest and satisfaction' as Meagher put it, 'and the corporal's features lit up with a glow of pleasure and enthusiasm, betrayed the gallant treason of his heart'.

Ten years later, John Mitchel sardonically reviewing all this in his book, *The Last Conquest of Ireland (Perhaps)* thought that the Hussars would have loved them better if the rebels had taken the Hussars' horses and arms, and gone elsewhere to collect more.

The later exploits of the Fenian organizers in subverting the Irish regiments in the British army suggest that Stephens in '48 may have first suspected the unexpected allies that made Fenianism a deadly menace in 1865, when the Fenian soldiers had to be held back from seizing the Dublin barracks, and Devoy could inform Stephens that he need not wait for arms from America or Great Britain since a bold stroke could place the British armories in his hands.

Kickham noticed several ominous signs of the slackening of the popular spirit before O'Brien and the other leaders left Mullinahone. The small army which had first gathered from the outlying districts to drill around the small town now melted away in hundreds, 'they saw no fighting to be done— no work of any kind', wrote Kickham to Gavan Duffy later, 'and had no idea where breakfast was to be had, except under their own roofs'.

There were, however, some hundreds still near enough to their homes to get food or who had money to buy it. The building of barricades had been suspended when O'Brien forbade the felling of trees without the owners' permission. One Protestant landowner gave permission, but pointed out that the trees of a magistrate, who had not given permission, on the other side of the road were spared, 'the boys felt the force of this appeal so strongly that only a few of the least valuable of his trees were cut down'. Kickham and a strong bodyguard escorted the car on which O'Brien, Dillon, O'Donohue and Stephens drove off a mile or so out of town. Dillon told the Mullinahone men to turn back when an escort of Ballingarry men marched up.

Kickham shook hands with Dillon and Stephens. He noticed that Stephens looked very cheerful and hopeful. And his last glimpse of Smith O'Brien was of a happy dreamer, smoking a cigar.

3 *Stephens at the Barricades*

IN the small hours of Wednesday, 26 July, or more precisely
Thursday morning, 27 July, James Stephens on duty at a
barricade near Ballingarry halted in turn Terence Bellew
McManus and John O'Mahony, and conducted them to
William Smith O'Brien, Dillon, Doheny and little more than
a dozen others, who at that late hour made up the Confederate
camp. The challenge and incident pass without comment in
Stephens's record, yet with these two men in the future he was
to make the most brilliant chapters in the story of the Fenian
organization.

McManus had arrived from Liverpool and landed in Dublin
two days before. It was his second visit to the capital when
bloodshed and turmoil threatened, and when the fate of an
Irish leader and his movement was to be defeat and disaster.
He had seen the end of O'Connell's Repeal movement, he was
now to see the end of Young Ireland. And on each occasion
McManus had been no idle spectator. In October 1843, he
had been in charge of a party of Liverpool Repealers, who had
followed another contingent of Manchester O'Connellites to
Dublin to assist in the expected resistance to the Government
plans to suppress O'Connell's last monster gathering at Clontarf
by a last-minute menacing proclamation, and the marshalling
of twenty thousand troops.

The parallel between the two events had an uncanny resemblance, and as he hastened towards Ballingarry, McManus's
feelings were sombre and intense. He soon learned that a large
force had assembled there the day before, and had been sent
home by O'Brien with orders to return next morning, pro-
visioned for two days. This force had never returned.

Two days later McManus was resting, fatigued and exhausted

after many false hopes, much marching and counter-marching, at a small inn in Killenaule, where the leaders had put up at midnight. At the foot of Slievenamon, five miles from the spot where they had proposed to meet Doheny with another contingent, they had sent home the score of followers remaining. Desertions and disaffection had reduced, mile after mile, the force of a hundred with which they had marched out of Mullinahone. Before their departure McManus had drilled some 'hundred and fifty slashing fellows' but of these a third vanished after some exhortations addressed to them at a hasty meal by the parish priest.

That morning at Killenaule Dillon and O'Donohue cured all McManus's aches and cold shivers by dashing into his bedroom with the news that a squadron of cavalry had surrounded the hotel. He dressed quickly and rushed to the street. The building was not actually surrounded but the cavalry could be seen advancing on the town. On the instant, he raised the cry of 'Up with the barricades!' With the help of about twenty townsmen a barricade of turf carts and timber beams was thrown across the narrowest part of the street. Dillon, Stephens, O'Brien and O'Donohue took charge of the construction of two more barricades.

McManus jumped on a horse and galloped off to reconnoitre the countryside. He soon observed, about a mile beyond the town on the main road, which he reached by a short cut, that the dragoons were already approaching the Killenaule barricades. He followed and collected some seventy men on the road. A barricade made of an iron gate and heaps of stone from a nearby wall was quickly erected. McManus and his party remained about half an hour behind this barricade in the rear of the dragoons, clearly visible to them. They continued their advance.

On his return to Killenaule shortly after, McManus heard the exciting tale of what had taken place at the barricade of which Dillon was in charge, and where Stephens had nearly precipitated an insurrection.

The gist of it all was given in the discreet and disingenuous military evidence at O'Brien's trial by William Parsons, a private of the 8th Royal Irish Hussars, the very regiment which

4

Meagher had beguiled at Callan, all marching, forty-five of them, under Captain Longmore from Fethard to Killenaule. Parsons was in advance of the others. On entering the town he met with the obstruction of a barricade, noticed about three hundred men there, and twenty yards behind another barricade. When Parsons reached the first barricade a man came forward with a rifle, told him to halt or he would blow his brains out. He halted till Captain Longmore came up.[1]

The man with the rifle was James Stephens, and the rifle in fact was the only rifle in all the variously armed host behind the barricades of Killenaule. Private William Parsons had somewhat exaggerated the strength of the first barricade, behind which stood some thirty men with two muskets, some pikes, pitchforks, Stephens and his rifle. The rest were a mere crowd of women and children.

John Mitchel in a famous passage on this incident in his *Last Conquest of Ireland (Perhaps)*[2] wrote the only complimentary words he was ever to write of Stephens, even if he there also succeeded in being as unjust to Dillon as he was to Stephens twenty years later. Stephens in his recollections does not dramatize himself at Killenaule. He even pokes fun at his conspicuous white coat as 'fit for a Lilliputian Bourbon'. He insists that he was a silent subordinate throughout, never giving expression to his doubts about some of O'Brien's actions, full of hope and ardour. His account agrees with that of McManus that Dillon and some others with great difficulty persuaded O'Brien to retire some distance before the dragoons could reach the barricade. Stephens saw Dillon go into the hotel. He told Stephens to take charge of the barricade while he prevailed upon O'Brien not to rush into immediate danger of arrest.

'I was not long in position', continues Stephens, 'when the cavalry came galloping up to the first barricade that we had constructed. I raised my rifle immediately, and covered the officer in command—ordering my men to hold themselves in reserve until the order for fire was given. This was willingly obeyed by all around me save one who was a collier, and who stood nearest to me that day. "General, in the name of J——

[1] *Annual Register*, 1848. p. 409 *et seq.*
[2] John Mitchel, *The Last Conquest of Ireland (Perhaps)* (Glasgow 1876).

and the Blessed Virgin, *will you give the word?*" "Steady!" I whispered.

'The collier was poor and ignorant, but he was a MAN OF THE PEOPLE. . . . The strata of society to which he belonged I did not know as well then as I did afterwards, but even my '48 experience convinced me that the further you delve into the ranks of the Irish people the purer is the gold you will find. If Ireland had ten thousand sons such as he the hour of her freedom would soon toll'.

The remainder of Stephens's story, after Dillon's return, on the whole follows that of McManus and Doheny. All are in contradiction to the evasive military evidence at O'Brien's trial.

McManus confirms Stephens's account in its details, and pictures the sequel:

'Captain Longmore rode to the barricade and asked that his troop might pass . . . Stephens covered the officer with his rifle, and held his piece at dead-rest. Dillon, who was standing on the top of the first barricade . . . entered into a parley with him, and demanded if he came to arrest O'Brien. He gave his word as a soldier that he had no warrant for O'Brien's arrest, and if allowed to pass quietly through the town, would neither molest him nor anybody else. After some consideration Dillon allowed them, one by one, through the barricade. The soldiers, being Irish, and evidently not hostile, the people gave them a cheer as they passed'.

Captain Longmore in his evidence at O'Brien's trial added no colour to the scene, merely saying, in language curiously like the official *Hue and Cry* description of Dillon, that 'a man rather tall and sallow, respectably dressed but unarmed, came forward from the barricade. He asked witness if he held a warrant to arrest him, to which witness replied "No". Nothing further was said'.

Doheny in his *Felon's Track* comments with some irony on the Captain's reticence and praises Dillon for assuming 'an ability he was unable to sustain' with such a weak and ill-armed force. At all events there was great elation in Killenaule as the cavalry disappeared from view. Stephens was a popular hero. Dillon addressed the crowds from a hotel window near the barricades to prolonged applause. Dillon finished but they wanted more speeches, and above all, cried out that they wanted, 'The little man in the white coat! We want the little man in the white coat'.

So Stephens, with due modesty, and with a promise of battles to come, spoke thus:

'Fellow-countrymen, this is not the time for words but for deeds. I am under my superior officers and whenever they give me any military command over you, if you do not find me at your head, put a bullet through mine!'

Yet although the enthusiasm excited by the diplomatic retreat of the dragoons, and the conduct of the insurgents at the barricades was widespread and fervent, even the sanguine McManus was disturbed after he had gathered fifty men, indifferently armed, and toured the district and neighbouring collieries. In general he was shaken by his all-day excursion. At the collieries, indeed, there were a hundred armed miners, half with firearms and half with pikes and other rude weapons from the coal pits. All these colliers, as Father Fitzgerald bears witness in his pamphlet on these events, stood by O'Brien to the end, ready to defend his life with their own. Stephens had already had an example of the spirit of one of them at Killenaule. McManus found a hero-worship of O'Brien widespread among the people, but he could not fail to notice, too, that they were practically unarmed and much of their physical courage was starved out of them.

When he returned in the evening to the camp this conclusion of his was confirmed by the latest arrivals, John O'Mahony, Michael Doheny, Meagher, Maurice Leyne, James Cantwell and others, all of whom reported inaction and collapse. O'Mahony, who had urged them all so insistently to strike at Carrick, was still in a fighting mood. He urged them that all might yet be saved if the leaders would fall back to his camp in the valley of the Suir, where they would be safer than anywhere else. He was confident that he could raise sufficient forces to check the disaster that every report confirmed to be very near.

Defections, the now open and vigorous opposition of the clergy, the enervating hunger that sapped the spirit of the population, the lack of arms, the divided mind of the leadership

—all this was clearly revealed at the final council of the Confederation leaders that evening, Friday, 28 July, held in an upper room of a public house near Boulagh Common, Ballingarry.

The members of the Council present were: William Smith O'Brien, Thomas Francis Meagher, Thomas Devin Reilly, John Blake Dillon, John O'Mahony, Patrick O'Donohue, James Stephens, James Cantwell, Michael Doheny, Maurice Leyne, Terence Bellew McManus, D. P. Conyngham and J. D. Wright.

'I gave no opinion whatever', wrote Stephens, in his memoirs, 'as I did not deem myself qualified to speak in a national council at that time'. His account is brief: the majority were for dispersing until the harvest ripened; O'Brien rejected an offer by Dillon to march on Limerick and go down fighting. When, at the close of the meeting, Dillon announced that at any rate he would go to Mayo and gather what support he could find, O'Brien smiled with joy, grasped Dillon's hands and said, 'Go!'

The final decision was an elaboration of this: the members of the Council, in particular Dillon, Meagher, and Doheny, should depart and discover whether various districts known to them could yet be roused to revolt. As Stephens, after a report had been received from Kilkenny that no blow would be struck there, was about to volunteer for service in that city, O'Brien checked him, and whispered, 'Mr Stephens, you will stay with me!' and then gave a similar order to McManus.

Doheny's description of this meeting in his *Felon's Track* differs in details from those of Gavan Duffy and Stephens. He emphasizes that although the discussion was a long and heated one, it ended without bitterness, and with a will 'to cope as best we could with a doom we were unable to avert'.

This doom was nearer than even Doheny suspected. That night on the very eve of the imminent and final clash that was to sweep their forlorn force from the field, even McManus, as he conversed with Stephens in a hut near Ballingarry, summed up the dark situation tersely, 'we are here in the centre of several military camps, the forces of which must eventually surround us, and we will be crushed. All I want is death in the field. If you survive tell the story of our struggle'.

At daylight next morning, Saturday 29 July, McManus was astir early, he fed and reviewed the small force of some hundred. He found they could muster only eighteen rude pikes, twenty guns and pistols with one charge of powder each, an even lower estimate than the parish priest of Ballingarry later gave of fifty guns and as many pikes. McManus discussed with Stephens and O'Brien the project of a march to link up with their sympathizers across the Kilkenny border at Urlingford, to attack, if possible, with these reinforcements a neighbouring police post, and make for Kilkenny, Carrick or Clonmel.

The police post in Co. Tipperary marked out for attack was at New Birmingham which Stephens agreed to survey. He prepared to leave as the main body began to move off. A horseman dashed up shouting furiously at them to halt. He was John Cavanagh, president of one of the Dublin Clubs, and his warning was an urgent one which changed their plans on the instant. A large police force was advancing in search of them from Ballingarry direction. Cavanagh, since he left Dublin on foot, had been in search of an insurrection. As he passed through Callan he thought the situation there favourable to an attack, and though he had noticed that the troops were alerted and new reinforcements pouring into Kilkenny earlier on his journey, he felt that there were possible opportunities there too. He was an optimist, as he had lingered in Dublin hoping against hope for action there. At a small hamlet beyond Callan he saw the police marching at their ease towards Ballingarry. He borrowed a horse and went furiously to Mullinahone and on through Ballingarry until he caught up with the insurgents at Farrenrory some miles beyond. Hearing a rumour that a second force of five hundred troops and police were on the way from Thurles, he did not dismount but galloped off on a scouting expedition until he had scotched that rumour at least.

Yet, although premature, the story was true. The force under Inspector Trant that Cavanagh had spied outside Callan had acted in advance of orders. Strong forces of police and troops were instructed to move from Thurles, Kilkenny, Cashel and

Callan, and arrest O'Brien and the other Confederate leaders on whose heads were now very tempting rewards. And it was insinuated later at the trial at Clonmel that this was the bait that lured Trant to a hasty departure, and to what only a most exceptional chance saved from being a humiliating surrender.

O'Brien decided to make a stand against the police. A barricade of timber and carts was thrown across the road where the police must pass from Ballingarry. Stephens and some musket men took up positions in houses commanding the barricade, at the front of which O'Brien stood with some more musket men. In a hollow on the left, pike and pitchfork parties were placed. McManus with some eighty men and women concealed themselves some hundred yards to the left in advance of the barricade. They were to lie hidden until the police passed and were fired on. Whereupon the pikemen were to charge and close in. Stephens was to load as many muskets as there was powder for, and stand by.

Even in McManus's account the ambush appears as an untidy and desperate scheme. Doheny's account suggests that it was even worse. A large crowd with some armed men appeared on the hillside as Trant's party came in sight. He sighted the barricades, and wheeled his men suddenly to the right, urging them on at full speed towards a large stone farm house on a hillside. Whatever plan existed broke down in a helter-skelter pursuit, without order, after the fleeing police, and with such speed that the retreat was nearly cut off. O'Brien was carried far ahead in the confusion. The Inspector's horse, with a brace of pistols in the saddle holster, was left outside as the police entered the Widow McCormack's farm house and prepared to resist a siege.

McManus, after reconnoitring the position, informed O'Brien that only artillery could carry it. Three additional factors made it impregnable: the kind heart of William Smith O'Brien; the Widow McCormack's visit to a neighbour that morning, leaving her five young children behind her as hostages for Trant's garrison; the attackers' neglect of obvious resources such as the supply of blasting powder in the nearby collieries, and sufficient tools to undermine the house.

Trant, in truth, was in a panic, and grossly over-estimated

the strength of his opponents. Yet Stephens, McManus, and John Cavanagh prepared a formidable plan of attack. Stephens, twenty men with guns and twenty pikemen aided McManus to break through stables in the rear. Stephens felt a reluctant admiration for the police on their prompt barricading of the place, the front in particular, and detected at once that the back defences were the weakest point. He remained with twelve of the gun party to cover the unbarricaded back windows from which the police quickly withdrew. The front was covered by Cavanagh's party mainly armed with pikes. The real stroke of the attack was to be an attempt to burn or smoke out the garrison.

McManus makes clear what Stephens omitted to state in his somewhat cloudy version where he even ignored his own movements related above. Among the crowd which followed O'Brien's party were a number of curious irresponsibles who were too cowardly to take action against the police behind their barricaded windows with menacingly jutting rifle barrels. They refused to help McManus when he asked them to bring up loads of hay, but hid behind the encircling outside stone walls of the garden near the gable ends of the house. McManus dragged up bale after bale himself and these were hurled against the back door.

Stephens and his gun party had intimidated the police in the rear from approaching the windows, McManus, crouching low, advanced and fired his revolver repeatedly into the bales. Stephens, with several others, joined him. Stephens cursed heartily when he found there was not a single match in the whole contingent. His bale would not ignite as in rage and despair he discharged his rifle into it. Smoke, however, began to curl upwards from McManus's shots, and a blaze was beginning when O'Brien appeared and ordered them to extinguish the fire at once and drag away the hay.

Five little hostages had, in effect, saved Trant and his men from capture, death or surrender, an advantage of which he grimly boasted in the parley that later took place between himself, O'Brien and Father Fitzgerald, then acting parish priest of Ballingarry. In one interview Trant, who professed indignation at the priest acting as a 'rebel envoy' said, to quote his own version, 'Father Fitzgerald remarked that they could burn the house over us. I replied that we had five hostages—five children . . . there would be a sufficient force on the ground soon to avenge us if we fell, and not leave a house standing in the county . . . We could fast and fight for forty-eight hours more'.

O'Brien's appearance was due to a frenzied appeal to him by the Widow McCormack. She had returned immediately when she heard that her house was besieged, and her five young children—the eldest no more than ten years of age—held within. She abused him like a madwoman, saying he was the man responsible for driving the police into her house and exposing her children to death. She wept in distraction. Both Stephens and McManus were moved when O'Brien informed them, not altogether accurately as it turned out: 'Here is the Widow McCormack, and she has been sent round by the police to say they will make terms'.

McManus and Stephens tore away the smouldering bales of hay, and the blaze died down. Then like a thunderbolt the scene was changed to bloodshed and tragedy. McManus was standing about seven yards from the building when he saw O'Brien stand on a front window sill and thrust his hand across the barricade. He shook hands with the police, and told them the insurgents did not want their lives but merely the surrender of their arms. Although the garrison were well armed and well supplied with ammunition they were panicky. From his very first view of them Trant thought that the attackers were some thousands strong, and it is clear that the police in general were very nervous of the threat to the badly fortified rear windows of the house which Stephens and his men had dominated shortly before.

While O'Brien was still arguing and pleading, the irresponsible groups of spectators who had refused to help McManus began to hurl stones. Some of the back windows were smashed. The stone throwers were safely sheltered under a wall. The police at once opened fire. One man fell dead beside McManus. John Cavanagh was severely wounded. O'Brien stood calmly within three yards of the house and escaped by a miracle.

At once McManus opened fire, and the men in the front of

the house followed his lead, but the windows were barricaded too high and too well for the attackers' shots to take effect. A second volley from the police answered, all forty rifles again from front and rear. McManus was struck by a glancing splinter from the gate and knocked flat. A rumour spread that either Dillon or Stephens had been badly wounded. Dillon, in fact, was then in the west and so far Stephens had escaped injury. John Cavanagh, whose wounds were grave, was taken in charge by a local man and brought into Kilkenny where he was hidden in the suburbs and treated by Dr Robert Cane. This was the origin of the legend that either Stephens or Dillon had been concealed and cared for in Dr Cane's house.

Father Fitzgerald had arrived on the scene to attend to the injured and dying. He feared a massacre of the garrison if the attack was resumed, and believed that the house would be carried by storm. He did his best to mediate, and interviewed Trant who rejected all his arguments and spat bitter threats against the insurgents. He knew reinforcements were on the way. He did not know that a police messenger was on his way with an urgent official order from Kilkenny to check Trant's 'imprudent haste', and with definite instructions that there must be no clash with the insurgents until the Thurles, Kilkenny and Cashel police contingents had linked up with Trant's force. On the contrary, he had narrowly escaped capture, expended two hundred and thirty rounds of ammunition, killed at least two men, and wounded more. His official superiors proved very cold to these exploits, as the venomous outcries in his pamphlet about neglect and dark Castle conspiracies against him prove.

A new stage of the conflict developed. McManus recovered and joined O'Brien. All the unarmed men had fled. Firing still continued from the windows. McManus urged O'Brien to call the attack off as his men had now expended all their ammunition. O'Brien stood defiantly and unheeding in the middle of the flying bullets, telling McManus, 'An O'Brien never turned his back on an enemy!' Stephens and McManus first entreated, and then, practically by main force, brought O'Brien out of range.

The insurgents as a body fell back to the rear of the house, and made their way to a boreen which they occupied spontaneously and without any orders from O'Brien. Stephens quotes O'Brien in his desperate mood as telling him, 'I shall never retreat, sir, from the fields where my forefathers reigned as kings!' Just before the retreat, O'Brien heard from Father Fitzgerald the result of the parley with Trant, listened with courtesy to a plea 'to postpone hostilities to some future time', and rejoined his officers.

Eventually, Stephens and O'Brien made their way to the small boreen. Stephens found a priest there haranguing the people 'in a violent fashion, fulminating ecclesiastical curses on the heads of any of them that remained'. Stephens suppressed his indignation and warned the priest that the police were making loopholes in the house and that he would be in danger if he remained. The priest then departed, and Stephens in recollection leaves 'all such to a justice more than human'. His warning was a serious one as he soon repeated it to O'Brien himself. McManus merely records that the priest was surrounded by the crowd whom he addressed and urged to retire to their cabins from a mad enterprise. O'Brien then made a speech and tried to rally them, but they would not respond.

'While the people were still hesitating as to what had best be done, news came that a second body of police were marching on us from the rear,' continues Stephens. 'I walked a few hundred yards to reconnoitre, and glancing ahead, saw a mounted cavalry man keeping watch on our movements. I immediately strode forward and ordered him to surrender at once. He looked at me at first with a fierce glare, but seeing that I had him covered with my rifle and that at my summons a few of my friends had come up to assist me, he quietly dismounted, gave up his steed and himself'.

Stephens placed the man in charge of a small group 'to keep him prisoner, but as they valued their lives not to do him injury'. He brought the horse to O'Brien, repeated his warning about the increasing danger from the loopholed house, stressed the more serious threat of the approach of the second contingent from the rear, and prevailed on him to depart on the horse. Stephens described his appeal to O'Brien thus:

'I have a horse,' I cried, 'that I captured from a policeman just now. Mount immediately and ride away, or else you will be taken. Give me the green and gold cap you are wearing, as it could be a target for the peelers, and take my hat in return'.

O'Brien shook hands warmly with Stephens, 'and both of us felt strange emotions while he was preparing for his departure'.

It was the end at last. Police reinforcements closed in, soon followed by strong military contingents. The last serious fight was led by Stephens who collected some forty or fifty men with very few arms among them. As the Thurles police came up, he divided his men into two equal bodies, and ordered them to hide on both sides of the wood through which the police, some forty-five of them, must pass. At his signal the few men who had guns and pistols rose and fired. Several constables were killed and others fell wounded. The police fell back, then recovered and poured a volley into the ranks of Stephens's force. Some men dropped dead at his side and many were wounded. He himself was struck by two bullets, one in the thigh. In the retreat that followed, pursued by vigorous volleys, Stephens was hit again, rolled half-conscious into a ditch, and lay there unnoticed as the police swept past firing after the scattering ambushers.

Stephens recovered and climbed out of the ditch. He could find only one member of his party. They exchanged coats for the sake of disguise. The famous white Lilliputian Bourbon coat had been too conspicuous in the fighting. He tore away the skirts of his shirt, bound up his wounds, said farewell to his companion, and limped across the fields towards Urlingford. On the way he stopped for some time at a cabin where two friendly men agreed to go with him most of the journey to Urlingford.

4   *Stephens and Doheny take the Felon's Track*

AT Urlingford Stephens came upon a group of armed insurgents and interrupted with vehemence the local parish priest who was thundering at them to disperse, 'lest hell be paved with your guilty souls!' It was then the turn of Stephens, who was denounced as a spy by the priest with such eloquence that the excited crowd were on the point of lynching him when an indignant Kilkenny friend brushed through the mob, roaring in fury, 'I know that man. He is a good Irishman'. He let loose such a tornado of invective and eloquence that the crowd changed front and in turn menaced the priest, headed by a sturdy six-foot insurgent, shouting: 'Pike him!' The parish priest thereupon galloped off on his horse and watched the gathering from a distance.

This Urlingford incident rankled in Stephens's memory for many years. It was the first among the Young Ireland clashes with the clergy and it gave him an inveterate distrust of the priests in politics, even when, as it happened, the priest some years later was pro-Fenian. Of one such case he wrote to a correspondent in December, 1870, 'I had much rather Father M——had kept to his special function, exclusively and for ever. For my maxim is unchanged and unchangeable'.

The now open hostility of many of the clergy led to bitter recriminations at the time, and were mentioned later in the records left by the Forty-Eight leaders. These accounts range from the ironical urbanity of William Smith O'Brien's, 'it is my sincere belief that it was through the instrumentality of the superior order of the Catholic clergy that the insurrection was suppressed' to the almost hysterical ravings of some of Meagher's letters from prison, and not least to Mitchel's vitriolic comment, 'you would have been free long ago but for your damned souls.' Mitchel, however, had no praise for what he termed 'that accursed Ballingarry', a trap into which, he said with emphasis, the Young Irelanders should not have walked. Nor had Mitchel any reproaches for his life-long friend, Father Kenyon, who was of the same mind, and who warned Dillon and Meagher that the hour for action had gone: 'Fight? Yes, of course I would fight, if the people showed themselves prepared for revolution; but it is not becoming in a priest to begin a bootless struggle'.[1]

Gavan Duffy, while sharp in condemnation of what he terms 'the handful of priests who stimulated the insurrection . . . committed to resistance more unequivocally than O'Brien or Dillon,' (a somewhat disingenuous shaft intended mainly for Father Kenyon) acquits those priests who were misled by John O'Connell's slander campaigns against the Young Irelanders or were convinced that the insurrection had no chance of success. He adds that after the struggle Dillon, McGee, Doheny and others escaped by the aid of priests in no way committed to their opinions, and that Meagher could also have escaped by their aid if he had wished to. An eminent ecclesiastic told him afterwards, 'If we hold back our people from a naked encounter with a tiger, it does not follow that we love the monster who ravages their fields one whit more'.

Stephens, strangely enough, was disturbed for years by an obviously idle tale that William Smith O'Brien had been a witness of the Urlingford attack on him from a nearby window and refrained from interfering. His judgment and knowledge of O'Brien discounted it, yet it was only long after O'Brien's death he got clear proof that it was mere fable. O'Brien at the time was hiding in a distant cabin, making plans for his journey home to Limerick, and was within a few days of his arrest at Thurles station.

Once convinced that the insurrection had missed fire in Tipperary and the adjoining areas, Stephens decided to make for John O'Mahony's home and the forces in the Munster

---

[1]Gavan Duffy, *Four Years*. . . pp. 669–70; Gwynn, *Young Ireland and 1848* pp. 257–8. L. Fogarty, *Father Kenyon* (Dublin 1920), pp. 118–22 replies to Gavan Duffy's criticism. John Mitchel, *Jail Journal*, ed. Arthur Griffith (Dublin 1913) and *The Last Conquest of Ireland (Perhaps)*.

glens and mountains which, he was told, were still ready for
further outbreaks. Doheny is very definite that Stephens's first
love affair was wrecked during the last stages of their flight to
exile together somewhat later, and so irrevocably that Stephens
who 'had braved every disaster up to that, broke under
disappointed affection and blighted love'.

Rutherford[2] probably distorts this story by dating it before
Stephens's departure from Co. Tipperary, embellishing it with
the malicious sneer that Stephens 'could not resist the temptation to waste some valuable hours in characteristic fashion. He
hastened off to pay a visit to the lady of his love'. This was
followed by a military raid, and his narrow escape from her
house four days later. Rutherford links all this to Stephens's
own account of a night in the open under a hedge with a
drunken tinker for company, and completes his chapter with
long quotations from Doheny's *Felon's Track*, apparently
without any knowledge of the far more dramatic events before
Stephens actually left Co. Tipperary.

In Bansha Stephens was sheltered by a friendly family,
which was often visited by a magistrate on very good terms
with the household. The family, trusting the magistrate, told
him frankly that their guest was a Young Irelander. Stephens,
not trusting the magistrate, took the precaution of warning one
of the servants to get in touch with the local Young Irelanders
and summon them if need arose. The magistrate pressed
arguments and questions on him, became very angry at his
replies, and threatened to have him arrested. The rescue party
were very soon on the scene, somewhat wary of Stephens until
one of them recognized and vouched for him, and the magistrate, much chastened, left under armed escort.

Another adventure with a dash of drama came as Stephens
strolled through a demesne on his way out of Bansha. He was
challenged by a gamekeeper armed with a fowling piece, who
abused him most aggressively in spite of the softest of answers.
Next, the gamekeeper accused him of being one of the Young
Ireland refugees and told him that he was a prisoner. There
were no more gentle answers, a pistol was clapped to the

[2]For Rutherford see Ch. 27.

gamekeeper's head, the fowling piece wrenched from his grasp, and he was left sprawling on the ground, thoroughly cowed, with orders to remain on that spot until Stephens was well out of sight. Stephens went on his way without further alarms. He bore off the fowling piece and threw it into the first convenient drain.

After a rapid journey to Co. Cork in which he covered some forty miles, Stephens at last met John O'Mahony, the man who was, for the rest of his life, his nearest friend and colleague. Since Ballingarry O'Mahony had been in touch with Michael Doheny who was still determined to consolidate effective forces for a new bid in the autumn. There were constant reminders of the alertness of the Crown forces. An urgent warning came even as O'Mahony and Stephens talked that first night that police and soldiers were pouring in from Cork city on a widespread search of the district, and that a large party was approaching the house. The two men decided to sleep out. O'Mahony told Stephens that on the way back from Ballingarry he and Doheny had narrow escapes, sleeping, now in the fields, now in a friendly farmer's house. Once, in a roadside cabin near Carrick, a scout roused them as raiders closed in. They made off barely in time, thanks to the extreme darkness, but not without a sharp tussle with some soldiers. This latest swoop disturbed O'Mahony. Until then he had moved about freely, no reward had yet been offered for him, and he still hoped to complete his preparations undetected. Slipping away, Stephens and he crossed the river Suir quietly on the one horse.

After resting for the night they pressed on without delay to Rathcormack where Michael Doheny, as arranged with O'Mahony, was waiting for them. In his account of this meeting, Stephens gives his final, and in O'Leary's opinion, his real, estimate of the man whom he calls 'the brave and dauntless', against whom so many bitter pages of the secret record of that American diary of 1859 were directed. There is perhaps some remorse and desire for amends in the intensity of the words written more than twenty years afterwards. Stephens declares that he can never forget the warm reception Doheny gave him:

'When he saw me, young as I then was, and possessed of a

light built frame with a face as delicate as a girl's, he could not resist the enthusiasm of his nature, and flinging his arms around my neck, while his eyes were dewed with tears, he exclaimed "Who could expect to see anyone like you here?"

'No man, I believe, ever made a more genial impression on me than Doheny, and the longer we remained together, the deeper and more enduring that impression became. I can never resist wondering at and admiring the heroic way he bore himself in the face of his difficulties and hazardous stands we were forced to make and confront throughout that felon's track of ours. It was nothing for a young man like me, without wife or child, to have gone on my way singing; but that he, having a woman he loved, and an interesting family he adored, to bear up as he did, as well, if not better than myself, raised him to a heroic level in my estimation. God be with him!'

At this conference at Rathcormack Doheny remarked that Stephens, even more than himself and O'Mahony, was against giving up the struggle until one more effort was made to rally what strength and resources remained for one last blow. O'Mahony after due discussion went off as the chief in charge of that mission. Doheny dispatched a messenger to discuss plans to smuggle Meagher out of Ireland, and then proceeded to the Comeragh mountains in search of Meagher himself. Stephens, who showed signs of exhaustion after his long journey, was sent to rest at a friend's house, where Doheny had sheltered, until the conference could be resumed some days later in the woods near Coolnamuck.

When O'Mahony met Stephens and Doheny there the situation had changed for the worse. O'Brien and Meagher had been arrested and the pursuit of the remaining leaders at large and the arrest of suspects was in full swing. He firmly advised them both to make for safety while he continued his efforts to gather a striking force. He was still less compromised than they were, but the hue and cry had become so fierce, after Doheny in particular, that he was convinced that he could not guarantee their safety. O'Mahony's stubborn hope had grown faint at last. His attempt to rescue the leaders at Clonmel had broken down. Twenty years later, indeed, he still claimed that if the leaders had made at once for his camp in the valley of the Suir

5

after Ballingarry, they would have been safer and he might have raised an insurgent force capable of redeeming the disaster. The discussions with Stephens and Doheny were interrupted by the nightly departures of O'Mahony to interview the chief men of the surrounding districts; by some scouting expeditions of their own to test the reports, promising and depressing, which reached them; and by the final news that plans for their possible escape from the country must be indefinitely suspended. O'Mahony at last insisted that they must take cover for their own safety, and if possible make their way to exile. The fight was off for the moment, and the secure refuges he could arrange for them were growing fewer and fewer while the iron circle of their pursuers steadily closed in.

In the end Doheny and Stephens gave way and parted sadly from O'Mahony to begin their famous 'felon's track'. They admired the determination and caution of O'Mahony, and knew that he would relight the insurrection before autumn had passed if any man in Ireland could, and he had promised them, 'If I succeed, and you have not left the country, you can return'. They knew, too, that O'Mahony would not come out into open revolt without a fighting chance.

While Doheny was in the *Hue and Cry*—with the unflattering description 'Barrister; forty years of age; five feet eight inches in height; fair or sandy hair; grey eyes; coarse red face like a man given to drink; high cheek bones; wants several of his teeth; very vulgar appearance; peculiar coarse unpleasant voice; dress respectable; small short red whiskers'—Stephens, on the other hand, was officially presumed dead and in his coffin. His friends had seen to that with the aid of a sympathetic obituary on 19 August 1848 in the *Kilkenny Moderator*—written, as he himself put it, by a 'rabid Tory who, however, could value honest services rendered to any cause such as that of Ireland's'. This writer was presumably the editor, George Augustus Prim, antiquary and founder of the Kilkenny Archaeological Association.

'Poor James Stephens', the mournful tribute ran, 'who followed Smith O'Brien to the field, has died of the wound he received at Ballingarry while acting as aide-de-camp to the insurgent leader. Mr Stephens was a very amiable, and apart

from politics, most inoffensive young man, possessed of a great
deal of talent, and we believe, he was a most excellent son and
brother. His untimely and melancholy fate will be much
regretted by a numerous circle of friends'.[3]

'This shocked my modesty', commented Stephens, 'and
should confound my critics'. A coffin filled with stones was
carried, he continues, by stalwart men to a graveyard under
the shade of St Canice's Cathedral. A simple stone bore the
inscription, *Here Lies James Stephens. Born at Kilkenny A.D. 1824.
Died from the effects of a wound at Ballingarry, 1848. Aged 24 years.
R.I.P.* When at last in 1856 he returned to Kilkenny, he
recorded that many refused to accept him as the modest young
man they had once known, and insisted that he was an imposter
or a ghost, so deep an impression had been made on the public
mind by his first funeral.

The adventures of the two fugitives have been told once and
for all in Doheny's *Felon's Track*. Their wanderings and dangers
until they parted in Co. Kerry that September were many.
Towards the close the pursuit of Doheny and the persistent
and widespread search of the Crown forces for insurgents on
the run grew keener and nearer. There was the diversion of the
detectives who knew Doheny best to Clonmel for the trials of
Smith O'Brien and other Young Ireland leaders. Doheny took
advantage of this and escaped by disguising himself as a
clergyman and boarding a boat at Cork for Bristol. From there
he made his way to France.

Of Stephens on that dangerous three months' flight, Doheny
wrote: 'His imperturbable equanimity, and ever daring hope,
sustained me in moments of perplexity and alarm when no
other resource could have availed. During the whole time
which we spent, as it were, in the shadow of the gibbet, his
courage never faltered, and his temper never once ruffled'.

Only once, as before noted, had Stephens been shaken on

[3]Quoted, with date given, T.F. O'Sullivan, *The Young Irelanders* (Tralee 1944),
p. 336; also *Mysteries of Ireland*, without date, p. 67. A later notice of Stephens in
the *Kilkenny Moderator*, quoted *Saunders Newsletter*, 9 September 1865, states that
his sister bought a shroud and mourning and the family spread the story of his
death as a blind. His comments and description are given, *Irishman*, 10 June 1882.
A footnote to Ch. III of his 1883–4 *Weekly Freeman* 'Notes on a 3,000 mile Walk',
credits the mock funeral to some very intimate friends.

that long and wearing trail. For the rest, one picture remained in Doheny's memory: the young man who had led him, singing gay songs while the hard roads cut the soles of his feet and the storms on bleak hills and mountainsides howled round them: 'My comrade, who had no life to lose but his own, and who of that was recklessly prodigal, provided he could dispose of it to good account, stepped blithely along and uttered no complaint, although he left behind him traces marked with blood. His terrible indifference soon restored my self-possession'.[4]

It was with the assistance of McCarthy Downing, later the attorney who defended the Phoenix Society prisoners in Skibbereen, and his sister-in-law, Mrs Washington Downing, a popular poetess, 'Christabel', whose home was in London, that Doheny and Stephens made their escape. After Doheny's successful departure, Mrs Washington Downing went on board the *Sabarina* accompanied by Stephens, who, in the character of her personal servant, carried her little boy. This led to the legend that Stephens escaped disguised as a lady's maid, a plan which was in fact proposed, because, as the *Kilkenny Moderator*, 21 September, 1865, explained with malicious delight in circulating this myth, 'being low of stature, and of slight build, effeminate in appearance and without a beard, the idea of dressing him as a female naturally occurred to those aiding his flight; and in the character of a lady's maid he accompanied a rather respectable female on board a vessel at Cork, and in the same capacity passed from the Dover steamer safely into France'. Stephens's comment on the myth was emphatic: 'I never donned a female's costume in my life, nor do I intend to!'

The *Sabarina* sailed, in fact, for Bristol from where 'Christabel' conducted Stephens to her London home. Mr Washington Downing welcomed him cordially. The following day Stephens landed in France and his long exile began, and also the career he summed up in the words 'I have been a nomad since 1848'.

---

[4]Michael Doheny, *The Felon's Track*, ed. Arthur Griffith (Dublin 1914), p. 216.

DURING his seven years of exile in Paris Stephens concentrated on three tasks: to keep alive, to pursue knowledge, and to master the technique of conspiracy. For some years the first task was the hardest and most urgent. Doheny, who soon afterwards left for the United States, joined Stephens and noticed that he spent all his time wandering through the Louvre galleries or looking at the statues of Versailles, forgetful of recent perils and defeats. Stephens knew from the reports which soon reached him that all hopes of another insurrection must be indefinitely postponed. He determined to bury himself in the Latin Quarter and become the 'most assiduous student that ever graced the Left Bank', and drink very deeply of 'the Parisian Pierian spring'. There were to be lengthy periods in the future when there would be little more substantial sustenance.

At first, he put up in a tavern in the Faubourg St Denis, the *Lion D'Or,* which later, with deep regret, he saw demolished by housebreakers and carted away. His wounds still troubled him, so seriously indeed, that he feared one of his feet would have to be amputated. He stayed in bed for a week and recovered. According to his own accounts, the following seven years were filled with varied and incessant study. He attended lectures in the Sorbonne in logic, metaphysics, ethics and philosophy. Kant, Spinoza, Berkeley, Descartes and Lamennais were his favourite authors, whom he studied in the hope that their systems 'might throw more light on the mysterious world beyond the grave. But I learned to change my mind on this'. At least, that was his mood and conviction in the eighties, when he deplored the time and attention he had given to such studies. In the Dublin of the late fifties, Stephens assured his wondering

friends that he was confident he had possessed himself of more
of the truth than most men.

The life of exile certainly was one of frugality and hardship,
and of the intensity of his studies there is little question judging
from his surviving notebooks and papers. Two accounts of this
time, sponsored or influenced by himself, throw some light on
all these aspects, allowing for some amusing exaggerations and
outrageous exhibitions of his skill with the long bow. A New
York pamphlet published in 1866, *James S. Stephens, Chief
Organizer, Irish Republic. An Account of the Origin and Progress of
the Fenian Brotherhood,* has an introduction by himself which
concedes that, some inaccuracies apart, the anonymous author
has treated the subject very creditably.

On the first Paris exile one passage reads:

> 'Mr Stephens's hunger for knowledge had never been satiated, and
> knowing full well that he had much to acquire to fit himself to be
> the successful leader of a popular revolution, he immediately on
> his arrival in Paris, again returned to his books. Shutting himself
> up in his own quiet room, he pursued his studies unremittingly,
> ignoring society almost entirely, and forming only such acquaint-
> ances as would contribute to the fulfilment of his plans.
>
> He was often cramped for even the necessaries of life, but by
> means of occasional services rendered to literary and professional
> friends, he obtained sufficient for his actual needs. For more than
> seven weary years did he remain in Paris, and nearly the whole
> of that time was devoted to his studies, and in attendance on the
> natural sciences, philology and literature. He became distin-
> guished as a linguist, being able to read readily in sixteen
> languages. During the later portion of his residence in Paris, he
> had contributed to the daily and weekly journals, his articles
> exciting much comment and admiration in the literary world . . .
> this added much to his literary fame, and contributed not a little
> to his purse'.

Apart from the characteristic flourish about sixteen languages, since Stephens could never refrain from a generous
multiplication of any figures he had to quote, these statements
are substantially true as more careful accounts of his own and
others prove. The famous war correspondent, John Augustus
O'Shea, drew a similar portrait from personal knowledge, as
did Michael Davitt.

Stephens soon joined John O'Mahony who had sent him and Doheny on the felon's track and then made one last effort to rally the forces of insurrection. Neither Stephens nor Doheny had heard in time of O'Mahony's last blow until too late, and they were already on their way into exile. After Ballingarry, O'Mahony, Savage and a small force held out and carried on a guerrilla struggle against police and military and the smaller military posts. After an attack on Portlaw police barracks in Co. Waterford with, as elsewhere, casualties on both sides, Dublin Castle offered £100 reward for O'Mahony's capture. Eventually he sent his men home and made for Wales where he waited weeks for a boat to France. He faced exile without resources. He made over his property to his brother-in-law, Mandeville, and henceforth drew no income from it, although from time to time, his sister Jane sent him small sums. Luby and Stephens made some bitter and resentful comments on the Mandevilles' treatment of O'Mahony which left him in exile resourceless, and, for long intervals, in the darkest poverty and semi-starvation.

The link that was formed between O'Mahony and Stephens in these years was never really broken in spite of sharp clashes, differences on policy, and stormy disputes between the two men. In his American diary, on 7 January 1859, Stephens wrote a decade later, 'O'Mahony, I say it absolutely, is far and away the first patriot of the Irish race'. And of the end of that first Paris exile, in the same document he wrote elsewhere, 'Unhappy parting! Had we stopped together how different our positions would now be! How different the influence we might now be able to bring to bear on the cause to which both of us have devoted our lives. *He* saw the importance of the work accomplished at home with the soul of a brother and a friend, and a patriot, and rejoiced at *my* having been the instrument of it as if it had been himself'.

The last sentence was written when the first phase of the Fenian movement had hardly begun, and was a dream upheld by two tenacious exiles against the incredulity of the surviving Young Ireland leaders. When that first phase had passed into history, and the movement of which he and O'Mahony had been the outstanding leaders had taken to other guides and other tactics, Stephens, in an even darker Parisian exile twenty-three years later, wrote again, 'In his grave to-day, John O'Mahony is dearer to me than any other man dead or alive'.[1]

One description of the early days of Stephens and O'Mahony in Paris is so minute and with so many traces of his own style, that it suggests it might have been written by Stephens himself, especially the final paragraph, 'Mr Stephens underwent an amount of physical suffering and exertion that will never be known on earth until the sounding of the last trumpet'. There is, however, one important message which appears verbatim in John Savage's *Fenian Heroes and Martyrs* (New York 1868). This description was reprinted in the Dublin *Irishman*, 3 March 1866, from an 'American paper'.

The house described in the opening paragraph is believed to be the Pension Bonnery in the rue Lacépède, a ramshackle old boarding house near to the Jardin-des-Plantes, where John Mitchel, John Martin, Kevin Izod O'Doherty and many Irish political refugees and bohemians stayed over the years. There Balzac had laid the scene of his novel, *Le Père Goriot*. John O'Leary, John Augustus O'Shea, and Mitchel's biographer, William Dillon, have written vivid and amusing pages on the life there in the sixties until, as O'Shea wrote sadly, under Napoleon III one Baron Haussmann in his improvement of the capital's streets saw to it that this bohemia was metaphorically sown over with salt.[2]

'One of the vilest streets in Paris', declared Mitchel on his first visit in 1859. The interior and inmates made him think of morgues and cemeteries. The *Irishman* account proves that ten years before it was then even worse.

'In a long crooked narrow street in the Quartier Latin there stands a rickety-looking house of many storeys—a strange kind of a house in a strange kind of a neighbourhood. A wide,

[1] *Irishman*, Dublin, 3 June 1882.
[2] John Augustus O'Shea, *Leaves from the Life of a Special Correspondent* (London 1885), Vol. 1. pp. 1–24, 54; O'Leary, *Recollections*, Vol. 1, p. 60; William Dillon, *Life of John Mitchel*, Vol. 2, pp. 136–7 237–8; Michael J. Lennon, 'Paris of the Irish', *Irish Ecclesiastical Record*, April 1955, pp. 260–5; G. M. Trevelyan, *Manin and the Venetian Republic of 1848* (London 1923); John Herron Lepper, *Famous Secret Societies* (London 1932).

winding staircase leads from cellar to skylight, and there are many steps in it on which you should not tread too heavily. If you have any one to guide you, and to say "look out" at the proper moment, you *may* go up with an unbarked shin; and after you have got over your heavy breathing, you may tap at the first door to your right, with all the "pinholes" in it peeping through the old black paint. It is six o'clock in the afternoon of a certain day in the winter of '48; and when the black door opens, a shrivelled old woman, in a poor though gay-looking old dress, salutes you politely, and inquires if you are looking for "Messieurs"; and tells you that, if so . . . "Messieurs" have gone out, and she does not expect them back till midnight . . . she sits in this room every evening . . . because this room has a gable window while hers has but a skylight . . . you are the first stranger she has ever seen visit them; and that they always meet their friends at the Café, Rue St *, No. ——, where they supped every night and gossipped and heard and read the news; and that "Messieurs" never leave their room at all in the daytime; for the gaslight best became their wardrobe; and "Messieurs" were poor, proud and (she believed) Irish, though one spoke French better than herself'.

As for the small room: 'A small can stands beside the fireless grate; a dilapidated table, without the falling leaf and fourth leg which it once boasted, leans crutched against the wall; two stools, invalided by loss of the backs which formerly made chairs of them, stand at each end of the veteran table; four broken plastered walls, scrawled over with charcoal diagrams; a litter of straw tied up in a rug in one corner on the floor, and a litter of books and papers, not tied at all, in another; this is the sanctum sanctorum of two Irish gentlemen . . . James Stephens and John O'Mahony'.

No life could be more miserable, declares the anonymous writer, than their hard struggle in a city which could break a stranger's heart 'with such pleasure, or starve him with such perseverence, politeness and dispatch'. Stephens as a teacher of English, and, eventually, as translator and journalist, O'Mahony as a teacher of Irish to students of the Irish College, and a few remittances from his sister in Ireland, survived 'to pasture comfortably enough, if not to live altogether "in clover". To be sure, every franc piece was the result of uphill head-work, but it was a God-send notwithstanding. At first they toiled without cessation; but their success soon enabled them to devote portions of their time to such recreations and pursuits as their natures craved'.

Then comes the most significant passage, which re-appears word for word in John Savage's book already mentioned. The statements in it seem to be indirectly confirmed by Stephens in his American diary, by John O'Mahony in his letter to Stephens in 1856, by such well-informed associates as Thomas Clarke Luby and Dr George Sigerson.[3]

This passage reads:

'At this period, the continent of Europe generally, and Paris particularly, were interwoven with a network of secret political societies, at once the terror and the offspring of the sway of tyrants. As a means of inviting and combining the people for the purposes of successful revolution, they had peculiar fascinations for those whose former attempt at rebellion proved a failure, simply for want of previous organization of the revolutionary elements. O'Mahony and Stephens soon conceived the idea of entering the most powerful of these societies and acquiring those secrets by means of which an indisciplined mob can be most readily and effectually matched against a mercenary army.

'Accordingly, they became enrolled members—and valuable ones too—of one of those very "dangerous brotherhoods"; and thus they became pupils of some of the ablest and most profound masters of revolutionary science which the nineteenth century has produced. How apt were the pupils, and how well they profited by their experience among the brethren, let their works tell. In one point alone they neglected to copy from their continental instructors—they devised no means of visiting with summary chastisement such members of their organization such as were led by ambition, arrogance, or cupidity, into treason or insubordination. In the Fenian organization due precautions were not taken against the admission of men who had never been initiated and who would endeavour to excuse perfidy, betrayal

[3]Luby, *Irish World*, 10 March 1877; Sigerson, *Modern Ireland* (Second edition, London 1869), pp. 26, 39; John Savage, *Fenian Heroes and Martyrs* (New York 1868), pp. 305, 315.

and mutiny, on the grounds that they had never been pledged to "obey implicitly the commands of their superior officers".[4]

'Stephens and O'Mahony worked night and day for some years. In the night to forward the cause to which they had bound themselves and to which they remained faithful to the last, though it was not an Irish cause; and in the day to supply current necessities and to lay up a little store for the work which was then in contemplation. They would have set about their gigantic project for Ireland at once were it not that both held important positions in the "great circle" which held them within its circumference, and desertions were rather against the law. They accordingly remained at their posts until the fall of the republic of February and the consequent disbandment of their circles'.

This somewhat grandiloquent passage is followed by an oblique reproof to the warring Fenian factions in the America of 1866, and illustrated by the edifying fable that a dispute between the two exiles as to which should organize Ireland and which America, was settled by the toss of a five franc piece, 'they were almost rich then, though they still stuck to the garret, "head" for Ireland, "tail" for America. Head it is—'twas Stephens that called.'

This passage is also the basis for Rutherford's legend of Stephens as the agent of international revolution perambulating Spain, Italy and Germany, and dropping over now and then with O'Mahony to London for a chat with the Central Committee of Universal Revolution. For good measure to his unacknowledged summary of the *Irishman* article, he throws in the myth that Stephens and O'Mahony travelled secretly to Ireland for the Lalor-Luby attempt at a rising in the autumn of 1849.[5]

In Rutherford's legend there was a grain of truth; in his added myth no truth whatever. Stephens in Paris in the autumn of 1849, or possibly later, had among his pupils of English a most competent guide to all the ramifications of European revolution, of those in Italy in particular, General

[4]Devoy, *Recollections...* p. 33, states that 'the organization got into several places without Stephens knowing anything about it, owing to failure to report it'. A Wicklow circle of some 1,500 Fenians, discovered accidentally by Devoy, startled Stephens.

[5]Rutherford, *Fenian Conspiracy*, Vol. 1. pp. 46–52.

Guglielmo Pepe. The general, like his chief, Daniele Manin, and like Stephens himself, was keeping body and soul together by giving language lessons. He taught Stephens Italian in exchange for language lessons, and it is pretty certain that he taught him far more than Italian. The only record of their meeting is a solitary line in Michael Davitt's *Fall of Feudalism.* A sympathetic historian said of the general that he was an honoured and venerable veteran of the Italian struggle at whom it was impossible not to laugh and impossible not to love.[6]

The general was then in his sixty-seventh year with only six years of life left to him. He had fled to Paris with his leader, Manin, to whom he had acted as commander-in-chief in the last stand of the Venetian Republic against the Austrians. It was the last militant episode in a life which had been given since his boyhood to Italian independence struggles. He had served as an Italian volunteer in Napoleon's army at Marengo in 1800, led a successful revolution in Naples twenty years later, fled then before the Austrians and had had many other adventures in the continental wars, in prisons and conspiracies. He wandered from Madrid to Lisbon, from Paris to London, after his flight from Naples in 1821, trying with little success to form an international secret league of all the republican and political reformers of Europe, a loose union by correspondence and conferences of these groups to be known as the Constitutional Society of European Patriots. He had worked with the Carbonari, with the French secret societies of La Fayette and Blanqui, but the greater part of his life had been spent in the Italian struggle and the secret work of Young Italy.

Dr Sigerson stated that Stephens and O'Mahony came in touch with 'some unquiet spirits of the continental secret societies' while Stephens worked as translator and journalist for the *Moniteur*; became enrolled members, 'and studiously made themselves acquainted with the best methods of secret

[6]*Manin and the Venetian Revolution of 1848,* p. 183: *Famous Secret Societies,* pp. 153–5; Davitt, *Fall of Feudalism,* p. 73. Davitt adds 'Stephens made the acquaintance of the leading European revolutionists who were found in Paris in these years'.

organization for ulterior purposes'. It has also been claimed that the society they joined was the famous Blanqui organization, the Society of the Seasons, with its secret Directory, circles and sections resembling the Fenian organization as Stephens later planned it.[7]

There has been much mystification and theorizing on this subject. Stephens's later references to his contacts with the French revolutionary Left during the Franco-Prussian war are vague and guarded although pointing mainly, in spite of his known membership of the International Workingmen's Association late in 1866, to political republican rather than to socialist groups. In the fifties, however, his admiration, due no doubt to General Pepe's inspiration, was given to Young Italy.

In his references to this time of exile and brooding over future plans for Ireland, Stephens remarks in an aside that he wished 'to take a leaf out of the book of Mazzini without in any way being a servile imitator of that great man'. He proceeds to a more definite statement: 'Once I resolved that armed insurrection was the only course for Ireland, I commenced a particular study of continental secret societies, and in particular those which had ramifications in Italy; for Italians have in a certain way perfected conspiracy, and I thought that with certain reserves they were the best models to follow. I proposed, however, not so much to make a slavish imitation of any known secret society as a selection of the good qualities of each, and fuse them into that I was creating'.[8]

There were, however, very definite reminders from Ireland itself in that very year of 1849 that the manufacture and even the models of secret organization were not a monopoly of France or Italy: Philip Grey, James Fintan Lalor, Thomas Clarke Luby, John O'Leary, Joseph Brenan and others had formed a small secret society and planned an insurrection for that autumn, for the embers of Ballingarry glowed however faintly yet. This small organization of Fintan Lalor and Philip Grey, or the amalgamation of two bodies set on foot in Dublin

[7]T. A. Jackson, *Ireland Her Own* (London 1946), p. 262; H. B. C. Pollard, *The Secret Societies of Ireland: Their Rise and Progress* (London 1922), p. 47.
[8]*Weekly Freeman*, 6 October 1883.

and Munster respectively by these two men and their helpers, was in a sense the real forerunner of the Fenian organization. It supplied two outstanding future Fenian leaders in O'Leary and Luby, and, in small groups of '48 and '49 veterans, it lived on until the magnetism and organizing genius of Stephens absorbed it and its members.[9]

The projected rising decided on by Luby, Lalor and the others at a convention in Clonmel for September in Cork, Limerick, Clare, Tipperary and Waterford was hampered completely by sudden public denunciations in the press and pulpit, and the mobilization was crippled before it could get under way by the Government drafting troops in force into Tipperary and Waterford. Brenan led an attack on a police barracks at Cappoquin but had to call off the attack after casualties on both sides. Lalor waited all night with a hundred and fifty men to attack Cashel, but had to abandon it when contingents from other districts failed to arrive. John O'Leary had to dismiss his small force because they were practically unarmed, but his scouts saved Grey's party by a timely warning just as the troops were closing in. Luby and O'Leary were arrested but released shortly afterwards. In spite of the death of Lalor in the last days of December, the organization was not buried with him. O'Leary and Luby kept Lalor's fame alive, however dimly, until Davitt, Henry George and Connolly discovered and applied his teachings in various ways to historic effect.

O'Mahony and Stephens declined to participate in or encourage the '49 attempt. Both they and Doheny had discussed the moral of the '48 defeat in the autumn of that year before the latter left for America; any new attempt must be based on what O'Mahony termed 'legions of liberty, silently enrolled'. Doheny agreed that he would do all he could for their ultimate aim in America, Stephens what he could elsewhere, although he and O'Mahony made it clear that they had no immediate intention of returning to Ireland. Philip Grey was also a

[9]For a detailed account of this organization, see *An Cosantoir*, April 1950, T. P. O'Neill, 'Fintan Lalor and the 1849 Movement', and the sources cited there; the *Irish Nation*, New York 1881–2 for Luby's first-hand account; and the Luby Papers. Also O'Leary's *Recollections*, Vol. 1. Ch. III–V.

refugee in Paris, and, as Luby made clear later, he formed a link between O'Mahony and the small secret organization at home. O'Mahony, according to the *Irish World*, 10 March 1877, remained in Paris during the 1849 attempt, and although in touch with Grey 'had next to nothing to do with' the affair.

Grey accepted Lalor's invitation through an envoy to return for the rising. O'Mahony refused. He wrote to Lalor that his conscience would not permit him to use the influence he possessed to lead his countrymen into any desperate and hopeless struggle. With all his courage he had caution, and deplored that his campaign after Ballingarry had been ruined by the precipitate action of some of his men. He concluded 'since the disgrace of Ballingarry, I am convinced it will take years to prepare the Irish race to meet their foe in arms.'

So Philip Grey returned to Ireland alone. The myth that O'Mahony accompanied him had no other basis than a rhetorical flourish in a speech of Kickham's. Grey, the forerunner, with Lalor, of the Irish Republican Brotherhood, died a year before its foundation. When he died, in January 1857, Luby wrote the almost only existing record of his life in Thomas Francis Meagher's New York *Irish News* and there, too John O'Mahony wrote:

'This Philip Grey I find to be the most untiring and most indomitable of all the men that ever took the field for Ireland. He could never be made to understand that we were beaten. It was he who worked hardest of all to retrieve the lost cause . . . He is also the man of whom least has been said'.

The link with the Fenian pioneers was complete when Stephens insisted that Luby should make his first halting public speech over Grey's grave in Kilglass churchyard in Co. Meath.

In December 1853, O'Mahony sailed for New York and arrived there in January 1854. In the same month John Mitchel who had reached America shortly before, after his escape from Australia, started his *Citizen*. He publicly gave O'Mahony a cordial welcome and they became life-long friends, in spite of Mitchel's later clashes with the Fenians, his sharp criticisms of their policy, and his hostility to Stephens in particular. In the early part of 1855, O'Mahony and Doheny created the Emmet

Monument Association,[10] and events more and more forced
O'Mahony into the leadership of Irish-America.

It is clear from their own scattered statements in their letters
and writings that both Stephens and O'Mahony deeply sympathized with the political and social ideals of the French and
other revolutionary leaders they met in Paris. O'Leary
describes O'Mahony as 'a strong democrat, and even much of
a socialist in opinion', and this is confirmed by O'Mahony's
frequent allusions to his 'ultra-democracy', as well as by his
preface to his translation of Keating's history, and such
declarations in his own New York *Irish People* as,

> '*Every individual born on Irish soil constitutes, according to Fenian
> doctrine, a unit of that nation, without reference to race or religious belief*,
> and as such he is entitled to a heritage on the Irish soil, subject
> to such economic, political, and equitable regulations as shall
> seem fit to the future legislators of liberated Ireland. From this
> heritage none shall be excluded'. (Quoted *Irishman*, 15 June
> 1868).

Neither Stephens nor O'Mahony left a detailed account of
their participation in the resistance to Louis Napoleon's *coup
d'état* in December 1851. J. P. Leonard in an obituary tribute
to O'Mahony in the *Irish World* in February 1877, recalled
how he had noticed O'Mahony in Paris as the fighting broke
out, walking through the streets, unconcerned by the flying
bullets. His own statement in his letter to Stephens in 1856—
quoted fully in the next chapter—is clear enough. The fall of
the French Republic and the rise of the Second Empire marked
the end of all hopes of the spread of the European revolution,
and the break-up of many of the conspiratorial circles in which
the two men had moved. And more and more the activities of
both of them turned back to fulfil the ulterior object which
had led them into foreign conspiracy.

[10][The title of the organization was a characteristic example of the Fenian
liking for mixing piety with concealment. It will be recalled that Robert Emmet's
immortal speech from the dock, after his abortive rebellion in 1803, concluded:
'Let no man write my epitaph . . . Let my memory be left in oblivion, and my
tomb remain uninscribed, until other times and other men can do justice to my
character. When my country takes her place among the nations of the earth,
then, and *not till then*, let my epitaph be written'. So the title of the Association
would signify to the knowledgeable that its business would initially include the
fulfilment of Emmet's prerequisite.] O.D.E.

Some years after O'Mahony's departure for the United States, Stephens, although he had established himself firmly in Paris, finally decided that the end of his exile was near. His closing days of the first Parisian exile are best described in his own words:

'Towards the end of my student career in Paris I devoted myself to the work of translating several volumes of modern French philosophy into English with a view to give them to the British public stripped of all the hideous and unmeaning Gallicisms which unfortunately but too often creep into English editions of French authors. Long before I ventured on the undertaking, however, circumstances made it imperative upon me to share my time between study and teaching in the English language. I used to spend one portion of the day at the lecture halls of the Sorbonne and another in several educational establishments of the city where I taught English. My nights were usually occupied with hard reading on the subjects treated of at the university, and later with the translations just referred to'.[11]

His struggle over the years of exile, he says, had been rugged enough at the start. His imperfect knowledge of the French language had hampered him, and more seriously, the small demand for foreign language teachers, as most of the French thought their own language and literature all-sufficient. Yet there was the exception of the Faubourg St Germain, 'where fashionable opulence, gazing Londonwards wished sincerely to understand the Londoner and paid many a Bohemian to gratify that wish. Democrat though I was, I was tempted to bask in the glare and inhale the Araby odours of the home of tinselled aristocracy, and succumbed to the temptation—not, be it said, because I loved the *beau monde* more but appreciated poverty less. Bohemianism, in short, was becoming exceedingly uncomfortable, and a ten sou dinner was a poor enough sauce with which to garnish thirty or forty pages of the Scholastics on the Science of Soul'.

After this candid admission Stephens explains he became a tutor to pupils from the aristocracy. Penury induced him 'to enter the ranks of that well abused but sublime profession which has for its special object the training of the young mind. I gave

[11]*Weekly Freeman*, 6 October 1883.

6

lessons in English to scions of the old Legitimist stocks and to
sprigs of the younger Napoleonic ones'. Yet, as his knowledge
of French increased rapidly, he had the second resource of
journalism. He became a member of the staff of the *Moniteur
Universel*, 'where my maiden newspaper efforts appeared every
morning under the title of "Faits Divers". While engaged on
this journal my chief occupation consisted in pursuing the
English exchanges, and giving the readers of the *Moniteur* a
succinct account of British intelligence, more or less condensed
to suit the exigencies of space. Subsequently, and while
Theophile Gautier was dramatic critic of this organ, the director
placed a *feuilleton* at my disposal, and I translated Dickens'
Martin Chuzzlewit for the journal—all my writings and translations being well received, and auguring for me (I may say it,
I hope, without laying myself open to the charge of egotism)
a successful career in French journalism'.[12]

Yet Stephens recognized that here was not his true vocation.
The lure of revolutionary politics dazzled him more than ever.
He grew to hate the sedentary life of the literary man, and his
desk became, he tells us, an instrument of torture and he longed
for action, more work for that Ireland of whose cause he never
despaired, for which he had risked his life, lost his career, and
for which he was to endure still more.

Through all his stilted and mannered prose that old fire
burns:

'The more brilliant my journalistic prospects became, the
more repulsive were their duties; for my mind was being more
and more weaned from the pen and the cabinet to the exciting
enthusiasm of the outer world. The ardour for philosophical
studies also cooled down under the influence of the feelings
which were then overpowering me. Every pursuit, every occupation, every other desire of my soul shrank into the merest
insignificance before this all-absorbing determination. At last,
not able to resist its powers any longer I gave it free rein, and
left Paris towards the close of 1855'.

[12]It was the *Moniteur* translation of *Martin Chuzzlewit* that led Taine to write an
article in the *Revue des Deux Mondes*, February 1856, which introduced Dickens to
Europe as an original and important novelist. Una Pope-Hennessy, *Charles
Dickens* (London 1945), pp. 330–1. Dickens himself praised the Stephens
translation.

6 Stephens tramps Ireland in 1856

EARLY in 1856 Stephens began his way back towards Ireland. Two questions he wanted answered could only be answered after a tour of inquiry throughout the entire country. Was a new uprising even conceivable? Had the time come at last for that secret revolutionary organization under his leadership? The old Ireland in which he had grown up had gone out for ever in famine, fever, depopulation, despair, and defeat. More recently, what hope survived these calamities was killed by the Sadleir-Keogh betrayal of a political and social movement on peaceful and parliamentary lines. A swindling banker, a place-hunting lawyer, and the politically conservative Catholic Primate, Dr Cullen, between them had wrecked tenant-right and all prospect of any popular movement on the O'Connell model. 'Till all this be changed' wrote Gavan Duffy in his farewell to Ireland the year before Stephens returned, 'there seems to be as little hope for the Irish cause as for a corpse on the dissecting table. I have done my best to change it . . . A preternatural apathy broods over the country, disheartened by corruption and pampered by a false and temporary prosperity. When all external circumstances favour a national movement, it is repudiated at home'.[1]

Because of their frustrated attempts to establish a revolutionary organization in America, Mitchel and other Young Ireland leaders, tended with some reluctance, towards a similar mood. This was deepened by the chaos, despondency and factionism among the disillusioned exiles and emigrants. O'Mahony and

[1] Charles Gavan Duffy, *The League of North and South. An episode of Irish History 1850–54* (London 1886) p. 364 footnote. [For a recent scholarly treatment of the constitutional movement in question and its failure, see J. H. Whyte, *The Independent Irish Party, 1850–1859* (Oxford 1958)]—O.D.E.

Doheny in the United States, Luby, Grey and their small groups at home, for all their tenacity, could merely hold on. John O'Leary, on the point of returning from London to Dublin, found he had lost all hopes of a national uprising, a conviction which ended only after his meeting with Stephens the following year. He believed ever afterwards that it was a sign of great moral and intellectual merit on Stephens's part that he refused to lose faith in the future.

Yet even Stephens, during his stay in London on the way back, had his own doubts as to whether Ireland was yet ripe for his plans. It might well be, he thought at the time, that the salvation of the country must come from without, the stimulus of revolution in Great Britain, or attacks from the Irish-American base and stronghold. In London he stayed at the home of Washington Downing whose wife had helped him in his escape from Ireland in 1848, and where he had sheltered before going to France. Washington Downing was on the staff of the *Daily News* and Stephens left with him the manuscript translations of those volumes of French philosophy done in Paris. The old revolutionary fervour and desire to see Ireland had once more asserted themselves with irresistible force.

While in England Stephens visited Manchester, according to Luby, and met again his old friend, Edward Hollywood, the weaver who had accompanied O'Brien and Meagher to Paris in 1848 to present an address to Lamartine, and who had later shared Stephens's exile in that city after the insurrection. From some of Stephens's conversations with Luby and others much later in the year it was evident that he had moved in some of the surviving Chartist and English Republican circles, since his talk ran on the prospects of a revolution in England and the small chance of a successful movement in Ireland until then, with much socialist, republican and universal philanthropic theorizing that thoroughly infuriated and disgusted Luby.

This meeting with Luby and the small surviving organizations of the '48 and '49 men was preceded by what Stephens himself described as his three thousand miles walk through Ireland.[2] In the opening days of 1856 he landed in Dublin,

[2]The account of Stephens's tour in the text is based mainly on his own account written in the *Weekly Freeman*, October 1883 to February 1884.

and was as much depressed by the universal lethargy in the capital, as he was later in the countryside. He made some brief contacts with old friends, and had a severe bout of illness which changed his appearance so much for the worse that John O'Daly, bookseller and Gaelic scholar, who had known him well in Kilkenny, wrote off to John O'Mahony in New York the alarming tale that Stephens ' was not long for this world'. O'Daly, at least, recognized him in spite of the stamp Paris had left on him. Often he was mistaken for a foreigner, which amused and annoyed him in turns as it was his boast that in spite of nine years abroad he had preserved his Kilkenny accent, irrefutable evidence of moral integrity and strength of character. The freedom of his language often startled his listeners.

As soon as he had recovered, Stephens travelled at once to Kilkenny. He was not a fugitive nor then sought or wanted by the police, and he remained openly in the city for several weeks. Since his exile he had not been in touch with his own family, and the news he heard almost at once overwhelmed him with grief. No word had reached him, he states, of his father or of the sister he had last watched sleeping when he stole away to the fight at Ballingarry. In search of news of them he paid his first visit to an old Catholic priest who had been a close friend of the family. When the priest heard his name he received a warm welcome. Stephens was not surprised that the priest did not recognize him. That was a familiar experience since his return, but in the warmth of this particular welcome he detected a pity and a sympathy that alarmed him. Then the priest told him that both his father and sister were dead. He rushed unceremoniously away and spent some bitter hours in solitude.

Later he learned from his only surviving relatives in Kilkenny that his father and sister had died shortly after the insurrection and Stephens's flight to exile. His reflections were bitter: 'Before the Young Ireland revolt a happy home was ours by the sparkling Nore . . . my aged father felt the rude shock severely, and, as I was then informed, never recovered from the shock. My only sister followed him to the grave in the prime of girlhood; and thus was a household ruined and broken up'. Stephens, in spite of all, could not regret the past, and realized that if at that moment the same decision had to be made, he would make it.

He stayed several weeks with his relatives, the Caseys, his uncle Patrick, and three aunts. He very soon discovered that the *Kilkenny Moderator* obituary of himself and his mock funeral to the shade of St Canice's Cathedral had made so deep an impression on many of his old acquaintances that the resurrected Stephens of 1856 was regarded by them as either an imposter or a ghost, and he declared with disgust that, in spite of all the evidence, 'there were incredulous Thomases in some groups who held out to the bitter end, and I had to give up the idea of ridding them of their ignorance and superstition'.

Kilkenny, too, he found deeply changed in national feeling and opinion from the enthusiastic city in which he delivered his Tholsel speech in 1848. It was now cold, dead, and passionless as if the Young Ireland frenzy had never swept through it and inspired it, or indeed had ever been. Among the middle classes there was a strong veering towards what he dubbed 'Repeal Whiggery', a contempt for the '48 men as rash and impetuous youths who had broken O'Connell's heart first, and then Ireland's, and an even larger number who said that Big Dan and the Young Irelanders were two plagues the country was well rid of, and that the old land could jog along quietly and finally secure the end of her grievances from the imperial legislature. The bourgeoisie of Kilkenny were split into these two groups. But the people, cried Stephens, were sound at heart. 'Artisan and labourer spoke to me with enthusiasm of the Club days and hoped to see them again before they died. I saw eyes light up to the glow of indescribable ardour when I spoke to them of their brothers beyond the seas, of the new and greater Ireland in the Western Republic, and reminded them that the cause which braved so many dangers had got enough life left in it to rise once more, in the near future, to the position it deserved to enjoy.'

He did not speak his whole mind here whatever important

place America had in his future plans, because in reality he had a very low opinion of the Irish-American political movement such as it was then, with squabbling factions and, what he loathed most, the pageantry of St Patrick's Day parades with bursts of flatulent rhetoric from exiled Young Ireland celebrities, and banquets where the shamrock was generously watered with whisky and champagne. Such were his opinions in 1856, when he certainly did not foresee that some fifteen years later he himself would be a wine merchant in New York making a brave effort to sell wine and, in particular, champagne to what he termed all 'Ramshackledom'. And such were his opinions in the eighties when the wine merchant venture was a thing of the past. These opinions of his were, in fact, enthusiastically shared by his friends, John O'Mahony and John O'Leary. Yet for all that, he regarded 'the new and greater Ireland' as his future base and source of supplies with a new and effective movement there as well as at home.

Indeed, towards the end of his tour, when he visited John O'Daly in his Dublin bookshop and learned from a letter that John O'Mahony had sent to O'Daly that O'Mahony had decided in disgust to give up for the future all political activity, Stephens wrote to dissuade him. O'Mahony's letter dealt in the main with books and material he required for his translation of Keating's *History of Ireland,* but one page was directed specially to Stephens himself. It may be quoted in full as it gives O'Mahony's true opinion of Stephens, reveals their common participation in the fighting at the barricades during the *coup d'état* in December 1851, and expresses the views both held on the Irish-American political scene as it then was:

'I was frightened at the account you gave me of my beloved friend and brother, James Stephens; for I love and value him more than any man that lives. I should feel quite despondent about him had my friend Doherty (Doheny?) not told me that he had received news that he was in Tipperary a few weeks since, and was looking very well. Stephens never, in my memory, had a very robust appearance; wherefore I ardently hope that you have been deceived in your opinion of him. Should my friend be cut off in the pride of his manhood, Ireland will have lost one of its brightest and clearest intellects and one of its truest and most uncompromising spirits.[3]

'You will be kind enough to send me his address by return of post, for I am still very uneasy about him. Send him also one of the Irish-American papers I forward you by this post. In this you will find an attempt of a speech by myself, that I intend as my farewell to Irish political agitation in America. He will see by it that I still hold the same political faith we both pledged ourselves to so often in our eyrie in the *Quartier Latin*, and for which we proffered our lives in the bloody days of December; in the *coup d'état* 1851. He is jealous of me, I know, for I have not written to him lately; but this resulted in no want of affection towards him, but because I had no good news to send him, either of myself or of the cause.

'My private course has not been very successful. I am sick of Young Ireland and its theatrical leaders, whose want of steadfastness of purpose and childish pettishness with the people that were disheartened by their own irresolution and want of forecast makes me more despair of my country than any fickleness of its populace. I am sick of Irish Catholics in America. I am sick of Yankee-doodle twaddle, Yankee-doodle selfishness and all Yankee-doodledum! The very names of parties are inverted here. Your slavery-man is a Democrat. A Republican *pur sang*—your abolitionist—is an aristocrat! Even in the anti-slavery party, there is nothing sound—they are mere political tinkers—would-be patchers-up of an old kettle they call a Constitution, that they should rather throw into the furnace and cast anew.

'It is refreshing to my heart to turn from Irish tinsel patriots, the people's leaders on *gala* days, and from American retrogression, to the stern front and untiring constancy of the continental apostles of liberty and the ceaseless preparation of their disciples. Verily, we Irish rebels ought to blush for ourselves and our people; but we must blush much more for our chiefs, who are little better than whipped schoolboys. A thought struck me to send this last sheet to my friend Stephens. Therefore, it is why I allowed myself to fall into the above political incoherencies. I don't want to discuss the questions they relate to just now—so

[3]Note by Stephens: 'The public will, I hope, be indulgent to me for not having applied the pruning knife to this rather luxuriant flattery'.

O'Mahony had retired from the Emmet Monument Association in the spring of 1856 to concentrate on the work of translating Keating's *History of Ireland* (D'Arcy, *The Fenian Movement in the United States*, p. 10.) The date of this letter is probably Autumn 1856.

you will be kind enough to let them pass without remark, even though you may not agree with me. You and I would pull much better on ancient than on modern Irish ground. Besides, I hate discussion. You will be kind enough to write me a long letter at your leisure on the subjects I mentioned; but take care and send me Stephens's address by return of post.

I remain, dear sir, very thankfully and very sincerely, yours,
John O'Mahony

P.S. I want Dr O'Donovan's and Dr Curry's addresses. Please send them. Tell Stephens that Doheny is well, and wishes to be warmly and affectionately remembered to him'.

This letter, indeed, Stephens did not read until the close of his tour on his return to Dublin towards the end of the autumn. Yet when he left Kilkenny some weeks after his first visit there, he was soon in the thick of discussions provoked by the political and social ideals he and O'Mahony had developed in their Parisian eyrie. During his stay with his old fellow-exile, Joseph Rivers, then a somewhat disillusioned farmer who lived at Tybroghy Castle, Co. Kilkenny, Stephens horrified his friend and a select company, quite as much as he did Luby and Philip Grey in Dublin later, with his philosophizing, and, above all, his novel views on social questions. His personal spell, indeed, proved strong. He was amused when Rivers shed his disillusion very quickly as soon as Stephens hummed or sang some old patriotic catch or ballad. Rivers would join in with spirit, and then round on Stephens for lighting the old fires within him, sadly admitting, 'It must be there all the time.'

He had cured Stephens of a mild fever in Paris during a cholera epidemic by insisting that he should try some old country recipe. Rivers very soon came to the conclusion that his old friend was afflicted with a mental disease far more dangerous than cholera or plague. He drew a very firm line at the advanced ideas and startling paradoxes that Stephens poured out with great conviction, and especially when Stephens said in argument that national independence, 'unless the Irish land were given to the Irish people was not worth the trouble or sacrifice of attaining'. 'Do you want,' thundered Rivers, 'to introduce Socialism or Communism into Ireland?'

Stephens explained that in general he would not give a red

cent for a parliament in the Old House in College Green or for a republic if in either case 'the toilers should owe or pay aught to State, king, or president, save what might be found necessary for the purpose of government'. And while the entire company joined with Rivers in denouncing him as a Marat, a wild utopian dreamer, and even a political criminal, he went on with assertions of his views that convinced them all the more that their charges were not at all wide of the mark.

'I am,' he told them, 'no Socialist, still less am I a Communist, but my faith is that every child born in a free state should have a place on his native soil whereon to gain an independent livelihood. At the same time, I may observe that I believe in the principle of association, for to my mind it is the only one on which the regeneration of mankind can be based'.

Yet in recording his discussions on these matters in his recollections, Stephens goes to some pains to explain that the Fenian movement had always a purely national and political objective. In 1856, in any case, he stresses, neither he nor the Fenians could have launched a land reform movement after the fiasco of the Tenant Right agitation some years before. Moreover, he found then a cleavage between the rural and urban workers. He could win over the Ribbon lodges to a national revolutionary effort, and the town workers, mechanics, tenant farmers and labourers, but to combine them all in a new social movement was a task beyond his power. Although Fintan Lalor was a living memory with Luby and the '48 groups with which Stephens was then in contact, he never mentions his name or doctrines or methods of organization, deep as the mark was that Lalor had left on the still existing secret societies. The name of Marx is absent from Stephens's writings. Frederick Engels that same year was conducting a tour of Ireland as extensive as that of Stephens but there is no record that they met. Their record of existing conditions, however, in the dead weight of landlordism, for example, is often similar.

Stephens's social ideals, in 1856, he protests nearly thirty years afterwards, remained his social ideals to the end: 'My ideas have remained unchanged on the land problem . . . People may here raise an objection, and ask me if I were so accentuated in my views on the comparative worthlessness of separation without the abolition of landlordism, why was it I did not start the Fenian movement with a view to such abolition. My answer is simple and I hope consequently clear. I did not think it possible at the time to inaugurate a land movement, for in the first place, Messrs Charles Gavan Duffy, John Francis Maguire and others had previously damned any little chance it might have by running it into a Parliamentary rut, and all but annihilating it there; and, in the second, I did not believe that I could unite the people on the issue of the land, as it was looked on just as Rivers looked upon it as the raving of a Bedlamite; and, moreover, I found the labourers and mechanics would never join the tenantry shoulder to shoulder in the enterprise.

'It is true', he continues, 'that in the columns of the *Irish People* several articles were written advocating peasant proprietorship; but national independence was certainly put forward as the point to be gained first, implying, of course, the immediate settlement of the agrarian question once separation was achieved; for it was my decided resolve, as well as that of nearly all who worked under me in the I.R.B., that if we were able to raise Ireland to the position of a nation, we would at the same time raise the Irish farmer to the position of Irish landlord, subject to a just and legitimate division of Irish property. Such is a synopsis of what I thought on this important subject'.

In this Stephens spoke for the Irish Republican Brotherhood in general, quite apart from that minority of Fenians, who like himself, and John O'Mahony, were in the latter's phrase, 'ultra-democratic'. The shadow of the social question, and in particular of the land question, lay over the Fenians, as it had lain over the Young Irelanders. The Ribbonmen and the landlords could never be ignored. Stephens's deep hatred of landlordism as he saw it on his journey, flashes out in many a line. Joseph Brenan and Devin Reilly in 1848 had spoken in the same spirit, and in the two Fenian leaders and in these two Young Irelanders was the same sympathy with certain reservations for the revolutionary struggles in Europe.

Reilly in the *Irish Felon*, and a writer, possibly Brenan, in the *Irish Tribune*, had written on much the same lines of the

June uprising of the workmen in Paris. The *Irish Tribune* writer
had recommended the military lessons of the outbreak to the
practical consideration of the Confederates, regretted that these
brave insurgents had been misled by utopians, and returning
to the social grievances of Ireland, added, 'We do not, however,
separate the settlement of the land question from that of nationality—for many reasons they are inseparably connected—and
the settlement of one necessarily settles the other'.[4]

When Stephens left Rivers and Tybroghy Castle and made
his way to Limerick, he learned that William Smith O'Brien
had returned to his home at Cahirmoyle from a long exile
abroad. It was during a visit there that Stephens realized the
conflict between the more conservative Young Irelanders and
the rising movement, and the gulf which lay between himself
and O'Brien on political tactics, and above all on those social
issues which since his return had led him into so many animated
debates.

[4]For Devin Reilly, see James Connolly, *Labour in Irish History* 182–5 (Dublin
1910). P. A. S(illard), *Life and Letters of John Martin* (n.p., 1893), pp. 76, 104.

For the *Irish Tribune* article, *Commission Court, Dublin, The Queen v. Kevin Izod
O'Doherty*, August 1848, 'A Lesson from the Insurrection in Paris', pp. 20–2.

THE outwardly tranquil seclusion of the house and demesne at Cahirmoyle misled Stephens. Here at least, he thought, William Smith O'Brien had a hard-earned haven after long and weary years across the seas. Near the front entrance two boys were playing and a girl on stilts amused herself. The barricades of Ballingarry and Killenaule, Trant and his riflemen, the solitude of Tasmania, the Clonmel dock, could fade into mere memories here. Then, when O'Brien came out quickly in answer to Stephens's message, that illusion died abruptly. O'Brien did not recognize Stephens at first but soon gave him a very cordial reception. The old leader was sadly changed, 'not much of the Smith O'Brien, the outlaw of '48 in this Smith O'Brien' writes Stephens, 'the crows' feet had been dealing harshly with that splendid forehead of his, and had ravished his features, his frame had lost its former litheness and activity, and he appeared to me to be broken down totally in the outer man'.

Half-reminiscently, half-prophetically, Stephens reflected that exile often sapped the most robust constitution. Yet O'Brien's old distant and dignified manner remained, his gentlemanly deportment, the eagle eye, knit brow, and pose of lips were still there. Something even more serious than all the physical marks of age and care wounded Stephens deeply: he sensed at once that O'Brien was still an exile, an exile isolated in his own home, his family hostile to his political ideals, and regarding him at best with pitying misunderstanding. The seeming tranquility of Cahirmoyle was on the surface. Pondering on this visit over a quarter of a century later, Stephens considered that only one of O'Brien's children had been true to their father's spirit, his daughter, Charlotte Grace O'Brien, the child of ten he had seen striding around on stilts. For the rest, Stephens dipped his pen in gall.

O'Brien, he felt, was stifling in disillusion and almost in despair, even if his own nobility of mind and character survived. Stephens would not have been at all surprised to learn even then that under the roof where he was, in some desk or other was a family tree with the entry after O'Brien's name in 1853, 'Now in exile in Australia, the ill-fated victim of misplaced patriotism'.[1]

When O'Brien introduced Stephens to his eldest son as one of his '48 friends, the young man responded coldly with a very formal handshake, and his father patiently explained: 'Mr Stephens was one of the few, *the very few*'—and here the words were spoken with marked emphasis—'who not only risked his life, but to the last, and in the face of everything, stood by me'.

There was a look of passing interest on the young man's face. O'Brien added: 'Had there been a hundred like this gentleman, things would have ended differently'.

O'Brien and Stephens then fell to discussing their old battles and adventures while the son listened in hostile silence to his kind yet somewhat heavy father and to the shabby and unwelcome guest.

Stephens recalled from the vanished forties memories of O'Brien's extreme personal courage and readiness to take every possible personal risk, combined with his fatal scrupulosity about commandeering food for hungry fighters or a tree for a barricade against an advancing enemy in a guerilla war. This inconsistency in O'Brien's character affected Stephens's judgment of O'Brien's errors in revolutionary leadership. O'Brien had erred on virtue's side, to be sure, but nevertheless,

---

[1]Quoted *Comhar*, Iúl 1958, 'William Smith O'Brien agus a Chlann', L. M. Mitchell (Smith O'Brien's great-granddaughter). The writer gives a similar picture in quotations from O'Brien's letters and from family tradition of political and personal divisions in the Cahirmoyle household. The quotations make clear that there was already tension between O'Brien's sons and himself when he was in exile after 1848. At O'Brien's funeral a relative commented, 'Except for a display of green knots and the waving of a green flag, I saw nothing one could take exception to'. Gwynn, *Young Ireland and 1848*, Preface, however, argues that O'Brien's journals and correspondence prove that his relations with his family were considerate and affectionate and that the contrary impression, though widespread, is false.

his error had led to a Ballingarry instead of to a Bunker's Hill.

Exile and conspiracy had clouded Stephens's judgment on one aspect of O'Brien. There was the old story that O'Brien had looked down from a nearby window and declined to interfere during an attack by a mob at Urlingford on Stephens. Only the timely intervention by a Kilkenny friend that day had prevented Stephens from being lynched as a spy. On what Stephens accepted as 'apparently good evidence', O'Brien was supposed to have watched in silence when one word from him would have calmed the mob. This idle gossip was in contradiction to everything Stephens knew of O'Brien's character, yet he dared not mention it in case it might be true.

Years later in America he learned beyond doubt that O'Brien had been elsewhere at the time and he regretted that he had not put the question. Once O'Brien casually mentioned Urlingford, an obvious opening for a direct challenge or even for a discreet inquiry. The opportunity was lost, and they went on fighting the rising all over again.

Then the son broke in peevishly but more mercifully than he knew:

'Would it not be better to forget these things? The country has not treated you so well!'

To Stephens's exasperation O'Brien seemed to give silent consent to this. 'The leading Young Irelanders', rasped Stephens in retrospect, 'had unwittingly fooled him into the belief that he was destined to be the Washington of his country!' His colleagues and his family alike had persuaded him that he was a martyr, and the sufferings of the Irish people who had deserved better leaders were forgotten! (Denieffe and Devoy were to pronounce much the same verdict on Stephens himself ten years later).

As their conversation continued the fundamental differences between Stephens and O'Brien on political and social matters became very clear, although Stephens preserved more reticence and tact than he would have shown in the case of any other man. O'Brien revealed himself as emphatically no republican, and he appeared to have given small attention to the social question in the abstract.

'His idea of a state was a King or President—a good resident

gentry, comfortable large farmers, and an active hewer-of-
wood and drawer-of-water class. (There was nothing, he said,
in a name, provided the thing was of the right sort). The
monarch, or some such chief, was necessary, he observed; for
an executive head was essential to the stability of government.
The aristocracy was also an essential in his eyes for it would
give employment to the masses and be a bulwark to the ministry
against popular madness. The comfortable farmer having, like
the landlord, a stake in the country, would be opposed to those
upheavals which Mr O'Brien regarded as most pernicious to
the proper development of trade and industry'.

When O'Brien pointed out the hundred-acre tenant farms
on the Cahirmoyle estate, and grew eloquent upon the cottiers
with their jaunting cars and whitewashed cottages, Stephens
diplomatically kept to himself his impression that 'the only
agreeable features in these fifteen by twenty foot cribs is the
whitewash!'

In the conversation, Stephens changed the subject twice,
from a desire to avoid wounding O'Brien in any way. First,
when he suspected O'Brien might think that Stephens had
come to sound him as to whether he would consent to be
leader of the new movement, and second, when O'Brien
mounted his hobby horse that, unless wisely directed, popular
movements turned to anarchy and Communism.

O'Brien's conviction that Ireland was then completely
'West-Britonised' was challenged by a direct question, and a
significant one because of the memories and experiences of the
two men:

'Would the people have fought in '48?'

Looking keenly at Stephens, O'Brien replied:

'Yes, if the priests had not influenced them. We had as
brave a set of men about us in certain localities as anyone
would wish to meet. But did you not see their arms drop and
their hearts fail them at the word of a Roman Catholic
clergyman?'

With unconscious irony, Stephens, who in a sense denied 'this
sacerdotal influence' over the people in the '48 struggle, made
in effect the same reply to O'Brien that Archbishop Hughes
of New York had already made to Mitchel and to D'Arcy

McGee in two violent controversies on the same problem. As
he knew O'Brien would not apply the criticism to himself, he
said:

'Had the leaders come to us in anything like numbers and
shown a determined front worthy of the cause they held dear,
the priests would have shrunk back or been bound to bless our
arms. In 1830 as you know, the Belgian bishops poured their
benediction on Belgian insurgents when the latter had their
chiefs at the head'.

The first statement was true, O'Brien agreed, and the second
accurate historically. Stephens refrained from pointing out that
O'Brien, if he had been a real revolutionary leader, should
have sent all the clergymen who dared to cross the path of the
insurgents immediately about their business. Both men agreed
that a distinction must be always made between clergymen of
all denominations as clergymen and as citizens. In their
religious role they deserved all respect, but in their politics no
more authority or power than any ordinary citizen.

A sceptical smile stole softly over O'Brien's face as they
talked, and again he lamented that all their debate was idle
as, after all, nationality must be looked on as extinct in the
land. Stephens was thrown off his guard, and he broke out
impetuously:

'I grant that there is a total absence of enthusiasm, there is
even great inertness and indifference in the country at present;
but I have been through several counties—counties by the way,
that have no great reputation for being rebellious—and I know
that disaffection is rife everywhere, and that even now it
would not be hard to stir them up to insurrection'.

These words seemed to stun O'Brien, and Stephens wondered, though nothing was further from his thoughts, whether
O'Brien suspected that he had come to offer him the leadership
of a new revolutionary organization.

'You see, Mr Stephens,' O'Brien repeated, 'the respectable
people of the towns especially are quite indifferent to, if not
hostile to Irish nationality'.

Incautiously, as he later put it, Stephens retorted, 'I never
counted on what is usually styled "respectable people". I
know you don't estimate men by their material possessions'.

7

'No! No!' cried O'Brien. 'Far would it be from my mind to do so. But I would labour for all; and, if not supported by the educated and influential classes, the movement could only degenerate into Communism, as there is in the instinct of the *plebs* a tendency to the equalization of wealth, and to other impossibilities'.

This ended any serious discussion. Stephens 'seeing him astride of Diderum (his political Bucephalus) contrived with as much courtesy as possible to extricate myself from a discussion in which a delicacy of feeling prevented me from saying what should be said'.

Later at the lunch table Stephens's delicacy and self-control were even more severely tested. Mrs O'Brien—'still good-looking, well-informed, and ladylike, who bore her years with much ease', made very plain with sly humour and sparkling eyes, her supreme contempt for the 'Ballingarry *fiasco*' and all her allusions to it were suavely derogatory. There were present also a governess, 'who appeared maliciously disposed to aim shafts of sly satire at myself', O'Brien's eldest daughter, 'grave and *distinguée*', the mugwump heir, and the heir's tutor. Out of respect for O'Brien, Stephens let them all have their way, and that 'with relative equanimity'. (Yet the insult, real or imagined, rankled deep, for nearly twenty years later he wrote to his own wife from New York 'how favourably my own sweetheart compares with the wives of other chiefs—of Mrs Smith O'Brien and Mrs John Mitchel, to say nothing of the smaller fry pitchforked into "a little brief authority" by me!')[2]

There was a final and prolonged conversation with O'Brien in the library. Stephens noticed his 'unrelenting haughtiness not unmixed with despair', yet with all the old beliefs intact. They discussed John Martin, Meagher, Mitchel and others. The irritated tone suggested to Stephens that O'Brien believed that he was abandoned by them all in the trying crisis of 1848, a suggestion indeed that should be taken with John O'Leary's 'grains of salt' for all statements made by Stephens in an explanatory and theoretical mood.

At last they parted. O'Brien drove Stephens to the station.

[2]Stephens to Jane Stephens, 27 March 1874. Nat. Lib. Stephens Papers.

There was a flash of the old fire when O'Brien's resentment flamed out at the town council of Limerick because it thought he might be pleased if it invited the Lord Lieutenant to a demonstration in his honour on his return from exile. 'What a monstrous sarcasm on my career!' he exclaimed. 'What toadyism!' 'Defeated but unconquerable', thought Stephens, 'too honourable to recant or bend'. They shook hands and parted, never to meet again. In the bitterest controversies of the Fenian movement in the coming years, Stephens preserved his old esteem and affection for William Smith O'Brien, and never relaxed that delicacy of feeling and restraint he had used at Cahirmoyle.

Yet as he resumed his journey, Stephens reflected with pseudo-Carlylean unction:

'Shade of the mighty Cromwell, what a contrast thou presentest to our own O'Brien! Methinks if thou and thy Puritans accepted and carried out such a code of military honour as this in Ireland, death and not victory would have lighted on thy standard!'

From Cahirmoyle he made his way to Adare, and visited the church to find Lady Dunraven at choir practice, which infuriated him even more than the lunch party at Cahirmoyle. He left Adare with many imprecations on the landlord system as it then prevailed. Lord Dunraven held full sway over the people of the district, and to 'hear him was to obey'. 'As I insinuated myself into the confidence of the inhabitants, I found they were mere serfs content with a pittance. I could not understand how such one-man power, such odious autocracy could be not only practised but looked upon as just and legitimate by many'. Landlordism, emigration, restrictions on the tenant's right to marry, he found accepted as in the eternal order of things.

'I asked myself often and often, as I did in '48, in the words of Jean d'Aquila of Spain—"Did Christ ever die for such a people?" But I warned back my evil angel and eventually went my way in hope, for despite all I saw and all I heard, I felt there was something within me that proclaimed that the Irish cause was not dead yet, and that it was worth one struggle more. Everything around me (on the surface) led me to despair, the people were in a state of hopeless inactivity. Political life was dead'.

The leisurely journey, stick in hand, knapsack on back, with many pauses and divagations went on. He rambled into King's County and Westmeath to inspect the famous ruins of Clonmacnoise. He stayed at a comfortable farmstead belonging to an octogenarian of wonderful physique, a Mr Molloy, who had known as guests in his house, Samuel Lover, Dr Petrie, Samuel Ferguson, and many other poets, travellers, antiquarians, foreign celebrities whose names were duly inscribed in his visitors' book.

Farmer Molloy, Stephens remarked, 'held opinions to suit his business', as 'a dependent of the upper classes though one of the masses'. He was disappointed sadly in Stephens, mistook his foreign appearance for 'perhaps a famous Pasha of the Ottoman Empire, a preacher of the Koran, or an Egyptian guide whose head was full of the Nile or forty centuried Pyramids'. When Stephens gave his name, Molloy's face fell: a mere nobody, another great name lost for the visitors' book.

At Lanesborough, however, there was one of the masses who entertained Stephens to several hours' delightful conversation, a small farmer, and rebel to the core, but a devout believer in St Columbkille's Prophecies, a fine edition of which had been published by Mr Stephens's roguish friend and Irish scholar, John O'Daly, that very year. Stephens found a widespread belief through Westmeath, Longford and neighbouring counties in these prophecies, especially in one which predicted, according to popular interpretation, that 'Ireland would wake from her trance and liberate herself',—'when the time comes' —a period with only a few years to run . . . 'no preparation was needed . . . Divine Providence would take the affair on its own shoulders and settle it satisfactorily!'

A conversation with two men from Connacht provoked Stephens to an outburst. They assured him that the flower of Irish virtue and chivalry resided in their province since Cromwell had banished it there. Local conceit and factionism! If there must be any choice, thought Stephens, he was for the Anglo-Celts!

He walked from Clonmacnoise to Athlone where it was

parliamentary election day at the hustings. Mr William Keogh, he reflected, the pious perjurer, had vaulted from there to the judicial bench, and here was a silly how-do-you-do for the misguided people to appoint some fiery patriot successor to the scoundrel in the House of Commons. Stephens betook himself to a tavern and relieved his feelings to his notebook in verse, a practice of his, generally satirical, but at times sentimental, on this occasion most satirical. He hastened on to Auburn where he paid his respects to Goldsmith's memory, and met a smith, also a believer in St Columbkille, but very much inclined to aid Providence in its design by his own strong right arm.

The smith was versed in genealogies and topography, and was indeed the son of the very smith in *The Deserted Village*, whose father had known Goldsmith and *his* father: Goldsmith was a blockhead with a father who 'was the best of men'.[3] There was hatred in the smith's eyes for the manors all round, a 'veritable agrarian revolutionist', whom Stephens judged to be one of the natural leaders of the people, and marked him down as a future lieutenant. The national cause, it seemed from the smith's talk, was still alive in the district except for the large farmers. On his return to Auburn, some years later, Stephens found the smith had died—and his spirit with him.

Stephens returned to Kilkenny to say farewell to his relatives before he set out on the final stages of his tour.

[3][Oliver Goldsmith's father, the Rev. Charles Goldsmith, died in 1747, when Goldsmith was something between 16 and 18. For the local smith to have impinged on Goldsmith, as a smith, he would have had to have been in his twenties, the relevant lines testifying to maturity of physique:

No more the smith his dusky brow shall clear
Relax his ponderous strength, and lean to hear;

One must therefore presume a birth-date for him of 1720 at the latest. We may, without straining the imagination, credit him with the capacity to beget a child at the age of 60, i.e. in 1780, which would make it possible, if not probable, for his son to encounter Stephens in 1856. But, as the author indicates at many points, Stephens was prone to exaggeration; nor does the smith by his account appear the man to spoil a good story by pedantic adherence to sober truth. Auburn is, of course, the name of the village in Goldsmith's poem; the real name of the village where he grew up was Lissoy—and Stephens's use of the poetic rather than the actual name adds to the air of unreality in the passage. Modern critics tend to dispute the identification of Auburn with Lissoy, or indeed any actual village; but many of the parallels are striking and such critics are unlikely to discover any inhabitant of Lissoy who accepts their view.—O.D.E.]

8 The End of the Three Thousand Mile Walk

BEFORE Stephens finally left Kilkenny to complete his tour at leisure, and make his way slowly back to Dublin, he wrote peremptorily to Philip Grey with whom he was in touch. He had heard that Grey proposed to open a memorial fund to enable Stephens to start a new militant national movement. He sent Grey and his friends a strong protest against this or any subscription towards his work or any public notice of his tour. His mind, he informed them, was not finally made up on the prospects of a new revolutionary organization, and he could not yet give anything but most uncertain findings on the result of his enquiry. He proposed to see more of the country, and meet Grey and his group in Dublin much later in the year. He remained in Kilkenny for some time longer. He spent much of his time with his uncle, Patrick Casey and his family. His cousins, Patrick, Joseph, Andrew and James were to be closely linked with his Parisian exile in the 'seventies and 'eighties.

The family memory, however, which haunted Stephens all his life was his last talk with one of his aunts, whom he knew was slowly dying, and of her he wrote with unusual feeling. The last sight of her face rose before him often during his years of exile. In Notre Dame, St Suplice, St Eustache in Paris, 'and in the wanderings of a restless life have I entered many a gorgeous cathedral along the banks of the Rhine, and elsewhere, gazing in reverie on the Madonnas in canvas and marble; but I do not think I ever saw any face so expressive in what I might call its celestial sweetness as hers was on that occasion . . . pale and haloed, the dark eyes rich in tenderness and beaming with a joy too pure to be worldly—their gleams lost awhile in meditations . . . and fixed at times on the little religious pictures of Christ and the Baptist that studded the walls of the quaint old room'.

And at last she came to the question that Stephens dreaded and to an appeal to him to turn back while there was still time from the dangerous path on which she knew well he had entered. She asked him to avoid all political activity in Ireland and to return to exile where he might use his talents on something better than a hopeless cause in a ruined land. His reply was frank; he could not give up the mission he was destined to fulfil.

This reply did not surprise her, and she said with resignation:

'Well, it is the old, old story. *It runs in the blood.* I ought to have known it does. Was not my own uncle a rebel in 'ninety-eight, and did he not suffer for Ireland?'

There was pathos in these simple words of farewell that pierced Stephens to the core as they parted.

Another experience during this visit to Kilkenny also left its mark on his future work. He spent many evenings with a family he describes as the K's, old and close friends of his father and mother, where he was always warmly welcomed. One evening he sensed a tension in the household, he was evidently unwelcome, his reception was frigid, and the conversation was extremely cold and forced. At first the frosty greetings and looks of disapproval puzzled him until he guessed the reason. He had been very friendly with many working people and had dared to walk down the Kilkenny streets with mere labourers, blacksmiths and the like!

He continued the conversation blandly, making a mock lament to himself for the petty snobberies and class distinctions of Ireland and Irish towns in 1856. He had found the old national fire burning mainly among the common people, and it was in the working class that he was to win his main support until the end. He had already reached the conclusion that, whatever their other limitations, the Ribbon societies were the basis for a popular revolutionary movement, and he determined to win them over. He looked also to the Dublin trade unionists as strong and useful allies in the future from his talks with the Hollywood brothers, Edward in Manchester, and William in Dublin, within the past few months. 'I was intimately

acquainted with both brothers,' he noted, 'and found them
fine specimens of the Irish artisan class'. It was Edward
Hollywood, the silk weaver, who had gone to Paris with
Meagher and Smith O'Brien with greetings from Young
Ireland to Lamartine and the February revolution of 1848.
He had also shared Stephens's exile in Paris, where he had
fled after the failure of the insurrection, to work as a silk
weaver there for some years.

Hollywood, as a leader of the Dublin trade unionists, whom
he represented on the Council of the Irish Confederation, was
to be a life-long friend and admirer of Stephens. He was one
of the pall bearers at that great Fenian triumph, the Terence
Bellew McManus funeral in 1861. In December 1846, four
months after the break between Young Ireland and O'Connell,
Hollywood addressed a remarkable letter to William Smith
O'Brien, full of the democratic spirit and non-sectarian temper
which Stephens claimed characterized Fenianism.

One passage urged the Young Ireland seceders from the
O'Connellites to raise a fund of £130 for the distribution of a
hundred copies of the *Nation* weekly for twelve months:

'To such of the Repeal Wardens in the North who have seceded
to be distributed by them gratuitously amongst their immediate
neighbours of the working class, who holding the elective
franchise are not yet Repealers, this I conceive would be acting
on that moral force principle so much canted of elsewhere by
self seekers, with far more effect. It has been said by Dr Griffin
of Limerick, [a Young Irelander and friend of Smith O'Brien]
that we cannot nor ought we succeed in repealing the Union
without the hearty co-operation of the Protestants of that
province, in the truth of that remark although a Roman Catholic
I fully agree, and I confess it has surprised me much, that the
Repeal Association, not only took no steps to win that portion of
the country to the National cause, but too often from their
proceedings aroused the prejudices and alarmed the fears of those
people. Let that body now take what turn they may, it is plain
the Young Irelanders' party have a great responsibility upon
them, and I think they would be doing much to fulfil their duty
to repeal by adopting such a course as I have suggested. Slow
indeed might be the progress of such a plan. I do not think it
would be the less sure nor would the success of our new repeal

missionaries end with them, the converts would in their turn become the preachers of Nationality and so on until the warm but mistaken people of Ulster would be.'[1]

Stephens's account of his tour is somewhat blurred with digressions on scenery and with purple patches, and is often very vague indeed on facts and essential dates. He travelled again over the scenes of the '48 rising at Killenaule, Mullinahone, Ballingarry, and visited Ballyporeen and Mitchelstown. In Cork he met another Paris '48 refugee, John Walter Bourke, and recalled that they had both been members of the Irish Parisian Association, and their veteran United Irishmen colleagues in that body were Arthur O'Connor and Colonel Myles O'Byrne, links with an older conspiracy and with Robert Emmet, and living memories of the insurrection of '98.

In Co. Cork, Stephens passed through Dunmanway, Bandon, and in Clonakilty was gratified when he tested some soldiers with 'an *anti-Irish* talk', to discover that these warriors were 'far from loyal to their Royal Mistress'. The 'O'Connellism among the peasantry' of Roscarbery and Glandore pleased him less, and he grew melancholy when he heard that the people were emigrating in 'thousands, fleeing the land as they would a pest house'. He proceeded to Kerry.

In Killarney he witnessed the inauguration of Bishop Moriarty as Bishop of Kerry, and in retrospect commented with some asperity on the bishop's famous sermon, in February 1867, on Fenianism and its leaders after the premature rising in Kerry that month, with the pointed reference to Stephens himself: 'men who while they send their dupes to danger are fattening on the spoil in Paris and New York—the execrable swindlers who care not to endanger the necks of the men who trust them, who care not how many are murdered by the rebel or hanged by the strong arm of the law, provided they can get a supply of dollars either for their pleasures or for their wants . . .', followed by the notorious passage which caused all the best theologians to look down their noses ever after, 'when we look down into the fathomless depth of this infamy of the heads of the Fenian conspiracy, we must acknowledge that

[1] Smith O'Brien Papers, National Library of Ireland, Mss. 437.

eternity is not long enough nor hell hot enough to punish such miscreants'.[2]

Mr Stephens, however, in that summer of 1856 as in the spring of 1867, had neither dollars nor gold, and felt the perennial pinch of poverty. He, however, had his talents as a linguist, and secured a post as French teacher in Miss Morris's School for Young Ladies in Killarney for two separate sessions. He states himself definitely, although he does not refer specifically to Miss Morris's establishment, that he taught French and other languages en route.[3]

That autumn Stephens concluded his tour after rambles through Queen's County and elsewhere, having spent some two months' rambling, teaching and summing up the journey. He concluded that it was as yet premature to start any serious movement, and that he needed more time and opportunities to test popular feeling and available support for a revolutionary organization. He so informed his friends in Dublin with the picturesque phrases 'the cause is not dead but sleeping' or 'the corpse on the dissecting table is a myth', or 'Ireland lives and glows, but lives and glows in a trance!'

His more considered and more private views were given years later in the concluding chapter of his reminiscences of the tour:

'My three thousand mile walk through Ireland convinced me of one thing—the possibility of organizing a proper movement for the independence of my native land. I found, of course, many circumstances to discourage me throughout my tour: the hostility of the aristocracy, the apathy of the farmers, the pigheadedness of the *bourgeoisie*; but the labourers and the tradesmen were on the right track, and the sons of the peasants were very sympathetic. With the materials I discovered in our favour, I came to the resolve that the attempt was not only worth trying, but should be tried in the very near future if we wanted at all to keep our flag

[2]Quoted more fully, T. D. Sullivan, *Recollections of Troubled Times in Irish Politics* (Dublin 1905), p. 84. Fr D'Arcy, *Fenian Movement* . . . p. 235 terms the sermon as 'ill-timed blast'. He adds that the wide publicity given to Dr Moriarty's 'intemperate remarks' probably won more recruits for the Fenians in America. Devoy, *Recollections* . . . p. 120 while condemning the sermon, quotes Gavan Duffy that Dr Moriarty 'was all right in 1848'.

[3]Donal Cahill, Killarney; *Freeman's Journal*, 14 November, 1865.

flying; for I was sure as of my own existence that if another decade was allowed to pass without an endeavour of some kind or another to shake off an unjust yoke, the Irish people would sink into a lethargy from which it would be impossible for any patriot, however Titanic in genius, or, for any body of patriots, however sincere and zealous, to arouse them into anything like a healthy existence.

'To save my race from this dream; to revive old hopes and awaken old aspirations; to propel the Irish people onward in the path of modern progress; to make them socially independent by infusing into them the spirit of manhood; to guide them as best I could to higher heights and teach them that political liberty inexorably demanded self-sacrifice as its price of ransom, and that they should be prepared to offer the holocaust—in fine to make my native land as free as any nation under God's sun— free alike from alien dominion as from wanton oligarchy and insensate communism.

'And once that aim was reached and that ambition satisfied, I desired nothing further from the people of Ireland save permission to retire for ever from public life. "If an end was made for ever to the old centennial feud", on these or such conditions, nothing would please me better than to see England and Ireland forget mutual pains, wrongs, and frettings, and insure their common future by an alliance offensive and defensive, by a union of the two peoples, and not by their amalgamation.'[4]

On arrival in Dublin, Stephens visited William Hollywood, with whom he breakfasted and discussed his tour. Then, as before mentioned, he visited his friend John O'Daly's bookshop, and read the remarkable letter from John O'Mahony before quoted. He wrote at once to O'Mahony to dissuade him from abandoning political activity in Irish-American circles. Almost at once he began a fairly successful career as a French tutor in Killiney where almost every day he gave lessons to the

[4]In the original article the obvious mis-print, 'as is wanton oligarchy,' etc. has been changed in that text above to 'as from', and 'people' to 'peoples' as the sense demands. The concluding sentence runs:

'How I started a movement which had such objects as these to attain, I shall reserve for a much longer work than this is. The history of the I.R.B. and Fenian Organization will be told by me with impartiality, and, I hope, justice to every man who figures more or less prominently in both.' Stephens made considerable progress with such a history after 1867 but refrained from publishing it, as will appear later.

Jebbs, the Jamiesons, and the Dobbs who in turn recommended
him to Mrs John Blake Dillon at Druid Lodge, Ballybrack,
Co. Dublin. He taught her two sons, John, whom he described
as 'the smartest', although this bright lad's activities as a
leader of the Land League and Irish Parliamentary Party in
the future were not to please him so much, and his brother,
William, later the biographer of John Mitchel.

One day in the library, John Blake Dillon met Stephens,
much to his surprise, for the first time since they shared the
barricades at Killenaule. They held some friendly arguments
and reminiscences. When later Stephens approached John
Blake Dillon on the subject of his new movement—the first
'48 leader to be sounded in the country—Dillon dismissed the
scheme as visionary and futile, and bluntly said so. There were
discussions again some years later. Dillon after some delibera-
tion remained of the same opinion and the relations between
the two men became cooler, and finally hostile. As a teacher
of French, however, Stephens won golden opinions in the
Dillon household where he taught for several months. [5]

Almost immediately Stephens met Philip Grey and his
group of '48 men at Peter Langan's timber-yard in Lombard
Street, and for the first time the man who was to rank next in
importance, although unobtrusively, to himself, his future
deputy in the Irish Republican Brotherhood, Thomas Clarke
Luby. Stephens does not record either Luby's name or his own
impressions of this meeting beyond a terse reference to a
conference with Grey and 'other revolutionary leaders' where
after 'an interchange of views, I gave it as my decided opinion
that it would be as yet premature to start any serious
movement'.

Thomas Clarke Luby's account, on the other hand, is most
vivid. Stephens appeared to him as a 'seedily attired personage,
long-haired, and of a somewhat Bohemian cut', who left a
most unfavourable impression on him, and on Philip Grey,
who, however, knew Stephens quite well from meetings in
Paris. Grey told Luby he disliked Stephens's attitude, especially
his Gallic freedom of speech and his frenchified manners.

Luby did not agree with this. Grey, in fact, was suffering from the rupture of a blood vessel on the previous St Patrick's Day and was to die within a few months. Luby had a much more serious fault to find with Stephens, even if Stephens's spell had already begun to fall over him: it was Stephens's very emphatic expression of his social outlook. Luby understood that Stephens had been in England 'for some considerable time' after he left France, and had been in touch with Edward Hollywood the weaver, in Manchester.

Luby had not met Stephens when he arrived in Dublin on the eve of what Luby dubs the 'so-called 1,600 miles walk'. It was Stephens who asked Langan to inform Luby he wished to meet him. 'So I called one night at Langan's timber-yard and abode in Lombard Street, Dublin. Lath-splitter Langan was a '48 and '49 man. On my return from Australia in October 1854, he and Phil Grey had again sought me out. After a short delay Grey conducted me into Langan's workshed, and introduced me to Stephens. At once Stephens and I tackled each other, he first referring to my old friend, Eugene O'Reilly, whom he had known in Paris, and who, he said, had spoken of me very eulogistically; of my metaphysical and martial tendencies, etc.

'This night, I remember, Stephens did not seem to think Ireland could do anything till a revolution occurred in England. He had evidently, I should observe, spent some time in England, between the date of his leaving France and that of his coming to Ireland. In Manchester, I think it was, he had seen Edward Hollywood, a Dublin silk-weaver and one of the Dublin Citizens' Delegation to the French Provisional Government in '48. Though he referred in complimentary terms to the *Tribune* newspaper, with which I was connected in the end of 1855 and the beginning of 1856, and affected to think its premature death a loss, he struck me as, at this time, going in for the idea of universal philanthropy rather than for that of Irish patriotism. I disliked his socialistic theories, too. In short, he impressed me on this night most unfavourably. He disparaged nearly all prominent Irishmen (authors and others), especially living ones. I thought him erroneous in his views of things in general, affected, dogmatic, and arrogant. By the way, he used to rather defend affectation'.[6]

This was the old argument waged with Joseph Rivers and his friends in Co. Kilkenny all over again. And three years later Stephens was writing in his American diary in January 1859:

'Since '48—since the day I became a soldier of Liberty—I should proudly, nay joyfully, have given up all even to life for my country . . . For *I* would fight for an abstract principle of right in defence of *any* country; and were England a republic battling for human freedom on the one hand, and Ireland leagued with despots on the other, I should, unhesitatingly, take up arms against my native land. In a word, the only countries I recognize over the earth are Toil and Privilege; the one of these I shall struggle for, the other against, with all the faculties of my being, while I can exercise them.'

The arrogance and self-assurance that Luby detected in Stephens became bye-words. 'I have no hesitation', he told Luby once, 'in saying that I think very highly of myself. I have grasped more of the truth than almost any other man'. This in retrospect provoked many a jest between John O'Leary and Luby in their correspondence in the 'nineties, as they summed up their memories of Stephens. 'The great Sir Hocus Pocus!' wrote Luby . . . and then the dramatic description and correction, twice underlined, that Stephens, despite all that, was *mesmeric*. 'Whatever sly digs I may have made, Stephens was our able organizer; a man who could *influence* other men to obey his will. I, for one, might have dreamed of an organization such as Stephens created. But I could never have done his work; nor do I know anyone who could. For me, my better qualities as well as my weaker ones would have incapacitated me from taking the initiative, or at least from rushing certain matters in his style'.[7]

This was a significant, if indeed a very modest self-judgment, from the man whom O'Leary placed next to Stephens himself in importance as an active Fenian leader. There was indeed a

[6]T. C. Luby to John O'Leary, 27 July 1890 (Luby Papers, National Library of Ireland).

[7]Luby Papers, Luby-O'Leary, 27 July 1890. National Library of Ireland.

curious dualism between the two men in the history of their organization for all their contrasts of character. Luby briefly sketched his own biography in a letter to O'Leary in July 1890, with the comment that Rutherford and the papers had it all wrong, while even their friend and colleague, Charles J. Kickham, had tried the same thing and made fifteen mistakes in a preface to the novel, *Sally Kavanagh*. Thomas Clarke Luby was born in Dublin on 16 January 1822. His father was a Tipperary man from Templemore, a Church of England clergyman, married to a Catholic. Luby's uncle was Dr Thomas Luby, Professor of Greek and a Fellow and Dean of Trinity College, Dublin, a true Tory, much distracted by his nephew's political wildness and failure to settle down into a sober citizen and good lawyer. Luby, indeed, studied law and put in the requisite number of terms in London and Dublin, won some reputation as a scholar, and took his degree.

Even his loyalist friends were fascinated by his witty and sometimes ironic powers in conversation although one wrote to a Limerick paper, after his conviction as a Fenian in 1865, to point out many good qualities with the reservation, 'His conversation also was interesting except when he touched on Irish Independence when he became so enthusiastic that one might suspect the soundness of his intelligence . . . Mr Luby was a somewhat sarcastic, but talented, pleasant, straightforward and gentlemanly little fellow, and I believe, a very estimable person in the domestic relations'.[8]

This anonymous friend noted that Mr Luby 'was well versed in literature, and had a profound knowledge of history and politics, in which unfortunately for him he took a deep interest, and at a period of life when he might have acquired deeper scholarship, or what is quite as useful a profession. I could never agree with him in politics but he was a very honest fellow'. The past tense no doubt indicated that twenty years' penal servitude was the equivalent of death.

The serious part Luby played in the planning of the '49 outbreak and his connection with the Grey-Lalor secret organ-

[8]Quoted *Irishman*, 23 December 1865, from the *Reporter and Vindicator*, Limerick. Luby was married to Letitia Frazer, a Presbyterian and daughter of the '48 poet, John Frazer.

ization has already been noticed. In 1851 he arrived in France to join the Foreign Legion to learn infantry tactics but found recruiting temporarily suspended. So he went to Australia for a year and then returned to Ireland where he remained in touch with the small groups of '49 men and Philip Grey. He made several attempts to carry out his old project of starting a revolutionary movement and a newspaper. From the end of 1855 he edited the *Tribune* founded by John E. Pigot of the *Nation* group, Father Kenyon and others.

Two objects set out in the first leading article in the *Tribune* were accomplished indirectly by the Fenian movement; the overthrow of the existing landlord system and disestablishment of the Church of Ireland. The main spirit of the paper was that of the *Nation*, which had first attracted Luby and eventually made him a revolutionary nationalist. Luby had a leaning towards Mitchel and Lalor, although after '48, like O'Leary, his views on social issues grew more conservative, as his reservations at his interview with Stephens made clear. The influence of Stephens over him increased, and on several journeys through the country his revulsion faded away, and he was thoroughly won over by Stephens's ability and success as an organizer. In January 1857 they both attended Grey's funeral in Co. Meath, where Luby, at Stephens's insistence, made what he himself regarded as a poor and halting attempt at a funeral oration. That same year a message reached them from America, a message that was to change their lives and the history of Ireland.

9 Stephens founds the Irish Republican Brotherhood

THE messenger who came in the late autumn of 1857 was a young man named Owen Considine. He brought a message signed by four Irish exiles in the United States—including John O'Mahony and Michael Doheny—to Stephens expressing confidence in him, and asking him to establish an organization in Ireland to win national independence. Considine also brought a private letter from O'Mahony to Stephens, which was, in effect, a warning which both Stephens and Luby at first overlooked. They both believed there was a strong organization behind the invitation rather than a number of loosely linked groups. This situation proved full of difficulties in the future, in slowly fulfilled promises and personal dissensions in the American branch of the movement. O'Leary, however, believed that Stephens would have gone ahead with his plans in any case because he thought the moment had come, and that the situation favoured a new movement under his leadership.

'Without him', said O'Leary of Stephens, 'nothing could have been done, and with him everything was done that could well be done under the circumstances'. The circumstances then were the collapse of the constitutional independent parliamentary body, political chaos and universal torpor. He noted, too, abnormal strength of will in Stephens, marred by arrogance, dogmatism, contempt for the world in general, including all Irish political leaders, with the exception of John O'Mahony. Yet to some of his intimates and to the rank and file of his followers, Stephens could be cordial, agreeable and flattering, especially as in the early stages of Fenianism, hero-worship and lack of criticism of the leader prevailed.

In his reply to the New York invitation all Stephens's will and arrogance appeared most unmistakably. He was already

8

in correspondence with Joseph Denieffe—Kilkenny man and
'48 exile—who had returned to Ireland with a somewhat vague
commission from the Doheny-O'Mahony organization, the
Emmet Monument Association, which the following year suspended its activities in the United States. Denieffe had left
New York in the spring of 1855, with full permission 'to do
what you can for the organization' from Doheny; with the
amazing announcement that he could tell all friends at home
that September would be the critical date with the arrival of
an expedition. 'We have thirty thousand men now, and all we
need is money, and arrangements are under way to provide it.
We propose to issue bonds, and some of the wealthiest men of
our race are willing to take them.'

This mythical expedition never arrived but it made Denieffe,
although he was in turn a '48 man and a lifelong Fenian, extremely critical of Irish-American prophecies for the future. In
Kilkenny he had been welcomed by Dr Robert Cane and John
Haltigan, and in Dublin by Luby and Langan. He found little
scope for political activity, and went to work in Co. Monaghan,
as foreman cutter to a merchant tailor in Carrickmacross, and
elsewhere in the north including Armagh and Belfast. Tiring
of the north and lack of news from his friends in New York, he
decided to return to the United States but was urged by
Stephens to delay his departure, and remain, if possible, to
await events.[1]

Two days before Christmas, 1857, Stephens summoned him
to Dublin for an important mission. The summons was
disguised as a business letter offering him a profitable new
post and urging him to break with his employer. He arrived
in Dublin the next day, and at a small meeting in Langan's
heard Stephens read his reply to the New York invitation.
Denieffe was informed that he was wanted to act as courier
because the reply was much too dangerous to be trusted to the
mails. Stephens had, for security or mystification, pretended
that he had written from Paris. At any rate the document he
read out was dated from there:

[1] Joseph Denieffe, *Recollections of the Irish Revolutionary Brotherhood*, (New York,
1906), Ch. 2. p. 14 *et seq.*

Paris,
January 1858

'My Dear Doheny,

As this is strictly a business letter, will you excuse the absence of all explanations of a personal nature. I reserve everything of the kind for some future occasion—perhaps the hour when I shall grasp your hand in mine with all the truth and fervour of our hunted days.

'To the point. Presuming the information given by Mr C. (Considine) to be correct, I proceed to state the conditions on which I can accept the proposed co-operation of our transatlantic brothers, and the great personal responsibility devolving on myself. Lest you should have over-rated my capability and influence, it may be well to inform you what I am convinced I can do in a given time, always provided you are prepared to comply with my conditions, which I believe essential. Bearer of this letter leaves by tonight's mail, and I undertake to organize in three months from the date of his return here at least 10,000 men, of whom about 1,500 shall have firearms and the remainder pikes. These men, moreover, shall be so organized as to be available (all of them) at any point in twenty-four hours' notice at most. It must be needless to say that such an organization as this represents the whole body of Irish Nationalists—even the indifferent would be inevitably drawn after us, the start once given. Nor do I hesitate to assert, that, with the aid of the 500 brave fellows you promise, we shall have such a prospect of success as has not offered since—I cannot name the epoch of our history.

'Now for the conditions. The first is money. There is a silent reproach in my words when I say: you ought to have foreseen this, knowing as you do that the men of property are not with us (of course, I speak but of the national men of property), and that we are without means, you would also have shown a wise foresight by sending us the nerves of organization as of war. I shall be able to borrow enough to go on with the work till I hear from you; that is, on a limited scale, and at great inconvenience to myself and friends, but anything like delay on your part will not only retard its progress, but otherwise injure the Cause and should you to be unable to come into my terms, the business must be given up altogether. You must then be able to furnish from £80 to £100 a month, dating from the departure of bearer, from New York. Had [I] a casting vote in your council, I should moreover, suggest you sending 500 men unarmed to England, there to meet an agent who should furnish each of them with an Enfield rifle. This, of course, would involve considerable expense; but were it possible it would so stave off suspicion that we might fall on them altogether by surprise. Of course, too, this money should come from you, and I beg of you, if possible, to raise it and act on my suggestion.

'A few words as to my position. I believe it essential to success that the centre of this or any similar organization should be perfectly unshackled; in other words, a provisional dictator. On this point I can conscientiously concede nothing. That I should not be worried or hampered by the wavering or imbecile, it will be well to make this out in proper form with the signature of every influential Irishman of our union. . .

N.B. Bearer may be trusted unto the death.'[2]

Denieffe reached New York at the end of January 1858. He found a condition of affairs in Irish circles which he tried in vain subsequently to make Stephens realize. Economic conditions were bad owing to a commercial crisis, unemployment had hit many Irish workers severely and the Irish-American press, with few exceptions, was hostile or indifferent to a new movement at home, and much immersed in American politics. Moreover, money in Irish circles was scarce and difficult to gather. At one meeting of the New York Committee, General Michael Corcoran, impatient at the slowness of gathering the funds for Stephens, emptied all the money in his pockets on the table and asked the others present to do the same, and the bulk of the eighty pounds which Denieffe brought back was then and there supplied.[3]

On 17 March 1858, Denieffe arrived in Dublin with the acceptance of Stephens's terms by the New York Committee and the eighty pounds. This subscription was his very minimum stipulation. Denieffe's report that there was no actual organized

[2]Denieffe, Appendix, pp. 159–60. An editorial note by O'Donovan Rossa states the letter is incomplete and, of course, unsigned, and in the handwriting of James Stephens. It is also stated that it was written in Paris on New Year's Day 1858. The letter, however, was handed as above stated, according to Denieffe's account, to him in Dublin by Stephens. Denieffe travelled to New York via Liverpool, and never visited Paris until 1859.

[3]Devoy, *Recollections* . . . pp. 18–19. Denieffe related many incidents and important facts about the early history of the I.R.B., which he did not give in his own book, to Devoy.

body of sympathizers in New York but merely a loose knot of associates, disturbed Stephens yet he went ahead at once, and that very evening the Irish Republican Brotherhood was established, in Peter Langan's timber-yard in Lombard Street. Writing to O'Leary on 27 July 1890, Luby's description of the event was that immediately after the return of Denieffe, 'at once Stephens began organizing. I had already made some provisional trips into Meath county; but 'twas on Patrick's Day 1858, that the I.R.B. movement was formally commenced. I drew up the form of oath, under Stephens's correction, in his room at Dennelly's, in the street behind and parallel to Lombard Street. The first text had clauses of secrecy and of obedience to all commands of superior officers not immoral. I swore Stephens in and he swore me'.

The original I.R.B. oath, as quoted by Luby and O'Leary, and which is among several versions in Stephens's own papers, ran:

'I, A.B., do solemnly swear, in the presence of Almighty God, that I will do my utmost, at every risk, while life lasts, to make [in other versions, according to Luby, 'establish in'] Ireland an independent Democratic Republic; that I will yield implicit obedience, in all things not contrary to the law of God [or, 'laws of morality'] to the commands of my superior officers; and that I shall preserve inviolable secrecy regarding all the transactions [or 'affairs'] of this secret society that may be confided in me. So help me God! Amen.'

This oath was drastically revised by Stephens in Paris in the summer of 1859. He made Luby draw up a new text, omitting the secrecy clause. 'Henceforth,' wrote Luby to O'Leary 'we denied that we were technically a secret body. We called ourselves a military organization; with, so to speak, a legionary oath like all soldiers'. The 'obedience to orders of superior officers' clause was, however, retained, and as O'Leary commented, the officers would naturally tell those under their orders to keep their mouths shut. The change was due to the violent denunciations of the clergy of secret oaths during the Phoenix Society trials. Mr John O'Leary held such decided views on oaths that he admitted he was possibly most peculiar. In due course he told James Stephens point-blank that he would take no oaths for any man, no blank cheque oaths so to speak. He had, in 1848, given and taken a simple oath to fight for Ireland, for his own small body, and believed in a shut mouth that caught no flies, but to swear to keep secret something the nature of which can only be surmised was another matter. Stephens in later discussions with John O'Mahony, who imposed merely a simple pledge on his Fenian Brotherhood, launched in the U.S.A. soon after the founding of the I.R.B., seriously considered dropping the I.R.B. oath altogether.[4]

The revised oath ran:

'I, A.B., in the presence of Almighty God, do solemnly swear allegiance to the Irish Republic, now virtually established; and that I will do my very utmost, at every risk, while life lasts, to defend its independence and integrity; and, finally, that I will yield implicit obedience in all things, not contrary to the laws of God [or 'the laws of morality'], to the commands of my superior officers. So help me God. Amen'.

The structure of the I.R.B. as sketched by Stephens bore some resemblance to that of the Blanqui organization in its original form in 1834 as the Society of the Families, and to its successors, the picturesque 'Society of the Seasons', with sections of six to twelve members under a chief, under an unknown directorate of three, Blanqui, Barbes and Bernard, with the aim of a democratic republic to be established by armed revolution. The qualification for membership was marksmanship and readiness to act at a moment's notice. After many mishaps, which included clandestine journals, gunpowder factories, abortive uprisings, police infiltration even into the leadership, the Blanqui organization developed into the formidable Central Republican Society which sparked off the February and June revolts in 1848, and played its part in the Paris Commune. There were, however, other secret societies, well known to Stephens and O'Mahony in Paris: Armand Barbès' Club of the Revolution and Raspail's Friends

---

[4]Jeremiah O'Donovan Rossa, *Rossa's Recollections*, (N.Y., 1898), pp. 269–281, which includes Stephens to O'Mahony, 6 April 1859. It was after this that Stephens introduced the second version of the I.R.B. oath.

of the People, and innumerable others with resounding titles, the French Carbonari, and the organizations of exiled Young Europe, yet all more or less deriving so far as their schemes of organization went from the original Carbonari as modified by Mazzini and Young Italy.

The scheme of organization adopted by Stephens shunned flowery titles and relied more upon the alphabet. A Circle was in charge of the Centre A, who had under him nine sub-centres, B's or captains, each of whom had nine C's or sergeants, while every C had nine D's or privates. The original intention, stated later in the rules of procedure of the organization, was to limit a Circle to 800 members, but in practice this rule was never observed as the circles consisted in some cases of 2,000 men. The unwritten rule that no recruit should be sworn in the presence of witnesses was observed rigidly but the rule that members should be known only to the members of their sections and circle soon broke down.[5]

Luby and Stephens immediately began a series of journeys through Leinster and Munster, sometimes together, and sometimes alone. They had many amusing adventures and met a large selection of the oddest types. Luby was much impressed by Stephens's unerring approach and power of sizing up possible recruits and sympathizers. One of their most crucial expeditions was to Skibbereen in May 1858 when Stephens won over O'Donovan Rossa, the Moynahans, Downings, and other members of the Phoenix Society. The Society consisted then of some hundred men, all of a revolutionary cast of mind, it was not oath-bound or secret. Stephens arrived in the town with a letter of introduction from James O'Mahony of Bandon to Donal Oge Macartie, one of the Phoenix men whom he swore into the I.R.B. Macartie next approached Rossa, told him of the meeting with Stephens, and swore Rossa in.

[5]O'Leary, *Recollections* . . . Vol. 1. p. 84 note; Devoy, p. 27. The rules of procedure of the I.R.B. were quoted by Chester Ives, on the authority of an anonymous Fenian, in the New York *Herald*, 12 August 1880. See *Devoy's Post Bag*, Vol. 1. pp. 546–8. The rules are also given Pollard, *Secret Societies of Ireland*, 279–89, and dated 1894. The references to 'A's' 'B's' etc. in these rules seem to date them as originating in Stephens's phase of the I.R.B. O'Leary writing from Paris, 5 November 1877, to the *Freeman's Journal*, stated that under Stephens, the I.R.B. had no constitution.

Stephens had told Macartie that the Irishmen in America had resolved to send arms and men to Ireland to aid in an insurrection if the I.R.B. had enrolled sufficient recruits for the task. The arms were to be landed and stored in hiding places known only to the centres before the revolt, and the rising would be backed by an invading force of from five to ten thousand. Military instructors were to drill and train the secret army. Within a month of Stephens's visit some ninety Phoenix Society members had enrolled. Rossa, Macartie and Moynahan became centres of three circles, and the movement spread quickly.[6]

Apart from the sequel to the merging of the Phoenix Society, until then mainly a social and debating club, with the I.R.B., this was an important date in Fenian history, inasmuch as O'Donovan Rossa became one of the most active of the Fenian leaders, and according to Devoy 'swore in more members than any ten men in the movement, and had a wider personal knowledge of the membership than Stephens himself'.

Another historic meeting on Stephens's journey, nowhere related by him, O'Leary, Luby or any other Fenian historian, is that given only by Rutherford whose account seems to be put beyond doubt by a lengthy quotation from an article of A. M. Sullivan's which appeared in his paper, *The Nation*, 19 April 1862:

'In the early part of the year 1858, I was waited upon one day by a man whom I had long reason to believe from himself and others, was largely engaged in establishing secret societies throughout Ireland. Indeed to myself he never concealed the general fact, and I know that a long time before the Phoenix Societies were formally introduced into Ireland, he had contemplated "getting hold of" the Ribbon Organization, and trying to turn it to his desperate purposes. There are reasons why, as an honourable man, I should now be silent on his faults, and say as little as is absolutely necessary of him at all. In what I am compelled to reveal, I shall be as rigidly exact as if I stood by the Judgment Seat, and I shall not reveal more than is imperatively required.

[6]Rossa, *Prison Life*, p. 6; *Recollections*, p. 150. O'Leary, Vol. 1. p. 84 and note; Devoy, *Recollections* . . . p. 20, 321.

'He, in the course of a long conversation, offered to join me to the Secret Society—the formal name of which was not referred to then. He, of course, approached the subject as prudently as he deemed necessary; and he quite as naturally avoided the revelation of particulars which could only be made known to me when I was sworn in. I rejected the proposition. I declined to take the oath, after which I would be told more that might make me think better of it. I did not rest satisfied with refusing. . . I vehemently endeavoured to persuade him from such an enterprise. He argued at great length the advantages of a secret organization—argued them better than I have ever heard them urged before or since. . . Failing to obtain me as a "member", the agent, with a cleverness that showed he had brains, and used them well—directed his attention to "covering his retreat"— preventing harm from accruing to his enterprise through the unsuccessful attempt just made. He sought to exact a promise from me that I would consider the interview as if it had never taken place'.

After Sullivan had replied that he would not reveal the circumstances of the interview, or what he had learned unless he learned it independently, but reserved his right to conduct his paper conscientiously according to his own ideas, the interview ended with a sardonic laugh and outburst, worthy indeed of Stephens himself in his most characteristic mood:

'You will not dare to allude to us openly in any case. If you say there are secret societies we will contradict you—and what will you do then? You must stand before the public as having made a false charge, or else divulge facts which the government can subpoena you to prove. You daren't. We will defy you to it!'

And when Sullivan candidly admitted all that was true, the finishing stroke came:

'Pause and consider well before you take your course. A secret organization could crush a newspaper or destroy a man in your position, without the possibility of your making a single retort; for you daren't avow you knew them. They could do their ends against you up to your teeth and before your eyes, and you would be obliged to keep silent and blind about them all the while'.

There is nothing at all improbable about this story, nor was A. M. Sullivan the man to invent it, nor does it fit any other leader of the Fenian movement of the time better than Stephens. At this period, he sounded John Blake Dillon and Father Kenyon. Dillon, at first sceptical, soon hardened into determined hostility. At first, after considerable argument and an eloquent plea to Stephens to abandon conspiracy, Father Kenyon to some extent gave his support. The story of the Sullivan-Stephens encounter was repeated by an unnamed 'Fenian' suspect under detention—possibly, from internal evidence, Richard Pigott—in a secret report to Dublin Castle, December 1865. There it was stated briefly that Stephens 'tempted the Proprietors of several newspapers. Among the last Alexander M. Sullivan of the *Nation,* who, being a sort of Roman official [sic] in Ireland, told Dr Cullen and rejected Shouke's [sic] offers'.

The only value of this reference is that it suggests the story of the Sullivan-Stephens interview was current in Fenian or near-Fenian circles. (Pigott, however, was not in jail before 1867).[7]

Luby and O'Leary described Stephens as exultant over the success and rapid progress of his efforts, and more and more Luby admired his organizing powers. The failure of the New York committee to carry out its agreement to send any further instalment of the financial aid promised hampered what gains had been made, and finally threatened many circles already formed with disruption, as it was difficult to preserve communications with them through lack of funds. Stephens was reluctant to use the mails to rouse 'the transatlantic brothers', although Luby and he considered the promises had been 'shamefully broken'.

In the end, Denieffe was sent again across the Atlantic, two subscriptions of twenty pounds each at intervals came after his arrival in New York, and finally he returned with a further forty pounds, and the work was resumed with enthusiasm.

[7]Larcom Papers, National Library of Ireland, 'Fenianism', 1865, Supplemental, 'The Story of the Fenian Brotherhood. By Nobody at All'. This production is a verbose mixture of gossip, distorted facts, and imagination, of which the Cullen myth quoted is typical. The anonymous writer claims to have been a contributor to the *Irishman* from 1861 onwards, and well-informed on Fenian affairs at home and abroad. Rutherford's story of the Stephens-Sullivan interview is given *Fenian Conspiracy,* Vol 1. pp. 267–70.

AFTER his return from his second visit to America in 1858, Denieffe accompanied Stephens and Luby on an organizing tour which set the Irish Republican Brotherhood going in earnest throughout the south, and which also led to one of the most serious checks of the movement in its initial stages. Denieffe and Stephens made first for Waterford while Luby travelled southwards towards Co. Cork. They visited Carrick-on-Suir, Clonmel, and Kilmallock and finally rejoined Luby in Cork city. On the way, Denieffe met Denis Cashman in Waterford and Denis Dowling Mulcahy at Powerstown near Clonmel, and at Cork Brian Dillon, Morty Moynahan and James Mountain, pioneers then and leaders in the future, and others, all men who made a deep impression on him as they were more advanced in their political ideas than any he had met in rural Ireland until then. He made other contacts at Kilmallock and Macroom.

With Stephens and Luby he listened to the Shandon bells, explored Cork and Cobh where he was depressed indescribably by the sight of Spike Island with its convict establishment looming away in the harbour. They made their way to Killarney by foot and jaunting car, by Glengariff and Kenmare with Stephens as an admirable guide to every point of interest. At Kenmare O'Donovan Rossa and his friend, Dan MacCartie, generally known as Donal Oge, held a short conference with Stephens in the small tavern where the party stayed. Denieffe noticed the unusual caution of some of the townsmen who also came to the conference and of the visitors in the little hotel. One visitor told him the reason: the perpetual vigilance of Lord Lansdowne's agent, William Steuart Trench, who was closely in touch with Dublin Castle, and had organized a very efficient system of espionage against the Ribbon Societies in the district, as he himself describes in his book, *Realities of Irish Life*.[1] There he gives a very different account of himself to Denieffe's 'one of the meanest and most contemptible petty tyrants that ever held authority over poor mortals,' or to the more detailed invective Rossa expends on Trench in his *Recollections*.

'This is a terrible place', said the visitor to Denieffe. 'The town of Kenmare, I mean. You can't move without you're watched and talked of'.

Mr Trench in his book also pictures himself as one much watched and talked of, a discriminating friend of the tenantry with a system of judiciously subsidised emigration of the poorer or more turbulent tenants. The Ribbonmen formed plot after plot against his life which he defeated by judicious bribery and extreme personal courage, going heavily armed on all occasions, and trusting to timely warnings from a strong body of informers. Rossa distributed some vigorous verse in English on printed slips about him which Trench, who never discovered the author, denounced as incitements to murder. This charge was based on pointed references to 'trenching tyrants', and to release 'by rifle and sword'. His clearances on the Lansdowne estate, by subsidised emigration during the famine of thousands of tenants and rigorous regulation of the lives, marriages, and movements of those who remained, were notorious. Sir Charles Russell found the popular hatred of Trench alive when he visited Kerry in 1880.

Trench himself would have been very uneasy if he had had word of the Stephens-Rossa conference in Kenmare that evening. He was soon to learn that James Stephens was far on the road to achieving what he admitted he himself had never achieved for all his informers, entry into the inner circles of the Ribbon Confederacy and a grip on that organization no political revolutionary had until then succeeded in gaining. Stephens, in turn, remembered before the year was out, with some reason, Trench's link with Dublin Castle.

Next morning the party made for the Lakes of Killarney. Denieffe very quickly made up his mind that, even in a talkative

[1](London 1868). Re-issued slightly abridged, with a preface by Patrick Kavanagh (London 1966). The original edition is that employed here.

land where all talk was very good, Stephens and Luby were not only unrivalled conversationalists but provided a very animated course of lectures in history, literature and poetry, 'not of English only, but of all the nations that had any to boast of, in ancient and modern times'. He took it all in, venerated these learned and worthy men, and thanked Providence for seeing such a beautiful countryside in such company 'on a noble mission for liberty, truth and justice'.

Stephens, moreover, had many happy and surprising tricks to shorten the road, indeed to shorten all the roads as he had learned them in his wanderings. On this trip he made the jarvey drive in by a certain road between the slopes forming a small valley on high ground, and then a sudden turn revealed the Upper Lake and all the glory of Killarney. He led his companions to Ross Island and Muckross, and explained so many things of history and legend that Denieffe thought himself in fairyland. And in one sense, as his memory later told him, Denieffe was in fairyland under the enchantments of Stephens, whom he cast off for ever in bitter revulsion some seven years later:

'He seemed to have me under a spell. He was the only practical man I had met in the Movement up to that time. There was earnestness in his every move. He was abstemious, frugal—in fact, in adversity his greatest qualities were shown to perfection. He was all that could be desired as a leader. If he had continued so, and lived up to the doctrine he promulgated and practised his own precepts we would have a different state of affairs now. But he was not a Wolfe Tone'.[2]

More serious business than history and local legends soon occupied Stephens. On his part, the tour became a series of interviews and secret visits to the most influential Nationalists in each town, to the younger Ribbonmen, to the old groups of '48 and '49 men ; a linking up of the centres already organized, and the revival of some which had lapsed through lack of communication and supervision from the Dublin headquarters. Many sympathizers were won over and persuaded to become

[2]Denieffe, p. 29. Denieffe's revulsion from Stephens's guidance which dated from 1865 makes his adverse criticisms unreliable. There is no evidence whatsoever that Stephens was ever anything but frugal and abstemious.

active local organizers. All meetings were carried out with due precautions behind closed doors. The indefatigable and magnetic Stephens at each meeting gathered the names of likely members and officers in the next town. Immediately after the foundation of the I.R.B. as before noted, Stephens had paid his important visit to Skibbereen and won over the small Phoenix National and Literary Society of which Rossa, the Downings, and Moynahans were the leading spirits. During the first Luby and Stephens tours Kilkenny and Tipperary had been organized. Already in the south Stephens was widely known under his romantic pseudonym as the Wandering Hawk or An Seabhach siubhlach, or Shook or Mr Shooks.

Denieffe, Luby and O'Leary all agreed that this organizing drive was the beginning of the spread of the I.R.B. throughout the entire south; that later what Stephens and Luby had done there with the aid of the Moynahans in south and south-west was to be repeated in the north and west within a few years by reliable and enthusiastic agents. Among these were to be such men as Andrew and John Nolan, who, with Frank Roney and James Blaney Rice, made Fenianism a force in Ulster while Edward Duffy was to gain the Ribbonmen of the west. These last triumphs lay some years ahead. Two warnings came in the summer and autumn of the first serious threat to the progress of the conspiracy.

First, Dublin Castle and the Catholic hierarchy suspected that the new secret organization had come into existence (in spite of all the precautions taken by Stephens), and took drastic measures accordingly. In addition, neither dispatches nor money had come from America. This was the position which faced the organizers when after some more Arcadian journeys with Stephens they all finally reached Dublin. Of the first danger there was as yet only a suspicion, provoked some time after their return by an adventure of Luby and Denieffe in Co. Meath, and which in itself did not warn them of the danger from the Castle and Catholic hierarchy. The American failure to send money and dispatches was regarded far more gravely. The fact that the very success of their organizing drive had aroused their enemies to action was not yet realized by them.

The first hints had reached the Castle—and through it the

Catholic hierarchy, in particular Dr Moriarty of Kerry—from Skibbereen and the Phoenix Society where the intense activities of Stephens and his lieutenants had alerted certain Dublin Castle agents made curious by rumours of the Wandering Hawk and the doings of Rossa and his men.

Rossa's own words tell the story:

'In two or three months, we had three or four baronies of the south-west of Co. Cork organized: Donal Oge, Morty Moynahan and I became centres of three circles. We had drillings at night in the woods and on the hillsides; and the rumblings and rumours of war were heard all round'.[3]

Minor rumblings had been heard already when Denieffe and Luby went to Co. Meath to interview a village schoolmaster whom they thought friendly. They had to leave in a hurry and lie low in Dublin for two months. They were warned, just in time and by a chance meeting with a Fenian farmer, that the schoolmaster had planned to have Luby arrested at sight. The schoolmaster had in fact denounced them to the parish priest of Drumconra who in turn denounced the two visitors from Dublin as agents of a secret society at Mass that very day.

The Fenian farmer who had warned them listened sedately. Their error had been to approach the schoolmaster to join the organization merely on the strength of Denieffe's good opinion of him. He had, in fact, agreed to join but had instead given Luby and Denieffe away not only to the parish priest but to the police. When Father O'Brien warned his flock a police sergeant and some constables at once left the church, placed guards on all roads leading out of Drumconra, and thoroughly searched the village. Both Luby and Denieffe read their names and descriptions in the *Hue and Cry* with an order authorizing any policeman to arrest them at sight. The pursuit soon died down although both men lay low for some months. O'Leary and Luby regarded the Co. Meath alarm as probably mere local officiousness.[4]

In the autumn Stephens decided to visit America and examine the situation on the spot. He left Thomas Clarke Luby

---

[3]Rossa, *Recollections*, p. 150.
[4]O'Leary, Vol. 1. pp. 93–4; Denieffe, pp. 41–3.

in charge of the organization in his absence. He called on John
O'Leary and explained his plans and hopes. He had been given
a letter of introduction from Father John Kenyon to John
Mitchel in the warmest terms. John Blake Dillon, according to
Stephens, at first favourable to this American scheme, finally
refused to give him any letters or support whatsoever. O'Leary
received this statement with 'some grains of salt' and considered
it of no consequence anyway as Dillon had every right to change
his mind, and Stephens might equally have believed that Dillon
had agreed because he did not altogether refuse at first.[5]

This memory led O'Leary into some pungent comments on
Stephens's truthfulness:

'It was often impossible to disentangle fact from fancy in his
talk. You could often not in the least believe what he said, but
you mostly felt that he believed it himself, and could seldom or
ever know that he didn't. Now, after half a lifetime, when the
glamour of Stephens's influence has quite left me, I know not,
any more than most of us know in the case of Mohammed or of
Oliver Cromwell, to what extent he was consciously untruth-
ful'.[6]

Asked by Stephens to meet him on a certain date in Boulogne,
O'Leary finally, but with some reluctance, agreed. This
brought the sceptical although sympathetic O'Leary definitely
into Fenian activities once and for all. He was to make arrangements for the custody of certain funds Stephens expected to
bring back from the United States, including a large sum at the
disposal of the Irish Directory of Forty-Eight Exiles in New
York. Among the members of this body were Thomas Francis
Meagher, Judge Robert Emmet, Richard O'Gorman and
Horace Greeley. This Directory Fund had been first raised in
1848. It had been used in the legal defence of prisoners in
Ireland that year, and in the organization of the escapes of
Mitchel, Meagher, McManus and others from Australia. It

---

[5]Dillon was the first person that Stephens approached in 1856 about his
revolutionary plans on his return to Ireland, but Dillon refused to have anything
to do with these projects (O'Leary Vol. 1. p. 71). Dillon himself told Gavan Duffy
that Stephens came to him at the outset of the conspiracy but that Dillon regarded
it as utterly futile, and declined to give any assistance. (Charles Gavan Duffy,
My Life in Two Hemispheres, (London 1898), II. p. 206).

[6]O'Leary, Vol. 1. p. 85.

also played some part in the unsuccessful schemes for arming the Confederate Clubs, after the February revolution in France, with the aid of the United Irishmen survivors then in Paris, General Arthur O'Connor and Colonel Myles Byrne.[7]

Contact had been maintained by the Directory with the '48 men in Ireland, and by these, or possibly by some of his American correspondents, Stephens had been informed that this money might be obtained for the new revolutionary movement at home.

Almost immediately after Stephens had sailed for New York, the government swooped on the Phoenix Society in the south. There were arrests in Skibbereen, Macroom, Kilkenny and elsewhere. O'Donovan Rossa and others were arrested. The *Nation* newspaper edited by A. M. Sullivan continued the campaign against the Phoenix Society in the south which had been followed by government action. The government had been informed in more specific detail and some colourful perjury of the workings of the secret society by another Sullivan, generally known as 'Goulah' from the name of his district. After some negotiations and delay, the majority of the prisoners, including O'Donovan Rossa, made a formal plea of guilty on the understanding that one of their number, Daniel Sullivan, who had been sentenced to ten years' penal servitude should be released. The blow shook the Fenian movement in the south, and had very unfavourable effects on Stephens's mission in the U.S.A. and above all on his relations with the Directory.

'Goulah', although much of his evidence had been inaccurate and perjured, had, however, thrown most unwelcome light on the activities of Stephens himself—invariably referred to by 'Goulah' as 'Mr Shook' with vague stories of that mysterious leader's plans for an American landing. The informer was sent under police protection to Clontarf. He persisted in hanging round public houses in that district and boasting that he was the man who had jailed the Phoenix men. This boasting became the talk of the neighbourhood.

[7]D'Arcy McGee writing to Charles Gavan Duffy from New York, 8 May 1849, informed him that the Directory had some £5,000 in whole or part available for an Irish purpose, 'clearly manifest'. Quoted, Gavan Duffy, *My Life in Two Hemispheres*, Vol. 2. pp. 5–6.

Langan and Denieffe and other Fenians discussed the matter, and finally decided that one of them should see the informer, warn him, and, if he again boasted of his treachery, shoot him. They urged Luby to sanction this, but he peremptorily refused and forbade such action, as Stephens's acting deputy. Denieffe never forgot Luby's words, as pacing backwards and forwards, he said with intense emphasis:

'My God, it cannot be permitted! The sacrifice would be too great—giving a good man for a scoundrel. Moreover, I will not take the responsibility for such a course upon myself'.[8]

In the meantime, Stephens reached the United States on Wednesday, 13 October 1858.

---

[8]Denieffe, pp. 44-5. There is an obvious slip where "Warner" is given instead of "Goulah" for the informer. O'Leary, Vol. 1. p. 94 quotes Luby's own statement that his 'consent was vainly sought to the killing of the original "Goulah" the informer. The wretch was then said to be living with the police at Clontarf.' O'Leary omits the names of Denieffe and Langan which occur in the original letter in the Luby Papers. O'Leary states that Luby's attitude represented his own and Kickham's on such assassinations. Warner, the later Cork informer, was similarly saved by Stephens's orders in 1865-6, but when Stephens left Ireland in 1866, a determined and almost successful attempt was made by a Fenian corporal named Tierney on Warner's life (Devoy, p. 150). Stephens also forbade any attempts on Nagle and Corydon.

THE first contact with American life, above all with the Irish movements and '48 exiles there, gave James Stephens a bias against all three which he never really lost. His misgivings about Mitchel, Meagher, and Richard O'Gorman, and about the leaders and rank and file of the chaotic medley of Irish clubs hardened into a hostile certainty. Fifteen years later he wrote to his wife from New York, 'How happy I should feel even in a garret in Paris . . . However humble my means of life, nobody would look down on me. Now here I could do nothing without wealth. This is an *upstart* people, and any ruffian with money, however acquired, is the superior of men whatever their virtues and acquirements. It is the country *par excellence* of upstart and ignorant brass'.[1]

When he landed that October morning at New York with some unidentified Irish friends, for the most part indifferent and unaffiliated to any political movement, Stephens, after a trying voyage, 'tottered at every step, as feeble as a child . . . as sick, too, as enemy could wish me'. After a brief rest in the Metropolitan Hotel, which he was to favour in his future tours in America, he recovered, looked up Michael Doheny's address in the directory, and went out to find him. His fellow-traveller on the voyage, one D.M., a friendly sceptic in Irish political matters, had not offended Stephens—after some non-committal confidences—by obviously regarding him and his new organization at home as the passing experiment of a dreamer, but Doheny's reception of his old companion and fellow-fugitive of ten years before was to prove a most unpleasant and disillusioning encounter.

[1]Stephens to Jane Stephens, 22 February, 1874.

Indeed, the opening pages of Stephens's American diary are the most violent contrast imaginable to his own account in the 'eighties of his flight in '48 with Doheny and with Doheny's own *Felon's Track*. This diary, to be sure, although one of the most revealing and best written of Stephens's writings, needs to be taken as an unrevised, incomplete, and unrestrained record of passing emotions in a strange atmosphere under considerable strain. As usual in his autobiographical writings, Stephens omits the most important fact from the record: that he, with one disappointing exception, succeeded in his mission. Only by inference, and by the definite assertions of John O'Leary, do we know that the mission was a triumph over great obstacles, and that Stephens, apart from the Directory and the '48 leaders, had reason to congratulate himself. He travelled widely on small resources and collected a considerable sum. The diary, in addition, is a personal defence, or partial draft of one, to be left with John O'Mahony against certain members of the Irish Directory and others, including Doheny, who, he believed, had conspired to wreck his mission. It opens with the date 7 January 1859, some three months after his arrival, and concludes with the entry of 25 March 1860.[2]

Apart from this suspicion of conspiracy and hostility against himself, O'Mahony, and their plans, there was the goad of an intense dislike of the America of that day, which he styled 'this Land of Self, Greed and Grab'. 'Ramshackledom' was his word for it, and 'Ramshackles' for the Americans with many disparaging comments on people, architecture, transport systems, public taste, manners and customs. There are several sharp references to the 'debasing influences' particularly in politics, which have ruined every Irish-American leader with the exception of John O'Mahony. Frances Trollope, the famous novelist's mother, and Charles Dickens had nothing to teach Stephens in anti-American invective.

[2]The quotations in the text from the diary are given by kind permission of the Deputy Keeper, Public Records Office, N.I. The original document—of which there is a photostat copy in the National Library of Ireland—is in the Public Records Office of Northern Ireland, Belfast, Reference D. 518. See also, *Report, Deputy Keeper of Records N.I.*, 1938–45, pp. 31–4. 'Stephens's American Diary', *Irish News*, Belfast, 6 May to 13 June 1950, and *Threshold*, Autumn, 1958, give two detailed accounts by Dr Brian A. Kennedy.

As the diary progresses, Hell yawns for Yankees, very closely followed by '48 celebrities and Irish exiles soaked in drink, humbug, and local politics, crossing all the 't's' and dotting all the 'i's' of John O'Mahony's outburst to Stephens in his letter of 1856. And particularly ferocious is the castigation of the 'puddle-pated or puddle-gizzarded members of that miserable Directory', those 'carrion knaves'. The indictment has an accent of sincerity and is not malicious, even if the writer admits that his views have become 'jaundiced'. It is, after all, the private brooding of the man who is yet to bind for nearly a decade in Ireland and the United States so many hitherto ineffective and warring elements into one formidable political and revolutionary force. Events were to prove that Mitchel, Meagher and the older '48 men were, in fact, blind to the greatness of Stephens and jealous of his success.

In his own jealousy of possible rivals, Stephens himself was quite as bad, and his judgment of Doheny is the most glaring and blameworthy example of it. There is some evidence that Stephens himself had a somewhat guilty conscience on this matter. O'Leary insisted that the tribute paid by Stephens to Doheny after his death, and repeated with emphasis most consistently thereafter, was Stephens's final view of his old comrade, and that of O'Leary himself and of Luby, with the significant qualification, 'whatever his faults'. There is also evidence that Stephens never quite trusted Doheny again and on impersonal grounds in which the fortunes of the Fenian movement were concerned. The funeral of Terence Bellew McManus was to be the most obvious example of this when Stephens over-ruled Doheny's and Roche's hare-brained project of an insurrection.

Stephens's matured and public opinion of Doheny has already been given in the account of their conference at the meeting at Rathcormack after Ballingarry. The 1859 diary almost from the opening pages is much occupied with describing Doheny's faults without any qualification at all, a minute, ruthless, and most envenomed analysis. When the October meeting took place, Doheny was about fifty-four years of age, Stephens some twenty years younger. The older man had only three years to live, and within those three years he

was to share in Stephens's most dramatic triumph, the Fenian
rally at the McManus funeral, although there, as noted,
Stephens was to interpose all his guile and authority to check
Doheny and his lieutenant, Roche, and indeed, as the malicious
declared, to keep Doheny from making even a funeral oration.

From the moment Stephens stepped into Doheny's office at
15 Centre Street, New York, a cloud fell between them.
Doheny's son, Michael—whose job, as Denieffe had seen at
once, was to protect his pestered and good-hearted father from
a host of cadgers and time-wasters—piqued Stephens with the
routine and cold reception and evasive answer. When
Stephens gave his name firmly and shook the boy by the hand
as his father's son, no interest was shown at all, and this aroused
the darkest suspicions. Denieffe had noticed, after a similar
reception, when he arrived with Stephens's reply to the New
York Committee in 1857, that tears came into Doheny's eyes
as he read Stephens's message, and that he summoned the
Committee with the utmost speed.

'In the midst of my conjectures', wrote Stephens, 'Doheny
entered. On meeting anyone for the first time, or whom I wish
to read, I always watch the *expression*, afterwards attending to
the features and other details. I carry the same principle into
art; it seems to me, for instance, that a poem should be read
right on to the end at first, then accurately to appreciate it,
analysed in all its constituents. Doheny's expression—always
equivocal—set me very much ajar. This effect was so rapidly
produced that before he could reach me (his step, too, was
hesitating and unsteady) I had time to note the confused
colour, the furtive peer, the bent head, the objectless motion
of the arms. His embrace, too, (for he took me to his breast)
had its *arrière pensée*. All this struck me and shot an indescribable
sensation through my whole frame. I don't think, however, he
observed this; for he is a wretchedly dull observer, *never* hitting
the mark . . .'

After several tortuous and verbose reflections on Doheny's
character, the diarist proceeds with the interview, after the one
plain charge:

'So, also, he is jealous, envious and false, while eternally struggling to be or appear free from everything of the kind; and so he is a patriot while plotting in such a way as to necessitate these notes, in order to shield my honour (my life—at least my liberty he has already doomed) from his enmity.

'I struggled and shook off the feeling alluded to above. "You have come?" he asked. The question requiring no answer, I briefly explained our position at home. He was evidently (as well he might) surprised; but it was painful to have to note how grudgingly he looked on the work I had accomplished.

' "Now", I said, "the Directors cannot refuse the money without proving themselves traitors".

' "Have you the letter from—"? he asked.[3] I said I had not. It requires a man to know both of us well, to believe what I have now to say of him true; at least that I may not have been mistaken. I have already said that my judgment of the man may have been more or less jaundiced. Spite of this, however, I am quite convinced that, on hearing I had not the letter, he manifested surprised pleasure, which it required an effort to suppress, and which reappeared again and again for some time. I remember distinctly, too, that his silence was longer than the announcement called for. At length he said: "Then they won't give the money!"

'Joe [Denieffe] told me before I left home that I should not get it without the letter in question, and that my mission would be a failure. I believe Joe spoke at random, or repeated what he heard others say; for with regard to the failure of my mission he could not have known it without (which is impossible) knowing the baseness of our great patriots here; as, without their hostility, I should, I firmly believe, have laid the basis of an organization which would, eventually, give us a hundred times the money in the hands of the Directory. I believe, too, that to this hostility alone is owing our inability to wrest the money out of the hands of the puddle-pated or puddle-gizzarded members of that miserable Directory.

'Our conversation took place partly in Doheny's office and partly on our way to O'Mahony's, to whom I asked to be brought after the first few words necessitated by such a meeting, and to

[3]Evidently John Blake Dillon, who had finally refused a letter to Stephens, as before mentioned, for which, as we have seen, O'Leary refused to blame Dillon, while Father Kenyon, on the other hand, had given a strong letter of recommendation to Stephens. There are, of course, no paragraphs in the diary, and those in the text are purely arbitrary, and for the reader's convenience. All Stephens's italics have been retained but not his ampersands, and initials for proper names, e.g. 'D' for Doheny, 'Mea' for Meagher, 'M' for Mitchel, etc.

whom I would have gone first had I known where he resided. For in him alone had I implicit trust, and to him alone would I wholly unburden myself'.

Denieffe's *Recollections of the Irish Revolutionary Brotherhood* are a corrective to Stephens's statements in his diary, first, as already noted, on Doheny, and, again, as to his reasons for warning Stephens against the difficulties of his mission in a time of depression and scepticism in Irish-American circles. He remembered too well the over-confident recklessness with which Doheny had promised 30,000 non-existent invaders for an Irish-American expedition in the autumn of 1855, and 'that some of the wealthiest men of our race' would finance the venture.

As Stephens's courier, Denieffe during his two trips to New York had lost all illusions on the immediate possibility of financial or physical support for a militant movement from the majority of Irish exiles. Their papers discouraged any such movement in Ireland, and collections were slow: 'the people had lost all confidence in such movements, and in the good faith of the leaders. Some of the Irish-American newspapers took a special interest in decrying any active movement in Ireland. They were, for various reasons, pandering to the local politicians, and, consequently, were not with us. The *Irish-American*, then the leading and most influential Irish paper in America, was, I remember, one of them. It took two months to raise four hundred dollars (£80)'.[4]

That was on Denieffe's first trip. On his second trip he raised £40. He warned Stephens 'not to depend on America for further assistance. "The Irish-Americans", I said, "will not subscribe until they are obliged to. They have been humbugged so often that they have lost confidence, and at present have no faith in attempts for the regeneration of Ireland" '.[5]

The critical passages on Doheny in the diary were written when Stephens was in a mood of deep resentment because Doheny had reproached him some nights before with over-estimating the power and importance of Mitchel and Meagher in Irish-American affairs, and with 'running after them', and thwarting Doheny. A further hint that Doheny thought

[4]Denieffe, *Recollections* . . . p. 22.
[5]Denieffe, p. 28.

Stephens did not wish to return to Ireland, a complaint that O'Mahony and Stephens were plotting against Doheny, and trying to destroy his influence as an Irish-American leader, roused Stephens to set down an account of his American experience in the diary. During the discussion, as Doheny enlarged 'on the time and money spent on running after Mitchel and Meagher . . . to O'Mahony and me, I took him up so as to astonish him rather'.

This meant, no doubt, the emphatic exposition of Stephens's own views on Mitchel and Meagher, which he sets out in detail and with much shrewdness in his diary.

Of the two, he prefers Meagher, in spite of what he deems a certain weakness of character. After Stephens had sent Mitchel a telegram asking for an interview, Doheny said disencouragingly that Mitchel would do nothing then as he had done nothing in Irish-American political life hitherto. 'It seemed to me' comments Stephens in the privacy of his diary, where his opinion of Mitchel proves far less complimentary than even Doheny's scepticism, 'that the argument, though not without some show of reason, was far from sound or just. I attempted to account for his inaction. Without a profound knowledge of the Irish people no man could have the faith in them that alone could justify continuous appeals to their manhood and nationality. Had Mitchel this knowledge? I found not'.

And from the many pages of the diary that follow on the subject it becomes very clear that Stephens has been discussing Mitchel with Father Kenyon and has read a very important self-confession in a long letter from Mitchel to Kenyon. (This letter is published in William Dillon's biography of Mitchel, Vol. 2. pp. 103–6). Mitchel had written it in a mood of deep disillusion when he sent Kenyon the prospectus of his *Southern Citizen*, and it explains his inactivity in Irish-American political affairs and his defence of slavery in the Southern States. Father Kenyon's name is left blank although the references in the diary leave no doubt as to the identity. Stephens, after reading the Mitchel-Kenyon letter, persuaded himself that Mitchel is a disgruntled egoist rather than an Irish patriot. Some pages before, Stephens has proclaimed himself a soldier of liberty and of universal freedom in such unqualified terms that some critics of the diary have rashly labelled him 'an international democrat rather than an Irish patriot'.

O'Mahony had warned Stephens that it was indispensable to win over Mitchel and Meagher, or make them pronounce one way or another before taking any serious step in the United States. If their cordial co-operation were won, the Directory would be forced to give in; if not, the Directory would not give a penny. Then other plans would have to be made. Stephens next advances the coldblooded confession:

'these were my own opinions before I left Ireland. I was certain of the co-operation of both Mitchel and Meagher. *Not* that I had a high opinion of—or even believed in—their patriotism. But I believed they would not *dare* hold out against the *facts* I had to state; they could not, because these facts held out the prospects of a career they could never aspire to elsewhere, supposing them ambitious, interested, or with any touch of salvation in them; they *dare* not, because by so doing, it would be evident to all that they were shams, had been shams probably at all times, and had abandoned their country. Let me here say a word in justification of the disbelief in their patriotism. I have read a letter of Mitchel to —— [Father Kenyon] in which he takes some pains to show *that he is not a patriot*; the motive of his conduct was an insupportable aversion to the state of things in which he found himself, and wherein he who should be free found himself a bondsman and the father of bondsmen; but there was no feeling for the rest of his countrymen—no detestable philanthropy. Anybody who has met him and knows his position here might well ask him *how* he is less a slave *now*, than he was in Ireland. His answer would be indignantly caustic and every one of his *followers* would cheer him to the echo.

'As to the "man of the Sword" he has performed such patriotic feats within the last lustrum as most assuredly make the angels weep. Still I must do Meagher the justice to say that I believe his heart infinitely more with everything generous, and even noble, than Mitchel's is, and but for his proverbial *weakness*, he would, as in his best moments, do good service to Ireland'.

Mitchel in his letter of November 1857 to Father Kenyon had shown at least that his egoism was not as self-deceiving as that of Stephens's. Mitchel sometimes had the wit to ask the question 'Can it be that I, J.M. am wrong, and the three

governments that jailed me right?' Stephens in like circumstances was always right: haughtily demanding from the
British government the return of his personal possessions left
behind in Richmond jail after his escape or denouncing with
fury the French government for listing his name with the most
abandoned criminals in its archives.

'Whatever it was that made me act and write as I did in
Ireland', Mitchel had written to Father Kenyon, 'I have
found that there was less of love in it than hate—less of filial
affection to my country than of scornful impatience at the
thought that I had the misfortune, I and my children, to be
born in a country which suffered itself to be oppressed and
humiliated by another; less of devotion to truth and justice
than raging wrath against cant and intolerance'.

Stephens could make allowance for Mitchel's retirement
from the Irish movement to the Southern States because all
Mitchel's Irish correspondents, with the exception of Father
Kenyon, told him 'in damnable iteration, how we had become
quite West-Britonised, prosperous and contented' and even
Father Kenyon had nothing better to tell Mitchel than that
'a vague aspiration after liberty was eternal in the Irish heart;
but that the Irish people would never fight for it'. Mitchel's
defence of slavery, however, horrified Stephens who did not
even consider Mitchel's arguments in the same letter.

Within a few years there was to be a final and bitter break
between Father Kenyon and Stephens. Stephens in his own
jargon was to dismiss Father Kenyon as an 'Aspirationist'. The
relations between John O'Mahony, Mitchel and Father
Kenyon were to remain cordial even if O'Mahony sided with
Stephens in the controversy. 'Aspirationism' had apparently
been preached to Stephens 'on that memorable night of our
first meeting when he [Father Kenyon] did all that in him lay
(his anxiety to succeed increasing as he was found, hour after
hour, to give me a higher place in his esteem) to prevail on me
to give up the work already begun; and whether he believed it
or not, or so wrote or not to Mitchel, and whatever it may
have been once,—[Father Kenyon] himself is now so little
disposed to, not to say capable of action, that his language must
have been in complete accord with that of Mitchel's other

correspondents.[6] Mitchel I believed to be *no organizer*. Indeed, his conduct, and far as I know, his words proved he did not *believe* in it. Nor were the attempts at organization here calculated to modify this. But—[Kenyon] who had been as incredulous as he on this head, has been forced to give in, in proof of which (though the note was by no means as *sanguine* as I knew—[Father Kenyon] to be, however guardedly he might speak or write) witness the note to Mitchel. When *facts*, on which he might rely, were placed before Mitchel he also would be compelled to believe'.[7]

These broodings are the prelude to meetings in due course with both Mitchel and Meagher, and these as described by Stephens are both diverting and exciting, which is by no means true of even the most emphatic of the same writer's soliloquies.

Two days after his arrival Stephens and O'Mahony set out at an early hour to visit Meagher, who then lived in Fifth Avenue, the sight of which caused an eruption of ultra-democratic rage in Stephens, who denounced it as the habitat of a monstrous aristocracy, a display of the almighty dollar, a servile imitation of European dwellings, the tinsel dream of tasteless upstarts, which even Dublin could teach in decoration and furniture. The architecture drove him to Rabelaisian jibes, and he summed up that, 'Art shrinks, shivering, aghast, at the mention of Columbia!'

Nor was his interview with Thomas Francis Meagher any compensation after O'Mahony had introduced him:

'As Meagher had met me but once in Ireland,[8] I was not surprised

[6]Stephens was well informed here, as letters quoted in Dillon's biography show. (Vol. 2 Ch. 3). See Mitchel's letter to Miss Marie M. Thompson 'Eithne' of the *Nation*, pp. 117. 18. 'Whatever indication do I ever receive from Ireland (save from yourself and one other) that does not show me how absolutely and scornfully Ireland has condemned herself and repented in sackcloth and ashes for having ever listened to the wild counsels of such as I . . . I do not feel impelled to keep harping on a string to which everybody is deaf'. Dillon gives Mitchel's chief correspondents in 1858 as Miss Thompson, John E. Pigot, John Martin, and Father Kenyon.

[7]Father Kenyon's letter to Mitchel, given to Stephens for his mission, as already mentioned.

[8]Meagher had met Stephens at the final Council of War on 28 July 1848 at Ballingarry, and apparently knew him well enough to recognize him earlier that day. See Doheny, *Felon's Track* ed. Griffith, p. 176; Gavan Duffy, *Four Years* . . . p. 667.

at his not being able to recognize me. On being presented he gave me a patronizing hand, inviting us up to his study. I had been told of his obesity; but, spite of this, he appeared by no means imposing on this occasion. The intellectual and moral portion of the head is small, and his measured way of speaking would scarcely reconcile one to the genius of Shakespeare. Briefly stated our position at home. He seemed greatly struck; pronounced me the Tone of our generation; expressed not only sympathy but a desire to forward my views far as he could. On hearing of the letter to Mitchel, and the telegram sent to him, was pleased, seeing the importance of his co-operation.

'He would present me to the Directory (for he also deemed it better to see Mitchel before applying for the money in the hands of the Directory) on my return, and, as a member propose that it should be given to me. All this, though pleasant, had one drawback; he said nothing about *going heartily to work with us.* He said, however, that he would give the matter his most earnest consideration. On leaving, he asked me to meet him next day at the office of the *Irish News.*'

A visit after this meeting to Doheny's office in Centre Street left Stephens in no better mood for praise when he reflected that this was 'the rallying centre of the Brotherhood', and finds the brethren presented to him worthy of 'credit for good feeling', but blames Doheny for passing them off 'as men of influence'. They were unknown in Ireland, with one exception, James Roche, one of the signatories of the New York call to Stephens, then helping Meagher with the *Irish News*. He was a former editor of the *Kilkenny Journal,* and according to O'Leary and Devoy, also editor of the *Galway Vindicator.* Roche, to Stephens, is a most qualified exception, for he declares with italics that after all Roche's influence is null *where he is known.* O'Leary who met Roche shortly afterwards is even less flattering, and so proves that Stephens is not merely malicious. Roche, O'Leary commented, was a slap-dash and effective journalist for those who required neither thought nor reason, and excessively ignorant.[9] A second exception considered by Stephens is also qualified: Oliver Byrne, another signatory of the New York call, mentioned favourably by Devoy for his theoretical writings on military affairs.[10] Stephens dismisses Byrne as important merely

[9]O'Leary Vol. 1. p. 104–6.
[10]Devoy, p. 17.

for his writings and as a man whose influence in Ireland would last for only one hour after he opened his mouth.

Stephens later clashed with Roche at the McManus funeral over a reckless project for immediate insurrection, and his instinct in his diary is thus justified.[11] At the back of Stephens's mind there lurked a resentment when he discovered that he had been misled by the New York Committee into expecting a stronger and more representative movement. Luby stated to O'Leary that Stephens and himself had indeed mistaken the real state of affairs by accepting the New York invitation at its face value. The complaint reiterated by Stephens throughout his correspondence with O'Mahony is that the movement in America has not fulfilled its promises or observed the conditions laid down by Stephens—a reproach made, in different degrees, by Luby, Denieffe and O'Leary.

A final outburst in the diary expresses Stephens's bitter opinion on the material to his hand, material, however, of which he made effective use before his tour closed:

'The oddest and most disgusting thing in this is that these men are taught to fancy they have as *good a right* to sign documents, sit on committees, nay, *lead* nations, as the wisest—the best of the children of men! We have too much of this deplorable pretension in Ireland'.

Rossa in his *Prison Life* writes with some humour of the dictatorial reaction of Stephens against any presumption in his followers. On the eve of Rossa's arrest in '65 some Carlow men remembering a previous visit by himself and Stephens to the Ballybar races, often used as a useful cover by the local Fenians for meetings, wrote to Dublin asking that Rossa should attend the next fixture. Rossa sent the letter to Stephens and received a peremptory order to go to America immediately.

'Why', wrote the Boss, 'should these Carlow men attempt to dictate to him? They should be taught they could not do that and it was for him to determine who was the fittest party to meet them'.

Rossa, who had recently returned from America, in July, and had been excused a second visit there in August, had no

---

[11]Rossa, *Recollections*, p. 237 gives an account of this plan and Stephens's determined precautions to prevent it.

desire to go to Carlow and was hurt when he detected signs of a little jealousy in Stephens. His arrest on the night of the *Irish People* raid on 15 September 1865, however, abruptly settled the trouble.[12]

This jealousy in Stephens of possible rivals was one of his blemishes, and less excusable than his arrogance. General Millen was struck by it at their first meeting and concluded that here was a man, so self-opinionated, so dogmatical in character and ideas, who even when he knew himself in the wrong would not admit it, but would prefer to see any project ruined, if his own plans were rejected for another's possibly better ones. Very soon after this meeting, Stephens expressed much the same distaste for Millen, who certainly provoked the Head Centre's jealousy.

As for poor Doheny's presumptions and errors, we read in the diary:

'Doheny is jealous of every man who would dispute the position he fancies he holds or may hold, as chief of the Irish people; and so unscrupulous—so madly culpable is he on this head that he would stop at nothing to ruin the man who rose or would rise, above him, nay, he would sacrifice the cause itself rather. Even of myself, I know D. to be jealous (it was palpable to a very ordinary observer) long before I came here.'

Yet in this Stephens was not altogether swayed by love of power or by conceit: the claim was based on a conviction of superiority which, in the early stages of the movement down to the crisis of 1865, was justified by results. He organized the semi-moribund Ireland of the 'fifties, and in spite of the outcries in his diary, this American tour was in fact to be a success, even if his hopes of winning over the Forty-Eight leaders in exile were to be disappointed. His distrust of the Irish immigrants who took to politics was shrewd and sincere, and in this Rossa, Denieffe, John Boyle O'Reilly and D'Arcy McGee were of the same mind as himself.

Meagher raised his hopes when, at their next meeting in the *Irish News* office the following day, 'the man of the Sword' said he had considered Stephens's proposals and was ready to throw himself *heart and soul* into the new movement. These were almost

[12]Rossa, *Prison Life*, Ch. V. pp. 35–36.

the first words spoken, followed by the appeal, 'But for God's sake, stop Doheny's mouth; it is the mouth of hell—no; hell keeps what it receives; but he can keep nothing'. This outburst was not surprising. Doheny and Meagher were not on speaking terms. Meagher insisted at some length on the importance of Mitchel's approval, and seemed very confident that Stephens was sure to get it.

There were minor irritations, and evidently a certain amount of mischief-making by some loose-tongued brothers who reported that Doheny was holding back funds for Ireland raised by lectures he had given, and a reported statement of Doheny's that infuriated Stephens, although he received it with some reserve, that the money would be held until important sums were raised when an envoy would be sent to discover how the funds already sent had been used. Stephens, too, resented the debts he had to incur because he was given no expenses; a tactless attempt by Doheny to settle Stephens's hotel bill on his own; and the great pressure that had to be used to produce money for the coming trip to meet Mitchel in Knoxville.

On a minor scale, this was a foretaste of the experience with O'Mahony and the Fenian Brotherhood throughout the years ahead, and of the added irritation of the many envoys sent from the U.S.A., which exasperated Stephens and the I.R.B. Yet, it is plain that until the Civil War the very funds were lacking or non-existent, and the American situation, as Denieffe had warned Stephens, was unpromising. Stephens's unconscious portrait of himself shows through many a hasty page that he was in fact the one possible leader no obstacle could halt. It also shows O'Leary's Stephens who never spoke good of anyone (except at this time of O'Mahony), and who assumed that he was Shakespeare and Julius Caesar rolled into one. Yet it was O'Mahony, in fact, who nearly won over the Young Ireland leaders. Mitchel was O'Mahony's ally to the end, and four years later O'Mahony initiated Meagher into the Fenian Brotherhood. Yet in Fenianism, temporary alliances apart, neither Mitchel nor Meagher ever played a serious part, and so far Stephens had summed them up correctly as men of the past.

12 *To Washington with D'Arcy McGee and Meagher*

On Friday, 15 October 1858, O'Mahony brought Mitchel's reply to Stephens's telegram: 'What business? Write by telegraph; if not by post'. Stephens decided to travel by Knoxville and have it out once and for all with Mitchel. Doheny, somewhat reluctantly to Stephens's mind, set about getting money for the journey. Meagher received Stephens with enthusiasm at the office of the *Irish News*, and highly approved of the decision. As he was going to Washington the following night, he invited Stephens to travel with himself and McGee.

This journey provides some of the most startling pages in the diary. Thomas D'Arcy McGee within the next decade was to be one of the bitterest enemies of Fenianism at home and abroad, but there is no hint of misgiving about him in the diary. Stephens spent many hours with him, found him not only kind and helpful personally, but judged him to be a man who, if left to himself, would serve the new movement in Ireland. McGee, in fact, was much under Gavan Duffy's influence politically, his part in the 1848 insurrection had been creditable, and his polemical journalism had upheld the Young Ireland cause after defeat with a rancorous fervour. Yet even in 1858 he had begun to reverse all his former revolutionary beliefs, was deeply disgusted with Irish-American politics as they then were, and had already sounded a conservative note in controversies with Meagher in the press on religion and republicanism. Stephens agreed with him thoroughly on the Irish-American politicians, otherwise their reactions and opinions were in violent contrast.

Stephens's first favourable impression of McGee—unlike that of Thomas Davis, spiritual father of the Young Ireland movement, who distrusted McGee at their very first meeting—

has its ironic side as the pages of the diary are shortly to be filled with devastating judgments on other Young Ireland celebrities he meets in McGee's company. It showed indeed a certain penetrating insight on the part of Stephens, even if McGee within the next few years became a venomous and most dishonest enemy of the Fenian movement, and of John O'Mahony in particular.

McGee was in June 1865 to describe the Fenian Brotherhood to the St Patrick's Society of Montreal as 'a seditious Irish society, originating at New York whose founders have chosen to go behind the long record of their ancestors, to find in the days of Pagan darkness and blindness an appropriate name for themselves'.

Already McGee, in an address at Ottawa in 1857, had declared that henceforth he would not be guided in the Canada he had adopted as his new country by his old inherited hostility to Great Britain. Stephens certainly would have forgiven McGee's future denunciations of Fenian schemes to invade Canada as the work of 'rotten members infected with political leprosy' as he used much the same language himself on that subject, but he sensed nothing of the McGee who was to deliver that anti-Fenian lecture of 1865 which goaded O'Donovan Rossa and the anti-Fenian, T. D. Sullivan, into a common unity of denunciation, and hurried a sharp rebuke from Gavan Duffy to McGee himself that he was better as a rebel at twenty than as a statesman at forty.

One passage in that lecture ran:

'The Ireland I loved in my youth is near and clear to my heart. She was a fair and radiant vision, but this Billingsgate beldame, reeling and dishevelled from the purlieus of New York, with blasphemy on her lips and uncleanness in her breast, this shameless imposter I resist with scorn and detestation'.[1]

The beldame meant James Stephens, John O'Mahony and all the Fenians on the face of the earth, whereon in 1868, three months before his assassination, Lord Mayo praised McGee as 'the most eloquent advocate of British rule'.

Yet Stephens may have perceived in McGee that side of him

[1] Alexander Brady, *Thomas D'Arcy McGee* (Toronto, 1925), quotes the full passage.

which made him one of the most remarkable exponents in his day of the cultural side of Irish nationalism, whatever political beliefs he recanted, the poet and historian who told the Canadian parliament, 'my native disposition is towards reverence for things old and veneration for the landmarks of the past'. This spirit provoked in the Canadian statesman the most extreme revulsion against the revolutionary spirit of '48 as in James Stephens it inspired the most extreme development of that revolutionary spirit.

There was indeed a confrontation of extremes in the Washington meeting of these two men, Stephens, the greatest Irish revolutionary since Wolfe Tone, McGee, revolutionary by accident in '48 though a most thoroughgoing one, who turned full circle, in the case of Ireland to an acceptance of the Union with England tempered by reform, and from a violent anti-clerical into a rabid reactionary who regarded revolutions everywhere as satanic.

Whatever his reservations on McGee, Gavan Duffy placed his mind next to that of Davis among the Young Ireland leaders 'in wide sweep of imagination, in the persistence and variety of his labours, in everything but the moral qualities'.[2]

By the autumn of 1860, it must be noted, Stephens's favourable impression of D'Arcy McGee had been drastically revised. A letter from Paris to O'Mahony dated 4 September, had this emphatic if obscure reference:

'Frankly your last letter has made me sick at heart. Granted that "there was much *exaggeration* in the representations made to you of his (McG's) remarks still as 'he stated his opinions to you *in substance much the same*,'" it is most difficult for me to understand your way of speaking about him. You wrong yourself—at least I would fain believe so—saying that, under like circumstances, you would act as he has. You wrong me—and deeply—when you say: "seeing how much *reason* is at the side of McG". There is no *reason*—not the faintest shadow of reason on his side; and the most painful thing connected with his low calumny is the fact of your having thought there was. . . Your way of speaking of him makes me *anxious*. You talk of his *steadfastness* and assure me that *he will do his duty*, etc. *wherever he may be*. I can scarcely believe my

[2]Charles Gavan Duffy, *Young Ireland*, (final revision: London 1896) II. p. 16.

eyes when reading these words. *Steadfastness!* How has he proved it? *Do his duty!* . . . But I will believe that you rather *wish* than expect anything from him'.

The journey to Washington with Meagher and McGee was uncomfortable. Stephens discovered that the accommodation on the main lines could not be worse. A good housewife, he agreed, knowing this would provide for her lord and master, in this case, Meagher, with food and drink. Meagher, however, he thought, spoke and partook of these with excessive enthusiasm, boasting he had paid three dollars for a bottle of brandy. A *gourmand* and nothing more, 'quantity not quality, filling not gustation is what he has a stomach for'. In addition, Stephens found the journey very trying, exhausting, full of insomnia, and felt quite worn out when they at last reached Washington, so much so that even in the hotel he could not sleep. After breakfast, Stephens accompanied Meagher and McGee on a visit to John Savage although Meagher had forgotten the address but was sure he would get it from 'one Dimitry'.

One Dimitry, whom Meagher assured Stephens had the intellect of a hundred men and the learning of a thousand as well as being a thorough good fellow into the bargain, also had an address of which Meagher had merely a notion, and the notion necessitated a walk of some miles. Dimitry, when found, kindly accompanied them all to Savage's house, but won no praise or thanks from Stephens, who by this time was in the mood to damn all Washington. He damned poor Dimitry as a fawning, patronizing, pseudo-intellectual Titan, 'naturally moulded for the ferule of a philomath and nothing more!' So soured was Stephens by this that he parodied the slogan of 'Washington, City of magnificent distances', by adding 'and shabby foregrounds!'

Stephens made some very sharp comments in his diary after Meagher introduced him to John Savage:

'I had time to observe this *artist* (he is under the impression that he alone, of all Irishmen, can write readable books, owing to the superior structure of his "artistic sentences") . . . A strange conformation of head is that of Savage's. So *small*, that you wonder where reason can have found a place at all: a narrow forehead; eyes well coloured but ready to pop out of their orbits; a small sensual mouth. Small and slight of person too; with the restlessness and gesticulation of a monkey. By the way, I noted that this gesticulation is looked on, by others as well as himself, as the best seasoning of his *wit*. On being presented to this specimen, he bowed slightly and stiffly, and with averted eye; instantly after which ceremony, he walked off on Meagher's arm'.

This disparagement of a man with as good a '48 record as Stephens himself, with a literary style far better than Stephens was ever capable of, one of the future leaders of American Fenianism, was indefensible. It was possibly, also, the echo of a resentment noted of Meagher's habit of always presenting McGee first. It points, moreover, to Stephens's sub-conscious urge to blacken any potential rival. The existing portraits of Savage do not support this malicious personal description; the portrait, for example, of Savage in 1848, facing p. 289 in Griffith's edition of *The Felon's Track*, shows a head and forehead with plenty of room for reason.

Even when Savage, almost immediately, turned round and apologized: 'did not know that I was *the* Stephens, was delighted to meet me, etc. I knew he lied; and that this change was owing to what Meagher had told him. What *had* he told him? This will some day come out'. A visit to Savage's house somewhat restored Stephens's good humour even if it left an edge on his wit. The house was neat and comfortable, he admitted, well furnished, with ornaments, prints, a piano, and all that. The edge of Stephens's wit fell on the devotion of the recently married Savage to his wife:

"Twas ludicrously delightful to hear him talk of his wife. She was adorable and a treasure to him. Before his marriage he was forced in his professional capacity to wade through measureless poetry and romance; since the date of his happiness, *she* did all that and gave him such exquisite abstracts of her readings, that *their* nights were like the Arabian Nights!! I was rather curious, and sincerely wished for a glimpse of the charming raconteuse. To my gratification, Jack, hearing a rustle, exclaimed that "she was coming".

'Instantly, a form: tall (for Jack), slender (not for Jack), pale of face, prominent of feature, blue-eyed, with light-coloured ringlets, floating to the library—borne of their own motion:

skipped into the room! A rapid greeting to Meagher; a rapid presentation of McGee and self; and the form disappeared as it had entered! What more is to be said? It seems to me, as in a dream, that Jack asked, if we didn't think her adorable. Long may he continue to find her so, every night proving more and more Arabian. And this though he is a very little crittur'.

After dinner at a hotel the same day the tour of Washington proceeded, and Stephens warmed up in earnest and had full scope for his powers of criticism and vituperation against all celebrities, Irish, American, and of the human race in general. They paid a visit to Dr Antisel, who, unfortunately for his record in the diary, had been spoken of as a very superior person indeed. Interpreted by Stephens this was an 'Irish patriotic way of praising to the stars every man who belonged to your party, and carried to a sickening extent by us . . . another and a bastard form of the great Anglo-Saxon bluster. I say a *bastard* form; for, after all, the *soi-disant* Anglo-Saxons *have* done the work of men; while these creatures—Bah! The exclamation applies to this Dr as to so many others. I don't know how to go about guessing such folk ever found themselves in the council of men. A more worldly specimen than the one in question 'twould be no easy matter to find. But enough of him'.

What Dr Antisel had done to deserve this scarification is a mystery. It may have been his sardonic wit and known friendship for Mitchel. He had been one of the founders and financial backers of the defiant *Irish Tribune* with Kevin Izod O'Doherty and Savage in the most dangerous crisis of 1848, which wrecked his Dublin career as surgeon and chemist. He escaped to the United States where he was to serve through the Civil War, become Chief Chemist in the U.S.A. Agricultural Department, and spend five years in Japan on a government commission. His Irish record had been honourable and hardly worldly. Apart from his connection with the *Irish Tribune,* he had been an active member of the Irish Confederation. He was also the author of pamphlets and addresses to the Royal Dublin Society on the geology of Ireland, reafforestation and the sanitary conditions of Irish towns. And he had been among those who joined in the public welcome to Mitchel in New York after his escape from Tasmania in 1853, and all James Stephens had for him was a Bah![3]

In the case of Savage, Stephens was as wrong-headed as he was in the case of other Fenians and Young Irelanders as good as himself in deed and word. In the case of Mitchel, Meagher, Antisel and other Young Ireland survivors, Stephens was on stronger ground, even if his private and public expressions of his feelings in this estranged many Fenians from what remained of Young Ireland. After his return from his first American tour, Stephens felt with good reason, as will appear, that Mitchel and Meagher had failed him while Smith O'Brien joined with A. M. Sullivan in open denunciation. Dillon had refused to back him and finally was responsible for turning Mitchel and the New York Directory against him. Nor was a clash with Father Kenyon to be long delayed. O'Leary, Charles J. Kickham and Luby never shared this anti-Young Ireland animus of Stephens and regretted it, feeling that Stephens had not all the right on his side against Mitchel and the rest in 1859 and later. John O'Mahony, who sided largely with Stephens, never expressed himself with the same rancour and malice, and preserved the most cordial relations with Mitchel to the very end.

When, however, the first phase of Fenianism had ended in defeat and Mitchel pitilessly jibed at Stephens as a discredited quack and his movement as mere sound and fury, it was O'Mahony who reminded Mitchel that only two Irish leaders in their time had given the Irish masses organization and leadership: Daniel O'Connell and the Fenian movement under James Stephens. Patriotic, devoted, talented as the Young Ireland leaders had been, they knew little of their countrymen 'except what they learned from books and newspapers'. And, in addition, when Mitchel and other leaders found out 'the inefficacy of fiery editorials and impassioned harangues' they never set about the 'silent and disciplined pre-organization' of the discontented masses at home and abroad. When they found, in Meagher's phrase, a revolution, they would not accept it,

---

[3]Mitchel, *Jail Journal*, ed. Griffith, p. 367; Dillon, *Life of Mitchel*. Vol. 2. p. 129, gives Mitchel's praise of his 'most intimate friend in Washington'. For a brief sketch of Antisel, see T. F. O'Sullivan's *The Young Irelanders*, p. 408.

and when Stephens organized a second revolution and made the Irish a force at home, in Europe and in America, they would not accept that either. And the isolation in which Stephens had been left excused his worst faults.

Stephens arranged to go by the train next morning and said his farewells to Meagher and McGee as if he would not meet them until his return to New York. The fare to Knoxville and back was sixty-three dollars, and Stephens had been, as he termed it, 'slenderly provided' with sixty-five. 'Two dollars', he exclaims, 'for travelling expenses!' McGee, discovering this, offered Stephens twenty dollars, excusing himself for not giving more to a cause he so deeply sympathized with. Stephens missed the train because the conductor forgot his instructions and landed him at the wrong station. Though far from well, as too often was his case, he decided to return to the hotel and wait for the night train. Meagher and McGee were pleased that he had not left and took him out visiting. Their first call was a public reception where Meagher seemed to take undue pleasure in fussing over President Buchanan by presenting Stephens to him.

'Have only this to say of Old Buck,' is the laconic comment, 'that he seemed not much better to me than a Yankee development of the Artful Dodger. That is in appearance: I could not speak of him otherwise, having had but a few moments' conversation with him'. Stephens remarked that the President bestowed unusual attention and observation on him, and a scrutinizing look. The President had just suffered a political defeat in elections in his own state, Pennsylvania, 'but whether from this cause or from excessive assiduity to his fair enslaver, he wore the expression of a philandering tom-cat'.

Carl Schurz, the German revolutionary and later American statesman, in his reminiscences in more decorous terms agrees with this description of the President. The German's verdict on Buchanan is that he was 'the most miserable presidential figure in American history' with 'moral weakness of the wise-looking kind', and a capacity for pronouncing 'common phrases with unctuous ponderosity'. Schurz had left the revolutions of Europe behind, completely disillusioned, and thrown himself into the anti-slavery cause in the United States. His description of

Washington as a city and of American conditions in general is near enough to Stephens's dyspeptic sketch.

Schurz quoted the 'city of magnificent distances' tag, and added, 'But there is nothing at the end of these distances, and excepting the few public buildings, very little that was in any way interesting or pleasing. In many of these streets, geese, chickens, pigs and cows had a still scarcely disputed right of way. The city had throughout a slouchy, unenterprising, unprogressive appearance, giving extremely little promise of becoming the beautiful capital it is to-day'.[4]

The Capitol Stephens allowed to be vast and imposing, and he had a word of subdued praise for some others, yet in general, finds detestable, if unspecified, monstrous agglomerations of stone, mortar and ugliness. Meagher in the presence of McGee paid him the unqualified compliment: 'Stephens, you have done me a great deal of good. Before meeting you, I felt as *if half my soul* were wandering I know not where; and you have given it back to me!' Stephens, when he wrote that down—very wise after the event—permitted himself to wonder whether Meagher's soul might not turn up on the shores of the Dead Sea.

Meagher, while still in possession of his soul, also gave Stephens a letter of recommendation to Mitchel:

'This will be handed to you by our gallant friend, Stephens— one of the truest of the true—and, I verily believe, the Wolfe Tone of our generation. And now, wishing every mother's son of us, a happy new year'.

Eventually Stephens set out, and after some adventures by boat and train, reached Knoxville.

---

[4] *Reminiscences of Carl Schurz* (New York 1907), Vol. 2. pp. 210–220.

13 *Stephens meets Mitchel*

On 21 October 1858, John Mitchel and Stephens met at Knoxville. Mitchel was on the point of removing to Washington. He was in the mood expressed to his friend, Miss Thompson, earlier in the year, 'an exile in my circumstances is a branch cut from its tree; it is dead, and has but an affectation of life. Neither are you to think that I have any tie, or am likely to have any here, which could prevent me from throwing myself into that cause again, if it were ever again showing life'.[1]

To the same correspondent, and to Father Kenyon, he admitted that his defence of slavery in the Southern States had been perhaps coloured by a tendency to be, 'exaggerative in expression, and in sentiment . . . the natural pleasure I have and always have had in hunting down and tearing to pieces all sorts of solemn cant'.

The great abolitionist, the Rev. Henry Ward Beecher, had been goaded to the very extremity of eloquent commination by Mitchel's jesting and 'exaggerative' crack that he wished he had a good plantation well stocked with healthy negroes in Alabama.[2]

'Once', thundered Beecher, 'you stood like some great oak, glory of all beholders and covert for a thousand singing birds. Now you lie with mighty ruptured roots, ragged and upturned to heaven. Fallen! Uprooted! Doomed to the axe and the hearth!'

'I may be like a dead tree', retorted Mitchel, 'but what if your Reverence is very like a whale, a whale of the blowing and

[1]Dillon, *Life of John Mitchel*, Vol. 2. p. 117.
[2]William C. Beecher and Samuel Scoville, assisted by Mrs. Henry Ward Beecher, *Biography of Rev. Henry Ward Beecher* (London 1894); T. M. Healy, *Letters and Leaders of My Day* (London 1929), I. p. 46.

spouting species—blowing and spouting as if you meant to quench the stars?'

Mitchel's version of his meeting with James Stephens is well known from Dillon's biography, and is short and terse:

'About two weeks before our migration a gentleman appeared at our door who announced himself as James Stephens. I had never seen him before and knew him only as having turned out with Smith O'Brien in 1848 with his pike in good repair. Glad to see an Irishman of such antecedents at Knoxville; and for two days he remained with us, telling me romantic tales of his armed, sworn, organized forces in Ireland. All he wanted was that I should publicly call on my fellow-countrymen in America for money and more money, and no end of money to be remitted to him for revolutionary purposes'.[3]

This belongs to the bitter and disillusioned onslaughts made by Mitchel on Stephens and the Fenian organization after 1867 —attacks such as he allowed no outsiders to the Irish movement to make on pain of verbal scarification in the style of his Ward Beecher inquest. It was written as late as 1869 in his *Irish Citizen*, yet is characteristic of his consistent distrust of Stephens.

James Stephens also left in the obscurity of his private journal an account of the meeting which suggests that both men misunderstood each other from the first. It proves that Mitchel's story of the meeting is unfair and misleading. Stephens certainly believed that exile and pessimistic correspondents in Ireland had depressed Mitchel unduly and made him too sceptical of the chances of any immediate successful Irish conspiracy. Mitchel, as in the 1869 quotation given above, concluded almost before Stephens left Knoxville that he regarded himself as the predestined leader, with Mitchel, Meagher and all Irish-America as the predestined paymasters. Stephens received the impression that Mitchel favoured his plans and accepted him as the leader of the revolutionary movement in Ireland and the United States.

Stephens reached Knoxville with only two of his hoped for letters of introduction, the one from Meagher, and the other from Father Kenyon, with whom his relations were then friendly, indeed Kenyon's letter, according to John O'Leary,

[3]Dillon, *Life of John Mitchel*, Vol. 2, p. 120.

was one of 'strong recommendation'. For some reason John
Blake Dillon, at first apparently favourable, had refused to write
any letter, and later wrote very critically to Mitchel about
Stephens. O'Leary's opinion was that both Dillon and Stephens
misunderstood each other, and that Mitchel—quite apart from
any criticism from anyone—was repelled by Stephens from
the first. O'Leary regarded Stephens as the greatest leader of
them all—and as the most arrogant self-deceiver O'Leary had
ever met. Luby, who had heard both sides of the later Mitchel-
Stephens clashes from the two men themselves, told O'Leary that
the truth lay half-way between their two stories. O'Mahony,
in any case, who had Mitchel's confidence, expressed himself
very strongly in Stephens's favour in the controversy.

Here is Stephens's description of his meeting with Mitchel
that October:

'Not *certain* of the result of my mission to M. decided on taking
a room for the night in Knoxville; as, should M. refuse to
co-operate with us, I should not have accepted his hospitality.
Besides, I had need of a wash and change of linen—especially as
M. was a benedict. My *toilet* effected, proceeded in search of my
man. Found at the *Southern Citizen* office that M. resided about a
mile outside the town and that I should find him at home. What
is to be said about Knoxville? *No* European, it seems to me, can
form any idea of *any* American town; much less a small young
one . . . Nor could the wit of man invent a word, or even a word-
picture, to give a European the least glimmering of what it is like.

'There is, however, *one* English word of so comprehensive a
significance that there is scarcely anything in Freeborndom to
which it may not justly be applied. Of course I mean the
immortal word, *ramshackle*. Now, to give a European an idea of a
young rising American city, I should say: given a number of
square or parallelogram sites (the archetypal *block*), stone, brick,
mortar, and a year or more of time, so many Freeborns, my life
on it, they will get you a young, rising city, that for ramshackleness,
shall most assuredly whip the universe! Of such a kind (and
numbering some 8 or 10,000 inhabitants) is Knoxville. There
are a few good stores in this town, and when I was there it looked
pretty stirring.

'It might have been three (or, by our Lady, even four) o'clock
when I reached M's. It drizzled all the way out; and, as it took
me a good while to get directed to the house, I was quite wet

when I stood at M's door. This, considering my looks and general
disarray, together with my then exhausted state, must have given
me a wild and ghastly appearance. I was conscious of the dis-
advantage; but, from what I had been told of M. I believed that
facts, more than the man, could influence him. Besides, I had
Meagher's and ———'s [Father Kenyon's] letters of recommendation.

'As I entered the hall, M., pipe in fume (he is as much of a
smoker as myself) stood up from the parlour fireside, and
advanced to meet me. Had I been ignorant of his antecedents,
I *might* have found it difficult to read his face; as it was, there
could be no mistake about the intensely passionate nature long
waging unequal war depictured in it. Wan, pale, emaciated, with
a frown occasioned by the constant tension of his faculties, or
some defect of sight.[4]

'He seemed to be asking himself were I friend or foe. *Introduced*
myself. His way of asking me in showed me that he had mistaken
me for somebody else. A few words of explanation showed this,
and then his manner was cordial. I soon came to the point;
giving him Meagher's letter to read. When he had got through
it, I handed him ———'s [Father Kenyon's]. This read, he
looked keenly at me and asked in a marked way "What does all
this mean?" Made my statement. The effect produced on him
was like what ——— [Father Kenyon] said I had produced on him
the first night we spent together. But with very opposite results;
——— [Father Kenyon] worked might and main for a whole night
to dissuade me from the work. Mitchel looked on it as good and
wonderful; grew hopeful, enthusiastic, warlike; would be with
us heart and soul!

'It looked a great triumph, and I had a time, spite of my
physical prostration, of intense joy. For what could Mitchel not
do here! I had been assured that his co-operation would give us
all we wanted; and lo! spite of all the doubts of so many of his
friends and acquaintances, here it was given! He would do all I
required, he said; and without waiting to hear what I did require,
said he would go to Ireland. What I wanted first of all, I said,
was that he would use his influence with the Directory to get me
the money in their hands. He would willingly do so, and asked

[4]This proves the closeness of Stephens's observation. Mitchel, in fact, was very
near-sighted, as William Dillon mentions several times in his biography. See, for
example, Vol. 2, p. 233, Mitchel did not recognize his brother William and his
two sisters when they paid him a surprise visit in Paris in 1865 through his extreme
near-sightedness.

(for he did not know) who were the members of the Directory.

'I had not been able to learn how many the members were; but five names had been given me, and these I mentioned. He would write a letter to each of them. As to his going home, for the present, we could not expect it as were not *certain* of being able to take the field that year; it would depend on circumstances of which we were not masters. For my part, however, it would be a great thing for me to have such men in Ireland, a short time before beginning the struggle, to share the responsibility I found so great. "Whether or not", he said, "*you* must have the responsibility; you have done the work and must bear the responsibility". This I looked upon as very noble. *He* had been the recognized leader of the Irish revolutionists'.

Stephens entered a parenthesis in his diary. He recalled the conversation the first night he stopped with O'Mahony after his arrival in New York. O'Mahony told him that Mitchel, shortly after his escape from Australia, had been appointed 'absolute director' of an organization then set on foot. O'Mahony, no doubt, referred to the Irishmen's Civil and Military Republican Union, which collapsed at the close of the Crimean war. It was short-lived, and its relations with O'Mahony's Emmet Monument Association were sometimes strained. Mitchel's relations with other groups were also strained. He had given up his newspaper after violent controversies with Archbishop Hughes on the one hand and with the Abolitionists on the other, and retired to farm in Tennessee in 1854. All hopes that Mitchel would lead the Irish movement in America were then abandoned. [5]

Admiration and gratitude overwhelmed Stephens. One of the outstanding leaders of the 1848 rising had abdicated in his favour, 'it seemed to cost him nothing to give way to one he had been taught to look on as mainly a brave young enthusiast! But I had done a man's work and the labourer was worthy of his hire'.

[5]See D'Arcy, *The Fenian Movement in the United States (1858–86)*, pp. 3–10; William Dillon, *Life of John Mitchel*, Vol. 2. p. 78, Mitchel to his sister Mary, 1 November 1855, 'I have nothing to do with conventions, with "Emmet Monuments". . . or the rest . . . yet many worthy fellows are connected with all those, and I would have no scruple in calling upon all for material aid in money or muscle upon a proper occasion. In the meantime, I am obstinate in keeping out of all that for the present'.

An edifying digression in self-defence was further inserted in the diary at this point:

'These notes shall be left in O'Mahony's hands, to be made use of by him, as I shall direct. Consequently, I have no misgiving as to the possibility of misconstruction. Were it otherwise many a sentence would lead one who did not know me to the conclusion that I am *gnawed* by ambition. This is far from the truth. I am far from desiring *power*—and Ireland once free, I would not be *forced* to accept it; if I do so even *now*, it is because I know nobody at once so practical and so devoted to the people.

'My firm resolution is to establish a democratic republic in Ireland; that is, a republic for the weal of the *toiler*. This once established, I shall retire from political life, refusing place, pension—recompense of any kind, and giving myself up to the development of my artistic, philosophical, and scientific plans. I shall live by my own labour; well, if that labour should be profitable; modestly or poorly, if it should turn out otherwise.

'Believing, however, that anything short of a thorough *social* revolution can effect but small good for the people, I shall, if granted, undertake the direction of a fraternal association, to be composed of volunteers sharing my faith and desirous of working with me. It seems to me that such an experiment should be made by our government; and, having thought deeply on the subject, and being, as I think it will be admitted, a practical man, I feel bound to place my personal plans in abeyance once more, for the sake of my fellows. If this be ambition, the thing has been much defamed'.

In these secret self-confidences we have the case for Stephens as Stephens saw it. He persuaded himself that Mitchel had accepted him as his successor as the better man, and, even if Mitchel after sleeping on the interview very soon had second thoughts, Stephens refused to see the significance of that. Even his own account of the conversation between them betrays an attitude that must very soon have antagonized Mitchel, for Stephens has said very plainly that while money is imperative, the presence of Mitchel and others in Ireland can wait until convenient to Stephens, and there is no ambiguity as to who will be the Wolfe Tone of the coming revolution.

Mitchel lived to say that Meagher and himself soon saw through Stephens, and were half-amused and half-resentful.

Unlike many of Stephens's autobiographical reminiscences, the
Stephens-Mitchel interview, as set forth in his diary, rings true.
There is no vagueness in it but sincere feeling. The mesmeric
power that Luby conceded to Stephens played in that first
meeting on Mitchel, always ready, given the opportunity, to
help hog, dog or devil against Carthage. Stephens in that long
undiscovered diary did give, in spite of his arrogance and itch
for self-deception, a more truthful memory of the event than
Mitchel's ungenerous distortion of it in 1867, quoted in part
by both Pigott and Rutherford:[6]

> 'Exactly nine years ago, James Stephens, came to this country
> to organize the American branch of the Irish Republican
> Brotherhood. He came to east Tennessee, stated his plans and
> resources, and required rather than proposed, that Meagher and
> myself should place ourselves at the head of the organization in
> the United States, appeal to our countrymen here for money,
> and plenty of money, and remit it all to him. This was cool. I
> questioned him closely upon the progress he had made in Ireland,
> and he assured me that he had then—nine years ago—fifteen
> thousand sworn confederates (they were not then called Fenians),
> all armed with rifles. I did not believe him. A few days later
> Meagher and myself met Mr Stephens by appointment, at my
> lodgings, in Pennsylvania Avenue, Washington. He demanded of
> us, in a somewhat high tone, that we should enter his conspiracy,
> and should use all the credit and influence that he supposed us
> to possess among the Irish citizens of the United States, in order
> to procure money for the purpose of that conspiracy. It was a
> startling proposal'.

Mitchel is here wrong on dates—he did not leave Tennessee
for Washington until some months after Stephens's visit to him
that autumn. Moreover, Meagher and Stephens had already
met. Time had telescoped many happenings. Mitchel now regarded Stephens as a humbug, a boaster and charlatan in the
management of revolution. It had not been so in Tennessee
in October 1858. Mitchel's attack on the fallen Stephens
continues:

---

[6]Pigott, *Recollections of an Irish Journalist*, pp. 100–2; Rutherford, *Fenian
Conspiracy*, Vol. 1. pp. 96–98. Mitchel's article, 'Personal Recollections of Thomas
Francis Meagher' in the *Irish Citizen*, is quoted more fully, *Irishman*, 11 January
1868.

'Unfortunately, for him, we could not believe his statements, and speedily arrived at the conclusion at which many others have since arrived, that he was a *humbug*. It was in vain he told us that our antecedents and the position we held (as he said) amongst Irish patriots imposed on us the duty to place ourselves in the hands of him, James Stephens, as the only representative of the Irish national cause, and with full confidence in him, his promises and pretensions, ask our country-men settled here for their hard-earned dollars, and plenty of them.

'Now Meagher and myself knew very well that the Irish-born citizens of the United States could be free enough with their dollars, if they only felt some confidence that their contributions would be honestly and intelligently used for the purpose of freeing their native land, but we had more than scruples in this case. It will always be a source of gratification to me, that my friend and myself acted alike on the proposition made to us by that most plausible gentleman'.

In fact, as Stephens shows in his diary—and John O'Leary makes the same statement in his memoirs—Meagher had already given a written undertaking of support to Stephens, which he later withdrew. This apart, Mitchel joins in the smearing of Stephens's personal integrity in money matters, a baseless charge from the former financial agent of the Fenian organization, even if his Paris letters to John O'Mahony in 1866 show that his correspondence with Stephens that year convinced him that Stephens had made mistakes that any intelligent revolutionary leader should have avoided.[7]

Mitchel ends his *Irish Citizen* article of 1867 with a statement —omitted by Pigott and given by Rutherford—of the real differences in policy between himself and Stephens:

'I told Mr Stephens that, although fully bent on taking advantage

[7]"Meagher . . . was weak of will, and, though he joined Stephens at first having certainly signed a document expressing confidence in that gentleman and conferring certain powers upon him, he afterwards withdrew, when he found that Mitchel was not favourable to the scheme' (O'Leary, *Recollections* . . . Vol. 1. pp. 96–106). Mitchel to O'Mahony, 10 March 1866 (Denieffe, Appendix. p. 220) expresses a very forthright condemnation of Stephens as a revolutionary leader, and lists his mistakes in 1865–6. Mitchel had warned Stephens that in his opinion an insurrection was impossible and refused to answer further questions for dealing with a crisis which Stephens had brought about against Mitchel's advice, or rather that Stephens knew well would have been Mitchel's advice, if asked before the crisis was brought about.

11

of any legitimate occasion and opportunity for liberation and destroying British power, we had never yet asked our countrymen to contribute to a revolutionary fund, because we had not any assurance that it would be properly and effectively used; that we believed that no opportunity whatsoever then existed for a revolutionary movement in Ireland (England being then at peace with all the world); that we declined therefore, to make ourselves responsible in the eyes of the whole Irish race, at home and abroad, by calling on them to pour into our hands their savings of years—as we knew they would—on the mere faith of his assurance that he was going to overturn the British Empire.

'Thereupon Mr Stephens attempted to assume a rather lofty and peremptory style of discourse; told us of our *duties*, and of the responsibilities to which we would some day be held. This tone did not answer. We declined to be informed of our duties by him; and he very soon took up his hat and left the house'.

This is obviously a second interview at a much later date. Mitchel insinuates that this second interview explains Meagher's attitude to Stephens and to his organization. Even the first interview as described in Stephens's diary disproves this:

'Mitchel, seeing my fatigue, proposed that I should go to bed immediately after dinner. My intention was to have started that night; and, spite of my exhaustion, I should have done so; but M. expressed such a desire to talk more at length with me, that I consented to give him a day. Was presented to Mrs M. She looks uncommonly well still, and must have been very handsome. Her reception of me was most cordial; and owing to this, and to the amiability and intelligence of the whole family, I should gladly have spent some days with them if I could. M. deserves all honour for the way he has brought up his family: for the reverence and love of the children for their parents; for the brotherly and sisterly love of the children for one another; and for the manners and information imparted to him. [*sic.* them?] Spite of his and Mrs M.'s trials, they ought to have as much happiness as falls to the human lot; for, besides the blessing of such a family, they themselves seem sincerely attached.

'Of course, his health and position makes them anxious about the future of their children. One of my oft-repeated curses of the social system that involves such a source of suffering. All the children are good-looking, too—as might be expected from parents, gifted in that way themselves, married young and married for love. The eldest daughter is as interesting—comely, gentle, and intelligent—a girl as I have met.[8]

'Slept but a short time; being too excited when I lay down to get any for a considerable time. I was, however, fast asleep when M. came to call me to supper. They had put off the meal long beyond the usual hour, not wishing to disturb me'.

Mitchel's mood had changed to the dismay of Stephens:

'Talked long with M. when the others had retired. He seemed to have changed his mind considerably—at least, he was by no means as enthusiastic, raised difficulties, etc.! This was most painful. I needed repose—could not have met the arguments of an able man without an effort sure to injure me. The effort, however, had to be made. Gradually I re-established his confidence, and even enthusiasm. He would do all he had promised. Meagher had promised the proceeds of a lecture; on hearing this M. would give a lecture for the same purpose.

'The night was a bad one—that is, a restless and feverish one. At breakfast, it was decided that M. should write the letters before going to town, where there was no special business to be done. I should have to depart midnight, there being no train sooner. While Mitchel was writing the notes walked about the grounds with Mrs Mitchel and the children. The house (a comfortable one in itself) is pleasantly situated, giving you vistas of forest scenery. The grounds are, with the exception of a small patch before the house and a kitchen garden, nearly in the primal state; but rich in tree, and bush and wild flower, it must be pleasant enough to dwell there with the summer beauty.

'Mrs Mitchel spoke of old times and places and friends. Like the O'Brien's, the Mitchel's (*his* mother had not tried to hide it) seemed to think the Irish people abandoned their chiefs in '48. The ladies (male and female) of the families feel (or, for their own purposes, *pretend* to feel) this most keenly; and they believe themselves more at liberty to express it than the chiefs. How sad is all this. Mrs Mitchel seems to believe that Ireland was lost the day the people allowed her husband to be arrested. Of course I

---

[8]Henrietta Mitchel 1842–1863. See Dillon, *Life of John Mitchel*, Vol. 1. p. 42. Vol. 2. pp. 147–9.

When Henrietta decided to become a Catholic Mitchel refused to prevent her, and silenced his relatives and friends who protested with a tart, 'If private judgment leads one into the Catholic Church, it is private judgment still'. He also informed them that—'and so much the worse'—there was no chance that he would follow her example.

had to speak guardedly on this subject. Another point (a cardinal one) on which it was absolutely necessary to be guarded was the *slave question.* Mitchel himself has been going on so madly in defence of slavery that *all* Irishmen must know of it, though they are not nearly so grieved or indignant thereat as they ought to be. Mrs M. shares her husband's views. She herself could very gladly place herself at the head of a plantation, but this, even if she had the means, would not do, you must be born to *it*, like poetry'.

Stephens left the Mitchel household with very friendly feelings, and indeed, Mitchel had shed his hesitations, and carried out all his promises:

'Mitchel wrote five letters: one to T. F. Meagher; one to Robert Emmet (the judge); one to Judge O'Connor; one to Richard O'Gorman, and one to Horace Greeley.[9] It would be a great relief to me to have these; they would fully justify (in the eyes of an enemy even) every step I have since taken. This, however, cannot now be; even Mitchel (knowing I should use them in my contemplated *impeachment* of the Directory, and even to Mitchel's disparagement, if the cause should need it) will not give me even a *copy* of his, and with all the others (save Emmet, who will act like Meagher) I have altogether broken. O'Mahony, however, to whom I showed the letters, can testify to the *sense* of what I shall here state. I take the letter to Meagher as embodying the sense of all the others, with fuller details, and written with the greatest confidence. The letter began by saying how and why he had stood aloof from Irish *organization* since coming to this country: nothing was doing at home, and he saw nothing practical here. The paragraph ended by a humorous hit at ——, who, Mitchel said, fancied on coming here, that they (the chiefs) had nothing to do, but, like the twelve apostles, get up and follow him. It also hit at the endless organizations of——etc.

'The second paragraph went on to say that *the time had at length come* when they were all called on to act, and how he had written to the other members of the Directory, in the most urgent manner calling on them to hand over the money still on hands to me. Then came a long paragraph beginning: "And now, between ourselves, I think Dillon has not acted fairly by Stephens". He then said how O'Gorman and Dillon had often shocked him by their way of speaking of the fund: they spoke as

[9]The original of the Greeley letter, since discovered in N.Y. Public Library by Owen Dudley Edwards in 1960, fully confirms Stephens's statement here. See text below, p. 139.

if the money had been placed in their hands to use it as they deemed fit, without owing an account of its debursement to anybody.

'In case they refused *my* application, it was his opinion Meagher should resign; had he influence enough with Judge Emmet he would get him to do the same. He ended by stating his belief that Meagher and he (Mitchel) by a general appeal to the Irish in America, and without saying exactly for what purpose, could raise 20 times the sum then in the hands of the Directory. This letter was, I said, all I could have expected, or even desired. It made me glad. The only thing notable in any of the other letters was a phrase in Judge O'Connor's: "In giving Mr S. the money you may rely on its being devoted to the right purpose, and with a capacity and integrity to make every pound tell for ten". Or words to this effect. He ended the letter to Greeley by telling him to preserve it if he pleased, "as I shall always be proud to be held responsible for what it contains". Or some such words.

'After dinner went to Knoxville. Mrs Mitchel accompanied us; and there was much feeling in her words and manner at parting; indeed I should say, that I left with most kindly feelings towards all; even the drawbacks in Mitchel's case, I construed in a friendly way'.

And there the diary becomes blank until it is resumed in Brooklyn on 12 January 1859. The Directory, obviously from the tone throughout this final section of the diary, remained hostile and quite unmoved by Mitchel's letters, and, as to Mitchel himself, who had in December left Knoxville for Washington, Stephens already had a hint that he too, had grown cold and unfriendly. The last definite reference to Mitchel in the diary is to a chance meeting in New York on 12 January:

'On the beat at the Fulton ferry met Mr Mitchel yesterday. He was standing in front of the beat; and, as I came out of the ladies' cabin, he may have seen me. I think he did; as (my eye resting on him for an instant as I looked round without taking particular notice of anybody) he averted his head. Why? Either from a wish to avoid me, or uncertain of the reception I should give him. If the former, he must have deemed it impossible under the circumstances. For he came over to me. He was told I had left New York last week. I said I had not been *able* to leave, and saw no better prospect of doing so *than* when I came; adding I supposed him aware of the object of my visit. He had a general notion of it, he said. I spoke a good deal about the business to him. His curiosity, if not sympathy, was stirred up; for he walked a good way with me, talking all about our position, prospects, etc. He left me in Centre St, proposing to call on me soon'.

And that is the last concrete statement made in the diary on the relations between the two men. John O'Leary binds the conflicting hints together as given to him in the versions of Stephens and some laconic and vague expressions of Mitchel. It is evident from the quotation just given that relations were already cooling, but that there had been no irrevocable breach. O'Leary could not find the exact truth but he regarded the break as most regrettable:

'Stephens asserted that Mitchel received him favourably at first, and promised his co-operation, but that, between a first and second visit, everything had changed, in consequence of a letter Mitchel had in the meantime received from John Dillon'.[10]

Long before the American visit Dillon had refused to aid or approve Stephens's plans, and he had not favoured Stephens's American tour. It is very probable that both he and Mitchel had finally united against the new revolutionary scheme and the entire Directory with them, because of developments in Ireland which were to disturb Stephens even more than the refusal of the '48 leaders to back him.[11]

Indirect confirmation of the truth of Stephens's version of the Knoxville interview was given by Mitchel himself in a letter from that place to John O'Mahony, dated 28 October 1858:

My Dear O'Mahony,
I had a very satisfactory explanation with Stephens. I am anxious to know how the potentates to whom I wrote in New York, treated his application. If he has not already written to inform me, pray let me have a line, such as may be explanatory to me though dark to the rest of mankind.

Faithfully yours,
John Mitchel[12]

[10]O'Leary *Recollections of Fenians and Fenianism*, Vol. 1. p. 96.
[11]In the quotations given in this chapter from the Stephens diary, paragraphs have been introduced, and such abbreviations 'Mea' and 'M.' for Meagher and Mitchel', etc. written where necessary in full for the convenience of the reader.
[12]A facsimile of this letter is given without comment in Arthur Griffith's edition of the *Jail Journal* (1914), p. 400. Also quoted, *Irish News*, Belfast, Tuesday, 23 May 1950, Brian A. Kennedy's *Stephens's American Diary*.

LOUD and angry outcries in his diary reveal how disturbed James Stephens was by the arrests of the Phoenix Society men in Skibbereen and elsewhere on 5 December 1858. He learned by degrees through letters from Ireland and the press reports that he himself had been gravely compromised by the evidence of the informer, Goulah. Moreover, this development gravely endangered his chances of success with the Directory. Nor when Doheny, with perhaps a touch of malice, informed him that he was figuring in all the Irish papers under the name of Mr Shooks, was he grateful to his old comrade.

In the second week in January, Roche of the *Irish News* called on him with a letter from a woman in Skibbereen about the Phoenix Society arrests, which Stephens regarded as indiscreet. It claimed that the informer Goulah had been staying in the house of one of the prisoners he swore against, and surmised that the informer, in a fit of remorse, had made an affidavit that his testimony was perjury. This, in fact, was mere gossip. Stephens was inclined to blame Lord Lansdowne's agent, W. S. Trench, for Goulah's treachery, in which he was wrong, although Trench as a magistrate had at once interested himself in the case. Stephens wrote in his diary on 12 January 1859:

'One part of the letter, seemed to express a desire to exonerate somebody from the *responsibility* of having founded the "Secret Society" and caused so much sorrow! The Phoenix, the letter stated, had been founded before the *somebody* (the name was illegible) came to Ireland. There can be no doubt that the person alluded to is Owen Considine or myself . . . All this it seems to me should have been kept for the *ear* of the lady's friend. And such letters are, doubtless, coming here in hundreds by every mail! Strange if the *authorities* do not know where to pounce. Of course, *I* shall be seized as soon as I lay foot on British soil. How gladly would I go into exile, how proudly meet death to serve this cause! But will the fools and traitors around me allow me to do so? . . .

'Have not seen any of the Irish papers to-day, but the *Irish-American* has an account from the *Tipperary Examiner* of the 22nd ult., which says that "On Tuesday evening the Fethard police escorted into Clonmel a young lady-like and extremely delicate girl named Anne Walton who was committed to jail on a charge of seditious letter-writing. One of these was written on the 20th ult. calling on her Majesty's forces to rebel and mutiny. Well done, brave Tipperary girl! May you love and be beloved by a laurelled hero".

'The approver, Sullivan, in his deposition, at the investigation begun in Cork County Jail on Tuesday 21st ult., spoke of the administration of *two* oaths to himself by a party after whom an active search is being carried on by the authorities . . . The terms of the oath (which the approver swore to from memory) were as follows:—I have something to tell you which will be a benefit to you and to the country—I can tell it to you if you promise to keep it secret. I have promised to keep it secret. An oath of secrecy was then administered after which the following:—"I, A.B. do solemnly swear that I will, to the utmost of my power, endeavour to subvert and overthrow the British government; that I will join and assist any foreign army who may arrive in this country with this object; and that I will obey and carry out the orders of my superiors in this Society to the best of my ability". No such oath as this has been administered by any true member of our organization.

' On being asked if he intended to keep the oaths, "He could not say; he may have intended to do so. He went to confession; the priest refused to give him absolution till he would break through them. It was at a suggestion of a police officer that he first went to Skibbereen". The priests again! Not the military, militia, or constabulary are holding Ireland for the English: your modern "Sogarth aroon" is the buckler and brand of Britain.'

Yet it was the paragraph that introduced *Shooks* into the evidence that really startled Stephens:

'The approver swore that he attended a meeting at the "Priest's Leap" on the borders of Cork and Kerry and drilled there, where members from Bantry and Kenmare met, the object of which was to take up arms as the Americans were expected at Christmas, who would be joined by the French, and Ireland was then to be an independent republic. He also stated that one of the patriots, who went by the name of Shooks, was making the necessary arrangements to rise when the Americans should land'.

And Stephens commented:

'This is the nearest approach to a knowledge of our doings, so near that, spite of certain distortions, I should infer from it that the wretch had been tested or tried to be tested, but for the Skibbereen lady's letter, which R. gave me on Sunday last. From that letter, it appears that, though *not* a member, the person with whom Sullivan had stopped, had, the friend, imprudently taken him into his confidence. How much did this person know himself? How much tell? Was he a member himself?'

Even in the meagre and distorted press reports and the garbled facts in the gossip's letter, Stephens had a shrewd suspicion of what had really happened at Skibbereen. When he learned the full story it led to the start of his life-long and harmful feud with A. M. Sullivan of the *Nation*, and intensified the strong anti-clericalism he had preserved since his wanderings after Ballingarry. It also caused him to coin the word, *felon setter*.

On 30 October 1858, A. M. Sullivan had written in the *Nation* a leading article which led Stephens and the Fenians in general to apply that bitter and deadly label to him for the rest of his life: one who points out or 'sets' political opponents or refugees to the penalties of the law. This article not only denounced Ribbonism and secret societies in general, but clearly stated that a political secret society existed in certain districts and in his own one in particular, which he declared he had visited to investigate the matter.

Indirectly this move was inspired by Dublin Castle and the Catholic Bishop of Kerry, Dr Moriarty. And one Catholic priest in particular had deserved Stephens's new label far more than A. M. Sullivan, who had acted under pressure against his better judgment and the irritation caused by the somewhat unscrupulous use of his name by some irresponsible members of the secret organization.

In fact, in the case of the Rev. John O'Sullivan, P.P., of

Kenmare, no epithet could be more deserved and more exact, even if Goulah the informer had lied when he mentioned a confession to this particular priest. Father O'Sullivan had not only refused absolution to members of the Phoenix Society— in fact by then of course, a regular Fenian circle—and denounced the secret organization from the pulpit, he had used the confessional to rush his penitents into giving him outside it, where no obligation of secrecy could bind him, the names of the members and copies of the oath. These particulars he gave to the local magistrates, Trench included, and to the Viceroy in Dublin Castle early in October 1858, some weeks before A. M. Sullivan's article in the *Nation*.[1]

Father O'Sullivan was genuinely astonished when the law was set in motion, and a Crown Prosecution followed. A. M. Sullivan shared this ingenuous astonishment. Nearly twenty years afterwards, in 1877, he revealed that the *Nation* article had been written on the insistence of Dr Moriarty, Bishop of Kerry, who during a visit to Dublin Castle had been warned that the government had discovered the conspiracy, and had very full information about it. The bishop persuaded A. M. Sullivan that 'a friendly warning in the *Nation* might disperse the whole business and bring these young men back to reason. At all events you will save others from being involved in the catastrophe.'[2]

Whatever his political animus, the bishop's short-sighted advice was humane and sincere. Even his notorious 'Hell-fire' diatribe against the imprisoned and exiled Fenian leaders eight years later, in February 1867, was tempered by an eloquent defence of the Fenian rank-and-file insurgents. Sullivan acted on his advice with hesitation, after consultation with John Blake Dillon, who advised him not to interfere publicly, and with William Smith O'Brien, who agreed that

---

[1][Jeremiah O'Donovan Rossa] *O'Donovan Rossa's Prison Life. Six Years in English Prisons* (New York, 1874), pp. 15–19 gives Father O'Sullivan's letters to the Viceroy and others on the matter. The Fenian organization captured the correspondence and published it. Father O'Sullivan never repudiated the correspondence but justified his action later in a controversy with A. M. Sullivan by claiming that he was the first to inform the Castle of the existence of the conspiracy.

[2]A. M. Sullivan, *New Ireland*, *(*1877*)* Ch. XVII; P. S. O'Hegarty (London 1952) *History of Ireland Under the Union*, pp. 417–23.

he should, and also sent him a letter for publication in the *Nation* in that sense. Sullivan was angered also to learn during a visit to Bantry that some members of the Phoenix Society were freely using his name and those of Smith O'Brien and John Mitchel to recruit others in the summer of 1858.[3]

Rossa in his *Recollections* clears up the mystery which perplexed Stephens as he read the approver's story. He explains that the informer came to Skibbereen from Kerry, and took lodgings in the house of another Kerryman, Morty Downing, from whom Rossa and the Phoenix men rented their club rooms. In fact, Goulah was acting with the stipendiary magistrate Fitzmaurice who had arrived in Skibbereen to prepare government action against the society. He had instructed Goulah to apply for employment as a clerk of the attorney McCarthy Downing—the very man who had sided with Stephens and Doheny in their escape in 1848, and whose chief clerk, Mortimer Moynahan, was a prominent member of the Phoenix Society.

Moynahan was deceived by this application for a clerkship which apparently explained Goulah's arrival in the town. A Kenmare correspondent sent a warning to Moynahan advising caution. This message urged that Goulah had been admitted into the organization at a fair in the Bantry district where his bad local reputation was unknown; that none of his Kerry neighbours would have tolerated his admission; that any business Goulah had in Skibbereen must be bad business. Moynahan, however, was misled by the alibi craftily provided by Fitzmaurice.

Goulah made himself very pleasant to the Morty Downing household. He fondled the eldest child on his knee, calling her his Kerry pet in Rossa's presence. A week before his arrest, Rossa had reason to suspect the link between Goulah and Fitzmaurice. It is also possible that Goulah was the 'dreaded

---

[3]Devoy, *Recollections*, p. 36 admits some Phoenix Society men probably used Smith O'Brien's name, but argues that the leaders were not responsible. A. M. Sullivan stated this specifically in a letter to O'Brien, 25 October 1858 (O'Brien Papers, National Library, 3058, Vol. 446). Rutherford, Vol. I. pp. 267–74 quotes at length Sullivan's account in the *Nation*, 19 April 1862, of his visit to Bantry and of Dr Moriarty. The interview between Sullivan and a Fenian leader there has already been quoted.

party' who gave the parish priest of Kenmare copies of the *two* oaths on 3 October, which Father O'Sullivan forwarded post-haste to the Castle, and then handed to the local magistrates. Stephens at once saw that these oaths were fabricated and spurious. Rossa later declares that Goulah also gave completely false evidence about drillings which had never taken place.

Mr Fitzmaurice, however, backed by a well-packed jury, and with ripe experience in securing convictions of Ribbonmen by similar traps and creatures, had no need to be particular, even if Goulah swore rather freely. Fitzmaurice had as assistant in the good work, one Everett, an attorney who went round trying hard to buy evidence and collecting insults for the most part. Mr Everett, above all, wanted evidence from eyewitnesses of drillings, and to Rossa's delight, was told by a poor woman hunted out of Skibbereen as a prostitute that she wanted no blood money, and had seen no drillings in the wood where she had taken refuge, although in fact she had seen Rossa and his men drilling there often enough.

Mr Everett wrote a beautiful copperplate hand, and Mr Fitzmaurice remembered all that good work in 1859 by forwarding a begging letter in that same copperplate hand to Lord Wodehouse in 1865 with a strong recommendation that the request be granted: a job for Mr Everett in Skibbereen as registrar of marriages. The Fenian trials were on in 1865, and Mr Everett waxed nostalgic for the fine work done in '59 with the regret that slackness since had led to Fenianism.[4]

Goulah, ex-process server, said in his sworn deposition, 30 November 1858, that an acquaintance persuaded him to join the society 'he asked me to his house to have a drink, that he had a secret to tell me; I went with him, and after having some drink he said he could not tell me without swearing me . . . I at first hesitated to take the oath of being a member; but when he told me that other respectable people that I knew—the editor of the *Nation*, Alexander Sullivan and such people—were members, I agreed to become a member, when he again handed me the book and swore me to following oath'.[5]

[4]Larcom Papers 1865. Supp.
[5]Quoted T. D. Sullivan, *Troubled Times in Irish Politics*.

'Dog and Wretch!' was Stephens's verdict on Goulah. A flash from Rossa completes the picture:

'Two stipendiary magistrates came into (Cork) jail and opened court in a room in the jail, and charged us with treason of some kind to something belonging to England. We had MacCarthy Downing for our attorney. Sullivan-Goulah was there to swear that we belonged to the Phoenix Society; that he saw me drilling three hundred men out near the New Bridge one night. He never saw such a drilling; there was never such a drilling took place; he never saw a drilling of any kind among us anywhere. 'Tis true, that he saw many of us at the rooms of the Phoenix Society, for he was lodging in the house where these rooms were . . . Fitzmaurice knew full well that he was swearing falsely . . . in fact made the swearing for him; and made the plot for him. Davis, the other stipendiary magistrate . . . seemed to have more of a conscience . . . for he used to occasionally say, "Oh, you unfortunate man! Remember you are testifying on your oath before your God." But it was all to no use. Goulah went along with his perjuries.'[6]

There was to be another letter from Skibbereen which exasperated Stephens almost beyond endurance. In his diary he writes of a meeting in Tammany on 20 January:

'I was very active endeavouring to give some time to many men present worth talking to; and everybody seemed satisfied. Everybody save one—a brother of Murty Downing, Skib. This fellow had received a letter from some female relation or friend in Skib, giving an account of the arrests, etc. Though the letter did not contain a tittle not given in the newspapers, the boor put on the important, deeming, or pretending to deem, *up* to everything going on at home! He was at the first meeting, and with this letter, and considerable drink, had well nigh kicked up a row. To the meeting in question he came, full not only of importance but of outraged dignity, owing to the little attention paid to his *knowledge* at the first meeting.

'On entering the room he sat apart, occasionally muttering something I could not overhear. But seeing that he was nursing mischief, I went over to him, with the intention of preventing a scene. On my addressing him, he lifted up his head, pursed up his mouth, and with an expression of drunken knowingness, said, "he was not to be gulled—he knew everything!" I bowed and

[6]*Recollections*, p. 218.

retired. It was my intention to tell him (so as not to hurt his feelings and prevent a scene in which he would have played an absurd part, and be found, perhaps, to do some mischief), that it would not serve his friends at home to speak of an understanding with them which he could not possibly have; that the members of our body were bound, *on oath*, to hold no correspondence with anybody whatsoever, (*even a member*) at home or abroad; that in saying they had corresponded with him, he accused them of nothing less than *perjury*, which, under the circumstances, was synonymous with treason; that the female who wrote to him had acted very imprudently, though she could not have told him anything that had not appeared in the newspapers. The fellow's words and manner prevented an explanation.

'He kept himself quiet till towards the close of the meeting. On hearing the Sec. read out his name (at the first meeting he had given it, and two others, each for $5) he stood up, and in an offensive way, said: "Not paid!" Everybody looked at him but the secretary went on. On hearing each of the other two names he had given read out, he said "Not paid!" in precisely the same manner. Some thought it advisable to put him out; but before anything could be decided on, he stood up and asked: "Will Mr John O'Mahony take the responsibility of the whole thing on himself? We all believe in him; and, if he consents, I guarantee $1000!" As O'M. had already been appointed, he stood up and said so. "Will you give your name?" the fellow then asked. O'M. said yes; and the fellow was got to sit down. But neither he nor his friends have given a cent'.

Stephens had more serious cares than that on his mind, and his mood was in turn sanguine and uneasy. Sometimes he dreamt of a million dollars by the autumn of 1859, the purchase of 25,000 to 30,000 Enfield rifles and ammunition, and, moreover, the dispatch of 10,000 men to Ireland!

This was not quite so fantastic as Michael Doheny's assurances to Denieffe two years before. Captain Michael Phelan, who afterwards subscribed to the Fenian movement substantially enough from his winnings as billiard champion of the United States, in an interview and correspondence with Stephens had discussed ways and means of approaching wealthy prospective subscribers, and of bringing strong pressure to bear on the Directory. And it was on these moves that Stephens counted. In the end the Directory refused to part with its funds.

Stephens, for all his energy, persuasiveness and tenacity raised in all from his tour some £600. The publicity of the Phoenix Society trials imposed secrecy and cramped any very public moves to raise funds on the lines proposed by Captain Phelan.

Stephens's accounts of his various meetings are vivid and unconscious self-portraits of his powers as an organizer and a personality. At a meeting on 19 January 1859, he had to administer a rebuke, courteously phrased, to a friend of Doheny's, 'a Captain Hogan—a dodger. For his plan of getting men together and raising money was this: Invite all you know to *a* meeting; have a few prepared to open a subscription with a *good* sum; the others would be *shamed* into giving something handsome! Doheny had introduced *me to* this person. On hearing his plan, I looked at him, and then turning to Ali [Rufus Aliboron, his nickname for Doheny], said: "This cause of ours is a holy one and we should do nothing to bring discredit on it. Let anybody who subscribes anything, however small, give it freely and advisedly—but let nobody be shamed or dragged into co-operation with us. This, being the most honourable, is the only *practical* course. By thus working systematically, men will work with us, lovingly and trustingly." Captain Hogan looked at me queerly—a slight defect in one of his eyes adding to the expression: evidently he was listening to a new language, and political hack though he be, for the moment he had a glimmering of the truth'.

Whatever his trials and disappointments, Stephens kept his sense of humour, even when hungry and almost penniless. There was, for instance, the comic tragedy of his trip to Boston towards the end of January, about the 20th, with letters of introduction from Meagher, O'Mahony, and others to some leading Boston Nationalists, mentioned, fortunately for most of their reputations, under the obscure descriptions of 'C', 'J. Br', 'O'N', 'Tr' and 'Lap'. Stephens arrived in Boston with broken boots, sleepless and weary. He found the city flooded, could not buy rubbers to protect his boots because the shopkeepers refused New York notes, and then discovered that his prominent Nationalists were very hard indeed to contact.

'C', who had already organized a Fenian circle of nine, was serious and friendly enough, but the hint that he dropped about the lack of serious intentions in 'O'N' turned out to be an understatement. 'Tr' was not to be found in his office. 'Lap' informed Stephens that if only Stephens could give him *faith*, then 'Lap' would answer for a hundred thousand dollars in Boston, but 'Lap' lacked faith, and would like to consult with 'Tr' and 'O'N'. He also mentioned an *excellent Irishman*, one Dr Smith of whom Stephens 'had an idea that this fellow helped to break up the Emmet Monument Association', but held his peace.

'Lap' brought Stephens in search of 'Tr'. He had not turned up. His partner and an unknown young man gave Stephens a warm welcome, and Stephens was taken to 'Tr's' house some miles away. 'His wife, looked care and discontent, but asked us in. Had a hint from the *unknown* on the way that "Tr" and some others (O'N amongst them) had been on the reel. The time it took "Tr" to make his appearance gave colour to this. He could keep his legs . . . shan't describe'.

After 'Tr' had dashed Meagher's letter of introduction on the floor, shouting 'your name is enough!' and then said Meagher had sent a second letter which stated that 'a gentleman of some distinction will call', Stephens arranged a meeting for the next day, and was conducted by the unknown eventually to 'O'N's':

'Found him in an even more unprintable state than "Tr": he was not sodden but in a maudlin excitement bordering on lunacy. On being presented, he exclaimed enough for the printers in the office, who were separated from us only by a thin boarded partition: "Stephens you come to a true rebel—the rebel of Boston! And a man coming to me on your mission is welcome to everything I have in the world, even my wife's bed!"'

'The bystanders (4 or 5—to all of who he introduced me without permission) laughed! Seeing this, he stood up, and with drunken energy said: "If the eternal damnation of my soul could free Ireland, I would stand on an altar (he uncovered his head), and there, in the presence of all men, allow myself to be eternally damned!" I was sincerely disgusted. This language even exceeded that of my heroic townsman, J—— D—— in '48: "I will never rest satisfied till I hunt the bloody English Myrmidons *down* (with tremendous emphasis) into the lowest chambers of hell". Said D—— was among the first who showed the white feather: it is said he hid himself in a cellar when he heard O'Brien's having taken the field; and, that not deeming himself safe even there, he delivered up the books of the club, or swore allegiance or something of that sort. I do not undertake to say that O'N is just a shameless poltroon; but I have little faith in men who talk so—even in their drink. Still, as nothing could be done in our way in Boston without his knowledge, told him of the meeting, and left with the understanding that he would attend'.

'O'N' did attend, and Stephens found that his view of 'O'N's' character was, if anything, a charitable underestimate. He knew before the meeting that 'C's' assumed belief that it was most unusual for 'Tr' to be as Stephens had found him was a most unfounded assumption. 'C' dismissed 'O'N' as 'a habitual—boon companion'. Far more important was the adhesion of 'C' and his group to Stephens's plan, even with a disturbing reservation: 'I was satisfied with "C's" friends. One of them, however, was very inquisitive, and seemed to attach great importance to Meagher's adhesion. "C", too, seemed to feel the necessity of having Mitchel's name connected with us; not that he (C) cares for it; but others are silly enough to do so. Told them how we stood (*at that time*) with Meagher, and that I believed that he and Judge Emmet would consent to act as auditors of the accounts (the Directory funds). This they considered quite sufficient, as if on the subject of money their doubts are awake'.

On Sunday, 23 January, 'Tr' and 'O'N' turned up at Stephens's hotel at eleven in the morning. They were if possible in a worse state than the preceding day! 'Seated in my room, "Tr" turned to me, and, with, as it struck me, a significant expression, said: "We come to know is it men or money you want? We can get you either". Said both were wanted: money first as with that we could get all the men required. They then proposed a *drink*. I may say here how frequently I have been hurt by persons offering to *treat me in my own room*, and, that however averse to this deplorable but almost universal habit of drinking, I find it inevitable to accept and give it. Got up *skins*, or brandy, for my visitors, taking ale myself. About noon, the gentlemen were so *tight* that I had to put both of them to

12

bed! Got them up, and to "Tr's" office. "Tr's" partner had promised to be in the office at half-past one; it was past two, and he had not made his appearance! The persons present (some 8 or 9) and I got impatient standing in the passage of a bitter cold day; seeing this "O'N" proposed that we should go to his place. Were overtaken on the way there by "C" who had stopped behind lest "Tr's" partner and others should come. Went back to the office'.

The meeting soon warmed up, and Stephens had to assert himself:

'During my statement, was frequently interrupted by the extraneous remarks and bye-pleasantries of "O'N" and others. Kept my self-control till convinced of the necessity of calling them to order, when I said: "Gentlemen, the business in hands is of the utmost importance, and requires to be treated with all solemnity". "O'N" interrupted me to ask, in a tone and manner most reprehensible in any but a drunken man: "Do you *dare*, Sir, to insinuate that it has not been treated with solemnity?" I advanced a step towards "O'N", and calmly but firmly answered, looking him steadily in the face: "I *insinuate* nothing; but I tell you bluntly it has not been". He leaned back in his chair, stooped his head, and said nothing. The business was looking like a hideous farce. I went on with my statement, however, and ended by telling them what was to be done. "Tr" was the first to sign his name—for $100. "O'N" did the same for a like sum. Two or three others signed for smaller sums, when jests began to circulate as to the improbability of the money being made! It was clear that parties present *believed* that it would not, and that the whole proceedings were a sham. Seeing this, I tore up the list. Then a few persons who seemed to be in earnest came to me and said: "We are willing to do what we can; but what is the use of signing our names after men who will not, and cannot if they would, meet their engagements with you?" "O'N." (quite stupid) had left by this time'.

And that was really the end of the meeting because the persons who seemed to be earnest all had to leave, except one, with promises to call on Stephens that evening: ' I gave the man who remained the necessary forms and instructions, and "C" assured me that the man was *whole-souled* (an eternal word with our countrymen here) and would do his work. "Tr" parted with me at his office without repeating the *sort* of invitation he gave me the day before—*to take tea with him before I left*! And that was the sum and front of the *kind treatment* requested of him by Meagher! "C" promised to be with me in the evening, and to bring one of the young men I had met with him the day before, who wished to ask me something about O'Mahony; this young man was from Mitchelstown, knew the O'Mahonys and has a full heart at the very mention of O'Mahony's name. Two of the parties who called in the evening impressed me very unfavourably, and I dismissed them politely as I could. A third I swore in, getting $5 subscription from him. This man's name is Donnelly (it gave me a pang when I heard it the day before in "O'N's" office), and "C" thinks but poorly of him; "C" admits, however, that he may be mistaken. We shall see. At all event, the man had been told as much by "O'N" and others, and heard as much in my statement. The Mitchelstown man was present, and when Donnelly went, he said that all he came to know was there. He was ready to go home when called on by O'Mahony; he is a tailor, unmarried, and can support himself. Alone, I began to think that there was no use in remaining any longer in Boston'.

And Stephens left the city with five dollars as reward of his efforts. With this, and with what small sum he had, he found that when he had paid his hotel bill and fare, just fifty cents remained, and he reached New York sick, cold, hungry, having eaten nothing on the journey. After a two mile walk he found a place to buy the only food he could afford, an oyster stew, cursing 'C' who had insisted on sending *his* $7.50 subscription direct by registered post to O'Mahony, thereby securing a double receipt, and good security for his character. Stephens reflected that the way these *whole-souled* Bostonian patriots talked about their characters would make the angels weep. 'N.B.' he wrote, 'Reflections on American climate, lakes. rivers with their adjacent *bottoms*, stones: contrasted with the fires and blessed waters of the Sacred Isle'. After supper at 'O'D's' Stephens went, as a climax to his agonies, to a meeting in Brooklyn with O'Mahony which was an even greater failure than a previous one.

O'Mahony the following night informed Stephens that Meagher had returned from the south, that Meagher as usual had promised to return immediately to the *News* office, and hurried off without any word about anything important. And 'as so often with me' reflects Stephens 'of course, O'Mahony saw no more of him', and was as disturbed as Stephens that 'our business' was not mentioned, felt it was strange and suspicious, and had a presentiment that Mitchel and Meagher were about to break with their schemes. Later that night O'Mahony and Stephens discussed for hours whether 'some if not *all* our distinguished brother patriots were plotting against us and the cause. Sad thoughts these!' Stephens was feeling the strain of his toils and disappointments. He discovered that no steamer, other than a British one, was available before March. He had some hopes, which proved later quite well-founded, of raising money by an organizing tour in as many of the states as possible, even as far as New Orleans.

There was a final meeting with Meagher in the *Irish News* office which left no doubt that O'Mahony and himself had guessed all too well what was in progress, 'that Meagher was not all right'. After an ambiguous hint from Roche, who told him Meagher's trip to the south had been a failure throughout, and one night he had only twenty-five at a meeting, Stephens called to see him: 'Meagher was in the office. I looked steadily and scrutinizingly at him as I advanced to give him my hand, and while addressing the first few words to him. He seemed to me at the time, and I am now *certain* that his face was *made up*. After a very short time, he said: "I left in a letter for you in case you did not call".

'He gave me the letter, which I opened with a misgiving. The letter ran thus:

New York, 26 January 1859.

My Dear Stephens,

I have come to the conclusion, after some days of conscientious reflection, that, if it be not criminal, it is unworthy of me, in any way, however trivial or indirectly, to urge or authorize a revolutionary movement, in the hazards of which, from a conviction of their utter uselessness, I feel at present no disposition whatever to participate. You will, therefore, be so good as to erase my name from the paper you did me the honour to submit to me for my signature a few weeks ago, since by this letter it is virtually withdrawn. And with sincere regards—and friendship,

Believe me,
Very faithfully yours,
T. F. Meagher.

To James Stephens, Esq.,
New York.'

And that last word of 'Meagher of the Sword', Stephens, some weeks before, 'The Wolfe Tone of our generation', placed as the most appropriate last word of his American diary without any comment whatever.

EARLY in March 1859, O'Leary and Luby arrived separately in France, and later met at Boulogne where they had arranged to await Stephens's return from America. He came at last, though somewhat later than they expected, full of hopes and plans, in the highest of spirits at the success of his tour, and with six or seven hundred pounds in gold. All his ill-humour and disappointment by this time was safely packed away in his diary, although he admitted that the dark spots of his tour had been his experiences with Mitchel, from whom he had hoped much, and Meagher's repudiation of a written agreement with him. He seems to have made light of these dark spots, and of the coldness of the other '48 exiles, and kept his grievances against Doheny to himself. O'Leary and Luby were, as they thought, more concerned than Stephens about the Directory's refusal to help and the '48 leaders' hostility. O'Mahony and Doheny, they understood, supported him but no other prominent Young Ireland exile did so. He spoke with enthusiasm of his successful tour, his ample funds for the future, and for all his plans. They spent a pleasant Sunday discussing the entire universe, and giving the Fenian movement a rest for the time being. The sun was bright and all of them were in fine fettle as they set out for Paris the next day. They settled down in due course in a hotel in the rue Montaigne, off the Champs-Elysées, and here Stephens stayed for the remainder of his sojourn in Paris.

Stephens soon set his plans in motion. He determined that constant communication should be established with America at once and, after some stubborn arguments on both sides, at last prevailed upon O'Leary to go out and take over O'Mahony's more routine official duties in the American organization. Stephens objected to Luby on the flattering grounds that his modesty allowed him to yield place to inferior and pretentious persons in ordinary affairs however strong his principles in general, while O'Leary notoriously stood no nonsense and never suffered fools on any scruples whatever. O'Leary grimly enough gave in, on his own conditions: he would work, and he would not 'travel through the States, spreading the name and fame of the I.R.B. for I had little knowledge of the workings of that body, and small faith as yet in its future prospects'.[1]

To his bewilderment, when he reached New York on 1 May 1859, in theory a secret envoy, O'Leary was publicly serenaded by the famous 69th Regiment, and was called upon to address an enormous crowd from the windows of the St Nicholas Hotel. He 'said very little and that little ill'. He was followed by several orators, including Michael Doheny, with assurances that it was all most secret because arrangements had been made that nothing would appear in the press, or at least O'Leary's name would not. One Irish-American paper, however, did reveal O'Leary's name and mission, to both his friends and enemies at home. From that time he detested the public receptions which were dear to the Irish race at home and abroad 'of more or less eminent or notorious characters'. He was unconcerned about the consequences to himself but he resented these ridiculous performances and others which he endured in the next twenty years of his life.

The three outstanding men in the Fenian Brotherhood were then John O'Mahony, Michael Doheny and General Michael Corcoran, of whom O'Leary saw much. The Fenian Brotherhood was, in effect, the American wing of the I.R.B., with John O'Mahony as its Head Centre and with much the same plan of organization into circles, except that a personal pledge replaced the oath and its proceedings were far more open. In Stephens's view the American organization was subordinate, including its Head Centre, to his orders as set down in his reply to the New York invitation to form a new organization in Ireland. This O'Mahony had with some reluctance accepted, with a reservation on policy. His own words in the detailed personal defence he made later in 1868 admit this:

[1] O'Leary Vol. I. pp. 92–6, 99 *et seq.*

'I accepted the position of Head Centre of the Fenian Brotherhood with the understanding that my duty should be to unite and organize, as far as possible, the Irish element in America, and to concentrate its moral and material forces, and to direct them systematically. The understanding was that the Irish Revolutionary Brotherhood should be organized *secretly*, with James Stephens as its leader and chief. They were to "make their own opportunity" by "landing a supply of arms and disciplined men in Ireland". No movement was to be made without this aid, or in the event of England engaging in foreign war. To this policy I faithfully adhered up to the year 1865'.[2]

Stephens, before his return to Ireland in 1859, had officially delegated O'Mahony as 'supreme organizer and Director of the Irish Revolutionary Brotherhood in America. With him alone as chief centre shall any communication be held from home, and I hereby notify to the members of the Brotherhood, that anyone writing to Ireland after having been made acquainted with this order, shall be looked on and treated as a traitor. This order is strictly carried out in Ireland, so that any member in America receiving a letter from anybody professing to be a member in Ireland, is bound to make known to authorized centre here the name of such correspondent, so that the men who trusted him may know they have to do with a perjurer, between whom and the traitor there can be no real difference with us at present'.[3]

Shortly after Stephens had left, O'Mahony changed the name of the American organization to that of the Fenian Brotherhood. Both men were in constant communication, and this step was no doubt taken with Stephens's full consent. A letter from Stephens on 6 April 1859 to O'Mahony which mentions 'the contemplated modification of our body' possibly refers to this change of name. The change in the form of oath is also announced, although in the case of the American organization, the wording is left to O'Mahony's discretion with the proviso that the 'oath of secrecy must be omitted'. There is also in the phrase 'the position you were placed in some months ago', a very direct statement of Stephens's view

[2]Quoted from O'Mahony's New York *Irish People*, in the *Irishman*, 8 February 1868.

[3]Quoted from the O'Mahony Papers, D'Arcy, pp. 12–13.

of O'Mahony's subordination to himself, even with the soothing addition, 'you are better known now than before . . . indeed I heard no one spoken so highly of.'[4]

There are detailed instructions for O'Mahony's conduct of his tour, including Stephens's life-long crotchet that every responsible envoy or representative of the Fenian movement must be smart in appearance: 'In connection with these details, I deem it necessary on account of notions of yours to tell—nay, command—you to procure clothes suited to the climates through which you have to pass, as well as to the ideas of the people you may come in contact with. Trifling as these matters may seem, the neglect of them might occasion deplorable consequences to the cause as well as to yourself'.

There is this candid description of John O'Leary, bearer of the letter for whom, 'I expect the highest possible courtesy, respect, and even deference, as my representative; and, through me, the representative of the Irish cause; you will perceive that he is an able man of high intellectual culture; his bearing, too, will prove—what I assure you of—his high principles of honour, and convince you how devotedly he loves Ireland. To you, however, I might say that, in spite of all these high qualities, our differences on many serious things are so very great that, had I a choice of men, of such intellectual calibre and honour, I would not urge on him a mission so little to his taste. For, in the abstract—as a matter of taste as well as judgment—he is not a republican . . . His faith in the success of the movement, too, is not at all equal to mine; but he believes the probability of success sufficient not only to justify but imperatively call on every Irishman to co-operate with us. Lastly he does not know that I am equal to the task I have undertaken; but, if not the most efficient of organizers, in his opinion I am second to no other Irishman of his acquaintance, and superior to anybody he knows able and willing to do the work.'

O'Leary, with unusual terseness summed up the contrast between the two leaders in character and policy. Stephens was 'far the more active-minded and resourceful man, ever planning and pressing his plans on others, while O'Mahony was

---

[4]This letter is given in full in Rossa's *Recollections*, Ch. XXI, pp. 269–81.

more slow, methodic and cautious'. And although, like most observers who came to close quarters with the two leaders, O'Leary preferred O'Mahony's idealistic and disinterested character, yet he conceded Stephens's superiority as a leader. Luby, General Millen, Father Kenyon, John Devoy, Frank Roney, the Belfast Fenian leader, and others, some of them, indeed most of them, reluctantly reached the same conclusion.

O'Leary's relations with O'Mahony were easy and friendly. On that visit he saw little of America beyond a brief trip to Philadelphia and spent his time in O'Mahony's office where, for the first time, he met John Mitchel, formally, as he puts it, as he had often seen and heard him in the stirring days of Young Ireland in the 'forties. Meagher, too, he met with O'Mahony. Mitchel and John Martin he met on his return to Paris in September, not at all formally yet with some constraint because neither they nor Stephens made any bones about the very low opinion they all by this time had for each other. The collisions of Stephens with '48 exiles and celebrities after his American tour became almost a principle with him. John P. Leonard and Father Kenyon, life-long friends of O'Leary, were soon added to the list.

As O'Leary left for America, Denieffe was summoned to Paris, and he has left a vivid picture of his memory of the city and Stephens in the May of 1859. 'Paris', he wrote, 'at this time was in its happiest mood—the Empire being in its halcyon days. We saw the army depart for Italy and return, covered with glory. Magenta and Solferino were victories the nation was proud of. As we were laying on oars, with little to do, we put in our time in the most profitable and best way—seeing everything of note.

'The Captain [Stephens] knew everything that happened in and around the city, and his directions were carried out to the letter. Sometimes he came with us himself to Versailles, St Cloud, Père La Chaise and the Bois de Boulogne. He took great pleasure in pointing out the bas-relief—all allegorical studies—on the Arc of Triumph, the Palace de Cluny, Sèvres and St Clotilde. These places were often visited by us afterwards. Wet days were spent in the picture galleries and art studios . . . The evenings spent in our quarters were also very pleasant. Our landlord and family, the Lacours, occupied the first floor, and we a suite of rooms. We were on good terms with them and visited them frequently. Stephens was always happy on these occasions, for he seemed to be at home in French society'.[5]

At the same time Stephens was full of plans. He considered bringing over all the 'A's', heads of circles, for a course of military instruction, and indeed, he also thought of establishing a special school for the purpose. This project was later abandoned although at intervals numbers from the centres from Ireland arrived on short visits, not at all with the approval of O'Leary who thought this a needless waste of time and money and little use for the visitors, with rare exceptions.

A cryptic letter from Stephens to O'Mahony late in 1859, seems to hint at secret feelers for assistance from the French Government. A letter from O'Mahony, apparently lamenting failure to increase or raise funds in America, provokes the outburst: 'This second letter came—to prove to me *almost*, that if we were to *strike* this year the means should be sought elsewhere besides America. My position here at the time was not a promising one—that is it promised nothing *immediately*; for the very parties I relied on for putting me in touch with those I had to expect anything of consequence from, were not here, and the letters I addressed to each of them remained unanswered. Hope, not to say *faith*, came with the Italian campaign. I succeeded in getting introduced to parties who, from the very first, showed a willingness to forward my views, of which disposition I found it impossible to avail myself, owing to my inability to meet the expenses incidental to important negotiations. Dan [MacCartie] will give you an idea of what I mean, *but you must not give the faintest hint of it to anybody; for all is not yet lost.*[6]

' I leave you to guess what I must have felt when, as the anti-English feeling rose, and the chance of turning it to account lay within my grasp, I could not stretch forth my hand to seize that chance. I remember saying (what looks like a *boast* now) to Doheny, Roche, and yourself, that once in France I should soon *complicate the* [*Franco-British*] *alliance.* When speaking so, I, of

[5]Denieffe, pp. 46–50.
[6]Dan MacCartie, 'Donal Oge', already sent as courier to U.S.A.

course, counted on speedy and somewhat solid assistance from America, *even before I set about the complication;* or, my calculation was that I might raise the necessary funds through my personal friends here. These two calculations having proved baseless, the great work I might otherwise have done remains for another day . . . Some of my creditors here were baying me, so as to render my departure impossible without, at least, part payment'.

Veiled allusions to the difficulties and progress of the Fenian movement were made in other letters.

The repercussions of the Phoenix trials were discussed in a letter from Stephens, probably late in 1859, when Dan MacCartie was sent out as a courier to O'Mahony:

'He [MacCartie who was to leave the following day on the *Arago*] will tell you that this whole district—the whole of Cork— so far from being cowed by the prosecutions, is in a healthier state than ever; that in said district two new centres have been added; and that we only want money to make our organization such a power as needs must needs accomplish the work before us'.

An admission follows which favours Rossa in a controversy which later arose between him, Luby and O'Leary. Stephens briefly states that his messenger was unable to contact Rossa and the other Phoenix Society prisoners until after their release. The messenger, in fact, was Luby who in July 1859 had left Paris which was bright with illuminations for the French victory over the Austrians at Solferino. His orders were to travel through Ireland, but in particular the south, and convey Stephens's orders to the Phoenix Society men still in jail but offered release on condition of pleading guilty, that this offer must not be accepted. Luby wrote somewhat sharply in his letters to O'Leary that 'it was impossible to prevent the unconquerable Rossa from pleading guilty', although he also stated that he had not seen him. Rossa in his recollections emphatically denied that any order from Stephens had ever reached the prisoners. They had repeatedly refused to plead guilty in conversations with their attorney, McCarthy Downing, the same man who had aided Stephens to escape in 1848. Downing again urged them strongly to accept the prosecution's offer as he had made an arrangement with the Government that Daniel O'Sullivan, already serving a sentence of ten years penal servitude, should be released if the others pleaded guilty.

Rossa and the rest, after long discussion, agreed. He contradicted O'Leary's version of the story based on Luby's somewhat testy remark. His account in his recollections emphasizes that, apart from strong local pressure on them to accept, their friends in Cork city gave them to understand James Stephens was in France and no message had been received from him, that the work seemed dead, and that the terms should be accepted. Referring to O'Leary's statement in his *Recollections* Rossa comments, 'He says that word was sent to us *not* to plead guilty. I can say and say truly that no such word ever reached us, and that we were obliged to conclude that the work, or the cause for which we were put in jail, was dead or deserted. So we decided to accept the terms of release offered, and we were let out of prison on the 27th of July 1859'.

Rossa makes no reference to Luby's later meeting with the Phoenix Society prisoners, nor to the campaign waged by A. M. Sullivan in his *Nation* to raise funds for the prisoners and against the Government prosecution and sentence on Daniel O'Sullivan. Stephens does both in the same letter. His messenger, he continues, when he met the Phoenix Society men after release, even then 'could give them but the oft-repeated assurances of what we should *still* do, nothing having been done up to that—at least nothing more than having kept life in our body; that our enemies, the *Nation*, etc., etc., who had put themselves before them and the public as their active friends and sympathizers, were busy, and though the *Nation* was held in something like execration by the prisoners, one and all of whom looked and still look on Sullivan as nothing short of a *National Approver*, still, this unsalted rascal must have had an indirect influence'.[7]

'The unsalted rascal' had been included in Luby's instructions for general denunciation as well as the spreading of Stephens's private account of his experiences in negotiations with Dillon, Meagher, Mitchel and the famous Directory, among the centres of the I.R.B. The amazing Captain in exile

[7] O'Leary, Vol. I. pp. 128–9; Rossa's *Recollections*, pp. 228–9. For A. M. Sullivan, P. S. O'Hegarty, *History of Ireland* . . . p. 421.

was as full of projects as he was of debts, and Luby saw at first-hand, on his return from brief visits in 1860, that the hardships Stephens and O'Leary's brother, Arthur, endured at times amounted to 'downright privation', a memory and experience which led Luby and others who knew Stephens at this time, into some spirited invective afterwards, when in many controversies what Luby called the 'luxury myth' appeared. This he told O'Leary—who had little need to be told—had its origin in American gossip and malice.

The debts that Stephens emphasized so frequently in his letters to O'Mahony were incurred by his stubborn use of the small funds that reached him on his organization schemes. At this time Luby warned him to slow down on a scheme he had arranged with O'Mahony for bringing back a number of Irish-Americans—and others from England and Scotland, several hundred men in all—to their native places as drill-masters and organizers. He argued that it was imprudent and premature although Stephens insisted, backed and aided in New York by the prudent and soon regretful O'Leary, 'that you must risk much in revolutions, that you must calculate on funds which may never come in, and act generally with an audacity which would be altogether out of place in ordinary private or public affairs'. Owing to the small general funds available and the weakness or non-existence of the organization in some places, these men finally made their way back to America and Great Britain after much hardship, embittered and demoralized by inactivity.

Shortly afterwards, however, Luby made a counter-stroke, which undid much of the damage the unlucky experiment had caused, by widening the recruiting area of the organization in Dublin where it had been limited mostly to Peter Langan and the Hickey's groups in Co. Dublin, and mainly composed of mechanics. Cornelius O'Mahony, a young schoolmaster from Cork, later Stephens's secretary, introduced Luby to James O'Callaghan, a drapers' assistant, and from their efforts the I.R.B. spread very rapidly among the shop assistants of the city until Stephens agreed with Luby that Dublin, previously one of the weak spots, was becoming one of the strongest. Among the recruits that Luby then gained was Edward Duffy who was later to become an extraordinary organizer among the Ribbon lodges in the west of Ireland.

After Stephens's return from America a gradual strain became evident in his friendly relations with O'Mahony, and within a year, great impatience developed on both sides. There was the perpetual question of the remittances promised which came slowly, and were expended before they came, and the number of envoys on special missions of inquiry into the conduct and condition of the organization dispatched by O'Mahony to the profound resentment of Stephens and his officers. Luby had, in the beginning, made a very determined effort to act as peacemaker, not only personally between O'Mahony and Stephens, but also in his reports of his tours of the south to New York and Paris, and by accompanying O'Mahony's envoys, of which at least three came in 1859 and early 1860, on their tours of inspection. He also checked an incipient revolt against Stephens's leadership amongst a section of the I.R.B. who were demanding immediate action—backed by others in the United States—a development which threatened O'Mahony's own leadership.

Stephens himself had mentioned such difficulties in the cryptic letter before quoted, written after O'Leary's return in September 1859: 'I give you once more to understand that we cannot possibly strike this year. I don't know whether anybody expects us to fight *in any case*, but if there be any man, thoughtless or guilty enough, to desire this, he cannot have been led to form any such wish by anything in me. My words have been that we would fight when we could.'[8]

Here in a few words is Stephens's ultimate justification for his actions in 1867, and the perpetual problem that faced him. Luby, Kickham and a score of I.R.B. leaders, crushed the danger to O'Mahony and Stephens by circulating a letter in Ireland and the U.S.A. reaffirming their confidence 'in John and James'. Reports spread in America that the I.R.B. in Ireland was dead and that all had died out with the arrest and jailing of the Phoenix Society men, were countered by Stephens's courier, Dan MacCartie, when he reached New

[8]Quotations from Stephens's letters, except where otherwise stated, are from Stephens Papers, National Library of Ireland.

York, and by a document sent to O'Mahony, also by Stephens's order to Luby, signed by twenty-four prominent centres all over the country, in September 1860, which expressed 'as local representatives in Ireland, of the Irish firm—over the American branch of which John O'Mahony has been appointed Supreme Director— . . . our unlimited confidence in the ability and integrity with which that gentleman has conducted our affairs in America; and, also, our admiration of the noble constancy with which that gentleman has enabled us to sustain our interests inflinchingly amidst the severest trials and in the face of the most shameful and unmerited calumny.

'We also testify, in the strongest manner, our approval of the conduct of James Stephens, in the general arrangement of the firm, under similar trying circumstances, and, finally, we confirm both these gentlemen in the authority originally conferred upon them; and express our unalterable determination to stand by them while they represent us, against all their enemies, whether open or disguised—their enemies being ours, also!'[9]

A previous letter from Luby on 25 August to O'Mahony described his discussion with O'Mahony's envoy, possibly Boylan of St Louis, a tour of the organization to collect signatures of the centres for 'the paper of confidence', the unlimited confidence of the 'principal shareholders' that 'our firm was bona fide and solvent' and their high opinion of their Irish and American Directors, yet concluded with the warning note, 'some few of our shareholders in the south are beginning to lose faith in your branch, and to think more and more every day of self-reliance. They are in sooth, a little disgusted with the great promises and little performance of some men on the other side who, let me add, seem so ready to censure shortcomings, for which in reality, they have only themselves to blame, and to believe the vilest slanders, backed by testimony, insufficient to convict the basest of mankind'.

In both Luby's letters a coming visit of O'Mahony is lauded as a 'prospect that delighted all . . . Nothing should prevent it

[9]Luby's letters and document are given in full, Rossa's *Recollections*, pp. 291–99. See also, Denieffe, p. 163; D'Arcy, *Fenian Movement* . . . pp.15–18; O'Mahony's statement, *Irishman*, 8 February 1868 *et seq.*

taking place . . . exhilarating'. Stephens's allusions to this were colder although he encloses a correspondent's letter in his own of 4 September 1860 with the comment 'you will see how much importance is given to your contemplated visit. I think it should decide you to go'. There are reproaches for ignoring Stephens's instructions and listening to his critics, 'the impudent statements in certain quarters from conceited or interested ramshackles'. Luby's coming statement of confidence of 'the shareholders in James and John' is forecast, yet all through there is a hint of the tension between the same 'James and John'.

Stephens was exasperated and discontented with O'Mahony's envoys, and on the scraps of paper where he let loose his seething irritation he described them as 'inquisitions', and when O'Mahony, just before the Christmas of 1860, reached Dublin, Stephens at length arrived in the city from Paris and greeted O'Mahony in the presence of Denieffe who described the scene thus: 'Stephens, after the formal greetings were over, asked a number of questions; wanted to know why the organization in America has not been kept together as a unit; he wanted to know why O'Mahony and his colleagues had not kept their promises to the men in Ireland and had not furnished the funds necessary for them to defray the cost of spreading the organization etc. To all these questions O'Mahony failed to give satisfactory answers, whereupon Stephens reproached him in words of the most cutting sarcasm, telling him of his shortcomings, feebleness and insincerity, and wound up by reminding him how he, Stephens, had dragged him out of obscurity and put him in a position he had never dreamed of'.

O'Mahony did not answer but showed he felt deeply humiliated. Denieffe hurried away before the close of the scene. Luby, however, supplied O'Leary with the details O'Mahony gave him. He had met both Father Kenyon and O'Mahony before Stephens arrived. Father Kenyon had just returned from Paris on a visit to Mitchel, and had also met Stephens with whom he had a final and irrevocable quarrel. He was infuriated with Stephens and made every effort to turn Luby against him. Luby introduced him to O'Mahony whom he met later with John Martin. O'Mahony, after the stormy interview

13

with Stephens, gave Luby the end of the scene of which Denieffe had seen only part. After Stephens had blamed him for failing as his 'subordinate' to obey orders and send over money, O'Mahony informed him flatly that there was no subordinate about it, and he would not be one. Then Stephens made a concession which Luby rightly thought was not seriously intended: regional councils to look after the purely local affairs of centres in Ireland and America, in effect a modification of 'the one-man' power claimed by him.

O'Mahony's description of this interview, which took place on the eve of his return, merely states that then he had 'my first definite understanding with James Stephens and the heads of the Irish Revolutionary Brotherhood, with respect to the exact amount of foreign or American aid that would justify an uprising of the Irish people'.[10]

Before he finally sailed for America in March 1861, O'Mahony had a last look at the country he was never to see again, spent cheerful days with Luby in the Dublin Fenian circles, and then travelled with him as far as Kilkenny, another flourishing Fenian centre, met Kickham and Denis Dowling Mulcahy in Tipperary, and spent the rest of his stay with his sister and her family in the mountainous Comeraghs on the Cork-Tipperary border.

O'Leary and Luby regarded O'Mahony's visit as of dubious value to himself or the Fenian movement. It is true that Kickham and Mulcahy were his firmest friends thereafter, and he had won the lasting esteem and support of Mitchel, Martin and Father Kenyon. Yet Luby's verdict showed that the old solidarity of the two leaders had been shaken as never before—although indeed in spite of even stormier clashes in the future the old link forged in the days of '48 and the Paris exile in the end survived.

'I fancy', wrote Luby to O'Leary, 'the Head Centre landed on Manhattan Island a sadder man than when he left it. I greatly doubt if he reached it a wiser one. From this date

---

[10]D'Arcy, *Fenian Movement* . . . p. 18, states that it was agreed that at least 5,000 men with competent officers should form the nucleus for the army of liberation, and a supply of at least 50,000 rifles to be put immediately into the hands of the insurgents. O'Mahony thought this could be done within a given time.

onwards, feelings of jealousy between himself and Stephens grew daily more intense and bitter'.

And then in the closing months of 1861, almost overnight, Stephens and the Irish Republican Brotherhood reaped the reward of many weary days and nights and won a resounding and spectacular victory which made Fenianism the most living force in Irish political life.

THE death of Terence Bellew McManus on 15 January 1861, in a San Francisco hospital, whether, in fact, he was or was not formally enrolled in the organization, was the real turning point of the Fenian movement at home and abroad. He had shared, as we have seen, the dangers of Ballingarry with Smith O'Brien and Stephens to the full, and made a concise and truthful chronicle of those days of doom and defeat. Thereafter his life had been one of poverty and obscurity. Since his escape from Australia in the summer of 1851, whence he had been transported for life after the trial of the Young Irelanders at Clonmel in '48, his career in California at his old occupation as shipping agent had been hard and uncongenial. Business life in America, he told his friend Meagher, was 'all wrong, wild, hazardous, false and desperate; and he would have nothing to do with it'. And this, noted Meagher in a commemoration lecture, explained all McManus's ill fortune and the heavy shadows on a face once full of light and pride.[1]

Yet his faith in his political ideal had never wavered. With the description of Ballingarry, which he sent to Gavan Duffy immediately after the event, McManus included a brief note, with some sentences prophetic enough: 'Do not despond at our present failure. I have got high hope, and am as light of heart— aye, and more so than when I stood on the Hill of Tara in '43. I have seen more in the last short campaign than you could learn in twenty years of a city life. I see elements at work, which to my mind, are indisputable evidences of the consummation of what we have begun'.[2]

[1]Quoted Webb *Compendium of Irish Biography*, (1878), p. 316. See also, Denvir, *The Irish in Britain*, (London 1892), pp. 134–8, 180.

[2]Gavan Duffy, *Four Years* . . . p. 699, note.

The Fenians of San Francisco, although their organization in 1861 was weak in numbers and influence, had the wit to launch an idea, when the news of McManus's death reached them, which gave point indeed to the fiery words McManus also wrote to Gavan Duffy in the letter quoted above: 'I will never lose sight of the glorious cause to which I have pledged myself. Whenever a death-blow is to be struck at this vile despotism that crushes our land, I trust in heaven I will be there to strike'. Only a year before McManus had heard of a move to secure an amnesty for him and had written to one of the promoters, John Francis Maguire of Cork, informing him that the amnesty, if offered, would be refused: 'I will never return to Ireland—if I cannot go without the consent of a foreign ruler'. The San Francisco proposal was that McManus's body should be taken home to Ireland and buried with full honours.

This proposal excited the active hostility of the Catholic Archbishop of Dublin, Dr Cullen, and, at first, was not favoured with any enthusiasm by such Fenian leaders at home as James Stephens and Thomas Clarke Luby. Dr Cullen's opposition was due to his experiences as Rector of the Irish College at Rome during the revolution of 1848, the virulent neo-ultramontainism, the absolutist theories, and hatred of the Carbonari he had learned there, and his acute perception that this move was a Fenian demonstration. The coldness of Stephens and Luby can be explained by their reluctance to reveal publicly to the Government the real strength and number of the organization, from their awareness of the impulsive insurrectionist projects of Doheny and Roche, and from their suspicion that their old enemies, 'the Aspirationists', might exploit the occasion to praise McManus and bury Fenianism.

The 'Aspirationists', were, of course, A. M. and T. D. Sullivan, Father Kenyon, John Martin, The O'Donoghue, and P. J. Smyth, all prepared to honour McManus as a '48 hero, and all, in varying degrees, hostile to the exploitation of the funeral as a Fenian demonstration. Moreover, Father Kenyon and the Sullivans feared, distrusted and detested Stephens. On this occasion, Luby and Stephens had already outwitted them by taking control of the committees in Ireland set up to welcome the dead patriot and his Fenian guard of honour on arrival. There was to be a determined struggle between the two parties, so bitter that Luby, much to his regret, was to be permanently estranged from his old friend, Father Kenyon.

O'Leary, years later, stated the issue clearly:

'The O'Donoghue and Mr A. M. Sullivan . . . seemed to have wished to make the funeral a mere commemoration of the past, having no significance in the present, and affording no lesson for the future. McManus had lived and died a rebel. 1848 was dead and gone, a mere thing of memory, and to many of them scarcely among the pleasures of memory. To Stephens, Luby, and their friends and followers, things, however, wore quite another aspect. They felt they were carrying out the principles of '48 to their legitimate consequences by reverting to that solider and sterner policy of '98, from which the '48 men had themselves so largely drawn their inspiration'.[3]

The organization of the funeral in Dublin was in the hands of the Fenian-dominated National Brotherhood of St Patrick, outwardly a legal and open organization. The mounting enthusiasm in Ireland, and the scenes as the body of McManus was borne from San Francisco across America to New York, obliged the more moderate party to take part in the proceedings. 'Aspirationist' and Fenian fought behind the scenes for control. At first Father Kenyon had met Stephens at Luby's house and appeared so much in agreement with their plans that he had agreed to deliver the graveside oration. When he made it clear that it would be tainted with 'Aspirationist' heresy another orator was selected for whom Stephens anonymously insisted on writing the speech, best described in O'Leary's restrained and damning phrase, 'bordered on the high-faluting, and I think this crossed the border sometimes'.[4]

The clash between Stephens and the moderates came to a head the week before the funeral at several meetings of the reception committee held in the Mechanics' Institute, where Luby, on behalf of Stephens who remained completely in the background, succeeded in securing the election of a Fenian

---

[3]O'Leary, *Recollections of Fenians and Fenianism.* Vol. I. p.156 .

[4]The speech is printed in O'Leary, *Recollections* . . . Vol. I. pp. 165–9, in irony 'to give the reader an opportunity of deciding this matter for himself'.

chairman, and defeated what he called Father Kenyon's 'damnable hole and corner caballing' conducted in 'balmy and glozing accents' either to kill any funeral oration or alternatively to have himself substituted for the American speaker, Colonel Smith. Yet finally, through his suddenly discovered eloquence, Luby carried all his points and Stephens had won the day. Luby, however, deeply regretted the violent and open break with his old friend with whom he and Lalor had spent such merry days on the eve of their adventure in 1849 in Co. Tipperary. Even then Father Kenyon had been much tried by Lalor, who, in spite of all protests, commandeered a Bible to swear in members of his secret organization.

Stephens in a letter to John O'Mahony on 16 November 1861, after the funeral, gave a glimpse of this contest:

'An infamous (I write deliberately) attempt was made on Saturday night to make the burial next day a failure. This attempt was the work of Father Kenyon, (the leader) John Martin, and such carrion as Cantwell, etc., even The O'Donoghue allowed himself to be wheedled into the affair, though he had since disconnected himself from the miserable clique, who were all utterly crushed by the wise and manful action of the committee. The scene on this occasion was equal to one of the stormy scenes of the French convention, and never before had the Irish people given such proof of their ability to govern themselves. Be your faith in them as strong as mine is. Kenyon lost his wits all out—he insulted every member of the committee, and when leaving in a rage threatened to prevent the funeral next day, declaring: "You shall have no funeral," etc.

'He and others then went to Miss McManus and by calumny, etc. endeavoured to prevail on her to interfere and have the body taken from the American delegation, Dublin committee, etc. They were miserably disappointed, having succeeded in nothing but making themselves odious in Miss McManus's eyes as well as in the eyes of every true heart in Ireland.'[5]

Although many Fenians, including John Devoy, regretted the Stephens-Sullivan feud, the bitterness aroused by the Phoenix trials, and A. M. Sullivan's open exposure of the existence of the secret organization in the *Nation*, could not be

[5]Denieffe, *Recollections* . . . Appendix V. p. 166.

allayed even if his brother, T. D. Sullivan, in due course achieved the double feat of fighting the Fenians and being their Poet Laureate at the same time.

The Fenian Brotherhood had organized formidable gatherings in every great city as the procession passed swiftly towards embarkation for Ireland. In New York, John O'Mahony, Michael Doheny and Thomas Francis Meagher, waited on the Catholic Archbishop Hughes, to make arrangements for a Mass in St Patrick's Cathedral. Although a year before, Dr Cullen, who tirelessly intrigued against the Fenians from the Vatican to the Thames, and incited so far as he could the American Catholic hierarchy against them, had sent the Archbishop a very solemn warning on the subject, 'beware of the Phoenicians!', the Archbishop remembered that he and Terence Bellew McManus were Monaghan men, and not only promptly attended the Mass but preached a sermon which delighted the Fenians and gravely embarrassed Dr Cullen.[6]

The style and sentiment in general surpassed the turgid and tawdry rhetoric Stephens was even then agonizing over for his puppet funeral orator, to the quiet amusement of Thomas Clarke Luby. One of Hughes's passages ran:

'It is a great deal for us to know, and to be able to state, that the deceased, whose remains are now before the altar, loved his country. In all times, in all nations, and under all circumstances, whether of savage or civilized life, love of country has always been held a virtue . . . Now this love of country has generally been understood as that by which men defend their native or adopted soil, and support the government, when that government is lawful, and not oppressive. If the government should degenerate into oppression and tyranny, then would come the love of

[6]D'Arcy, *The Fenian Movement*. p. 19 and footnote which states that the text of the sermon is given in Michael Cavanagh, *Memoirs of Thomas Francis Meagher* (Worcester, Mass. 1892). The sermon is quoted at length Rutherford, *Fenian Conspiracy*, Vol. I. pp. 187–191; more briefly, Pigott, *Recollections of an Irish Journalist*, pp. 111–12. Rutherford apparently gives the full text of the sermon. He insinuates that the Archbishop was seeking to capture the Fenian Brotherhood through John O'Mahony, 'a devout Roman Catholic more than inclined to place his organization under clerical sway'. It is added that O'Mahony's visit to Ireland in 1860 was mainly to win Stephens to this view and Stephens 'did not absolutely say no'. Father O'Flaherty, whose bishop already frowned on his Fenian activities, is also named solemnly as an agent in the same scheme.

country—but not of government . . . Some of the most learned and holy men of the Church have laid it down with general sanction and authority, that there are cases in which it is lawful to resist and overthrow a tyrannical government . . The young man, whose brief and chequered career has come to an end in a distant land, to whose memory and remains you pay your respects, was one who was willing to sacrifice—and I may say did sacrifice—his prospects in life, and even his life itself, for the freedom of the country he loved so well, and which he knew had been oppressed for centuries. When the effort was made, it is true, he did not dally to enquire about the circumstances, as laid down by St Thomas, but he went into it disinterestedly, and willing to undergo all the risks and responsibilities of the contest . . . and it now only remains for you to unite your prayers for the repose of the departed soul . . . and reflect that all must reach the same goal at last'.

The body of Terence Bellew McManus, accompanied by Michael Doheny and other American Fenians, reached Ireland on 31 October, and, after impressive scenes in Cobh and Cork, was placed on the train for Dublin. Rossa marched in the procession to the train and saw, as he passed along the quays, a small boy cause much commotion among the watching crowds by climbing up the mast of a ship in the river flying a Union Jack and tearing it down. On the train Rossa noticed that the American delegation was stationed in the compartment next to the coffin. Among the delegation was Colonel M. D. Smith, selected by Stephens as official orator. Rossa and some others were warned by Stephens's orders as he learned that a section of Fenians, inspired by Doheny and his old acquaintance on his first American visit, James Roche, were in favour of using the funeral as a signal for an insurrection. Their plan was to seize the coffin at Limerick Junction and bear it to historic Slievenamon, calling on the country to rise in revolt. Stephens was waiting with his armed guard in the same carriage as Rossa when the train rolled into the station. Waiting also were another armed guard of Tipperary Fenians to reinforce his order if the attempt was made. His stage management was perfect. As the bell rang in warning for the train to restart, Stephens dramatically and reverently called on the crowd to kneel down and say a Pater and an Ave for the dead, and while the crowd was on its knees, the train steamed out.[7] And in the speech to be delivered by Captain Smith was written impressively:

> 'Here I beg to allude to an incident of such touching beauty that I shall never think of it without a fresh delight. At midnight a large body of men met at Tipperary Junction [i.e. Limerick Junction] the train that was bearing the hallowed dust. No voice or stir of any kind was heard, but all, uncovering their heads, knelt and prayed awhile. Then they rose, and, with heads uncovered and the silence of the dead, they remained in their places till the train drove away, when they knelt again, and so we saw them praying with earnest reverence till we were borne out of sight'.

This did not argue undue cynicism on the part of Stephens, who even mentioned 'the sublimely touching sight at Limerick Junction' to John O'Mahony. The appeal he evoked by his stage management genuinely moved him as did many of the scenes on the journey as the train left great crowds standing silent and bareheaded at the small stations. 'The most favourable account', he informed O'Mahony in his first letter of 16 November, 'is far below the reality. The funeral procession in Cork numbered from 80,000 to 100,000, about 8,000 walking in regular order. Such men as Denny Lane, John Francis Maguire, John O'Donnell of Limerick, etc. were thunderstruck. They could not have believed such a demonstration possible without the co-operation of the clergy, at least, if not the leaders. Still, the opinion of such parties was that Dublin—rotten Dublin—would be a blank failure!' Even Rutherford's description of the scenes in Cork corroborates Stephens here, 'the procession was immense . . . and the sympathizing crowd still larger. There was funeral music, and plenty of it; flagstaffs with banners drooping, half-mast high, rose in all directions; every breast bore the tokens of mourning'.[8]

When the train reached Dublin before daybreak Rossa saw a city ablaze with torchlights. The body was conveyed to the Mechanics' Institute to lie in state until the funeral. Dr Cullen,

---

[7] Rossa, *Recollections*, pp. 237–8; also Rutherford, Vol. I. p. 195.
[8] Rutherford, Vol. 1. pp. 193–4.

regarding the proceedings as a mere Fenian demonstration, declined to allow the remains to be admitted to the Pro-Cathedral or Mass celebrated for any ceremonial lying-in-state. Similarly in Cork, the local bishop, Dr Delaney, had refused the Cathedral for that purpose, whereupon the coffin was removed on arrival to a church at Cobh under the jurisdiction of the more sympathetic Dr Keane, Bishop of Cloyne, who, like Dr John MacHale, Archbishop of Tuam, firmly refused to penalise the Fenians, and neither of whom later ever promulgated the papal rescript condemning them.[9]

For the funeral itself on 10 November, Luby could find no parallel than 'the second burial of the great Napoleon', and then reflected that that had been backed by all the power and resources of France while the McManus funeral 'was the unaided effort of a populace trampled on or expatriated'. In his letters to O'Leary he recalled the triumphal procession of some 50,000 marchers, with hundreds of thousands of spectators in the streets, through which the bands, horsemen, processionists tramped seven miles in slush and dreary weather: 'dense masses of men, and fresh masses, endlessly, as it seemed . . . I felt as I never felt before or since, the grandeur, the magnetism of an immense crowd of human beings, when all are, for the time being, gloriously animated with one and the same noble aspiration and conviction'.

Luby's description and impressions, as given by O'Leary from the original account at some length, are rounded off with the burial by torchlight, and some simple prayers by Father Patrick Lavelle at the graveside:

'The regular chaplain of the cemetery, pursuant to archiepiscopal orders, I suppose, is conspicuous by his absence. Next Lavelle takes it upon him to deliver what he deems a patriotic harangue, which perhaps it may have been more or less. I catch none of the words . . . Captain Smith set to work like a Trojan. "In order to arrange my ideas the better" quoth he, "I have reduced my thoughts to writing". He stumbled only once over one word. The effect of the torchlight gleaming on the dark excited faces around the grave was superb'.[10]

[9]Devoy, *Recollections* . . . p. 119, For the papal condemnation see D'Arcy, *Fenian Movement* . . . pp. 329–332.
[10]O'Leary, *Recollections* . . . Vol. I. pp. 160–5.

The most significant words in the Stephens-Smith oration were:

'That coffin speaks of more than hope today, for it gives us faith and sheer resolve to do the work for which McManus died'.

Father Edmund O'Flaherty and Michael O'Brien were among the three hundred guests at the reception held in a Dublin hotel after the funeral. These two men, in their different ways, were to be numbered among the casualties of the Fenian movement, Michael O'Brien as one of the Manchester Martyrs in 1867, Father O'Flaherty as almost the last Catholic priest to identify himself with the Fenian Brotherhood publicly. He had come from John O'Mahony that year as yet another confidential envoy of the Brotherhood. On 5 October 1861, he had already sent a very favourable report after an inspection of I.R.B. circles in Dublin, Carlow, Wicklow, Waterford, Tipperary, Cork and Kerry. He added a warning on the dangers of merely spasmodic aid from Irish-America: 'I must tell our friends candidly that it is their negligent mode of proceeding—their periodical fits of action and inaction that have clogged the wheels of the movement in Ireland'. On his return Father O'Flaherty met with ever-increasing hostility from his superiors. His final act was to launch a crusade for the relief of distress in the south and west of Ireland which brought him the thanks of Father Lavelle who had been so prominent at the McManus funeral, and, in addition, a letter of thanks from the Archbishop of Tuam, Dr John MacHale, to 'the charitable Brotherhood'. Yet the tension between Father O'Flaherty and his bishop had almost reached breaking point when he died in 1863. Stephens was to say grimly to Luby, 'Father O'Flaherty was lucky. He has died just in time'.[11]

None of these future shadows troubled the rejoicing Fenians at that Dublin reception where they felt that Ireland at last was theirs. Above all, as James O'Connor reported somewhat acidly later:

'Stephens was king. He wielded his sceptre with suppressed ecstasy—which was yet apparent. He smiled and smoked, and

[11]Luby Papers. Father O'Flaherty's report is quoted from the O'Mahony Papers at length, D'Arcy, pp. 23–5.

walked about among his devoted lieutenants, receiving their congratulations, returning them in his most bewitching accents, his small eyes twinkling the while with a delight which only lovers of fame and human worship can understand. He moved that night in a sphere of glory; but his joy was full to the brim when taking them by the hand, one by one, he led them to the top of the table to speak words of peace and hope to the cream of the young Fenian army'.[12]

Denieffe remarked, too, that after the funeral Stephens was the most jubilant man in the city, and that the American delegates were astounded at the change in public sentiment within a decade:

'The demonstration proclaimed the I.R.B. supreme over all the land. The Sullivans, the Grays and the prelatists were *hors de combat*. The people had at last risen to the occasion and saved the honour of the country'.[13]

'That day,' wrote A. M. Sullivan later, 'gave the Fenian chiefs a command of Ireland which they had never been able to command before'.[14]

And, moreover, the outbreak of the American civil war seemed to promise new opportunities and resources to the rising and triumphant movement.

---

[12]*Irishman*, Christmas Supplement 1874; January 1875 *et seq.* 'Fenianism Photographed'.

[13]Denieffe, *Recollections of the Irish Revolutionary Brotherhood.* p. 71.

[14]A. M. Sullivan, *New Ireland*, Ch. 20.

17 Courtship and Marriage of James Stephens

THE Fenian historians, for the most part, have been unsympathetic and almost silent about Jane Hopper whom Stephens married in the autumn of 1863. John O'Leary was the most courteous although unenthusiastic, Devoy and Denieffe were openly hostile, Luby was dubious, and James O'Connor was venomous. Yet Stephens's affection for his wife showed him at his most human and least pretentious; and the long quarter of a century correspondence between them is poignant and revealing reading. Sometimes, semi-ironically, Stephens addresses his Jane, with inverted commas, as 'my old woman', but more often, 'Beloved heart', and now and then, 'my own soul'. Their life together—with the exception of the last four years which ended with her death on 13 November 1895—was a life of hardship, danger, separation, exile, and hope defeated until almost the last.

In these letters to his wife Stephens comes most to life, with many sharp and amusing sidelights on his political vicissitudes and on his friends and enemies. On 12 July 1864, he wrote, 'I can verily believe that as you did not cease to love me under all changes of health and circumstances—nay, loved the man, perhaps, for what would have alienated most women's love—you will go on loving me however I be'. And he tells her that the hardships he has caused her are his 'eternal anxiety'. Jane Stephens's theme can be summed up in the one undated letter where she writes, 'Another Christmas finds us apart, but please God, we may be happier next year, and whether parted or by your side, my heart is ever with you, darling, since first I loved you, and *will be till it is cold.*'

The courtship of Jane Stephens has in part been described

by James O'Connor, maliciously, by Thomas Clarke Luby, most urbanely, and by John O'Leary, impartially. Stephens, as lover and bridegroom, shocked the rank and file of the Fenians, partly—according to Denieffe—because Stephens had been understood to frown upon his followers making love or marrying until the imminent and final establishment of the Irish Republic, which was, in any case, the more urgent business, yet mainly—according to O'Leary—because they considered that their Chief was 'marrying, as they chose to consider, beneath him—Miss Hopper being the daughter of a tailor in a small way of business'. And O'Leary laughed in his sleeve at those 'furious democrats in theory, but not without a certain leaven of that aristocratic feeling, which I think, lies deep in the breasts of most Irishmen'.[1]

John O'Leary, beyond question the most aristocratic of all the Fenians, most aristocratically slaughtered in public those same furious democrats when they expressed such a sentiment in the Fenian press. In particular, Mr James O'Connor, book-keeper and writer in the *Irish People*, who chose in the first of a series of articles, 'Fenianism Photographed', in the *Irishman*, Christmas Supplement, 1874, to lampoon both Stephens and his wife by a malicious picture of their courtship. O'Connor, as one of the Dublin Centres, had been closely in touch with Stephens and had an intimate knowledge of the *Irish People* office, and in addition, used material from a manuscript history of the Fenian movement. Like Denieffe, Devoy and others he had turned violently against Stephens, and personal partisanship coloured every line of his portrait, which was used afterwards against Stephens by such writers as T. D. Sullivan very disingenuously, and the scathing repudiation of it by O'Leary and other lieutenants of Stephens suppressed or ignored.[2]

O'Connor, whatever his distortions of facts, at least presented a picture of Stephens a-wooing which, amended by the amusing additions to be found in Luby's letters to O'Leary, is diverting and of human interest. O'Connor tells first that Stephens, in

[1]O'Leary, *Recollections* . . . Vol. I. pp. 244–6; Denieffe, p. 84; The Luby Papers, *passim*; Devoy, *Recollections* . . . p. 274.
[2]T. D. Sullivan *Troubled Times in Irish Politics*, (Dublin, 1905), pp. 51–2, 82.

1860, was obliged to change his lodgings in Lennox Street for
security, and found—thanks to Luby, although O'Connor does
not mention this—furnished rooms in Charlemont Street
where the Hoppers then lived, and goes on:

> 'Stephens took up his small bag, his only luggage, and walked
> down to his new quarters. I was with him. Having knocked at
> the door it was opened by a young person, pale of complexion,
> black-eyes and pensive looking. She was picture-like in her
> wanness and melancholy aspect, but her deep dreaming orbs,
> though unbrilliant and slow-moving, shed a softening light upon
> a countenance which seemed to me sad from some secret cause.
> Besides being pallid, she was thin and slight. In after years she
> became entirely changed, for she grew round, rubicund and
> dumpy. Stephens, who always yielded easily to women's charms,
> must have been smitten on the spot. His glance was quick and
> sharp; he saw before him a black-eyed houri of paradise, such
> as Moslem fancy paints her; he smiled and spoke blandly in his
> best Parisian accents. The sharp twinge of the Kilkenny brogue,
> which clung to his tongue in spite of foreign sounds, was sup-
> pressed for what may be thought a more insinuating modulation'.

The malicious sketch describes the rapid progress of the
courtship which leads Stephens to quit his Fenian business
with O'Connor and other lieutenants abruptly, leaving them
desolate to the sounds of a social evening with the Hoppers in
another room while Stephens dances with the ladies and his
beloved 'his landlady's daughter', as O'Connor in true furious
democratic style puts it. The attack in 'Fenianism Photographed'
was published when Stephens was a half-starving exile in Paris
and Mrs Stephens was living in London. The sketch proceeds
to exonerate Mrs Stephens for her husband's alleged inactivity
for two years after the marriage, and without being very
specific holds her 'blameless'. She had, indeed, become very
cold and distant to the writer—whose pseudonym in the
Irishman was the Irish equivalent for Truth, 'Firinne'—after
Mr Stephens beyond a doubt reported Mr O'Connor's appeals
and warnings to him to keep away from one quite unsuited to
him. Instead Stephens rushed to his doom, and whiled away
the time with Mrs Stephens in a little cottage at Harold's

Cross which the Fenian Centre, Hugh Brophy, had found and decorated for him, and Stephens, an eager horticulturalist, cultivated flowers and gave up to blooms and love precious hours lost forever to the Irish cause.

Devoy and Denieffe in their memoirs, if somewhat more restrained, were as critical as James O'Connor. John O'Leary intervened in the *Irishman* controversy with two sharp and curt letters in which he tore 'Fenianism Photographed' to shreds on some very evident distortions about himself, in particular the invention that he had gone to the United States, masquerading as Stephens to throw the Head Centre's pursuers off the scent. The attack on Mrs Stephens he regarded with contempt, and did not mention it, although he wrote some forthright letters to Luby and Devoy. In his memoirs he intimated that Stephens's love story and marriage were his own affair, so much so that although he himself had been best man at the wedding, he scorned to recall the date or look up the newspaper files to find it. He yawned, too, at Mr Stephens's idyll in the cottage, not bothering to check where the cottage was, and intimating that Stephens's gardening experiments had been grossly exaggerated. Con O'Mahony, Stephens's former secretary, joined in the defence of the silent Chief, while 'One of the Old Guard', Middleton, Co. Cork, told O'Connor that he was a Reptile and a stinging Serpent Mrs Stephens had detected at a glance, and no Irishman!

Luby with some wit and delicacy confided to O'Leary the comedy of Stephens's courtship. One scene he recreated took place the night of the great September excursion to Delgany to celebrate Stephens's return in '64 from America, when the assembled Centres had 'quaffed so royally', and 'the Captain amid resounding cheers propounded to us the deluding words, "You know that next year is to be the year of action"'; Luby, in right merry form at a family reunion in Dublin of the Hopper household, 'quizzed and mystified old Mrs Hopper: "She should be eternally obliged to me for the great honour I had procured her family. This referred to the fact that 'twas *I*, who had first engaged lodgings in her house for the "Captain".'

There is none of the malice of 'Fenianism Photographed' in Luby's amusing picture of meeting Stephens in one of his

14

lodgings before his marriage. The landlady, 'that fool!' had objected to any more visits to her house 'of that young lady' under any circumstances. Stephens met Luby in a most frantic and agitated mood. Jane was due that very day! Stephens would not go out in case he missed her on the way. He implored Luby to meet and detain her. He feared she might call, be insulted and her sensitiveness was such that Stephens would not answer for the consequences. Luby must detain Jane until Stephens arrived. Luby intercepted her at Merrion Square successfully and most diplomatically. She concluded that James had some sudden and 'strange', (i.e. Fenian) guests, and suspected nothing, lulled by Luby's pleasant and entertaining talk until Stephens arrived. Mr Stephens gave very prompt notice to his landlady that her rooms were no longer required and removed to Mount Street where there was no trouble about 'that young lady'.

Stephens was married to Jane Hopper on 11 November 1863, at the Church of St Michael and St John's, Exchange Street, Dublin, by the Rev. John O'Hanlon, with John O'Leary as best man and Miss Mary Hopper as bridesmaid. The parents of the bridegroom were given as John and Anne Stephens (both dead), and those of the bride as John and Rossanna Hopper. The address of the bride was given as that of her parents, 83 Upper George's Street, Kingstown.

The only description of the wedding is that of John O'Leary:

'I turned up in the church of the parish about six or seven in the evening. There was nobody in the church but the officiating priest—the Rev. John O'Hanlon—the bride and bridegroom— a young sister of the bride—myself, and, I think, the father and mother and two brothers of the bride—but certainly the father and one brother. After the marriage ceremony, we adjourned to Stephens's lodgings which appeared to me a strange sort of proceeding, and there I spent a few more or less dreary hours in not over-genial company.

'But I may as well have done with this wedding business. I should scarcely have mentioned it at all but for the fact of its having cropped up at my trial. I suppose I felt Stephens's selection of me for his best man as a sort of compliment at the time, and the thing had something of a mild air of mystery about it, somewhat marred, however, by a certain grotesqueness in the whole surroundings'.[3]

After a somewhat chilling admission that the event had 'a considerable and perhaps not altogether fortunate bearing on the life of Stephens, and so no doubt having some bearing on Fenianism too', John O'Leary abruptly dismissed the subject. So far as Mrs Stephens was concerned, however, he had already pronounced judgment: 'Of this lady I do not know that I am called upon to say much either here or elsewhere, for she played no direct part in Fenianism whatever, and such small indirect part as she may have played, through such natural influence as she may have had with her husband, rather belongs to his story than to mine'. And in a footnote, O'Leary adds, 'I could never make out that she had much influence with Stephens, though Luby and others, I think, thought differently'.[4]

Mrs Stephens's letters, written, often under the strain of anxiety for her husband, or illness or exile, sound simple, trivial and colourless, apart from her affection for Stephens, reveal little about her, though among the Fenian martyrs she most certainly earned a high place, a unique and lifelong one. The idyll which angered the austere Fenian critics was short indeed, and the alleged two-year inactivity of Stephens was filled with the organizing and launching of the *Irish People*— into which Luby noted that Stephens threw himself very thoroughly and skilfully—his tour of the Union armies in America within six months of his marriage, the strain of the Fenian split in U.S.A., his arrest and escape and exile once more. Mrs Stephens, from the early seventies, spent a life of poverty and suspense between her father's home in Dublin, in London, and with Stephens in Paris. In the crisis of '65 she was made the victim of the legend that has persisted to the present day that she was indirectly responsible for the arrest of Stephens: Dublin Castle espionage was wrongly supposed to have trailed her to Fairfield House. In the disgraceful campaign

[3]O'Leary, Vol. I. p. 245–6. See also, *Evening Press*, Dublin 21 November 1958, 'Where was James Stephens Married?' for letters by Martin D. O'Connor and D. F. Moore.

[4]O'Leary, Vol. I. p. 244.

launched against Stephens after the crisis of '67 she was, next
to him, the target for the most reckless and unfounded charges
of living in luxury on Fenian funds in exile, wrapped in furs
and studded with jewels.

It is when Jane Stephens is in question that Stephens shows
the profoundest feeling, in his letters to her or to his closest
friends like Luby and Edward Walsh. Megalomania and
affection are the constant notes of his letters to his wife, who
fully approves and shares these sentiments. One example is
typical of all. On 27 March 1874, he wrote from New York:

'Is it not a blessing—a priceless gift of God—for you to be able
to write after all your trials, how sure you are that you can cheer
our home—"our happy home, darling, be it rich or poor".
These words filled my heart to overflowing and thrilled me with
delight. Another passage in your last dear, dear letter not only
made me very happy, but proud of you to boot. It is this: "You
must do justice to our poor people in thinking they are true to
you; they are, dearest, if they only knew what to do (and when
they are true to you they are true to Ireland), only they are *led
astray*". These are noble words, darling. For you know only too
well that no people more foully wronged their chief than ours;
but like myself, the knowledge of this does not stir one drop of
bitterness in your heart. And yet it would be almost pardonable
in you—a woman and my wife. How favourably my own sweetheart compares with the wives of other chiefs—of Mrs Smith
O'Brien and Mrs John Mitchel, to say nothing of the smaller
fry pitchforked into a little brief authority by *me*.

'With honest pride I read this passage for some friends of mine,
last night. And talking about "my old woman" to another friend,
on Friday evening, I told him that, had I to live my life over
again, my choice of a wife, should be *you*, *dearest*. Such talk as
this is rare with me however as I deem it exceedingly bad taste
in a man to praise his wife to others. Only an uncontrollable
out-gush of the heart is natural and excusable, and very sure I
am my "old woman" won't set it against me. Sweet love, I
repeat, "You are fully up to my heart"—Is not this enough and
more than enough about ourselves? I might write ever so much
more in the same strain if I was sure no other eye but yours
should see it. But I write not only for you, but for all the family
—all who love us—though not one word for those outside
ourselves. Dearest heart, it would be an agony within all my

agonies to think that any but our own true and sympathetic kindred knew anything that I write to you in love'.

In the same letter comes this spontaneous flash of sympathy for his wife, and a sudden portrait of his own loneliness in exile:

'In this last letter, and spite of all efforts to hide it from me there . . . seems a current of sadness that goes to my heart. My noble, loving and devoted wife has been terribly tried. This I know only too well. I say nothing of *my* trials. But, dearest heart, you must admit that, however, terribly tried, you have at least your own around you. Whereas I, however surrounded by good and true friends, have been utterly alone. What should I not have given in this eternity of agony for the presence of a father or mother, brother or sister? You have had all this around *you*. I know only too well that the true and loving wife or husband must be forever and always alone without the presence of the true and loving husband or wife . . . Darling, you are more to me than father or mother'.

And then comes the hint of his nostalgia for Paris and for the hundredth time the assertion that the mass of the Irish people are true to him, and if he could place matters, that is his leadership—in their hands all would be well. No man seems to have lived more on hope than Stephens. There is always some hope of an influential friend or a favourable foreign political situation etc. around the corner, in a month or so, next week.

In a letter to John O'Leary, then living in London, dated 7 August 1863, Stephens made two urgent requests, first, to act as best man at Stephens's wedding, 'though, of course, I would not put you to any great inconvenience for this alone,' and second, to take the nominal proprietorship of the *Irish People*, which he suddenly told his closer colleagues, Luby, Kickham, and some others, he intended to start. In the end O'Leary became editor, Luby and Kickham his assistants, and O'Donovan Rossa, manager. The office, characteristically, was situated almost at the gates of Dublin Castle, at 12 Parliament Street. O'Leary sometimes was paid his small salary. Rossa, as manager, often in the beginning paid the expenses of the paper and insisted that subscribers, and there were many such, who were poor, should go on the free list.

'To the devil with your business reasons', said Rossa to critics of this policy, 'the organization can't be run on business principles, and we must push it in every way we can'.

Stephens had some hopes of converting his printers to a similar altruism. Once when they threatened a strike for what Luby considered an extortionate demand for overtime, Luby sent for Stephens who addressed them thus:

'I had hoped to treat you as Brothers. You insist on being treated as tradesmen. Be it so!'

O'Leary and his staff were relieved when Stephens, who had first announced he would act as super-editor with the rest subordinate to his literary instructions, decided to leave the writing to them. John Devoy had been puzzled and alarmed by the leading article in the *Irish People*'s first number. This, 'Isle-Race-Doom,' had been written by Stephens, and was described by an irate reader in a letter to one of the staff as 'all dashes, commas, and bosh'. James O'Connor, in his 'Fenianism Photographed', declared that Stephens spent a fortnight in preparation, reading De Quincy for style, some chapters of Mrs Hall's *Ireland* for general local colour, and especially for Killarney and the Golden Vale of Tipperary, 'and then rummaged all his own stock of poetical knowledge for fancy touches of grace and ornament'. Finally on the day before going to press, Stephens sat up all night writing, with a messenger ordered for next morning at six sharp. The messenger by mistake called at three and found Stephens still on his second page. Long after dawn, and when the day was bright indeed, 'Isle-Race-Doom' was handed to John O'Leary, who had to endure two more such contributions, and then the Head Centre 'relapsed into a silence which I never after urged him to break'. O'Leary became editor 'being clearly, if not the fittest person for the post, certainly the least unfit'.[5]

Both Denieffe and Devoy have recorded the extraordinary reckless atmosphere of the *Irish People* office; the eccentric 'Pagan' O'Leary sleeping there at night and casting bullets in the daytime, while the Dublin Castle detectives hovered like birds of prey at the very door. Once Luby, while he wrote

[5]O'Leary's *Recollections* are the most detailed account of the *Irish People*, in particular the second volume, with the possible exception of the Luby Papers.

upstairs, heard an extraordinary outburst of blasphemous obscenity from the printing room downstairs, and descended in a rage. It happened that two of the most pious and long-tongued gossips in Dublin were at that moment in Kickham's room, and Luby feared the appalling outburst would reach them. Then 'in the folding room behind the front office whom should I see but the Pagan stamping round furiously and blaspheming with all his might. He was taking the name of God in vain . . . enough to freeze the blood of anyone short of an atheist of devilish bad taste'. Luby, after a fierce pursuit through several rooms, cornered the Pagan, and spoke:

'If you choose to go out into that street, you may, if you like, stand on your head, and blaspheme God and the Virgin and all the saints. I can't prevent you doing so. But *this is my house* (Luby was the nominal proprietor of the paper), and as long as it is mine, I'll allow no one to blaspheme in it'.

'Oh', retorted the Pagan, 'since you are turning me out of your dirty house, I'll never set foot in it again. Damn you and it!'

'And damn you, too!' cried Luby, kindling into almost as violent a rage as the Pagan, who strode out, and never spoke to Luby again until they were both fellow-prisoners in Mountjoy jail. The Pagan's version of this reconciliation was, to Luby's delight, 'Why did I speak to the Doctor again? Why, he craved my pardon, and I forgave the dog!'

The Pagan, for all his eccentricity, which came from a bullet wound in his head in the Mexican wars and the belief that St Patrick had ruined the Irish race by teaching them to forgive their enemies, was the most able Fenian agent for subverting the Irish soldiers to Fenianism, 'horse, foot and artillery', as Luby wrote, 'incaution was the secret of Pagan's success'. Long years after Luby had his last meeting with the Pagan O'Leary in a New York street—a pathetic ghost of an ancient fighter, at peace with St Patrick and then living in an American naval home in the south—trembling with nerves at the busy traffic, toothless and half-blind. Luby's eyes filled with tears as the Pagan tottered out of sight.

While the Pagan was undermining the British army, and Luby, John O'Leary and Kickham with many able writers were making the *Irish People* a force in the land, hardly a week passed without a financial alarm. Sometimes the paper was saved by intermittent American aid from O'Mahony, some-times it was on the point of closing down, yet it always escaped by luck or a miracle. More than once Stephens thought the end had come.

In these *Irish People* days, Luby had a sly thrust of a parti-cularly infuriating self-delusion of Stephens. He used to tell Luby he scorned 'to live on the movement', and suffered in hunger and poverty, with occasional help from 'influential friends'. 'Public funds!' thought Luby, 'what humbug!' On one fortunately very dark night, Stephens again told Luby this tale of woe. He and his wife had had no breakfast that morning and he congratulated himself that he had not lost the stoicism to endure silently and unthanked.

'It happens', replied Luby, 'that I have in my pocket some pounds of *Irish People* money. As proprietor of that journal am I not entitled to advance a loan of one pound, so that you and your wife can have breakfast to-morrow morning?'

Stephens with some decent demur, and after much fencing, agreed, and then as Luby handed him a pound note, asked in a low voice: 'Could you make it thirty bob?'

And Luby, rejoicing that there was no bright moon to show his face, 'forked out another quid!'

SHORTLY after the establishment of the *Irish People* Stephens decided to visit America again. His main object in which, according to O'Leary, he was to be very successful, he professed to be the collection of 'the sinews of war' for the new paper. He had, moreover, received an invitation to attend the Chicago Fair organized by the Fenian Brotherhood in that city, announced for 26 March 1864.

There was, however, an even more serious reason for the journey. The relations between himself and O'Mahony had become worse and worse, and the proceedings of the Fenian Brotherhood convention in November 1863 had been a polite but unmistakable challenge by O'Mahony to Stephens's hitherto undisputed supremacy over the entire movement at home and in America. Ever since O'Mahony's visit to Ireland in 1860, the difference between the two leaders, partly personal, partly on policy, had grown steadily. O'Mahony, in a letter to Charles J. Kickham, then on a visit to the United States, had written on 19 October 1863, that he could no longer submit to 'dictatorial arrogance' from Stephens, and that, as chief officer of the Fenian Brotherhood in America, O'Mahony's powers 'must be set on an even keel' with Stephens's authority over the Irish organization: 'I will no longer consent to be accountable to him for my official conduct'.[1]

O'Mahony made his meaning very plain in three secret resolutions adopted by the November Convention in terms most flattering to Stephens, unmistakable in meaning, and phrased in the best Fenian ritualistic, long-winded vocabulary:

The first resolution read:

[1]Letter quoted from O'Mahony Papers, D'Arcy *Fenian Movement* . . . pp. 33–5.

'Whereas, it has been proved to the Fenian Brotherhood, not alone through the authorized reports of its Head Centre, but also through the forced acknowledgments conveyed in certain recent denunciations emanating from the enemies of the Irish race, that there exists among the MEN OF IRELAND a numerous and widely-extended national Irish organization, which was heretofore named the Irish Revolutionary Brotherhood, but which having grown in numbers and power, in subordination to its constituted authorities, and in discipline under the wise and able directions of its central executive, is now known as THE IRISH REPUBLIC, be it

'Resolved—that we, the Centres and Delegates of the Fenian Brotherhood assembled in this Convention, do hereby proclaim the Republic of Ireland to be virtually established; and, moreover, that we pledge ourselves to use all our influence, and every legitimate privilege within our reach to promote the full acknowledgment of its independence by every free government in the world'.

The second secret resolution proceeded to business, and blandly put James Stephens where O'Mahony wanted him. It noted that 'the principal national organization on Irish soil' existed there 'almost entirely' because of 'the devoted patriotism, untiring labours, and indomitable perseverance of its Central Executive Officer, convinced thereof by the knowledge that he has raised Ireland from the prostrate condition in which she lay a few years since to her present proud and defiant attitude,' the said Central Executive Officer, which, of course, was James Stephens, was thereby acknowledged as 'the Representative of the Fenian Brotherhood in Europe, and the Supreme Organizer of the Irish People'.

In many words O'Mahony had asserted his independence, and refused any longer to be regarded as subordinate to Stephens. The third resolution crowned the good work by an invitation to Charles J. Kickham to present the two resolutions to Stephens when he returned to Ireland with a pledge of undivided support and entire confidence, respect for his person, and unalterable gratitude for 'his superhuman labours, eminent sacrifices and unexampled success in organizing the Irish Republic'.

Stephens expressed his opinion of all this voluble insolence in a private letter to Luby, which was unfortunately captured in the raids and arrests of 1865, and given the fullest publicity during Luby's trial. It was a letter for which Stephens later publicly apologized to O'Mahony whom it wounded deeply; he had indeed chafed under Stephens's yoke, desired freedom for his policy and organization in America, yet at heart his praise of Stephens was sincere. On this clash between the two leaders certain Irish-American politicians and the hidden evil genius of O'Mahony and the outstanding traitor in the Fenian movement, Red Jim McDermott, were to play to the ultimate defeat and ruin of both O'Mahony and Stephens and their cause.

After some sympathetic allusions to 'the death of our friend which for private as well as public reasons, I sincerely regret,' —a reference to General Michael Corcoran, one of the founders of the Fenian Brotherhood with O'Mahony and Doheny, who had been killed by a fall from his horse in December 1863— Stephens, in this letter to Luby, very soon warms up on O'Mahony and his new policy. The loss of the unnamed friend at an earlier stage would have been an inestimable loss, and 'is even now a serious loss, still by no means an alarming one, at least to those who understand our position, better late [*sic*] than navel-eyed seer beyond the wave'.[2]

After this contemptuous and obvious stroke at O'Mahony, and an equally obvious examination in the Fenian correspondence code idiom of the position and use of the Fenian Brotherhood as regards the I.R.B. in Ireland for the recruiting of officers in the Union army camps and money supplies, Stephens proceeds:

'How long shall the good and true—the able, too, by might of brain and heart, or both combined—be doomed to grope blindly through interminable mazes and glooms of Ramshackle? One thing is certain, whatever hope we might have nursed, in our friend's lifetime [Corcoran's] of coming to the light and on the open way—in other words whatever our expectations of such proceeds yonder, we might reduce that business [the Fenian Brotherhood] to a merely *partial* failure, there is no hope at all, now that our friend is no more'.

[2]Special Commission, Dublin, 1866, *Trial of Thomas Clarke Luby and Others*, Appendix, pp. 1078–9.

Then follows an exhortation to Luby, who during his American tour from February to May 1863 had acted as peacemaker between Stephens and O'Mahony, and Stephens's opinion of those secret resolutions:

'Are your eyes open at last? You have nothing whatever to blame in *yourself*. In your place and acting as *you* were instructed to act, in accord with *him* (O'Mahony), *I* should have had the same story to tell. He is our standing drag-chain and stumbling-block. The worst of it is, that for some time at least, there is no remedy. Well then we are absolutely thrown on our own resources at last. The great organizer, statesman, patriot, martyr, sage, seer or oracle, has spoken, and bids us hope no more from *him*. And he announces this in a style of levity to make a stoic shiver—actually launches what he deems a wit-shaft at us—bids us laughingly and we be wise to build no more castles in the air! Even for his sake one would wish to spare him the exposure of such lunatic fatuity. Doubtless *he* is building daring castles on adamantine rocks!

'Lunatic fatuity is what *that* is surely, for the strong foundations of our house are *here*—mark me well, here,—and if those foundations should be moved to any purpose, then topples down the edifice he complacently claims as *his*, and too fondly gazing at which, his eyes grow dim and his brain is addled. I am sick—almost to death—of the man and his ways'.

Yet with much more invective of the kind, Stephens assures Luby that there will be no break with O'Mahony and the Fenian Brotherhood; 'with him, still less with the firm he directs. This, though worthy of the insane insanity we wot of, would be quite unworthy of us'. He attacks O'Mahony's policy 'which involves, on the one hand the assumption that we require but little—that it would be unwise to entrust us with much; and on the other that whatever our requirements, *he* is not bound, could not be expected to try and furnish them . . . On an average the receipts of the house yonder have not reached £250 a year. And what have we not been compelled to endure for this?'[3]

O'Mahony in 1868 published his own account of his leader-

[3]O'Leary, *Recollections* . . . Vol. I. pp. 135–6 gives the American financial aid to the I.R.B. for the first six years as less than £1,500.

ship and the Fenian Brotherhood in America as a defence of himself and his policy. It appeared in his own paper, the New York *Irish People*, and in violence of language and personal feeling quite equalled the intensity of Stephens's letters to Luby.[4]

Before his departure for America, Stephens confided a fateful document to Luby which the latter filed and promptly forgot. Later on, with some cynical amusement, Luby vaguely intimated its existence to O'Leary but did not bother Kickham at all about it as there seemed to be no necessity. He enclosed it in an envelope with the secret resolutions that had so annoyed Stephens, never suspecting that herein were the trump cards of the prosecution at future Fenian trials.

The document was in Stephens's own handwriting, and read:

EXECUTIVE

I hereby appoint Thomas Clarke Luby, John O'Leary and Charles J. Kickham, a Committee of Organization or Executive, with the same supreme control over the Home Organization (Ireland, England, Scotland, etc.) I have exercised myself.

I further empower them to appoint a Committee of Military Inspection, and a Committee of Appeal and Judgment, the functions of which Committee will be made known to each member of them by the Executive.

Trusting to the patriotism and ability of the Executive, I fully endorse their action beforehand, and call on every man in our ranks to support and be guided by them in all that concerns our military brotherhood.

J. STEPHENS

Dublin, 9 March 1864.

Stephens arrived in the United States on 23 March. On the 25th he wrote to his wife from New York:

My Own Janissa,

Here I am safe. Everybody I meet will have it that I look better than they have ever seen me. We got here the evening before last. The passage was very rough till Patrick's Day. By the way, I

[4]This statement was used with generous quotations, and many characteristic distortions in both volumes of Rutherford's *Fenian Conspiracy*. It was reprinted in the *Irishman* from 8 February 1868 onwards until late the same year, over 60,000 words in length.

should say that Patrick's Day is not only memorable but has always been lucky to me. So on this occasion, the weather took up suddenly on the 17th and continued favourable till the night before our arrival. We were 13 days and nights. For the present I can say nothing more about the passage and very little about anything else. I am greatly improved and in such cheer as would make your pulses bound did you only realize it. This evening (or afternoon—5 o'clock) I leave for the Fair which now is certain to exceed all expectations—an immense success.

Could I only be sure that you have borne and shall continue to bear my absence even tolerably, I should be happy as I could be, away from my darling. But I will believe that, in all things, she shall be found worthy of her own James. Darling, I must for the present conclude with best love. But you shall have a long letter from me soon.

Your own James.

O'Mahony at the time of Stephens's 1864 visit was under the severest hostile pressure from the Chicago Fenian 'Men of Action' section. He knew, too, that Stephens and his followers at home resented the secret resolutions even more than the Chicago Fenians, and both repeated the taunt that O'Mahony was 'the drag-chain and stumbling-block,' and pressed for an immediate fight in Ireland within a year. As he wrote later:

'The first convention of the Brotherhood had scarcely adjourned, when the "Men of Action" repenting of their participation therein, set about undoing its work. Steps were taken by them towards holding a Fenian fair in Chicago where their faction was strongest, and without consulting the central council or myself, they dispatched the late H. O'C. McCarthy[5] to Ireland, ostensibly for the purpose of purchasing and collecting goods, but really to invite James Stephens to America, in order to aid them in precipitating a fight in Ireland. The latter gentleman arrived here in McCarthy's company in '64, attended the fair in question and made a long tour through the States, visiting the Circles of the Organization. He everywhere proclaimed that the revolutionists in Ireland would either fight or dissolve their organization within the coming year. War or dissolution in '65 became his watchword. This cry was taken up eagerly by the sanguine and

[5][Probably a newspaper misprint for 'H. O. C. McCarthy' otherwise known as Henry Clarence McCarthy mentioned below.—O.D.E.]

unreflecting masses of our countrymen. It was fostered by the knavish and the designing. I believed the proposition impracticable as matters stood, and discouraged it as far as I could without coming to an open rupture with its originator.'[6]

Stephens had, in fact, mounted a team of tigers, and willy-nilly, spurred them on. And O'Mahony, in one point at least, was right, the team was a very mixed one indeed. Devoy summed it up concisely in his sketch of O'Mahony's associates and hangers-on:

'His associates may be described thus: clever men like P. J. Meehan of the *Irish American* (then the leading Irish paper in America, though Patrick Donohoe's Boston *Pilot* had the largest circulation), who was not fully convinced of the possibility of an Independent Irish Republic; William R. Roberts, a successful dry-goods merchant, who was vain and shallow, but showy; the Scanlan brothers of Chicago; Henry C. McCarthy, a State Senator in Illinois and an able man; P. W. Dunne of Peoria, big-hearted and forceful but impetuous; James Gibbons of Philadelphia; B. Doran Killian of New York, an able lawyer and others—all men of standing in the communities in which they lived'.

And also, as Devoy deplores, in much milder terms than Denieffe, certain 'good fellows enough but poor advisers', O'Mahony's camp-followers, who hovered round the Chief like flies round a honey-bowl, 'tale-bearers, flatterers, and gossips'. O'Mahony's violence and bitterness of language in his detailed defence of his leadership is indeed painful reading. Yet more so is his power of self-deception and blindness to some of the worthless and, in fact, treacherous associates high in his councils. He had a real grievance against the ambitious and shallow politician, Roberts, whose main feat in Fenian history was to split the movement and launch the fatal policy of an invasion of Canada with the help of the guileless 'Men of Action' and the Stephens-O'Mahony estrangement. O'Mahony was warned against both the folly of flirting with the Canadian policy and the traitors in his ranks by Stephens.

[6]Quoted, *Irishman*, 8 February 1868 from O'Mahony's defence in New York *Irish People*.

Denieffe in his inquest on the Fenian failures of 1865 and '67 wrote in disillusion:

> 'In analysing causes and results, I decided that Stephens and O'Mahony, who never worked in harmony, were both of them unfit for the great responsibility they had undertaken. In my opinion, it was mainly O'Mahony's fault. He always kept around a lot of flatterers, an imbecile pack, who were no use whatever to the movement, who could not get the confidence of anyone but that one good-natured soul who loved to listen to flattering stories of himself and the chieftains of old, without taking a single lesson from their misfortunes and ultimate extinction.'

Frank Roney, former Belfast Fenian Centre, very active in the Ulster campaign of the '60s to win over the Ribbonmen and Presbyterians to the Fenian ranks, and, later a labour pioneer in California, in his recollections is as severe on O'Mahony and the Fenian Brotherhood in general, and wholly pro-Stephens throughout:

> 'The members of the American branch of the organization had made themselves ridiculous by forming what they called a *de facto* Irish government with a president and cabinet houses expensively in New York city. The funds contributed to aid in Irish liberation were wasted on this fantastic government got up to flatter the vanity of an honest but foolish and weak old man, crazed with the glories of a line of patriotic ancestors, Mr John O'Mahony, "President of the Irish Republic" located in New York city, committed a prodigious blunder when he assumed that title and called into existence his sham government. He did more than that when he permitted the frittering away of vast sums of money to uphold the portentous dignity of his Lilliputian outfit'.[7]

Roney here was unjust to O'Mahony in repeating the taunt that he was responsible for the costly Moffat Mansion establishment which was imposed on him in 1865, when Roberts and his supporters deprived him of his powers on the way to Roberts's successful intrigue to oust him from the presidency of the Fenian Brotherhood. O'Mahony, as his statement proved, protested bitterly against the ostentatious expenses of

[7]Denieffe, *Recollections* . . . pp. 149–50; 185–6; Devoy 268–9; *Frank Roney Irish Rebel and California Labour Leader*, ed. Ira B. Cross, University of California Press. 1931, pp. 111–12.

the scheme, which was starving the arms fund for Stephens and his men in Ireland. 'I fear the Moffat Mansion', he said, 'will be the tomb of the Fenian movement. It is want in Ireland, and waste in New York'.[8]

Luby, Rossa, O'Leary, Kickham and Devoy, whatever their criticisms of O'Mahony, had no regard for the intriguing wrecker, Roberts, who had retired from the dry goods business a millionaire. Eventually, after many political campaigns, he retired into private life, late in the 70's, minus the greater part of his fortune.

An amusing description of Roberts spell-binding the Fenians in Febuary 1871, was given later by an Irish priest, the Rev. M. B. Buckley of Cork.

'Went to the Cooper Institute to hear Mrs O'Donovan Rossa read for the benefit of the widow of J. J. Geavny (a Cork Fenian) who died here by falling into a boiling vat of soap. A crammed and most enthusiastic house—General Tom Burke in the chair . . . In one of the intervals there was loud cries for "Rossa". He at length came forward and said he was not going to make a speech. "Deeds, not words" was his motto, but he would read a letter he had just received from a gentleman, addressed to his wife (Mrs Rossa). The writer was Mr Bashford, and he presented a cheque for fifty dollars for the object of the meeting. Loud cheers for Bashford, the modest, retiring, unselfish Bashford. But lo! a gentleman steps forward, kisses hands to the audience. This is the modest Bashford, advertising himself . . . But modesty is a virtue unknown in Yankeedom. Behold another sample of it. There are loud cries of "Roberts, Roberts!"'

'This is the famous Colonel Roberts, once the head of a Fenian split of a split. I learn afterwards that the gallant Colonel had a lot of fellows paid to call on him. The air was filled with cries of "Roberts", and at last the Chairman came forward and asked was Colonel Roberts in the hall. The Colonel who was at one of the doors modestly concealed, then marched the whole length of the hall, appeared on the platform, took off his outside coat, and with a voice of thunder made a rattling speech on "Irish Nationality". He gave all the old claptrap, "these gallant heroes", "England's accursed tyranny", "Ireland's imperishable rights, founded on the principles of God's eternal justice", etc. etc. . . all

[8]O'Mahony's statement, *Irishman*, 21 March 1868, pp. 598-9.

15

well committed to memory. He paced the stage, and if England
saw him then she would have trembled for her very existence. All
this was a bid for the Irish vote! All got up by the astute Colonel
himself. Curious engraftation on the programme of the evening,
but puffing and advertising is the great Yankee notion. General
Burke in returning thanks to everyone, thanked Mr Weber for
the loan of his splendid piano. Fenians, buy your pianos at
Weber's!'[9]

O'Mahony, as soon as the Chicago Fair had finished, aided
Stephens on his long tour of the country by giving him letters
of introduction although he shook his head over Stephens's
fatal slogan 'Insurrection or dissolution in 1865...' The previous
year Luby had toured the Union armies, and Stephens now
made an even more extensive tour. He was given passes by
sympathetic officers, and was well received everywhere.

The second American tour was a repetition, on a more
successful scale, of his first organizing reconnaissance through
the Ireland of the 50's. It showed his genius as an organizer as
he honeycombed the Union armies with Fenian circles, and
toured the States even more widely than Luby had in 1863.
To John O'Mahony, Brother and Friend, he showed himself,
too as the unerring Brother, and most candid Friend, in his
letters. He wrote from Chicago, 1 June 1864:

'My visit to Memphis, was a successful one. I did not find so
strong a circle there as I had been led to expect, but the men are
good and acted spiritedly. Mr [Henry Clarence] McCarthy was
with me; and on our return to Cairo, he saw and addressed
that Circle again with good effect.

'I got here last night. Fortunately the 23rd are here and I meet
them tonight at Fenian Hall. Tomorrow I leave for Milwaukee,
my course will be as follows: Detroit, Friday evening; Toledo,
Saturday evening; Sandusky, Sunday evening; Tiffin, Monday
evening; Cleveland, Tuesday evening; Buffalo, Wednesday
evening . . .

'You, also, mention having had a visit from a Kilkenny friend
and a Callan friend, and how you don't like what they say about
the spirit in their districts—how you fear a cry is being raised of

[9]Rev. M. B. Buckley, *Diary of a Tour in America . . . in 1870 and 1871.* ed. Kate
Buckley (Dublin 1889).

their being abandoned by their chiefs in the hour of danger. For many reasons you should not have written this, though one reason alone will suffice to prove it; it cannot possibly be. So that your fears on the subject, if expressed even to me only, would hardly be worthy of a thinking man. You must have written in a hurry, or you would have recollected that there is but one chief absent. My absence is by no means calculated to raise the cry in question. It is well known why I am away. It is, moreover, known to all who have a right to know it, that my absence had become a necessity—that I should either come out here and do what, at the risk of my life, I have been doing, or let the work of my life become a total wreck.

'I repeat: there was no alternative between my visit to America and utter ruin. Again, those who should know this are aware of it. I fear nothing from the cry in question. Nor can the Clique—lay or clerical—make much of such a cry. Have faith in the People, friend, at home especially, they are not the base and stupid things this fear would make them. Provided I realize the objects I came out for, all will be well, and hitherto I have fully realized them.

'With regard to the emigration it is appalling. Nor can it be stopped in any way but one. To prepare to take that one and only way soon as possible should be our constant labour. If not the first man to see, I was certainly the first to teach Irishmen that, if we did not make ready and fight for our cause and race, a few years would realize the ruin of both. The wretched men who opposed us so bitterly from the outset are now beginning to dread what I dreaded years ago and have devoted my life to prevent. They make overtures to us now, when they can do us no harm'.

Stephens wound up with a warning to O'Mahony to be on his guard, and some generalities about conciliating and gaining the active co-operation of all good Irishmen as their common aim and labour. Yet *good* Irishmen, it would seem, were scarce, as Stephens peremptorily advised O'Mahony to keep such persons as John Finerty, even if he had joined the I.R.B. in Kilkenny before arriving in U.S.A., in their places in the ranks, 'be sure and give him no prominence'. And a sidewipe at Finerty's friend Peter Gill, editor of the *Tipperary Advocate*, as 'perjured', which probably meant no more than that he was too colourful an individualist to toe the Head Centre's line.

And that both Finerty and Gill were personal friends of Father John Kenyon, which since the McManus funeral was to Stephens sufficient condemnation.

Most of Stephens's letters to O'Mahony were in the same key, a record of intense organizing activities and stern personal advice. It may be that O'Mahony endured more from James Stephens than he would have tolerated from another, although it is evident that some of the advice and the over-bearing tone in general would have infuriated a saint. One wise warning of Stephens's O'Mahony ignored with deadly and almost fatal consequences, to the Fenian Brotherhood in particular, and to the Fenian cause in general.

In a letter written from Louisville, Kentucky in May Stephens wrote:

> 'I have heard today that Mr James McDermott has announced his intention to go on a lecturing tour. This move is so highly injudicious, so calculated to do injury, now especially, that I cannot believe that it has your sanction. Whatever Mr McD's zeal and activity—he has not the weight and steadiness—the ability and other essential qualifications to represent us creditably. Not having these, he injured us in his former efforts in this way, and would injure us seriously now. As to going "on his own hook", it would be still worse—it would be making a trade of his connection with us, as, without us, he could not have even entertained the notion at all.
>
> 'It would be disreputable for an able and accomplished man to go trading in this way. How much more so for one who can give no value whatever—in thought or words—for the money received. You are certainly bound to look to this and give Mr McD. to understand that you are quite opposed to it. Should he not be got to apply himself to some calling for which he is fitted? It is deplorable to see men led astray in this way'.[10]

Every Fenian historian in due course deplored that O'Mahony himself persisted in supporting Mr James McDermott. Apart from the warnings of Stephens, 'Red Jim McDermott' had been denounced to O'Mahony by many close observers, and sound judges. The year before six Dublin Fenian Centres had sent an explicit intimation to O'Mahony that McDermott was

[10]Both the preceding letters are quoted from Denieffe, Appendix, pp. 183–86.

untrustworthy. When John O'Leary told O'Mahony that, all else apart, the man was notoriously a blackguard, the reply was that morally 'Red Jim' was a bad man, 'but *politically* I have never been able to see anything wrong with him!'

From its inception, the Fenian movement had been dealt heavy blows by British espionage, and the heaviest blows were inflicted by this glib-tongued, handsome, intelligent, unprincipled son of a Dublin coachman. 'Red Jim' was adventurous enough to win the Cross of St Sylvester in the Papal Brigade of 1860. In the '6o's he entered the Irish movement and the British secret service with equal thoroughness and enthusiasm. In the first, he waved the green flag, boosted dynamite, and tickled all the groundlings. For the second, he fanned up the flames of discord at the Chicago Fenian Congress of 1863; sold the secrets of the Fenian Brotherhood to Mr Archibald, British Consul in New York in 1865, including ciphers, the most confidential documents, and the location of arms stores; helped to complete Le Caron's wrecking of the Roberts wing schemes for a Canadian invasion in 1868 and 1870; betrayed O'Mahony's Campo Bello expedition devised at the same time as a counterblast to the Canadian invasions against Stephens's most emphatic orders; toured London with some of the Clan na Gael 'Triangle' dynamiters of the '8o's as they inspected public buildings; and pursued his career in the most brazen manner in spite of public denunciations by Rossa, Devoy and Michael Davitt, and several determined attempts on his life into the '9o's. Nothing could shake the confidence of O'Mahony in 'Red Jim' whose uncanny influence over him survived to the end.

In his apologia in 1868, O'Mahony wrote:

'James McDermott, the "Assistant-Secretary" was the best abused of all my subordinates. This arose from the fact that it was through his evidence that the existence of the great conspiracy in Chicago was made known to myself and the Central Council. For this neither P. J. Dunne nor Michael Scanlan, whom he confronted face to face before me and their colleagues, could ever forgive him. He was, moreover, exceedingly and demonstratively devoted to me personally. I found him an indefatigable worker and strictly scrupulous in all his pecuniary relations with the

Brotherhood. His youthful and giddy exuberance of spirits sometimes caused him to use rash and indiscreet language out of doors, of which his enemies and mine were in the habit of taking unfair and malicious advantage'.[11]

Writing on the death of Stephens in his *United Irishman*, Rossa recalled that when he returned to Dublin in 1894, Stephens presided at a lecture he gave in the Rotunda, and introduced Rossa to the audience as one of his old comrades in the work of organization. 'In that work', commented Rossa, 'Stephens was single-minded and zealous. I have heard people say he hoarded money "for a rainy day"; but he did no such thing; he did the thing that was the very contrary; he borrowed money all round him, to forward the work of organization. He went to America in the springtime of 1864. I was the registered publisher and manager of the *Irish People* paper, and while he was away I did my share of hustling to gather money enough to run the concern.' Rossa's article continued:

> 'When he came back from America in the autumn of 1864, he brought with him some $50,000. I saw him apportioning it out for the work of organization in England, Ireland and Scotland; I told him he should keep something for the needs of the publication of the paper, and he gave me a kind of scolding for telling him so. He told me that by his arrangement with the American side of the house, he was to receive a certain amount of money every month, and that he was going to work up to that arrangement. He did work up to that arrangement; he worked ahead of it, for the money that was promised did not come.
>
> 'He, in America, told the men of the organization that there would be a fight in Ireland in 1865. At a meeting of the county centres in the organization in Wicklow, after his return from America, he told the men there that next year, the year 1865, was to be the year of fight. There was no fight in 1865. There is no good my saying any more over the Fenian grave of James Stephens— but I may say: he did not hoard, or save, or put by any Fenian money for "a rainy day" in his life; the organization he directed embraced most of the best men in every county in Ireland'.

[11]*Irish People*, New York; quoted *Irishman*, 14 March 1868. For 'Red Jim's' biography and misdeeds in detail, see, Davitt, *Fall of Feudalism*, Ch. 35; Devoy, p. 269; D'Arcy, p. 41, *passim*. Also, *Devoy's Post Bag*, Vol. 2. pp. 202 *et seq.*; 342 *et seq. passim*. [P. J. Dunne may be a slip for P. W. Dunne—O.D.E.]

In August 1864, after some amicable discussions with O'Mahony on financial and organizational schemes, Stephens returned to Ireland, and went on an intensive organizing tour. After his return the *Irish People*, staff and management, O'Leary noted, were 'little hampered through want of money henceforward although Stephens, then as ever, did little to husband such money as he got'. Drilling in the stores hired by the Fenians for secret arms depots, the manufacture of pikes, the search for arms, the steady subversion of the Irish regiments proceeded with an intensity hitherto unknown. And Stephens repeated his slogan on every possible occasion 'Next year will be the year of action'.

LUBY commented tartly on the Stephens prophecy that 1865 would be the year of action: that it was very true except that it was the year of action for the British Government, and not for Stephens or the Fenians. On the night of 14–15 September Dublin Castle struck at the organization and its leaders in Cork, Dublin, and other centres. The raid on the *Irish People* was one of the most damaging blows, not only because of the arrest of the staff and suppression of the paper, but because many compromising documents were seized, including even more compromising evidence elsewhere, notably the 1864 'Executive document', appointing Luby, O'Leary and Kickham as responsible heads of the I.R.B., in the absence of Stephens. This was found by mischance at Luby's house. He had disposed of other documents but carelessly placed the Executive document in an envelope intended for the love letters of himself and his wife. Thinking the half-crazy production of an eccentric non-Fenian journalist, one C. M. O'Keeffe, urging the Fenians to organize a general massacre of landlords, which he rejected for the *Irish People*, was 'a literary curiosity' he neglected to destroy it in spite of his wife's warning. On these two documents the Crown built an indictment that the Fenians planned wholesale murder and confiscation. The foreman of the jury at Luby's trial interrupted Judge William Keogh to inform him that the jury could not take the O'Keeffe document seriously. It sent poor Mr O'Keeffe to penal servitude, however, as the Executive document sent Luby, Kickham and O'Leary.

Through one trusted agent of both Stephens and Dublin Castle, Pierce Nagle, who worked in the folding department of the *Irish People* and had been giving information on Fenian affairs since the previous March, the Government came into possession of a letter of Stephens's dated 8 September 1865 to the Clonmel Fenians, which added to some routine instruction an urgent order for the B's or captains to select a candidate for A, or colonel, and dispatch him to Dublin for approval at once. Then came the all familiar exhortation: '*There is no time to be lost. This year*—and let there be no mistake about it—must be the year of action. I speak with a knowledge and authority to which no other man could pretend, and I repeat, the flag of Ireland—of the Irish Republic—must this year be raised. As I am much pressed for time, I shall merely add, that it shall be raised in a glow of hope such as never gleamed around it before. Be then of firm faith, and the best of cheer, for all goes bravely on. Yours fraternally, J. Power.

N.B. This letter must be read for the working B's only, and when read must be burnt'.

The B's never got the chance to burn it. Pierce Nagle stole it from a foolish messenger, who had gone on the spree, and was sleeping too deeply in the *Irish People* office.

The letter was delivered to Superintendent Daniel Ryan in the Castle, under standing and strict instructions from Under-Secretary Larcom to pay Nagle well for that information which had proved so useful since the spring. The Superintendent did not think very much of Mr Nagle, and though hostile in general, yet respecting the Fenians, thought this scoundrel made money all too easily. The message to the B's alerted Larcom and Lord Lieutenant Wodehouse. They were alarmed by other evidence: the power of the Fenian organization shown, for example, in wrecking, on occasion, Rotunda meetings held by A. M. Sullivan for such patriotic objects as erecting a statue of Grattan in College Green to keep out Prince Albert. Even more dangerous documents had come into the Viceroy's hands. Two envoys of O'Mahony's 'Men of Action', Messrs. P. J. Meehan and P. W. Dunne, had arrived to discover whether the situation in Ireland was favourable enough to insurrection to justify a final call to the Fenian Brotherhood for the funds urgently pressed for by Stephens if there was indeed to be war in '65. Behind this question and delay was the subtle hand of Roberts, intent on his Canadian schemes and the overthrow of O'Mahony and Stephens alike.

Dunne and Meehan were honest men, and reported favourably back to O'Mahony for Stephens's demands. They verified similar reports by General Millen, Colonel Thomas J. Kelly and O'Donovan Rossa. Of this nothing leaked out to their enemies. Meehan, however, unfortunately lost, through over-anxiety, O'Mahony's simple letter of recommendation and drafts to the value of £500 which were handed to the police. The actual text of the documents alarmed Wodehouse who decided to swoop at once. They read:

HEADQUARTERS OF THE FENIAN BROTHERHOOD

11th July 1865,
22 Duane Street, New York

To the C.E.I.R.

Brothers,
I beg leave respectfully to present to you Messrs. P. W. Dunne, of Peoria, Ill. and P. J. Meehan, of New York, both worthy and trustee members of the C.C.F.B. (Central Council, Fenian Brotherhood).

They are delegated to you by the H.C. (Head Centre) and C.C.F.B. (Central Council Fenian Brotherhood) with full powers to treat and arrange all existing relations between the organizations they represent at the I.R. (Irish Republic. i.e. I.R.B.). They will present you with copies of the resolutions, in virtue of which they are sent to Ireland. They will also fully explain to you verbally the objects of their mission.

For many reasons I will confine myself to bespeaking for them a cordial fraternal reception.

Your obedient servant,

JOHN O'MAHONY, H.C.F.B.

P.S. I enclose herein £500 sterling.

Enclosed in this letter of introduction were a draft for five hundred pounds and a personal letter from O'Mahony to Stephens asking that O'Donovan Rossa, who returned to Ireland on the same boat as Meehan and Dunne, should be sent back permanently to the F.B. headquarters in New York:

To James Power Esq.

Brother,   12th July 1865.

It is with extreme reluctance I let our friend O'Donovan Rossa leave me at this crisis. It is absolutely indispensable that I should have here a man like him, in whose honour I have implicit confidence, and in whose friendship and fidelity towards yourself your faith is unshaken. Send him back at once in view of prompt and cordial work.

JAMES MATHEWS.

The draft was in these words:

New York,
£500   July 11th, 1865

Three days after sight pay this our first of exchange, second and third of same tenor and date, unpaid, to the order of George Hopper, the sum of five hundred pounds sterling, value received as advised.

Per pro Auguste Belmont and Co.

W. LUTTZEN.

To Messrs. A. M. Rothschild and Son, London.

Shortly after the news of the *Irish People* raid and arrests reached O'Mahony on 24 September, a dispatch from Stephens, marked 'confidential and private', and dated 'Saturday night, September 16' arrived.[1] It related in Stephens's diffuse and melodramatic style the news of the arrests and raid with the usual implied reproaches for O'Mahony and the transatlantic friends and brothers.

O'Mahony's summary, with the exception of two startling phrases gives its sense: 'Another dispatch from Stephens detailing the extent of our losses, including the "drafts", and requesting an immediate reply to be sent by hand, and that a trustworthy man be selected without delay and sent to Paris as our financial intermediary for the future. He attributed the immediate cause of the entire misfortune to the loss of the

[1] Quoted, Rutherford, Vol. 2, pp. 108–109 in part with errors and omissions; more correctly and at length, D'Arcy, pp. 76–7.

documents by "Plenipotentiary" P. J. Meehan. There can now be no doubt that it was so'.[2]

The first startling suggestion coldly summarized by O'Mahony ran: 'In our opinion, an agent should be at once sent to Paris and placed in communication with us. To this agent all large sums of money should be made payable. Should John Mitchel be available (and an effort should be made to have him so) he is the man'.

The second suggestion is a magnificent Stephens flourish:

'Well, long as I am free, I answer for everything. But once you hear of my arrest, only a single course remains to you. Send no more money from the States. Get all you can, though, and with it purchase all the war material you can. Gather all the fighting men about you, and then sail for Ireland. The heads here may be in the hands of the enemy, and much confusion may prevail; but with a Fenian force to rally them, be sure that overwhelming numbers shall be with you. But this must be done before next Christmas, after which date I would have no man risk his life or his money.'

For two months after the raids Stephens remained a free man. Even Nagle could not help his paymasters to discover the Captain's hiding place, although he had sounded Luby frequently on the eve of the swoop. He was living a peaceful, retired life with Kickham, Edward Duffy and Hugh Brophy, at a Dublin centre in Fairfield House, Sandymount. Then at last the news came to the Fenian prisoners in Mountjoy jail that the Chief had been taken, and Denieffe exclaimed in bitterness, remembering Nagle, 'Who is the wretch this time'?

This was a shrewd guess and it was true; Stephens had, in fact, been betrayed. The general belief, however, was expressed by A. M. Sullivan in his account, *New Ireland*, that Mrs Stephens had been closely shadowed and finally tracked to Fairfield House, and the explanation seemed so plausible that even Thomas Clarke Luby accepted it, with the comment that it was strange Mrs Stephens or her sister, Mary Hopper, had not been detected sooner. Luby only surmised this and thought Stephens himself had made an imprudent arrangement by

[2]*Irishman*, 22 February 1868.

sending his wife and sister-in-law to the *Irish People* office with notes and messages. He recalled Nagle's persistent questions and knew in this case Nagle was innocent for lack of opportunity. 'The wonder was that the Philistines did not beset his house before', he wrote to O'Leary.

Mrs Stephens and her sister, then and later, showed great skill in eluding their shadowers and eavesdroppers behind screens on jail visits to their relatives. Until the evening of 9 November, the Castle authorities had no suspicion that either the Captain or his wife or a nest of Fenian celebrities were in Fairfield House. Even the reference given to the landlord for his quiet and respectable tenant, 'Mr Herbert' by Mr Joseph Denieffe, tailor, South Anne Street, Dublin, had been no clue. Mr Denieffe, in spite of his Fenian activities, had enough personal circumspection and such conservative business connections that he was regarded as a most respectable citizen. When the detective Clifford arrested Denieffe in the general swoop on the Fenians, it was with an apology, and the words, 'I am sorry to see a gentleman like you connected with such people!'

In 1910 the recollections of John Mallon were edited and published by Frederick Moir Bussy as *Irish Conspiracies*. When a serial version of this appeared in 1909, John Devoy, in the *Gaelic American*, made a sharp and critical examination in a series of articles. Devoy accepted the version of the arrest of Stephens given by Mallon, and recalled that it confirmed the suspicion current in some Fenian circles that Stephens had been betrayed.

Bussy and Mallon disguised the actual discovery in a vague statement that the informant was an old man who went to the police and reported 'that three or four men whom he had occasionally seen about the steps of the *Irish People* office before the raid, were in the habit of arriving at Sandymount station and crossing the line there to a lonely house that was close handy'. A detective disguised as a policeman, proceeds the tale—as the conceited Stephens would never expect a mere constable to be concerned with him 'instead of the entire paraphernalia of the whole British Secret Service'—won the confidence of the gardener, and obtained a description of 'Mr

Herbert' which the 'G' division man, Dawson, who knew Stephens well, at once identified, and the raid and arrest followed.[3]

Superintendent Daniel Ryan's report of this to Larcom revealed a more malign animus at work against Stephens than that of a law-abiding old man telling the police he was afraid the Fenians were up to mischief. He never received the hundred pounds reward offered by the Castle for information about Stephens. Bussy merely states 'that he was well looked after by the police authorities, and his position in his line of life considerably enhanced.' He was probably a casual tout. Ryan described him as a man who called into the detective office in the Castle on Thursday evening, 9 November, and told Inspector Hughes that a gentleman named Herbert was living in Fairfield House, Newbridge Avenue, Sandymount, ever since the beginning of July. Mr Herbert and his wife used to go into the city every day until the *Irish People* raid, but were since then seldom out of doors, and then only at night. The man thought he had seen Mr Herbert standing at the door of the *Irish People* office once, and that he might be Stephens, although this surmise was merely suspicion. This was quite obviously an evasion or fear because the report proceeds to note that the informer 'would not wish his name to be mentioned'. He then gave on request such a minute description of Stephens and his wife that Superintendent Ryan knew he had located the Captain. The informer was thanked and sent on his way. Stephens had been sold cheaply enough but he was soon to teach his pursuers that economy in such matters never paid.

Superintendent Ryan happened to know Mr Nathaniel Halbert, the landlord of Fairfield House, who told him that Mr Herbert had taken the place in July, and given as a reference, Mr Denieffe of South Anne Street, known at once to the Superintendent as one then in custody for high treason! Sadly had Mr Halbert been deceived by the respectable Mr Denieffe, who led him to believe that Mr Herbert was one of the Herberts of Muckross, Killarney—although Mr Stephens,

[3] F. M. Bussy ed., *Irish Conspiracies, Recollections of John Mallon, the Great Irish Detective*, (London, 1910) pp. 20–1; Devoy, *Gaelic American*, New York, 21 August 1909; Denieffe, p. 110; Luby Papers. p. 118.

in a pleasant interview, made no such claim. Mr Herbert paid the rent in advance and appeared to be a gentleman of means and position. Halbert's description of 'Mr Herbert', with his now suspicious reference, convinced Ryan that it was indeed Stephens.

A shrewd detective of the 'G' political division, one Rothery, was disguised as a plain clothes policeman on duty in Sandymount district. He soon became friendly with the gardener at Fairfield House, and a few chats supplied enough evidence to justify action. Between six and seven o'clock on Saturday morning, 11 November, the entire 'G' division under Colonel Lake, ten constables from another division, six inspectors, and Superintendent Dan Ryan, all very pleased with themselves, surrounded Fairfield House. The six inspectors climbed over the garden walls and approached the hall door. All around the house, in suitable positions, were stationed the 'G' division and their ten auxiliaries.

One of the inspectors knocked at the hall door and a voice from within asked whether it was Carrigan, the gardener, who came early every morning.

'No, it is the police!' said one of the inspectors, Acting-Inspector Hughes. One of his clerks, Michael Breslin, was a Fenian agent, who was soon kicking himself in Hughes's office for grave inattention to his Fenian duty. His brother Niall was a Fenian centre, his brother John was a hospital steward in Richmond Prison, his four other brothers, including Thomas, a policeman, were all Fenians.

After a pause, Stephens told the police that he could not open the door as he was undressed, and Hughes then threatened to break it down. The door was opened by Stephens who said he was Mr Herbert, and asked their business. He went back to his bedroom followed by Acting-Inspectors Dawson and Hughes.

'How are you, Stephens?' asked Dawson.

'I am Stephens', came the sharp answer, 'and if I had notice of your coming I might have surprised you. But who the devil are you, sir? Oh, *Dawson*, yes, I have seen your name in the papers'.

Turning to his wife and sister-in-law he told them he would

not see them again, and forbade them to ask permission from the prison authorities to visit him. 'Die first, and so will I !'

Dressing at leisure, he assured his captors that he did not propose to offer resistance, adding with a glint in his eye, 'If I had anticipated your visit, I should soon have discovered whether you are men. And if I escape, you will have a damned hard job to catch me again'. All of which Superintendent Ryan duly related to Larcom.

A glance through the windows had shown Stephens that escape or fight was impossible, there was a strong guard of police on every side, and from other rooms came sounds of search. Some documents were found in Stephens's coat pocket but none elsewhere. Two loaded six-barrelled revolvers were found in a room adjoining Stephens's bedroom, and two more on a dressing table in the room occupied by Kickham, Duffy and Brophy. The raid was entirely unexpected. The quiet two months in Fairfield House had given the garrison a false sense of security. The prisoners were driven direct in cabs to the Commissioner's office in the Lower Castle Yard, and appeared before Mr Stronge, Chief Magistrate, who remanded them to Richmond Jail until 14 November.

Two days later, Inspector Hughes and a colleague were standing at the door of the Head Police office in Exchange Court, Dublin Castle, near the City Hall when an indignant Fenian, Tom Frith, opened fire and wounded him slightly. Hughes fell stunned and lay for a moment on the sidewalk. Frith walked to a waiting sidecar and escaped. Devoy and others had known of Frith's plan and tried to stop him as he was acting against the standing order that no attempt of the kind should be made nor resistance offered to arrest. Devoy, who had something more serious on hands, hurried Frith out of the country the next day.

Devoy had been in charge of the Fenian organization of the Irish soldiers in the British army, and in close touch with every barracks in Dublin and the main garrison centres in the country. He was in touch with some thirteen thousand sworn Fenian soldiers, and like General Millen, head of the Fenian Military Council, and Colonel Thomas J. Kelly—both envoys of O'Mahony and busy on the preparations for revolt—

regarded these as the Fenian trump card, and as the shortest and surest source of Fenian armament. He was very soon in touch with Michael Breslin who had interesting conversations with his brothers Niall and John.

Niall, the Fenian centre, met his brother John, the hospital steward in Richmond Jail, some time after Stephens's arrest. John had a conversation with Stephens the day after the arrest, and was greatly impressed, although he was not a sworn Fenian. Niall, who saw great possibilities in this brotherly link with Richmond Jail, suggested schemes for the release of Stephens, but these were coldly received by John who demanded proof from some superior authority, 'of more importance than you', that Stephens was an irreplaceable loss to the organization, in which case an escape possibly might be arranged. Niall put John in communication with Devoy and Colonel Thomas Kelly, and soon afterwards Michael Breslin, in his police uniform, acted as Fenian courier between Stephens and them.

Before this contact was established Stephens and the other Fairfield House captures were again before Mr Stronge. After some formal proceedings, Mr Stephens electrified the court with the emphatic declaration:

'I feel bound to say in justification of, rather than with a view to my own reputation, that I have employed no lawyer or attorney in this case, and that I mean to employ none, because in making a plea of any kind or filing any defence—I am not particularly well up in those legal terms—I should be recognizing British law in Ireland. Now I deliberately and conscientiously repudiate the existence of that law in Ireland—its right or even its existence in Ireland. I defy and despise any punishment it can inflict on me. I have spoken!'

And Stephens was there and then committed for trial on 27 November, and sent back to Richmond, then one of the strongest jails in the city. He was quite unaware when he spoke that any rescue plan or escape was possible, and his outburst had been spontaneous. Certain precautions were taken in the prison, yet they all broke down in the presence of one sworn Fenian, Daniel J. Byrne, night watchman, and John Breslin, already won by Stephens's magnetism and the careful plans of

16

Colonel Kelly and Devoy. It was useless to lock up the keys of the corridor in which Stephens's cell was located—when Byrne had already made wax impressions of them; or to instal a convict with a gong to be rung at any suspicious sign in the next cell or to place a guard on doors which led to the body of the prison.

Ten days after his defiant speech Stephens was free. John Devoy, at Kelly's request, chose nine men as a bodyguard for Stephens, and turned up outside the walls of the prison on the night of 24 November, all armed with revolvers and with a rope ladder. It was a dark and rainy night and the wait for the signal—a handful of gravel over the wall—for the ladder to be thrown across, was long and wearing. At one o'clock Breslin left the hospital ward, opened the door into the corridor and entered Stephens's cell. The police guard outside the other door of the corridor heard nothing. McLeod, the convict with the gong, candidly informed the reproachful Governor Marquess next day that he had heard someone unlock Stephens's cell, and gave the unanswerable apology, 'Whoever could enter one cell could enter mine and cut my throat!' Breslin led Stephens to the prison yard. A high wall between this yard and the Governor's garden had to be crossed before the outer wall was reached. A ladder in the yard relied on for this now proved too short as Byrne by an oversight had not tested it. Byrne, however, was on the alert, and when Breslin hurried back to tell him about the ladder he helped him to bring out tables on which the ladder was placed, and Stephens crossed in safety, and in turn gave the signal, grasped the rope and was soon among his rescuers. Kelly and he hurried to their hiding place, the house of Mrs Boland, whose brothers James and John O'Connor played a prominent part in Fenian history.

Stephens's final destination, where he remained until he left the country, was the house of Mrs Butler, a fashionable dressmaker in Kildare Street, nearly opposite the loyalist Kildare Street Club.

When the news became known, the Viceroy, Lord Wodehouse, wrote to Larcom: 'All our work is undone!'

THE police were quite baffled in their search for Stephens, in spite of the reward offer issued in a proclamation by Larcom, of one thousand pounds for the capture, and three hundred pounds for information of Stephens, who was thus described:

'James Stephens is about 42 years of age, 5 feet, 7 inches high, stout make, broad high shoulders, very tight, active appearance, fair hair, bald all round the top of his head; wore all his beard which is sandy, slightly tinged with grey, rather long under chin, but slightly round jaw approaching the ears, tender eyes which defect seems to be constitutional, and has a peculiar habit of closing the left eye when speaking; high cheek bones and rather good-looking; hands and feet remarkably small and well-formed, and he is generally dressed in black clothes'.

T. D. Sullivan immediately suspended hostilities with Stephens and the Fenians, and mocked Larcom in verse:

Forth went the royal mandate to all the British lands,
    Saying his shall be One Thousand Pounds who brings into our hands
A wicked Irish rebel, five feet seven inches high,
    Light haired and fresh complexioned, who winks with his left eye.

Wodehouse wrote privately to Lord John Russell that he was mortified that the Fenians had proved that their boasts that they had agents everywhere was only too true, and that there was not much hope of the recapture of Stephens. He also wrote to Larcom that the only course about another humiliating event was for them both, Viceroy and Under-Secretary, just to say nothing. It had been revealed at a Cork courtmartial on a Fenian centre and some Fenians for swearing in soldiers, that one Fenian had indiscreetly assured one of the soldiers that the arrest of Stephens did not matter because there were five

Fenian warders in Richmond Jail and that, in fact, the escape of Stephens had been arranged. The soldiers had given information of this and a police report on the matter was lying unread in the Castle even as Stephens crossed the wall. The story, in fact, of the coming rescue of Stephens had reached certain Fenians, two hundred according to Devoy, and the Cork centre had heard it on a visit to Dublin. One of his circle, who heard it from him, somewhat nettled by a remark of the soldiers that perhaps the Fenians were not as strong as they thought when their leader was in jail, rapped out the truth, adding four warders for good measure.

And the ballad makers were rubbing it in around the Dublin streets with the impudent question:

> *Perhaps you'd like to know,*
> *Says the Shan Van Vocht,*
> *Which way did Stephens go,*
> *Says the Shan Van Vocht.*

As for Stephens's actual movements, Devoy and Denieffe vary greatly in their statements. The escape and the Fenian trials had keyed up popular enthusiasm, and thousands of new recruits were sworn into the Fenian organization, even from sections which had until then held aloof, the commercial and professional classes, while the mass of sympathizers grew steadily. The rank and file of the organization believed that the Captain would carry out his promise of insurrection before the end of the year.

Yet, according to Devoy, Stephens was deeply depressed by the split in the Fenian Brotherhood in America, where O'Mahony's leadership had been threatened, and the Canadian policy faction triumphant. Stephens and O'Leary realized that this was a fatal blow to the movement in Ireland in the very hour of greatest promise. Devoy, too, realized the gravity of this event, and, with justification, blamed Stephens for making it worse than it need have been. All three men understood at once that the funds and equipment intended for Ireland, as well as a number of Irish-American officers, would be diverted to the Canadian effort. Support for the I.R.B.

from America henceforward could come only from the much
weakened O'Mahony wing.

In what way was Stephens responsible for aggravating
the split? He made a grave miscalculation that his personal
influence, expressed in most peremptory and intemperate
language, would decide the issue and restore O'Mahony's
tottering leadership. He appointed O'Mahony Chief Agent
and Representative of the Irish Republic in America, in a
document drafted in unconciliatory terms, with a covering
personal letter denouncing O'Mahony's opponents in such
violently provocative language that the split could not be
avoided.

This letter—which the *Irishman*, 27 January 1866, published
with the comment, 'the great Irish leader of the Fenian movement is not only safe, but in a position to exercise the executive
powers in his office'—opened with an apology to O'Mahony,
and gave Stephens's summing up of Fenian fortunes:

'The only misunderstanding ever possible between you and me
has been occasioned by what I deemed your drag-chain policy.
Knowing the absolute necessity for action within a given time,
and aware that you did not agree with me in this, it has been a
constant fear with me that, so far as the Fenian Brotherhood is
concerned, the time would come and find us unprepared. This
apprehension has kept me in a state of pain and apprehension
also, and so I have often said and written things which must have
hurt you most keenly. For all this I now sincerely ask your
forgiveness. Let me add, however, that I would not do so, though
you were on your dying bed and I on mine, if you had not
entered, albeit very late, on the only path of salvation for our
land and race. Treason and baseness in every shape have been
at work around you, and to such effect as to have put the cause
of Ireland into serious peril. Before my escape from Richmond
Bridewell, I should have looked on the actual state of things as
all but certain ruin. That event—for it is nothing less—has given
such marvellous strength to our work, and to me such influence,
that I can now undertake to hold our forces together for some
time longer. Still it is of the utmost urgency to make the delay
as short as possible'.

This important statement of Stephens's mood and plans after
the escape is followed by violent denunciations of P. J. Meehan,

Michael Scanlon and other members of the anti-O'Mahony Senate F.B. wing, well peppered with exhortations, 'I would lash them from me like so many dogs', 'Away with all such fools or rogues', 'kindred carrion', 'cowardice and treason', 'may they never pollute our shores', 'cut and hack the rotten branches around you without pity'.

The document of appointment more coherently expressed these sentiments:

IRISH REPUBLIC

To the Members of the Fenian Brotherhood, and the friends of Ireland generally in the U.S. of America, Canada, etc.

Dublin, 23 December 1865.

COUNTRYMEN AND FRIENDS: Aware that certain members of the Fenian Brotherhood, and notoriously the 'Senate' of that association, have madly and traitorously moved to a mad and traitorous end, raised the cry of 'to Canada!' instead of the cry 'to Ireland!'; and aware that John O'Mahony, known as Head Centre and President of the Fenian Brotherhood, has, wisely and firmly, as in duty bound, opposed this mad and traitorous diversion from the right path—the only path that could possibly save our country and our race, I in consequence hereby appoint the said John O'Mahony Representative and Financial Agent of the Irish Republic in the United States of America, Canada, etc., with ample and unquestionable authority to enrol men, raise money, and fit out an expedition to sail for Ireland and reach Ireland on the earliest possible day, and in all other ways in which, to the best of his judgment, he can serve Ireland—that land to which he has devoted life and honour—I hereby authorize and call on him.

JAMES STEPHENS
C.E.I.R.[1]

Denieffe, who grew even more anti-Stephens than Devoy during this time, states that two days after the escape, Stephens held the largest meeting of Fenian centres and American

[1]Denieffe, Appendix, pp. 207–8. The *Irishman*, 27 January 1866, published this document as well as Stephens's letter, but with the reference to enrolment, money and an Irish expedition deleted.

officers he had ever held in the city. The meeting took place in the evening. During the day Stephens met provincial centres from all parts. And all discussions were concentrated on one question alone: the alternative of immediate insurrection or further postponement.

'I was more than surprised when Stephens selected me to give my opinion first. I told him I had only left prison two days before he did, and had not seen many friends, but would cast my vote with the American officers, who had closely investigated the situation, and were well posted on the true condition of affairs. All the Americans and all the Dublin centres expressed themselves in favour of immediate action until he came to Denis Cromien who was the only one at the meeting that argued and voted for delay. Stephens evidently was glad that our opinion was not unanimous and, to our surprise, endorsed Cromien's views.

'Notwithstanding, the majority were in favour of immediate action, and our discussion took up considerable time, it was eventually decided, mainly through Stephens's influence, that we would postpone the rising and wait. This resolution, to me, seemed simply a hocus pocus. Stephens plainly did not want to fight, and I made up my mind that he did not want to proceed any further; in fact, I concluded then and there that Stephens's work was done, and his usefulness ended on that night of 26 November 1865'.

This account cannot be reconciled with Devoy's memory of Stephens's movements at the time, nor with the known police reports which surmised that the Captain was lying very low indeed, and probably communicating with his followers and issuing instructions through his more confidential delegates. In one such report John Hickey of Kingstown was mentioned as the most probable channel. Hickey was the Fenian centre for Kingstown district, and one of the '49 group with which Luby worked in the fifties before Stephens returned in 1856. The police report was a mere guess as Devoy shows. He names Colonel Thomas J. Kelly, Chief of Staff, as the link between Stephens and the centres, adding that Kelly gave no hint that Stephens was deeply depressed in their daily interviews. Stephens, in truth, was in despair and almost in a panic. Invariably, in times of stress, his chronic dyspepsia asserted itself, and his complaints about his ill-health in his letters to O'Mahony make painful reading. So it was in '65 and so it was to be later in '67, even if in both cases, Stephens had good reason for hesitation and, possibly, for non-action.

In '65 Denieffe shrewdly sensed the sudden change of spirit in Stephens, who, in fact, was even pestering Mitchel in Paris with queries two months later, similar to those which disillusioned Denieffe. Mitchel was exasperated by Stephens's letters because Stephens knew Mitchel's opinion very well already; without American aid in a powerful expedition, impossible in the conditions which existed then, insurrection in Ireland was a hopeless gamble. Moreover, the British Government had struck a staggering and demoralizing blow at the leadership in the *Irish People* raid, and, what was even worse, pursued the process of determinedly wearing down the organization by constant raids and arrests of important officers.

On 10 March 1866 Mitchel wrote to John O'Mahony:

'The last letter but one I had from him [Stephens], the beginning of January was to ask my advice as to whether the outbreak should begin then, within a day or two, or be postponed for a month, when he said he was sure of being much better provided with material. Now, he knew my opinion at the time he wrote . . . So in my reply I told him I must decline to give any advice now on that point that he knew best what his resources were and what engagements he had taken . . . Again he wrote to me a few days later stating that neither he nor anyone else in the movement thought for one minute of settling down without a fight—that the question was only whether they should fight then or in the beginning of February. It is now near the middle of March, and the government has now, I suppose, made any respectable fight impossible . . . the prompt action of the English government was precisely what they ought to have expected—what they ought to have been prepared for—what they ought to have anticipated by striking two months ago—if they were to strike at all'.

In a long letter to Mitchel, in January 1866, Stephens sent a minute account of the I.R.B. organization in Ireland, a denunciation of the 'Canadian faction' in the U.S.A., the appeal mentioned for advice, with some characteristic flourishes: 'Our strength exceeds two hundred thousand sworn men in

Ireland alone . . . fifty thousand thoroughly trained men . . .
Of the enemy's garrison we have nearly one-third. We count
fully a third of them in Dublin. Rely on these figures, and
then say we can do nothing till France or America goes to
war with England'.[2]

Mitchel, so far as is known, made no further reply. He had
memories of a somewhat similar process and tragedy in 1848.
He saw, too, the significance of the Fenian Brotherhood split.
O'Leary similarly was to say later that this split meant that
the Irish cause was then temporarily lost.

In Stephens's figures to Mitchel, however, there was an echo
of discussions with a certain Fenian, who was most certainly
not of the opinion that the cause was at all lost, who had
played some part in the most effective counterstroke to the
Fenian trials and the British swoops on the Fenians, the rescue
of Stephens. This man, John Devoy, had at least a clear and
concrete plan which he pressed on Stephens and the Fenian
Military Council. As one of Stephens's chief agents in the work
of subverting the Irish soldiers in the British Army, he had
faithful helpers inside every Dublin barracks. He advised
Stephens and his lieutenants to wait for no problematical
American aid or expeditions, but order the Fenian soldiers to
seize the arms and war material within their reach, take over
the barracks and launch an insurrection in Dublin forthwith
as a signal to the rest of the still intact organization in the
country. Otherwise, the last chance was gone. This remedy was
a drastic one yet the situation was a desperate one, too.

Devoy regarded Stephens's tactics then with misgiving and
had reached the same conclusion as Denieffe. He was consistent in his own policy of using the Fenian soldiers, on the
recruiting of whom Stephens had at first frowned. Even those
critics of Fenianism, who afterwards dismissed it as an inefficient
and make-believe conspiracy in general, agreed that the one
dangerous element in it lay in the effective Fenian permeation
of the British army. Frank Hugh O'Donnell in his *History of the
Irish Parliamentary Party*, quotes a conversation with an American

[2]Mitchel's letter to O'Mahony is given Denieffe, Appendix, pp. 220–21; also
in part, Dillon, *Life of John Mitchel*, Vol. 2. pp. 231–33 where a brief summary of
Stephens's letter is added.

general. The general declared that the British military historian George Hooper informed him that in 1865 there 'was real danger of a surprise of the three chief arsenals in Ireland by several companies of disaffected soldiers, and the distribution of 30,000 stands of arms which would have given the conspirators what they wanted most.'[3]

This claim is confirmed by Devoy's memoirs, backed by some pointed facts and figures. His main plan concerned Dublin where he aimed at the capture of several barracks from inside, coinciding with a Fenian swoop on Dublin Castle, and the Pigeon House Fort where 30,000 rifles were stored, and a subsidiary project to capture Athlone military barracks from the inside where another 30,000 rifles and a battery of artillery were available, besides two hundred Fenian soldiers out of the light infantry guard of five hundred men there. In the Curragh Camp Devoy and his agents had won over twelve hundred men out of three thousand. Among the regular British forces in Ireland, who numbered some 26,000, Devoy listed 8,000 sworn Fenians; in the British establishment outside Ireland, 7,000 I.R.B. men; and of the 12,000 militia in Ireland, some 6,000. He adds that the records of the courts-martial on many of these Fenian soldiers, the long terms of imprisonment they endured, and the measures taken by the British Government, proved the sincerity of these men. Moreover, the trials also proved that all the Fenian keymen he had selected for his proposed seizures of military centres turned out to have been thoroughly reliable without a single informer among them.[4]

The discussions in Fenian circles are given more clearly by Devoy than by Denieffe in his recollections. According to Devoy, Stephens suddenly announced through Colonel Kelly towards the end of December, that he wished to meet the Dublin centres, and ordered them to be brought to Kelly's lodgings in Grantham Street in groups of not more than two

---

[3]F. H. O'Donnell, *History of the Irish Parliamentary Party* (London 1910), I., p. 5.
[4]Devoy, *Recollections of an Irish Rebel*, p. 130. Devoy gives the third section of his book, some six chapters, to a description of the Fenian organization in the British Army. Denieffe, p. 144, declares that the courts-martial revealed 13,000 sworn Fenians in the British forces in Ireland. A Fenian informer's Memo to Larcom in 1865, based apparently on hearsay and gossip in sympathetic circles, gave the Fenian strength in the regular forces at 4,000 and 11,000 in the militia.

or three, each group to retire as soon as the Captain's business with them was done to make room for another. This procedure was explained by the evident need to avoid attracting attention. Devoy suspected, that obvious as that need might be, the real explanation was that Stephens wished to avoid discussion and a vote. With Stephens at these interviews were the Fenian Military Council: Colonel Michael Kerwin, Colonel William G. Halpin, Colonel Denis P. Burke and Captain Doherty. Colonel Thomas J. Kelly as Chief of Staff was present at all these meetings.

Stephens's general arguments subtly insinuated into his informal discussions with the centres might well be summarized in the letters already quoted to Mitchel; how the split in American Fenianism had interrupted the supply of funds on which he depended to buy sufficient arms; messages he had sent to America might bring about better conditions in the organization there, so therefore a delay of three weeks or a month would be necessary for a correct judgment on the course of action; if at the end of that time the situation in America had not mended, then, of course, the fight must come off without American help.

And Stephens asked each centre in turn the equally subtle question, which Devoy grimly assumed had been framed by Stephens, with his black picture of the crux caused by the transatlantic faction fight, to suggest the answer: 'Could the centre hold his men together for three weeks or a month longer and keep them in condition for a fight at end of that time?'

All the centres, though a few reluctantly, gave the required answer, and to one truculent doubter who bluntly snapped at Stephens that he supposed he must give the answer Stephens intended him to give, the Captain, after a moment's dismay, smoothly assured this Matthew O'Neill, centre of one of Dublin's largest circles, and one of Stephens's rescuers from Richmond Jail, that after this short postponement, the fight would come off.

The American officers of the Military Council held their peace while Stephens spoke. They had already given him their real opinion before the centres arrived. Nothing could be secured by further delay, nothing Stephens could say or do

would heal the American split. Halpin and Kerwin had even
appealed to Stephens to give the word for an immediate
insurrection before all the Irish-American officers were
arrested, before the British authorities grappled with the
Fenian regiments, not one of which had yet been moved, and
before the constant raids and arms seizures crippled the
organization beyond repair. They urged him to make no more
postponements, but to make 1865, as he had promised, the year
of action, and reminded him they were meeting in the very
last week of December. They offered on behalf of the Military
Council to take full responsibility. Stephens listened with all
deference, said that the men themselves must decide, and they
decided as Stephens intended they should decide. And the
process was repeated with the country centres in interviews
with Stephens in a Dublin hotel, and with the same result.
And the 'Year of Action' passed out.

In February 1866, as in July 1848, Habeas Corpus was
suspended in Ireland, and raids, arrests, searches followed fast.
Most of the 150 American officers still at large were rounded
up, and some of the leaders of the Fenian soldiers, notably
John Boyle O'Reilly, detected and arrested. One decision of
Stephens, Devoy believed, prevented a spontaneous insurrection, an order that revolvers should, except in the case of a few
Fenians on special duty, be given up and stored in small depots.
This, in Devoy's opinion, prevented the assassination of the
more zealous and obnoxious detectives on anti-Fenian espionage work, clashes with raiding parties, and such a widespread
resistance that the Fenian soldiers would have deserted *en
masse* and joined in a bloody outbreak, 'the result would have
been bloody, but could not possibly have been more disastrous
to Fenianism than the most bloodless Rising of 5 March 1867
—a year later'.

Even as it was, Devoy, on several occasions, had to visit the
Dublin barracks disguised in soldier's uniform to restrain the
seething Fenians. He was somewhat exasperated by Stephens's
constant demands for descriptive reports about conditions
inside and the spirit of the Fenian soldiers in the British army,
instead of the brief cipher summaries of essential military
information regularly sent to him by Devoy. He obeyed this

order, which he considered a useless and dangerous one, with reluctance when he was compelled to confront his chief with a very critical and alarming report indeed, of threatened mutiny and widespread discontent with Stephens's waiting policy.

Among rank and file Fenians Devoy had clear evidence of growing tension, and also among the Dublin centres. Yet he was horrified when two of the centres, one among the soldiers in particular, asked him point-blank to 'pitch Stephens to the devil', and call out the Fenian soldiers at once. Devoy warned Stephens at once in general terms in a report on 20 February, and insisted that to end the tension there would have to be either a definite postponement or immediate action. Otherwise the Dublin organization could not be held together.

Stephens took the warning seriously, and three conferences were held, at which the two remaining members of the Military Council still outside prison, Halpin and Kelly, Devoy himself, and four important members of the organization, Edmund O'Donovan, Mortimer Moynahan, David Murphy, and John Nolan and Mrs Stephens were present. The conferences were held in the house of Mrs Butler, nearly opposite the Kildare Street Club in Kildare Street, the very centre of ascendancy and loyalism, overlooking which Stephens sheltered unsuspected for several months.

Devoy pressed his plan again at these conferences, but finally even Colonel Kelly and Halpin felt forced to side with Stephens against him on the grounds that a simultaneous attack on the Dublin barracks was out of the question, because the 8,000 Fenians in the city had only 800 rifles, and about a thousand other weapons, shotguns, revolvers and pikes, in all, and that it was not immediately possible to bring over some 2,000 rifles stored in Liverpool—in which case Kelly and Halpin would have agreed to an amendment of Devoy's plan by an attack on Pigeon House Fort and Richmond barracks with inside help from the Fenian soldiers. The wholesale arrests of the American officers since the earlier conferences in December, including Colonel Kerwin, who was the most persistent advocate of insurrection, weighed much with those who opposed Devoy's proposals. In his opinion, when a majority of the meeting, after a discussion late into the night of 21 February, decided there was no hope of a successful start, the last chance of a rising in 1866 was thrown away, or of any effective Fenian move in the immediate future. Late the following night he himself was arrested with a group of his Fenian soldiers when police and military in strength swooped on Pilsworth's public house, James's Street, one of his regular meeting places. He was taken to Mountjoy Jail.

James Stephens decided to go to New York and impose unity on the riven movement in the United States. Devoy had noted during those long all-night conferences how intensely Stephens believed that he alone was absolutely necessary to the success of the movement, and must be the only arbiter in deciding its course.

EARLY in March 1866, John Flood, one of the Richmond escape bodyguard, approached his old friend, Captain Weldon, of Baldoyle, Co. Dublin, and arranged with him to sail James Stephens and Colonel Thomas J. Kelly to a port in northern France on his two-masted coasting collier, *Concord*. The vessel was aptly named since Stephens's mission was to restore American Fenian unity. The adventure appealed to the Captain because his own grandfather had helped in the escape of the United Irishman leader, Archibald Hamilton Rowan, by boat to France in May 1794. Weldon knew that the watch on coast and port was exceptionally vigilant. From end to end the Dublin quays were placarded with Larcom's second proclamation offering two thousand pounds for the capture of Stephens, or a thousand for information leading to his arrest. The crews of many of the ships that left the port were on the alert for these prizes.

To cloak the presence of Stephens, Kelly and Flood on board the *Concord*, Weldon discharged three of his usual crew, which left him two men, a boy, plus, as he put it, 'three nautical duffers'. He acted boldly when he discovered that two revenue cutters on each side of the Poolbeg lighthouse challenged and boarded any suspicious outward-bound craft. On 11 March, a pilot unsuspectingly told him that a ship had been thoroughly searched that day. On 12 March Weldon had the *Concord* in the river, ready to start. At 9 p.m. on Tuesday the 13th, he was on a landing steps on the Dublin quays by appointment. Stephens, Kelly and Flood stepped into his boat, and he sculled them to the *Concord* as quickly as possible. He cast off his moorings, and had the vessel hauled to the north side of the river to make sail. Yet manfully as his three nautical duffers worked at the winch, their lack of skill considerably delayed operations. It was not until 1.30 p.m. on Wednesday the 14th that they hailed the revenue cutter to ask the time, and gave the ship's name without attracting unwelcome notice. They sailed gaily between the two vigilant revenue cutters in the bay, unhailed and unmolested. Then a stormy and nightmare voyage followed, and they had to abandon hope of reaching France. After some nerve-racking misadventures, including gales and near-shipwreck, Weldon's overstrained imagination transformed an innocent Derry steamer into a pursuing British gunboat. Stephens, Kelly and Flood gripped their six-shooters with vows never to be taken alive, suddenly recognized the steamer, and laughed heartily. The three-day ordeal ended happily when Weldon landed them all safely at the Scottish port of Ardrossan, shook hands briefly, and never saw Stephens and the others again.

Such is Denieffe's version of the episode, which does not differ much from Colonel Kelly's two letters about it in the press, 21 March 1866. They all slept that night in Kilmarnock, took the mail train next morning to London where they stayed at the Palace Hotel near Buckingham Palace, arrived in France on Monday, 18 March, and reached Paris the same night. A more picturesque description was given by A. M. Sullivan in *New Ireland*, and other contemporary writers. In these accounts Stephens, as befits a hunted Fenian Chief, escapes under Fenian escort, heavily disguised and armed. He travels from Dublin in a coach and four for the coast and the lugger, France and freedom. John O'Leary commented ironically on this description that it was 'nearly as pure a piece of fancy as anything in Mr Rutherford'.[1]

Mr Rutherford, however, never sponsored that piece of fancy, but relied upon Colonel Kelly's letters for the event, even if he threw in some particularly nasty fancies about the Colonel directing Fenian murders from brothels, and planning massacre, sack and slaughter for the citizens of London. His account of the escape and Stephens's movements in Paris, however embroidered, was near enough to the mark. Colonel

[1] John O'Leary to the editor, *Freeman's Journal*, from Paris, 5 November 1877, printed in *Freeman's Journal*, November 1877.

Kelly was indeed breathing contingent fire, dynamite and sword in many a letter to the press—often it must be suspected with his tongue deep in his cheek, yet often indeed seriously enough, and with flamboyant prophecies, very briefly and grimly disproved:

> 'The next time James Stephens touches the Irish soil, he will show the British that their barbarous treatment of Irish patriots but added fuel to the national flame already kindled all over the island . . . Sir Hugh Ross the British Commander-in-Chief in Ireland will find, when he attempts to commit such devilish barbarities as those of which he was guilty in India, that he has not sepoys to deal with . . . Let him dare to carry out his black-hearted intentions . . . and there will be such a retribution, not alone in Ireland, but in the heart of the British Empire as will not be paralleled in history. The enemy left no stone unturned to make us fight before we were ready; they played a desperate card and lost. Just wait and see the effect of the arrival of Mr Stephens in America, and you will see I speak correctly. All is well for Ireland yet. Next Christmas I have confidence I will dine with you as a free and independent citizen of the Irish Republic'.[2]

Stephens blended conspiracy and social life in this short visit to Paris. Larcom's files in Dublin Castle were filled with the most contradictory collections of press cuttings on the Fenian leader's activities. The *Irishman*, 21 April, for instance, quoted the Paris correspondent of *The Times*, who gave the impressions of an unnamed French writer who had spent some hours in Stephens's company one evening at the house of an illustrious Academician 'who desired to surprise his guests by the presence of one who at this moment causes so much disquiet to the English government'.

The anonymous writer gave his impressions of Stephens: an elegantly dressed gentleman, of modest demeanour, who waited to be spoken to before speaking, and then replied in a simple and natural manner. When asked for details of his arrest, imprisonment and plans, Stephens spoke, according to

---

[2]*Irishman*, 31 March 1866; also quoted, Rutherford, Vol. 2, pp. 236–7; For Captain Weldon's account, see Denieffe, Appendix, pp. 208–11. For A.M. Sullivan, *New Ireland*, Ch. 22, 'The Richmond Escape'.

17

this none too favourable source, with both force and delicacy:

'My arrest took place because I wished it. For many hours I knew that the police were on my traces, and it was my pleasure to be arrested in order to prove that I could escape with the greatest ease. While in prison I was treated with the utmost regard. I wanted for nothing, and in this respect I cannot too highly praise the English government. But it was absolutely necessary to depart. I had expressed my desire to do so to a person of whom I was sure, with whom an unexpected circumstance put me in communication, and the prison doors, so to speak, stood open before me. I don't know whether anyone meant to stop me, but around me I saw only accomplices.'

A listener interrupted: 'But once out of prison, how did you manage to leave Ireland?'

'Once out of prison', explained Stephens, 'I fled to the country. Money and a revolver were given me. I then heard that a reward of £40,000 was offered for me, and that anyone who discovered me was to bring me to Dublin, dead or alive. I remained up to the time of my getting on board ship in the country, living during the day in a hut, and going out at night to reach another. In every place where I took refuge I was well known, indeed, I was expected there. Notwithstanding the large sum offered by the Irish government for my apprehension, nobody ventured to inform against me; and this single fact proves that Ireland was at my disposal'.

'And what are your plans?' asked the company.

The response, whether invented or truly reported, had the authentic Stephens ring:

'I am going to America for an army of 250,000 men who are expecting me, and I will return with them to deliver Ireland, my country, from the British yoke!'

The *Irishman*, 19 May, quotes with irony an 'assertion' from the Rome correspondent of *The Tablet* that Head Centre Stephens had been received by the Emperor Napoleon III in an audience which lasted about an hour, and that Stephens was also in lengthy consultation with M. Drouyn de Lhuys, Minister for Foreign Affairs. This report was rounded off by the insinuation that Fenianism was fostered, subsidised, and kept alive as much by Paris as New York to 'prevent England from taking an effective part in the great game of European politics by occupying her at home'.

On his arrival in Paris Stephens had been entertained by the wealthy and eccentric Marquis de Boissy, senator, anglophobe, epicure, and by several members of the French Academy, including Jules Sandeau, with whose family Stephens had been friendly during his first exile. The Marquis lived in a famous mansion in the Rue Saint-Lazare where the floors were richly decorated with quaintly designed carpets and fountains played in the main rooms to preserve the guests from boredom. His wife was Teresa Guiccioli, who had once won the heart of Byron—indeed she was the last of all the women who won his heart—and inspired some of his poems, to the great edification of the Marquis who admired Byron even more than he detested England. The French astronomer, Camille Flammarion, in his memoirs described the household. He noted with kindly scepticism, in spite of his lifelong sympathy with psychical research, that the Marquise, whom he described as still beautiful in the 'sixties, was always elegant, amiable, gracious, well-informed, and erudite. She had a boundless faith in spirit-rapping, believing herself to be in constant communication with Lord Byron, who advised her well and wisely on her financial affairs, gave most reliable tips for her speculations on the Stock Exchange, would do anything for her, and always sent the most cordial messages to the Marquis himself.

Whether Stephens, in spite of his avowed hostility to the Second Empire, was in touch with the French government or not, is a question he passes over in silence in his brief published references to this Paris visit, although he mentions his conference with de Boissy, Sandeau and other public men 'whose sympathy I found to be unreservedly on the Irish side'. He is silent, too, on the resumption of the old links with the French Republican Left. It was possibly at this time that he came in touch with the agents of the International Workingmen's Association which he joined later in the year in New York. It is known that Cesare Orsini—half-brother of Felice Orsini, the would-be assassin of Napoleon III in January 1858—who actually enrolled Stephens in that organization, was then in Paris. Cesare Orsini was a friend of William O'Donovan (known as

Dr Hamilton), the Fenian financial agent in the city. O'Donovan was one of the sons of the great Irish scholar, John O'Donovan.

John Augustus O'Shea relates an amusing visit of Orsini and O'Donovan to Alexandre Dumas. Orsini came to collect for a fund in aid of distressed Italian revolutionaries, and was cordially invited to take 'whatever the gods send you on the mantelpiece'. Orsini looked very glum when he found there five francs and a few sous.

'Money has wings!' said Dumas, 'but you know, Orsini, if it had been fifteen hundred francs, you would have been welcome to it. Is your young friend an Italian?'

O'Donovan said that he was from Ireland where he had known a member of the Dumas family who was a universal favourite there. Dumas was astonished until O'Donovan named the Count of Monte Cristo, whereupon Dumas kissed him on both cheeks and shouted aloud that the Irish were as witty and civilized as the French.[3]

Nearly two years later, in his weekly letter to the *Irishman*, 25 January 1868, O'Shea, with his tongue in his cheek, solemnly pointed out how absurd a report in a Belgian paper must be that documents seized during police raids in Paris proved that the chiefs of Fenianism in France were 'one Hamilton—a member of the Irish branch of the same family as the Duke of Hamilton—and Cesare Orsini, said to be in Paris conducting Fenianism', since Orsini had been in the United States for months, and no Irish branch of the Duke of Hamilton's family existed. In a second message O'Shea hinted that the French police had inspired the rumour. Indeed, a secret agent cornered by a group of Irishmen in Paris admitted that he was really engaged on inquiries about possible collusion between the Fenians, French Republicans, and other foreign revolutionaries. From later letters in the 'seventies it is clear that Stephens was friendly with these French revolutionary circles during the Franco-Prussian war, both before and after the fall of Paris. The Fenian informant, who recklessly or maliciously gave away

---

[3] John Augustus O'Shea, *Leaves from the Life of a Special Correspondent*, Vol. I. pp. 95–99. O'Shea mentions Orsini and Stephens were in Paris about the same time in 1866.

so many secrets to Chester Ives during an interview published in the *New York Herald*, 12 August 1880, declared there was no longer any connection between the I.R.B. and continental revolutionaries although Stephens once had an understanding with them.[4]

Stephens's membership of the International Workingmen's Association was broadly insinuated by Devoy in his memoirs, although that astute conspirator said nothing of his own membership of the same organization in 1871, after his release and arrival in New York:

'Dr Cullen based his assumption of an alliance with the Carbonari on the fact that James Stephens while a refugee in Paris had fought at the barricades in the Red resistance to Louis Napoleon's Coup d'Etat in 1851, and claimed that he was an enrolled member of the Communist Party. Even if he were, he never tried to convert the Fenians to Communism, and his chief lieutenants, O'Leary, Luby and Kickham were most conservative men'.[5]

In the last statement Devoy was completely justified. Luby publicly repudiated any attendance at or sympathy with the International in a letter, published in John Mitchel's paper, the *Citizen*, 30 March 1872; John O'Leary saw nothing in common between Ribbonism, Fenianism, and even the Land League, except illegality, and after '49, lost all sympathy with the Mitchel-Lalor views of the land question; Kickham, in spite of his sympathy with the tenants against the landlords, like O'Leary traced all Irish troubles to English political rule, and opposed Davitt and Devoy when they linked up the Fenian rank-and-file behind the Land League in the 'eighties.

Indeed, Stephens himself by then took up the very same hostile attitude, and his later statements suggest that his mind

[4]*Devoy's Post Bag*, Vol. I. pp. 546–8. Davitt was later informed by Chester Ives that the information was given to him by James or Joseph Mullett, both Dublin Fenians who afterwards became Invincibles. The interview gave a fairly accurate outline of the I.R.B.'s work from its foundation, including a summary of its constitution, with long quotations from its early rules of procedure. The interview was inspired by hatred of Davitt's Land League activities and revealed his expulsion from the Supreme Council in 1880.

[5]Devoy, *Recollections* . . . p. 118. Luby's letter to Mitchel is reprinted *Irishman*, 20 April 1872.

had grown more conservative or more disillusioned. His relations with the French Republican Left or other secret revolutionary bodies were never, apart from the vaguest of hints in some of his letters and diaries, explicitly set out by Stephens himself, while the interpretation of Fenian policy in general in his writings agrees with Devoy's own just quoted.

However, the membership of Devoy and Stephens of the International is proved by certain documentary evidence. Karl Marx in a letter to Engels, 17 December 1866, informed him that Cesare Orsini had reported to the Central Council of the International that he had enrolled Wendell Phillips, Horace Greeley, Charles Sumner and the Fenian Head Centre, James Stephens, 'the most doubtful of our acquisitions'. In a second letter, 4 July 1868, Marx told Engels that Orsini had been acting as agent for the Fenians and was in controversy with the Fenian Colonel Nagle over his conduct of this work.[6]

This somewhat obscure flirtation of Stephens with the International came to a head on 10 May 1866, one month after his arrival in the U.S.A. on his declared mission to restore harmony in the ranks of the Irish-American organizations. He was appalled that O'Mahony had allowed himself to be stampeded into the bungled and betrayed expedition to seize Campo Bello and anticipate the projected Canadian foray of the Roberts wing. The Campo Bello attempt was betrayed by Red Jim McDermott; the schemes of the Roberts wing in due course, apart from the independent espionage of Le Caron, were to be revealed by Rudolph Fitzpatrick, assistant secretary of war. Both McDermott and Fitzpatrick were on the payroll

[6]These references to the Marx-Engels correspondence are taken from an article, and some further references supplied to the writer by Paul O'Higgins, *Irish Workers Voice*, Dublin, October 1953, 'Fenian Leaders and Marx and Engels'. A letter from Marx to F. A. Sorge, North American secretary of the International, 12 September 1871, is quoted in the same article, asking him to hand an enclosure from J. P. McDonnell, then Irish Secretary of the International to Devoy. It is noted that when Sorge later published the letter, a footnote gave Devoy as Irish delegate in the I.W.A. North American Central Committee. See also, *Devoy's Post Bag*, Vol. I. pp. 19–22 for Sorge's address from the I.W.A. to the released Fenian prisoners, New York, February 1871; and p. 42, Sorge-Devoy, 23 June 1871 inviting, 'Friend and Colleague Devoy' to a General Meeting of the North American Central Committee, I.W.A. as delegate of Section VII, presumably the Irish one.

of the industrious Mr Archibald, British consul in New York.[7]

In a letter written to an unnamed correspondent in U.S.A. four years later, 28 March 1870, Stephens claimed with some justice that the Campo Bello fiasco had saved the Senate (Roberts) party but robbed the I.R.B. of 'a fair chance, not to say certainty of success', in Ireland yet added that O'Mahony had acted with the best intentions, that he had been placed in a false position by Stephens himself, who was compelled to place him there. Stephens insisted, however, that O'Mahony must resign in his favour and censured him severely for condoning Campo Bello against Stephens's orders.

A hostile writer in the London press greeted Stephens sarcastically as engaged in 'the great work of liberating Ireland in America', and then warmed up thus:

'Mr Stephens will receive only such attentions as are dictated by curiosity, and not such as are dictated by respect. The interest felt in him will be that which might be felt in a political Jack Sheppard and a political Barnum combined—in a clever prison breaker and clever charlatan. He has the gifts which impose on maid-servants and on ploughboys, and which seduce turnkeys and policemen from their duties'.

This critic had a historical sense for he ponderously conceded that Mr Stephens was the result of misgovernment. Irish history had made a conspirator of a man, 'whom nature had intended for a clever bustling attorney, fertile in expedients, and not over scrupulous in employing them, who with a more legitimate opening might have been a respectable local notability, in due time, it may be a borough magistrate, very hard upon offenders, and especially upon all promoters of privy conspiracy, sedition, and rebellion.[8]

A more shrewd critic and colleague of Stephens at this time, who accompanied him on many of his lecture and speech-making campaigns in the summer and autumn of 1866 judged him with more wit and depth. This was the man tartly summed up by John O'Leary as 'the inevitable and invariable

---

[7]See D'Arcy, *Fenian Movement* . . . pp. 136–141 for Campo Bello; pp. 260–61, Fitzpatrick.

[8]Press-cutting, *Daily News*, 25 May 1866, Larcom Papers, 'Fenianism', 1866.

Cluseret', whose account of his connection with Fenianism and Stephens, O'Leary indeed summed up with asperity as 'full of bad feeling, ignorance and misstatement, whether conscious or unconscious I know not'. Devoy took the contrary view both regarding the General and, above all, on his account of Fenianism and Stephens which Devoy with more justice found somewhat cynical but truthful in the main.

General Gustave Cluseret was later military leader of the Communards during the Paris Commune of 1871. He had been a specialist in wars and revolutions from June 1848, when he commanded a battalion of the Mobile Guard during the suppression of the Parisian workers' revolt. He won the Legion of Honour for carrying eleven proletarian barricades and for many ruthless exploits against the insurgents under their red flags, a most unexpected beginning for the man whose name was used later to link Fenianism in general with fabulous international conspiracies. His enemies in all camps agreed that he was a good fighter, a champion liar, able, tyrannical, vain and cantankerous.

Cluseret fought in the Crimea, in Algeria, in Sicily under Garibaldi, in the American Civil War under McClellan who made him a Brigadier-General, and where he also became a close friend of General Phil Sheridan.

In the wars and on his travels, Cluseret became a soldier of fortune with a turn for revolutions, a dislike of orators, and a weakness for describing his colleagues as imbeciles. He had been struck off the French Army list after the mysterious disappearance of a great number of military stores. Temporarily he returned to civil life to manage an estate for a trusting baron, but was dismissed when an entire flock of sheep under his charge most mysteriously disappeared. So he went back to the wars with a somewhat shady reputation.

Early in 1866 Cluseret arrived in New York from Mexico and met James Stephens. The General had already been in negotiation with the anti-O'Mahony Fenian wing which planned the Canadian invasion; but the invasion collapsed so quickly that, although Cluseret's assistance had been 'offered and accepted—my good intentions only were engaged'.

After several meetings with Colonel Thomas Kelly, Cluseret

held his first conference with Stephens in the house of a French republican refugee, Pelletier, later author of a history of socialism, and friend of the semi-mystic social reformer, Pierre Leroux. Cluseret thought that the Fenian leader, as an organizer, was indeed a man of superior merit, but also, as Cluseret wrote in a cynical mood in *Fraser's Magazine* in 1872, 'vain, despotic, and over-bearing beyond any man I ever saw. As regards action, he was worth nothing. I left the house, much disturbed in my mind'.

For all his cynicism and his personal distrust of Stephens, Cluseret was sympathetic and he accepted the military leadership of the proposed rising on the clear condition that he was given ten thousand armed men to lead. He submitted plans for a campaign based on the seizure of strategic points backed by flying columns. He appointed two military advisers, Fariola and Vifquain, Civil War veterans like himself, as his adjutants. Finally Cluseret sailed for England with a commission, obtained through Fenian influence, to inspect military organizations abroad for the State of New York. With documents issued by the American Legation in London, Cluseret gained permission to visit Woolwich Arsenal and Aldershot, and facilities to inspect militia, volunteer, and regular army depots in Great Britain.

Stephens had passed into political eclipse before Cluseret terminated his connection with Fenianism, which may be briefly summarized here. The information given by Corydon about the Fenian plans to capture Chester Castle and its armoury as well as the outbreak of the premature Fenian insurrection in Kerry earlier in 1867, cut short the Cluseret-Fariola inspection. Fariola suspected that Massey—later an informer—had treacherously leaked the Fenian plans the same year to the London correspondent of an American paper.

Early in March 1867, the horrified Anglophile American diplomats learned that Fariola and Cluseret, whose visit to Britain they had unwittingly aided, were under suspicion as Fenian agents, a suspicion soon verified at the Fenian trials.

At the trial of Thomas Bourke in April 1867, Lord Chief Justice Whiteside remarked as he imposed the death sentence: 'The 5th of March was fixed on for this rising in arms, and in the proclamation of your directory—an appeal was made to the workmen of England to assist the disaffected in this country in the intended insurrection'.

Massey, in evidence, described conferences of the London Fenian directory and meetings with Fariola, Cluseret, and Colonel Thomas Kelly. At one meeting in the Colonel's lodgings Fenian delegates discussed one proclamation complaining of the wrongs of Ireland; calling on the people of Ireland to take up arms; and invoking the aid or sympathies of the workmen of England. Massey did not believe that it was ever distributed or published in Ireland.

In fact, the full text appeared in the London *Times*, 8 March 1867. This document bore all the traces of General Cluseret and some Irish-American Fenians with strong land nationalization and semi-socialistic views in earnest collaboration, by its mingling of styles and phrases and a pooling of ideas by no means common to the Fenian membership as a whole. The final passage read:

'Republicans of the entire world, our cause is your cause. Our enemy is your enemy. Let your hearts be with us. As for you, workmen of England, it is not only your hearts we wish, but your arms. Remember the starvation and degradation brought to your firesides by the oppression of labour. Remember the past, look well to the future, and avenge yourselves by giving liberty to your children in the coming struggle for human freedom. *Herewith we proclaim the Irish Republic*'.[9]

Yet in the end, thoroughly disillusioned because the promises made to him had not been kept, Cluseret, on the eve of the 1867 rising, returned to France. At a final conference in London with the Fenian directory there, Cluseret, supported by Vifquain, as a military man advised against an insurrection in the existing circumstances and with the failure of the organization to secure supplies and arms. William Harbinson, Ulster delegate and colour sergeant in the Antrim militia, agreed with this opinion also on military grounds. The London directory rejected the objections, and Cluseret's proposals for

[9] For full text, see *Charles Bradlaugh* by his daughter, H. B. Bonner, (London 1906), Vol. I. Ch. XXV, where an interview with Cluseret and Colonel Kelly, who sought Bradlaugh's legal advice on this proclamation, is also described.

a working agreement with the Reform League, some surviving Chartist groups in Great Britain, and certain French, German and Italian exiles. Most unjustly, a furious Communard writer later accused the General of pushing the Fenians into revolt and then leaving them in the lurch. It must be admitted that although his military leadership of the Commune while it lasted was more competent than that of his rivals, and that he made a genuine attempt to save the hostages, in particular the Archbishop of Paris, from slaughter by the ruthless and bloody-minded Ferre and Rigault, his contemporaries, including detached critics like E. A. Vizetelly, suspected that he was in negotiation with the Germans and later with Thiers during the sieges of Paris.[10]

Before he wrote his cynical criticism of Fenianism, as a disillusioned exile after the Commune, Cluseret had expressed a more sympathetic mood towards the Fenians and their leaders in an article in the *Courier Français*—quoted and translated, *Irishman*, 25 January 1868—and showed some sympathy with Stephens in eclipse:

'That all my sympathies are with the Irish Fenians I do not deny. I feel proud of avowing that I am acquainted with their chiefs in America. I also confess that I have a knowledge of their principal men and their designs . . . I have known Stephens, Bourke, Kelly and many others. Although some of them have been sacrificed to the blind passion of party, they are yet gallant men who have made sacrifices for the cause of their country and liberty, unhappily unheard of in this age of selfishness and mean ambitions. Some of them like Bourke, are of the true Roman mould, and will be transmitted to posterity, as the ideal of self-abnegation and sacrifice. Mere errors of judgment, following undoubted proofs of devotion and self-abnegation and sacrifice are forgotten by the people, others, more or less perfect, will be engraved on the memory of the Irish people for services rendered to their common country . . .

'Whether Fenianism be the work of Stephens, continued by

[10]E. A. Vizetelly, *My Adventures in the Commune* (London, 1914); *Republican France 1870–1912* (London 1912), *passim*. Cluseret's sharp and sardonic *Fraser's Magazine* attack on the military and political aspects of the Paris Commune provoked its historian, Prosper Olivier Lissagaray, to most vitriolic comments. *Histoire de la Commune de 1871* (Paris 1896) *passim*.

Bourke and Kelly, and perfected by new victims and martyrs or not, it does not deserve the less credit from free nations, because it has established itself in Ireland—a country hitherto a stranger to any sentiment except the faith and clerical rule.

'The programme of actual Fenianism is grounded on three principal points, first, complete independence of Ireland from English power; second, a free church and a free state; third, the republican form of government'.

SOME thirty Fenian officers were present at the stormy New York meeting summoned by Stephens for 15 December 1866. These included those more directly engaged in preparations for the much publicised and long-announced insurrection, his deputy Colonel Kelly, Captain John McCafferty, Godfrey Massey (or Condon), General Thomas F. Bourke, and General William Halpin. Some hours of bitter and violent argument ended in his removal as Head Centre of the Fenian Brotherhood in America. His overthrow as head of the I.R.B. at the hands of the same group was not to be long delayed, to the cry of 'Stephens does not mean to fight', and a split in the leadership of the group that overthrew him. His life was threatened. Only the intervention of Colonel Kelly saved him when Captain John McCafferty, future founder of the Invincibles, former confederate officer and the most desperate man in the entire Fenian movement, drew a pistol to dispatch Stephens without more ado. McCafferty had been infuriated when Stephens had urged that insurrection must be again postponed because the Fenian Brotherhood had failed to supply the minimum of arms and funds stipulated and agreed upon.

Essentially Stephens was right in his decision which he must have foreseen for several months. In spite of all his strenuous seven months' speechmaking and campaigning in America, some few thousand pounds—four thousand according to O'Mahony, two thousand and five hundred according to his own —had been transmitted to Ireland. And as serious again were the figures he gave to the meeting of the war material in the Fenian Brotherhood's arsenals, which amounted in all to less than one-fourth of the minimum laid down by him, which was thirty thousand rifles.

Of the men who deposed him, Halpin was the most friendly;
Kelly almost insanely embittered, since he was soon to be
hurling the same reproaches as Stephens, with far less restraint,
against the American Fenians; McCafferty the most impetuous,
a freelance whose individualism was to tangle up the plans of
the foredoomed insurrection, (the funds for which were to
amount to some few thousand pounds realized on the sale of
one of the Brotherhood's steamers sold, according to Cluseret,
for little more than the engines alone had cost). Well might
John Mitchel describe the plight of any supreme Fenian leader
just then as a man holding wolves by the ears. Mitchel still
nursed his animosity against Stephens, resenting his flamboyant
campaign, and refusing bluntly to countenance by his influence
the intended insurrection. He advised the Fenian Brotherhood
leaders privately against any action whatever, 'while England
is at peace with America and France, all invasions and
insurrections will be in vain. It is not that I stand for
"civilized" warfare. The Irish have the clear right to strike
at England anywhere or anyhow, in Canada, in Ireland, in
London, by steel or gunpowder or firewood. But I hold that
those who undertake any such warfare at present, whether
civilized or uncivilized, must perish and perish in vain. With
these views you must see that I could not join in any new
appeal for money for war materials, or any new representations
of the near approach of an insurrection or invasion'.[1]

If Mitchel had read Stephens's egotistic and semi-hysterical
description of his deposition, he would have claimed he was
justified in his bitterest judgments on the man. And it is
painful reading, and, as usual with Stephens's apologias,
wordy, rambling and full of everything except the important
point even when that important point is his best defence.
Three accounts, apart from anonymous ones, mostly published
after his death, exist of the meeting: Massey's evidence as an

[1] D'Arcy, *Fenian Movement* . . . pp. 225–6, Mitchel to Mortimer Moynahan,
28 January 1867, quoted from the O'Mahony Papers. Mitchel also ironically
said he had kept silence on Stephens's activity 'lest I should discourage our
honest fellow-countrymen here from sustaining him in case he should, after all,
mean what he said'. Mitchel agreed that the Irish-American impatience for
immediate results rules out a Fenian organization exclusively agitational, run at
minimum expense, and patiently awaiting its opportunity.

informer at the trial of Thomas F. Bourke in Dublin, 1867; Stephens's own; and a brief one by Cluseret, all of which agree in general—the most favourable and the most truthful being that of Massey, the informer. Massey and Stephens were present, Cluseret apparently not, although closely in touch with Colonel Kelly, and a frequent though silent observer at similar conferences.

Massey gives the figures on Fenian armament and funds quoted before, which Stephens omits completely from his account, as he also omits the threat to his life, although he admits there were words, hints, and reproaches. Massey, while silent on McCafferty's attempt to shoot Stephens, makes very clear the clash between the two men.[2]

Cluseret in his *Fraser's Magazine* articles, 'My Connection with Fenianism', July 1872 (later republished as a pamphlet and quoted in part, *Irish Freedom*, Dublin, October 1913), states clearly that Stephens's life was in danger. His brief sketch of the crisis does full justice to the unselfish and headlong idealism of the anti-Stephens leaders of the 1867 insurrection:

'Stephens, who, as it would seem, by no means deceived himself about his material resources, began to blow cold, and he had hitherto blown hot. So long as it was a matter of going onwards the American Irish had been tolerably obedient to the despotic requirements of their Head Centre, but the moment they imagined they saw symptoms of coldness in him and as month succeeded month and the end of the year approached, and yet no announcement had been made of the campaign, they became indignant and enraged; in short, they deposed him and his life was even threatened.

'Kelly through whom I had become acquainted with Stephens, and who had been the means of assisting him to make his escape from prison, Halpin, Bourke, McCafferty, and several others were at the head of this movement, the majority of them having been Confederate officers . . . As will be seen hereafter, these men knew what they had to trust to as regards the material means and resources of the administration—they did not deceive themselves as to what would be the result of these intrigues, or the fate that

[2]*Report of the Trials of Thomas F. Bourke and Others* . . Dublin Special Commission, April 1867 (Dublin 1869), p. 167 *et seq.*

awaited them—they were men capable of self-sacrifice, heroes in
the full chivalrous meaning of the word'.

Massey's evidence makes clear that there were, in fact,
several meetings, three in all—December 15–17—at one of
which Cluseret was present, the last two meetings being held
in Stephens's lodgings, No. 11. West-Eleventh Street. Stephens,
and this extraordinary statement is confirmed by himself,
'objected to open the fight, as he had promised; but to prove
his fidelity to Ireland, he offered to come to Ireland, put
himself in the hands of the British authorities and get hanged. . .
The proposition was scouted by everyone present'. An uneasy
truce seems to have resulted. Although Stephens was deposed
as American Head Centre, he still remained head of the Irish
Republican Brotherhood in Ireland, and civil head as opposed
to military chief of the Fenian Brotherhood in America,
although his policy was rejected by the leaders who had
decided on insurrection in Ireland. That the meetings were
held at Stephens's lodgings, where he lay low the preceding
month while the Fenian leaders spread the story that he was
on his way to Ireland, disproves Rutherford's highly coloured
story of pickets on a luxury hotel where Stephens hid from his
infuriated colleagues. Stephens, in fact, had gone into hiding
on 28 October after a final burst of rhetoric at a Fenian rally
where he stated that he would next be heard of when he led
his army in Ireland into action. The British Government had
alerted all its consuls in the U.S.A. to convey immediate news
of Stephens's departure from any American port, his destination, details of the vessel in which he travelled, to the British
Consul at Washington who was instructed to communicate the
information to London immediately. Many arrests of suspects
were made in Ireland, military reinforcements poured into the
country, and Stephens's words on his disappearance in October
widely believed: 'My last words are that we shall be fighting
on Irish soil before the 1st of January, and I shall be then in
the midst of my countrymen'.

Only once in all his whirling speeches had he hinted at the
hard choice that was slowly being forced upon him, and few
seemed to have noticed the warning. In a speech to the women's

auxiliary Fenian organization, the Fenian Sisterhood, at Jones's Wood, New York, on 22 September 1866, his words, in view of what occurred three months later, not only revealed his real thoughts, but were indeed the sentiments of a supreme Fenian leader holding wolves by the ears:

'I will not say anything else except that it is my deliberate intention to go to Ireland this year, and let no man be mistaken in this. Some men have said that if I were in earnest I would not make it public; but these are men who, either by their treachery or their blunders, made it a necessity for me to do so. I chose this course only as the least of the two evils forced on me because if I did not make a definite statement, I could not hold the men in Ireland together, they have been so much meddled with; nor the men in this country either; their complaints have reached me, and it is therefore that I am forced to say that I will undoubtedly be in Ireland this year, for I fully believe that if I did not go over, they could not be held in over there, and the fight would go on without me.

'If I thought it would be any gain to delay, I would do so and risk all my popularity; but I cannot for they are determined on fighting this year, and I am fully determined on being with them, come weal or woe. No matter what others say, take my word I will be in Ireland, and the people will strike a blow for liberty'.[3]

Stephens's arrogant and impetuous self-confidence had led him into a fatal trap. O'Mahony, as we have seen, had always condemned the slogan of 'we fight in 1865, in 1866—or we dissolve'. General Millen, as one of O'Mahony's envoys, after his first interview with Stephens in May 1865, had been staggered that he had committed himself publicly to action at any particular time, 'as a revolutionary movement from the nature of it was a secret one, and such as prevented a leader from saying even to himself, much less to his friends, that he would take action at any given time'.[4]

The deposition was a blow to Stephens's pride which unnerved him, and in the crisis of 1865, provoked an attack of his old enemy, dyspepsia, and at the critical meetings during December and January he looked haggard and ill. His writings

---

[3]*Irishman*, 13 October 1866.

[4]*An Account of Fenianism from April 1865 to April 1866 . . . by one of the Head Centres for Ireland* (Millen) Nat. Lib. M.S. 5963, p. 34.

18

of this time reek with self-pity and are full of complaints of his ill health, in spite of which, one acid commentator remarks, he managed to survive another thirty-four years. Such comments are inevitable on a reading of his *Statement made in January 1867, in New York by James Stephens, Chief Organizer, Irish Republic, as to the reasons why he had not returned to Ireland in 1866.*

Several copies—with slight variations—of this statement, which is in his own handwriting, exist; one from the O'Mahony Papers, cited in part by Father D'Arcy in his *Fenian Movement in the United States*, pp. 218–20; a second in the Devoy Papers in the National Library of Ireland. Pigott in his recollections quotes two of the most damaging lines he can find from this statement which he styles 'dispatch to the Fenian Centre in Cork'.[5]

On the contrary, the document headed to 'All whom it may concern', and opening 'Friends and Brothers' was obviously for all the I.R.B. centres. Whatever copies reached Ireland, and from Pigott's reference some obviously did, were probably forwarded by George Hopper who was sent to Paris by Stephens with instructions to inform Mrs Stephens and his sister-in-law, Mary Hopper, that they must embark at once for Le Havre, and meet him in France.

A close reading of the document proves that Stephens is playing for time, and indeed to postpone the insurrection. But the passages quoted by Pigott, or summarised by him with a certain malice, leave a very damaging impression. This is reinforced when taken in combination with Stephens's previous admission that at the meeting of 17 December, chiefly of Fenian military officers, he 'asked these to volunteer to go home and the majority did so, and in making such a request at such a time, it must be evident that I meant to bring on the fight as soon as possible'. Yet such an adverse impression is essentially a very false one of his actual conduct and motives.

There was no need to tell the assembled wolves, whose ears had slipped once and for all from his grip, to take the course they had decided on, and whether Stephens went through the ritual of 'ordering them to Ireland on the pain of their

---

[5]It is possible that the Devoy and O'Mahony versions of this statement are drafts of a final version. Stephens had a mania for revision.

allegiance', as Devoy reminded him for the rest of his life, matters little. They no longer heeded what the fallen Chief might tell them, and he had grown so used to unscrupulous flourishes in his heart-breaking campaign that one flourish more or less hardly troubled him, and the word 'possible', sounding like a litany through the message, meant 'impossible' screened by much warlike invective.

The essential paragraphs of this statement dated January 1867, from New York are:

'This would be addressed to a friend in Dublin [Edward Duffy, his deputy in Ireland] but for the uncertainty of finding him, and the necessity of making known its contents without delay . . .

'I trust there is no man in Ireland so ignorant, base and ungrateful as to think I would not keep my promise and fight by the New Year's dawn. I meant it and but for the breakdown in my health would have kept my promise to the letter, as in the spirit it shall be kept . . . I left this city about the 15th of last November, the cry was raised immediately I was gone to Ireland. As this was calculated to serve us of course we favoured it.

'But I continued almost helpless myself, so that when wealthy sympathisers were brought to me they found a man apparently not long for this world, and consequently not calculated to impress them as a revolutionist. Still I did my best, hoping and trying to keep and realize my promise.

'On the 14th December, I returned to New York, when I directed Colonel Kelly to bring certain friends to confer with me the following evening. During my absence from New York, Colonel Kelly had the absolute control of affairs here. He could not tell me exactly how we stood, but he knew enough to tell me things were in a desperate condition. When the other friends met me on the evening of the 15th I found that matters were even worse than my apprehensions. We had nothing like what I promised and expected, and the little we had we could not forward.

'I then proposed to go to Ireland by the next boat, even though I should be taken and hanged, seeing it was of great, if not vital importance, that I should keep my word to be on Irish soil on the 1st of January. All who spoke condemned the proposal, on the ground chiefly that if I were disposed of, all would be lost. No particular plan, that I can now recollect, was proposed by anyone that night, and so we parted without having determined on anything definite. I met another party of men, chiefly, if not all officers on the following Monday evening. I asked these to volunteer to go home, and the majority did so; and in making such a request at such a time, it must be evident that I meant to bring on the fight as soon as possible. Questions were asked by these officers, words fell from Colonel Kelly and others, and hints were given me by parties, then wavering in faith and undecided which side to take, from all of which it began to force itself on me, most reluctantly and sickeningly, that something was seriously wrong . . . this most revolting belief was growing on me that Colonel Kelly and others, were deep in a plot to set me aside and put Colonel Kelly in my place. How had it come to this? Colonel Kelly and his backers got up the cry that I had abandoned the cause in despair, or through cowardice shrunk from the struggle, frightened by the powers I had created . . . The simple facts are that I had not resigned my position as C.O.I.R.[6] and that I was resolved to bring on the fight as soon as I possibly could.

'Why, then, you may well ask, the astounding course taken, and the still more astounding calumnies resorted to by Colonel Kelly? Remember that all this time for six weeks from the day I left New York until the 29th of December, I was shut up in my room, and generally supposed to be in Ireland or on my way there; to come out and expose Colonel Kelly would have been certain scandal and probably ruin. I was bound to bear all however bitter, even unto death for the good of the cause, and I have borne more, I believe, in this way than has ever fallen to the lot of man . . .

'. . . Colonel Kelly then became reserved and avoided my society. Several times I sent for him, but he sent evasive answers and stayed away. I wanted a full explanation, for even at this time I could do little more than conjecture what he was doing and had done. This explanation was not given until the 29th of December, and was then made in such a manner that we quarrelled and parted in anger—is this to be wondered at?

'He had given proof not only of insubordination, but of being at the head of a plot to depose me, and ruin my reputation. And he was to take my place. So far as America was concerned, he had *actually* deposed me and was in my place. Seeing this, I said I

[6][C.O.I.R. stood for Central Organizer, Irish Republic. The initials of C.E.I.R. which were apparently used in the 1860's as an alternative to it may have arisen from confusion, from an employment of 'Executive' as a synonym for 'Organizer', or simply from the Fenian liking for proliferation of nomenclature.—O.D.E.]

would not be responsible for the F.B. as I no longer controlled it. Thereupon it was spread abroad that I had resigned my post. Not the supreme direction of *home* affairs, friends, but only of an office requiring what I could not give without scandal, if not ruin, my presence before the public on that same 29th of December. I was to have left for Paris in order to get into communication with the men at home and get these soon as I could.

'And here was one of the main points between Colonel Kelly and me—the other main point need be no further explained than by stating that, if acted on, it might bring shame and ruin on all concerned. The point I may fully explain, however, is this. Colonel Kelly would commit the men at home to the fight without letting them know how we stood here. Now, nothing could be expected from this side till we took the field and gave proof of being able to hold our own. Deeming this a betrayal of the great and sacred trust reposed in me, I would not commit the people to action till I told them exactly how I stood. But having so informed them, I would add that we were bound in honour to fight if possible, and that if we did not fight it would be highly detrimental, if not ruinous to our cause'.

This was Stephens's real case, and it is evident that he was fighting a delaying action to stave off an insurrection which he knew could only be a flash-in-the-pan, which had not the resources for any sustained campaign, for which the arms and resources promised and expected by him had not been furnished, for which the British Government was prepared and ready. He dared not say so openly nor publicly call off the insurrection which had landed so many of his followers into jail in Ireland, which had been fed on false hopes and on his own promises of action as part of his American campaign to secure funds and war material. He had only one weapon left: silence, in the hope that the majority at home might not move without him, even if this exposed him to the charge of cowardice and desertion of his cause in the hour of danger. Ultimately, Stephens used this weapon, and remained silent until he died. Yet even this weapon he only used in the last extremity, and he did not use it in time.

The man who knew that the I.R.B. in Ireland had scarcely more, if as much, as the two thousand rifles, some thousand shotguns, a few hundred revolvers, and the large number of pikes it possessed in 1865, and that the Fenian Brotherhood, above all the O'Mahony wing, had not one ship to act as blockade-runner, could only at the most muster five thousand stand of arms and a few field pieces, ended his apologia with a blatant outburst of downright falsehoods:

'I would still further add that we have plenty of men, sufficient war material to enable us to take and hold the field till assistance came from this side, and in spite of all that has happened, sufficient assistance—all the assistance we could possibly need, if we have the manhood to begin the fight ourselves.

'If there be a man in our ranks to disprove of this sense of duty on my part I pity him for he could not be a patriot. Well, Colonel Kelly and I quarrelled on these and on matters of less importance . . A meeting of the officers was called at which I was deposed—this was only for appearances—for I was deposed already. But you have learned all this scandal through the press, everything gets into print here.

'Before matters came to such a pass that I could be silent no longer an understanding was come to between Colonel Kelly and me, it was to this effect, I was to hold my position of C.O.I.R. and direct civil affairs. Colonel Kelly with some others were to have accompanied me to France. We were to leave together on Saturday last (12 January 1867), the boat sailed two hours before I thought, and I was left behind. Believing the understanding was come to in good faith it was certainly so on my part.

'I have written the preceding explanation solely to set myself right with you. Should Colonel Kelly reach Ireland before me, and acting in good faith he calls you to arms to fight for honour, freedom, and the salvation of our race, I call on you to rise and prove to the world the faith and stuff that is in you, that is if possible rise every man, but if only a tenth of our strength should take the field, rely on being able to hold your own whatever comes to you. Brothers, be as one man in your support of those who first raise the flag, and once raised, let it be death or freedom for every man now living on Irish soil.

'Soon as possible by the first conveyance I shall leave and be with you, I trust, soon after Colonel Kelly reaches you. Would to God we had been over together and when you arise smite with a will and stamp them out.

Ever yours,
Fraternally and faithfully,
JAMES'.

By the time Stephens had written this letter the break between himself and Colonel Kelly was common knowledge. The news that he had been deposed from the Fenian leadership was published in the New York press on 7 January, together with an account of a public denunciation of Stephens by Kelly as a coward whom the Colonel had prevented from absconding to Paris with the Fenian funds. This was the beginning of a defamation offensive against Stephens in which the Roberts wing, whose head was notorious for his gutter press tactics, joined even more outrageously. Insinuations and inventions about Stephens's luxurious life in the United States and his even more luxurious intentions when he should reach Paris, as well as fables about the furs and jewels lavished on Mrs Stephens from the Fenian funds, wounded Stephens deeply.

Kelly learned that Stephens had reached France in February, and he wrote from Dublin on 10 March 1867, with reproachful scurrility to Halpin, who remained friendly with Stephens at the crisis in spite of their differences.

'Little Baldy has at last given up the ghost, and acknowledged that if he came to Ireland the people would be certain to make short work of him. The rascal is in Paris, taking his ease with his wife while the destiny of Ireland is in the balance. The money he squeezed from the men of New York, through you and others under pretence that it was necessary "to procure a boat", he coolly pockets, together with the proceeds of the "Hopper drafts" (which I am almost certain have been drawn), he now uses to take his ease in Paris where he denounces the Irish-Americans as "dogs' dung and devil's scum". . . Stephens is repudiated and denounced by the entire home organization. Look out for any future vindications of himself which he may now offer to an American public'.[7]

The Fenian drafts mentioned were in fact held by the American banker, Belmont, who eventually on a legal technicality avoided payment. Stephens obtained a ticket from the Fenian headquarters with which he dispatched his brother-in-law George Hopper to France—an action which exposed him to serious criticism. In spite of his complaints against

[7]Denieffe, Appendix, p. 278–80.

Kelly's 'trickery' in sailing away on 12 January, two hours too soon, there was no reason why he should not have gone to France instead of his brother-in-law. He was enabled—as he relates to an unknown Irish-American correspondent, in a letter, dated 25 October 1867, from Paris—to leave the United States through the help of a Brooklyn friend, Thomas N. Dwyer, who also sheltered him for a while. From this letter and another, republished from the American press in the *Irishman* on 23 November in the same year, it is clear that he laboured under extreme mental stress and hardship; that he visited St Louis and Philadelphia; that with some difficulty he raised some twenty pounds to send to his wife who Hopper had informed him, presumably after arriving in France, was in a state of destitution; that he feared the Hopper family, then it would seem still in Dublin, had been 'utterly ruined, and in the utmost distress'; that he summoned his wife and sister-in-law, Mary Hopper, through his brother-in-law, to proceed direct to Le Havre under the pretence that Stephens was in France or going there—as he then believed that he was going to Ireland—'no place for her during the struggle'.

Towards the end of January, Stephens sailed to France, which he reached on 8 February. An old friend, a Frenchman, gave him an advance, but could not find him a private yacht to take him to Ireland. Other friends were colder and he found little assistance. When his wife and sister-in-law landed at Le Havre that summer on 3 June, they could not get into communication with him for nearly three weeks. They had some weeks of hardship until he found them and rescued them. They proceeded to Paris and stayed with him until the autumn when they returned to Dublin. His health broke down. When he had recovered he insisted that his wife and sister-in-law must no longer share his semi-hunger and destitution. 'I could not be sure they might not die of hunger here soon, and it is little short of a miracle they are alive even as it is'. So, reluctantly, he felt compelled to send them back to what he called 'the shelter of their father's more than morbid house' in Dublin. The family's fortunes had been completely broken and within the next few years his father-in-law and George Hopper went to

London where with the help of George's brother, John, their tailoring business was for a time re-established.

Henceforth Stephens had to face the monotonous and galling experience of evictions from lodging after lodging, the darkest poverty, and persistent espionage. But in spite of all this, and notwithstanding his querulous complainings about his ill health, and his outbursts against persecution and conspiracy, he retained his belief in himself and his old self-confident arrogance. He also retained much more dignity than did his critics in Ireland and America: A. M. Sullivan gloating in the *Nation*, the Roberts faction spewing venomous libels in the *Irish-American* and elsewhere, the howling New York *Herald* and *Tribune*.[8] All of whose revelations were most conscientiously extracted and filed in innumerable volumes for the guidance of Dublin Castle, and Under-Secretary Sir Thomas Larcom. 'I could live down the calumnies of a whole world of such beings, God pity them!' wrote Stephens, in that letter of 25 October. 'Calumny is fatal to the weak alone,' and the comment was just.

And even in this darkest hour, he had loyal and unshakeable defenders. A very large number of the Fenian rank and file, his Old Guard, stood by him as the true and only Fenian Chief. 'He was a good man,' said one of them, who in extreme old age limped out to join the insurgents of 1916. 'He had not arms, he had not money, and we did not think it right to blame him'. His former Ulster lieutenant, Frank Roney, wrote in his memoirs:

'Stephens was a learned, able, and indefatigable worker, devoting his life to Ireland's independence, and dying in comparative obscurity. Some of those who responded to his call to visit him after his escape from Ireland condemned him for not ordering the "rising" in 1865 and called him a coward. Stephens was a conscientious man and was possessed of complete knowledge of the strength of our movement. He knew that our inability to secure sufficient arms for the uprising would only result in the butchery of the revolutionary forces and retard for a hundred years our dream of an Irish Republic'.

[8][The *Herald* and *Tribune*, of course, obtained their Fenian revelations and their biases from Fenian journalists on their staffs, and the contacts these latter possessed. Devoy, for instance, was to find a place on the *Herald*.—O.D.E.]

This was a not uncommon view among the Fenians. Even a Fenian centre and a supporter of the Roberts party in Great Britain felt compelled to write in the *Irishman*, 31 August 1867, over the pseudonym, 'One of the Late Provisional Government':

'At last the final moment came when it was necessary to plunge Ireland into a hopeless struggle or sacrifice the pledges which had been rashly given. James Stephens had still a little conscience left, and redeemed a great many of his past errors by sacrificing himself and his great reputation rather than lead the people to annihilation'.

From the early months of that second exile until the very end of the year Stephens watched the first forlorn uprising of Fenianism, and its defeat; the second series of Fenian trials, with the moving orations of Thomas F. Bourke and William Mackey Lomasney, and another procession of victims to penal servitude; the daring Manchester rescue of Colonel Thomas Kelly and Captain Deasy; the hanging of Allen, Larkin and O'Brien for the death of the police-sergeant Brett in the rescue; the Clerkenwell explosion;—events which swept England with hysterical anti-Fenian panic, and Ireland with a new national anthem and a new spirit, which fired among many more an unknown young Irish Protestant landlord, Charles Stewart Parnell, to lifelong and significant activity. 'The Fenians made only one mistake', he said in admiration. 'They never should have fought'.

The rising was outwardly a fiasco, drowned in a hurricane of snow, bungling and treachery, yet the iron will and enthusiasm of the hundreds of Fenians who marched to battle almost unarmed, impressed the insurrection of 'sixty-seven on the popular memory as a magic and historic date. Even the mistakes and blunders of the Fenians worked eventually in an uncanny fashion to their advantage. An informer in Dublin betrayed the project of the Manchester rescue to Dublin Castle, and the consequent Dublin warning reached the authorities just late enough to neutralize loose tongues. An impetuous Fenian brawled with detectives outside the court as the prison van waited for Kelly and Deasy, and the police guard was increased, without the military escort which would have made any rescue attempt impossible. Thus, although the rescue without the brawl would have been a bloodless one, yet there was a rescue. The same spy in the Dublin Fenian circles sent full warning of the coming rescue of Burke and Casey from Clerkenwell, whereupon the prison authorities confined the prisoners to their cells, and thereby saved their lives from the results of a crazy miscalculation in the amount of gunpowder to be used, which was to turn the district into a shambles. The date of the insurrection was changed without due warning from 11 February to 5 March. Kerry rose prematurely. Its insurgents scared the loyalists of the area to ignominious flight, learned from a captured police dispatch of the changed date and demurely faded away through the British cordons, being helped in some cases by friendly Highland regiments. Allen, Larkin and O'Brien, innocent of the accidental shooting of police-sergeant Brett, were hanged on evidence perjured so recklessly that the prisoners' counsel, the Chartist Ernest Jones, threw up his brief and left the court. Yet the executions fanned Ireland and Irish-America to such a flame that the errors of the Fenian leadership were forgotten, and Gladstone pondering on Clerkenwell and Manchester changed his mind on the Irish issue. John McCafferty in his freelance way, without sanction of his colleagues, summoned the Fenians of the North of England to a raid on the armoury of Chester Castle with its several thousand rifles and considerable ammunition, all in the care of a weak guard. The seizure was to be followed by a dash on captured trains and the Holyhead mailboats for an arms landing on the Dublin coast. McCafferty, who had not learned of the altered date, filled Chester with his Fenians on 11 February, was betrayed by the informer Corydon, for long a trusted and loyal Fenian, and was delayed by the troop train rushing heavy reinforcements to protect Chester Castle against his raiders—mostly successfully dispersed when McCafferty arrived several hours late. Thence his way led to Dublin into the arms of the waiting detectives and penal servitude. Colonel Kelly in a confidential letter to Halpin after McCafferty's arrest in 1867 spoke sharply of McCafferty's 'madness' in rushing the Chester attack, 'a fiasco', against the wishes of the Provisional Government—that is against the group of officers in charge of operations—and concluded that it was an 'attempt to make an individual reputation'. As McCafferty was then in prison, the escapade had to 'be looked on in the mildest possible light'.[9]

General Halpin was in charge of the operations in Co. Dublin. There was no fighting in the city itself, and with some relief the Castle authorities allowed the Fenians to march out of the city, to the Dublin hills. At Tallaght a large body of Fenians attacked a police barracks at midnight, and were driven off by a volley from some sixty rifles which demoralized and scattered them, wounding twelve and killing two, Stephen O'Donoghue and Thomas Farrell. The attackers were some thousands in number, mostly unarmed, and proceeding without scouts or advance guards or any precautions. The night was pitch dark, the rifle fire came by surprise, and the small number of Fenians who had rifles could only fire wildly at the flashes. A second volley, and further casualties, completed the rout. The main body of insurgents retreated to Dublin over the heavily guarded city bridges where they were arrested and taken to the Upper Castle Yard to sink weary and exhausted on the damp ground. Halpin and Niall Breslin, who were waiting with sixty men some miles away at the appointed assembling place, told Devoy later that the march through Tallaght was an inexplicable blunder, and O'Donoghue, who took charge, was not a Fenian officer. Halpin guided his sixty men back to the city safely late the same night, infuriated by the disaster.

Elsewhere in Co. Dublin the Fenians gave a better account of themselves and attacked police barracks at Dundrum, Glencullen and Stepaside, capturing the two last with great efficiency and determination, suffering no fatal casualties and seizing many rifles. Lennon, the leader with John Kirwan, several times threatened to shoot any of his men who did not treat the police prisoners with humanity and respect. After he had inspected the surrendered barracks at Glencullen, he came out and discovered the local parish priest haranguing his

[9]Denieffe, Appendix, p. 279; Pigott, *Recollections* . . . pp. 224–25, states that the Chester Castle attempt had not been included in the general plan of the rising nor sanctioned by Cluseret when he was still commander-in-chief.

Fenians and ordering them home. Lennon stepped up to the priest, clapped a revolver to his head and said with an oath, 'If you don't get out of here, I'll give you the contents of this'. The priest promptly took the advice. Some years later, he met a friend of Lennon's, and said 'That man knew his business, and I've no hard feelings against him. If I didn't do what I did, Paul Cullen would be after my scalp, but that man did know his business!' Lennon returned to Dublin after the fighting, was arrested and sentenced to fifteen years' penal servitude. Before his arrest he rescued his fellow-officer, John Kirwan, who had been wounded in the Dundrum attack and taken to a Dublin hospital under police guard. Kirwan made his way to New York.

In Cork, Limerick, Clare, Tipperary and Kerry, the Fenians rose as best they could, ill-equipped but dauntless, and leaving behind the memory of the encounters at Ballyknockane barracks which was captured and burned, at Kilmallock barracks, at Ballyhurst Fort in Tipperary, at Kilclooney Wood in Co. Cork, and many minor clashes elsewhere.

By the end of March the rising was technically over. Its last engagement ended with the death of Peter O'Neill Crowley in Kilclooney Wood. The revolt had in reality faded away within twenty-four hours in spite of minor incidents in a week of pitiless snow unknown in the country for years. Colonel Kelly continued to send frenzied appeals for aid to Irish-America in terms as bitter as Stephens ever sent to O'Mahony. Communications were slow, news of the actual progress of events was scant, yet one phrase in Kelly's letter of 15 March 1867, moved the Fenian Brotherhood to a successful and romantic act. 'Don't believe', Kelly had written in desperation, 'a tenth of the vile newspaper reports about complete suppression—utter routs—overwhelming defeats. What do our countrymen in America want? Will they wait until the last man is slaughtered before sending aid? . . . Fit out your privateers . . . I say, don't mind what the newspapers say . . . We took the field on little more than a thousand rounds. If those scurvy Irish millionaires had done half their duty we would now be recognized as belligerents . . . When the word of the present extensive business reaches you, there should be certainly immense work done. A landing in Sligo at the present time would be infinite service. That section has been reserved for just such an event, and if Fortune should only guide your ships in that direction it would just suit our purposes'.[10]

The O'Mahony wing, with a depleted treasury and no ships then at its disposal, nevertheless made a spirited response to Kelly's appeal. Through some unexplained influence they persuaded the American customs authorities to hand over to them a vessel, the *Jackmel Packet*, which had been seized by the New York collector of customs with its cargo, apparently on suspicion that it was a Mexican gun-runner. Whether by purchase or otherwise, the ship came into the hands of the Fenian Brotherhood in April, and on the 12th of that month sailed from New York with a cargo of 5,000 stand of arms, three small pieces of artillery, and a large amount of ammunition, packed in piano cases, sewing machine cases, and wine barrels, labelled as consigned to merchants in a Cuban port, which duly satisfied the scrutiny of the customs. The ship sailed with the usual crew, and the search had happily been completed sometime before departure from the quayside. Otherwise a group of very busy carpenters preparing berths to accommodate a large number of men might have aroused suspicions. As the ship lay to at Sandyhook for a favourable wind, with its crew and officers—all good Fenian naval volunteers—a small steamer came up and lay under her stern. Thirty-eight Fenian Civil War veterans came aboard and the voyage began. Nine days out from New York the ship was renamed the *Erin's Hope*, a green flag with sunburst hoisted, and thirty-two guns fired, one for each county in Ireland. It was decided that in case of serious risk of capture, ship and cargo should be blown up after the crew and officers had taken to the boats, or, if the pursuit was in such strength that capture was unavoidable, the nearest pursuing vessel should be rammed as the ship's engineer, S. R. Tresilian, Orangeman, Freemason and Fenian, touched off the powder magazine.

[10]D'Arcy, quoted from O'Mahony Papers, p. 243. The account of the '67 rising in the text is largely based on Devoy's *Recollections* . .; the writer's *Phoenix Flame*; Pigott's *Recollections* . . .: and some additional details from a lecture of James Hurley, Cork, 'Cork and Limerick in 1867'. For the *Erin's Hope* expedition, see also, *The Cruise of the Erin's Hope*, M. J. O'Mullane (C.T.S. Dublin 1916).

A messenger was sent to Kelly in Dublin to warn him of the coming landing. Neither O'Mahony, the other New York leaders, nor the *Erin's Hope* men would believe that the insurrection had been suppressed, and that all Ireland was quiet without a single Fenian band still in the field. Thirty-two days later the *Erin's Hope* sailed down the Irish coast past Donegal Bay to Sligo and entered the bay on 23 May. Kelly's envoy, Colonel Ricard Burke, boarded the vessel and informed the invaders that the insurrection for which they brought aid had been finally suppressed two months before. The *Erin's Hope* turned back to the ocean, and after some narrow escapes and the capture of one landing party near Dungarvan, Co. Waterford, reached America safely with its cargo intact. Several attempts to land the cargo broke down. Captain Kavanagh made the double-edged comment on his return, 'There is no point of the coast at which I stopped during this time but where I could land any amount of men and arms, were there preparations made to take them from me'. One consolation for the captain lay in the fate of the Fenian landing party which had been arrested at Dungarvan. It had disregarded his instructions to land only after dark. But being all American citizens the captives turned out to be such a Band of Tartars and legal embarrassments between the British and American Governments, that the weary British sent them back to the United States, but not before they had delivered some most seditious and inflammatory orations in Great Britain and Ireland immediately after their release.

Such was the mournful saga that Stephens was compelled to watch in silence from afar. He remained in Paris, a needy and harassed exile, nor even yet like his beaten and scattered Fenians would he admit final defeat in the face of bitter and crushing calamity.

23 Stephens during the Franco-Prussian War

AFTER the end of the 1867 rising, Stephens finally preserved absolute silence in public in the face of continued attacks on him. In one of his letters of the time, indeed in several of them, he explained that he feared a full statement of his case might injure the imprisoned Fenians. This was one of the reasons for his silence. In fact, it was only slowly that Stephens reached this decision. By the end of 1867 he had not only completed but had made arrangements for the publication of an apologia of himself and for his refusal to sanction the rising in '67, and his opposition to it at the three December meetings which ended in his deposition. He found a French publisher and arranged for an English edition. His friend John Augustus O'Shea had reported progress, and finally announced in the *Irishman*, 11 January 1868, that 'Mr Stephens has completed a defence of himself, and a tract on the later stages for the French public, and has an English edition prepared for the press'.

A letter from Stephens in New York, dated 12 October 1871, to an unnamed 'Brother and Friend' also in the United States, refers to this work and to his life at the time:

'I come to what may be termed my silent period. I think that silence and its consequences make up as hard a trial as any man has outlived. What I call its "consequences" means amongst other trifles the danger of death through sheer want any week for years. The Second Empire was not only upright, but actually seemed to many in its palmiest state, kings and rulers flocking to see the beauties and glories of the world's capital. I was in no favour there, and some who should have looked for and befriended me weakly or criminally held aloof.

'There was only one certain way out of this darkness into light.

The way was easy enough and would have immediately led from misery to affluence. In the weakness of my agony, I determined on the one only course of salvation—that by which my misery would at once be ended and my reputation triumphantly vindicated. I resolved to write and publish a book on Fenianism. My literary friends (Frenchmen) said it would be a great success, all being mad to know what we meant and had done, and my name being so well known; and a Paris publisher of celebrity before I had written a word of the book, gave me such terms for the French edition as made my literary friends open their eyes. I could readily have found a publisher in every civilised country in Europe and for the English edition secured £5,000. Affluence was within my grasp and the power of making myself thoroughly known to my countrymen. I set to work; and working hard— working myself almost to death, want straining still harder on me than the work—in less than two months the book was more than half written. I had refused to bind myself to time as to the publication, something like an inner monitor or Socratic demon warning me that I might not be able to publish at all. And so it happened.

'For the more I wrote, the clearer it became to me, that however it might serve the cause generally (and I am confident the book would have done this largely) it would certainly doom our imprisoned brothers for years. Once convinced of this I wrote no more, then my trials thickened and I don't know where I found the strength to hold out . . .'

In spite of the old Stephens self-deception and exaggeration, this decision was highly creditable to him, an honourable and understanding scruple. Certainly, whatever need, and appearances were strong against him, he had to defend his utterances and actions, a full statement over his own name which revealed the weakness of the Fenian resources in Ireland, and the conduct of the final New York meetings in 1867 would have exposed Bourke, McCafferty, Halpin and others to odium and discredit. Stephens withdrew both books, or rather laid their completion aside, and held his peace. It is true that his private explanations to his supporters in Ireland and the United States were published in part in the press of the time, and that the violent personal attacks on Stephens in speech and print by Colonel Kelly and others in the 'sixties, and by Devoy and

the released Fenian prisoners after 1871, might well have
justified Stephens in breaking his silence or in publishing his
side of the story. Hoping, in his own phrase, that 'when the
blind passion of the hour has passed, the People would do him
justice', he decided otherwise, as William Smith O'Brien had
done before him.

Then came the outbreak of the Franco-Prussian war. In his
letters to Fenian correspondents and in brief public statements
Stephens is guarded, yet something can be read between the
lines and in what he admits and half-suggests. He still
regards himself as the one indispensable Fenian leader, and
remains in touch with his Old Guard. He is still the Stephens
of the American diary, the republican democrat at heart with
the ideal of a democratic republic for the weal of the toiler,
and sharing the intense sympathy for France widespread in
Ireland from the outbreak of war.

Sometime in December 1870, he wrote to an unknown
supporter that he had left Paris in September by the last train
just before the German investment of the city, and heard the
bridges blown up behind him. A rumour had appeared in
some foreign papers 'of my having offered a Legion to the
Emperor was utterly without foundation. The elder Brutus
could not possibly be less disposed to serve or brook a King.
But the Emperor was down and the flag of the Republic raised
once more in revolutionary France. I put myself in communication with "the Committee of National Defence"; but so as
to give no offence to England. That was my duty, knowing the
deadly odds against which France was struggling, and that
policy—the policy of the hour at least—called on the French
Government to conciliate "Perfidious Albion". My "co-
operation" they said "would be now with England". I knew the
contrary but could not press my offers'. Stephens continued:

'Before I went, and for some time afterwards certain influential
friends of mine were anxiously looking for me. What for? To
place me at the head of a certain combination which might have
largely affected the destiny of France. Had my friends found me
I should have left Paris in the balloon with Gambetta[1] and played

[1]Gambetta left Paris, 7 October 1870 by balloon on a mission to rouse the
provinces against the invaders with M. Spuller.

a part only second to his own. My conviction is that I could have rendered serious service to the Republic—possibly have changed the result of which all lovers of liberty have since deplored. But of all these things another time. I started for Brest where I arrived Sept. 20 with the sum of *ninepence*.'

There is a haze of mystery about Stephens's exact movement at this time. It is known that he lived in the south of France after the fall of Paris until the end of the war; that after his visit to Brest that autumn, he made his way to Bordeaux. His own reference to his relations with French political parties will be quoted later. The purpose of his journey to Brest appears to have been to use it as a centre of communication with the pro-Stephenite groups in Ireland and the United States. At Brest he stayed at the Hotel des Voyageurs, under the name of J. Bishop, and on his way to Bordeaux visited Nantes.

One of the many letters that Stephens wrote from the United States in 1871 to inquirers and sympathizers gives some account of his outlook and life in these years, and, especially, of the intricate Fenian factions and his relations, friendly or otherwise with them. This letter is dated 12 October 1871:

'In June 1870, I went with my wife to Reims where certain republican friends procured me something to do, and where we were living very modestly and contentedly and hoping for better, when the Franco-Prussian war broke out. Immediately my friends began to stir—all Ireland was profoundly moved; and word was sent to me that the friends wished to know what I meant to do. One of my Reims friends, a wealthy and distinguished man, on hearing how matters stood, gave me money to go to Paris, whence I sent home my wife with a sort of manifesto to the friends at home. They were delighted, but did not follow my instructions. I had told them to go to work at once, but only with my staunch friends at first, allowing my enemies and even the doubtful to go their own way for a time.

'There were three Fenian parties then in Ireland—my friends, for the greater part unorganized; the "Party of Action" men, numerous but ignorant, and loosely held together; and followers of the "Supreme Council", not powerful but having money (mostly received from this side)[2] and blended together firmly as

2That is, from the United States.

lies can do it. My friend, instead of setting to work as instructed, had the imprudence to hold a meeting to which, not only the "Party of Action", but the S.C. were invited to send representatives. At this meeting the representatives of the S.C. declared themselves to be my implacable enemies—they would have nothing to do with me under any circumstances. The representatives of the "Party of Action" were more practical and patriotic—indeed these men had always been more or less friendly to me, and had formed this party solely in the belief that I had abandoned the cause for ever—a calumny industriously circulated by the truthful patriots of the S.C. Their representatives on this occasion declared themselves favourable to an amalgamation with my friends and promised to consult their chief on the subject. This they did by letter, and his answer was: "Accept him (meaning me) at once, and you will be supported". He promised various sums of money from various places at the same time.

'Three weeks having gone by without any further sign of life from him, he was written to and asked what he meant. The answer was that I was a despot and he would have nothing to do with me; such rule as mine being only tolerated in Russia, Turkey, China, Japan, etc. etc. etc. This did not satisfy his officers. They called a Convention to which this chief was summoned; and then and there it was unanimously voted to act under my guidance. The chief voted with the rest, but then resigned, his resignation being accepted. The "Party of Action" then merged into the more legitimate I.R.B. and pledged allegiance to me. They promised me support and went to work as best they could.

'Meantime the Prussians were advancing on Paris. I wrote home to the effect that I should like to stand the seige and that I would not leave Paris unless my friends were sure they needed my services. Their answer was that my services were required. At the same time I received letters from several parts of these [United] States and England asking what I meant to do, and requesting me to put myself in communication with them. Everything considered I selected Brest as the best point of communication between France and my friends at home and abroad'.

There is no mention in these letters of the generally accepted story that Stephens during the war was appointed an Inspector of Fortresses, a position the German advance on Paris rendered useless, although he mentions, as will be seen later, a visit to the frontier in a New York interview in 1871. His picture of the Fenian factions in Ireland is certainly correct. Even Devoy's hostile report to the Clan na Gael on the position in Ireland in 1879 admitted that the Stephens party immediately after 1867 had been able to draw the I.R.B. circles in Dublin, Louth, and Wexford away from the Supreme Council. Some 1,500 men, mostly in Leinster, had recognized only the leadership of Stephens. Devoy claimed that at the time his report was made the Stephenites had dwindled to a few hundreds.[3]

Until late into the 'eighties, Stephens made every effort to recover his leadership. The majority of the Clan na Gael and I.R.B. made equally determined, and in the end successful, bids to defeat this ambition. Stephens himself at heart, for all his protests, must have felt that the events of '67, however strong his case, and however sincere and inevitable his own action in that crisis, were a formidable barrier to his return to his old position.

John O'Leary[4] looked him straight in the eye, listened patiently to his long and verbose explanations and told him on more than one occasion that not only was a second period of Stephens's one-man rule impossible in the future but undesirable. Stephens was prepared to concede John O'Leary a right to say and think what he liked. For the rest, Stephens conspired and ruled so far as he could, and even in the midst of the war sent advice to Dublin on the chances of importing arms from France, even if he could not see that the chances amounted to anything.

[3] *Devoy's Post Bag*, Vol. I. pp. 312–13; 404–7; Sir Henry James, *The Work of the Irish Leagues*, p. 65. Dr Mark Ryan, *Fenian Memories*, pp. 66–70, in his account of his meetings with Stephens in the 'eighties in Paris states, 'he was appointed Inspector of Fortresses in Paris during the Franco-Prussian war of 1870'. Dr Ryan quotes with approval Luby's judgment on Stephens to O'Leary in his letters, 'in spite of all his blemishes, I most sincerely admire the "Captain".' Dr Ryan adds, 'He was accused of being arrogant, vain-glorious and theatrical; but he retained the respect of every member of the Supreme Council'.

[4] [O'Leary and Luby had been sentenced to twenty years' penal servitude in 1865, at which time Rossa was given a life sentence. But following an intensive Amnesty movement, they were released in 1871, together with most of the civilian Fenian prisoners of 1865 and 1867. O'Leary and Luby travelled initially to Brussels; subsequently O'Leary settled in Paris, and Luby in the U.S.A.—O.D.E.]

From his hotel in Brest Stephens on 22 December 1870 wrote one such letter to a correspondent bearing a name sometimes seen in the Dublin *Irishman* as an advertiser of toys, fancy goods, and for Fenians, in particular, of meershaum pipes, one Keevil, possibly very interested, from Stephens's phrasing, in 'disposing of rifles' to the French, but more probably from the tone of his letter in gun-running for the Fenians at home. Keevil is evidently a regular contact and correspondent as he is thanked for a letter of 19 December, and two previous ones. 'I had been in hopes of going to Tours where I believe that I could have sent you cheering news. At present I am doing all I can to get to Bordeaux, and if I do, I am almost certain of being able to advise you to your advantage'. Bordeaux, although Stephens does not mention the fact, had been just then selected as the headquarters to which Gambetta and other members of the Delegate Government for the provinces had gone from Tours. Paris, Stephens continues, for the first six months was the best place in all France for Keevil's purpose and his own, matters had completely changed, and he could not advise Keevil to come to Brest, 'it might be different if you could treat on a larger scale with the authorities, but you have already told me that you could not do so'. After suggesting Nantes, through which he will probably pass on his journey, for a meeting with Stephens when Keevil could learn further of the prospects for his mysterious purpose, he congratulates Keevil on 'your good luck about Rouen'.

Then Stephens even in this modest business note lets himself go:

> 'How miserably that glorious old city has fallen! Think of the descendants of *your* conquerors—of the times which the Norman sword made glorious through the world. Can anything whatever be said in extenuation of the actual Norman degeneracy? I know what *I* think. Be good enough to give me your opinion'.

There had been considerable and very bitter criticism in the French press because the city had been left defenceless by retreating French forces, and a humiliating surrender by the municipal authorities some weeks before, and Stephens's sympathies and opinions are very clear.

Then up flamed some ancient enmities provoked by the mention by Keevil of 'the Irish Ambulance', with which A. M. Sullivan, P. J. Smyth, and John Martin were associated on the national committee: 'What', exclaims Stephens, 'should anyone expect of those who sent out that Ambulance? I am surprised that such folk could find in all Ireland a hundred earnest men to be guided by them, but the poor fellows' hearts were thoroughly with France no doubt'. Then with thanks 'for information on another matter' Stephens gives his address 'for the present' as the hotel at Brest.

Whether Stephens had been misled by a controversy raging in the *Irishman* about the Irish Ambulance corps and ambulance sent to France, or the fog of war or ancient spleens had blinded him, or whether his tongue was deep in his cheek, must be guess work. What is certain enough is that some volunteers for that corps had been much surprised on arrival to find that they were expected to carry rifles rather than stretchers; and a large number were most certainly not surprised at all, as they had come for that purpose. Among the latter were some very old, if not altogether friendly, colleagues of Stephens himself, 'their hearts thoroughly with France', and all for lessons in the art of warfare with the same ulterior aim as John Devoy in the Foreign Legion and the Fenian recruits to the Union armies in the 'sixties.

One Fenian colleague, not then friendly to Stephens, even if his views on the wisdom or rather the unwisdom of '67 were exactly Stephens's own, arrived in France at the outbreak of the war to organize an Irish Brigade—James J. O'Kelly. And close on his heels came volunteers for the Irish Ambulance Corps which A. M. Sullivan, P. J. Smyth, Lord Mayor Bulfin, John Martin and others, on a very mixed committee, had organized with much publicity. 'You go', ran one manifesto of the committee, 'in this hour of her dire distress to France, to assist in the care and relief of her wounded soldiers. You go to prove the sympathy which Ireland feels for France. But your work is one of humanity; and on the battlefield you will go to the relief of all the wounded whom it may be in your power to save—even of the enemies of France'.

For many of the volunteers and organizers of the scheme, in

spite of Stephens's impatience with them, it was something
else, a variant of Daniel O'Connell's old trick of driving a
coach and four through an act of parliament; in this case
ambulance wagons through the Foreign Enlistment Act, with
such decent trimmings, according to the *Freeman* report of the
departure in the French ship *La Fontaine* from the North Wall,
as 'a surgeon in chief, four assistant surgeons, thirty-two
experienced medical students, and over two hundred young
men of good character'. At Le Havre there was a civic reception, an oration by Mr P. J. Smyth who formally presented
the ambulance corps to the French nation from an ancient
ally. A local newspaper wrote enthusiastically, 'Henry VIII
and Cromwell go this day under the names of William and
Bismarck'. The French Government more calmly intimated
that it would gladly accept the surgeon in chief, the four
assistant surgeons, the thirty-two experienced medical students
—and forty of the young men of good character. Captain
Martin Kirwan, a Fenian from Great Britain, arrived some
days later and marched off with most of the others in his Irish
Brigade to Caen, and fought throughout the remainder of the
war down to the last engagement. Edmund O'Donovan,
Arthur Forrester and some hundred other Irishmen joined the
Foreign Legion and found themselves in the forefront at
Orleans, Gravelotte and Sedan.[5]

Whether Stephens met any of his old colleagues at Tours,
where Edmund O'Donovan became the leader of the Irish
recruits who joined the Foreign Legion there, is not known.
It is improbable, as the Legion had left to take part in the
Orleans fighting in mid-September, according to a letter from
O'Donovan published in the *Irishman*, 22 November 1870,
dated 12 October. As O'Donovan belonged to the Colonel
Kelly wing of the I.R.B. his relations with Stephens were then
unfriendly. Nor is it on record whether in his journeys Stephens
met the Garibaldians, who with their chief had also arrived in

[5]The official account of the Committee is given in M. A. Leeson's *Reminiscences
of the Franco-Irish Ambulances*. (Dublin 1873). Also, John Denvir, *Life Story of Old
Rebel*, pp. 160–3. *Freeman's Journal* and *Irishman*, October–November 1870. Devoy,
Recollections . . . p. 337. For Edmund O'Donovan, see R. Hayes, 'Famous Irish
War Correspondent', *Studies*, March 1947.

Tours, and revived any old links with the Italians knit through Pepe and Cesare Orsini; or met his old colleague, General Cluseret, who, since the fall of Napoleon III was busy stirring up the Reds of Lyons and Marseilles with no very great success, until his brief and effective military leadership of the Paris Commune. What Stephens's final relations with the International were is not yet established. It is very clear that Stephens had even less sympathy with the more extreme factions of the Paris Commune than Cluseret himself revealed in his later statements.

Stephens always remembered his Fenian leadership. Years later on his return to Ireland he wrote 'Fenianism was wholly and unequivocally democratic, although the utopian or childish theories of continental socialists did not by any means form part and parcel of its programme'. This, no doubt, was aimed at those enemies of Fenianism, like Rutherford and Monsignor Dillon, who indulged in imaginative hysterics on Stephens and the Fenians as Reds wrapped in green flags, although the statement just quoted was the mere truth so far as the majority and programme of the organization were concerned. Yet Stephens was personally 'ultra-democratic' and his references to the French Reds of the time though reticent were not hostile. Nor would the angry description of the official historian of the Irish Ambulance Corps, M. A. Leeson, of the Garibaldian legionnaires in France as 'the scum of Italy' and 'international cut-throats' have lessened his contempt for the Committee as expressed to Keevil.

The first plain statement of Stephens's life and doings in France at this time is given in a letter to his wife from Rheims, at the *Hotel du Lion d'Or*, 21 June 1871. He declares with enthusiasm that the hotel is opposite the great front of the Cathedral of which he can never see enough:

'I could almost worship the stone alone, for it embodies, perhaps the most ideal dream of Gothic beauty in the world. I remember, though, "my old woman" used to say, in thorough disgust of Reims, that people could not live in a town for the sake of two old buildings (St Remy and this!). Right enough; but when fortune brings us to a town of the kind, Providence is good to us through this beauteous work of man. I rejoiced yesterday morning on finding my boudoir looked out on this glorious pile. *L'Hotel du Lion d'Or* is the finest hotel here. What a triumph'.

And in the same letter there were other triumphs, past and present to relate, with some glimpses of France emerging from the shock and ruin of defeat, 'the weather is an additional trial on France but she will get over everything. The two milliards (£80,000,000) loan was all made up yesterday. Her day will come before long. God send it soon'. Then Stephens mentions the name of M. Lelegard, an old friend of them both, and M. Delacroix, who had seen service at the front, and endured the seige of Paris, 'and these two spent many a day looking for me—not merely as friends. They had (or Lelegard had) a great plan in which I was to have played the leading part. Had we met, I should now be a dead man—a death to glory in—or the leading man in Europe. But of this when we meet. I wish my friends, and *enemies in the cause*,—only knew what I am thought of in Europe. Dr Thomas, Dr Henrot (the big *slob*, who spent the Sunday with us at Verzy), and Dr Brebant (the honest-faced gentleman who accompanied Dr Thomas the evening we made his acquaintance at Delacroix's) were all arrested here by the Prussians and sent for some months to one of their feudal prisons. All these gentlemen were quite well. Dr Henrot is Deputy Mayor here, all the Corporation being republican. Dr Thomas is one of the members for this Department, and took me through the Chamber of Versailles on Saturday'.

In Bordeaux Stephens had entered into partnership with a M. Carvallo and finally persuaded him to open a branch of the business in New York. M. Lelegard 'whose vaults gave me my first notion of this wine business' although on the point of retiring, offered to hold on and work with Stephens, out of sheer friendliness, but the New York experiment had already been fixed with Carvallo.

In September 1871, the *Perieire* of the Transatlantic Line arrived at New York with a full list of passengers, including Mr James Stephens.

THE return was triumphal, and the moment seemed well chosen. Stephens went at once to his old headquarters in Broadway, The Metropolitan Hotel, as he had gone on his first visit and when he came to tour the Union Armies. A newspaper account recorded that Mr Stephens was assigned to No. 441 on the third floor 'by the courteous little grizzly Marsh', and then with some friends went off to Delmonico's where together they enjoyed 'one of those fine dinners without eating of at least once a man cannot expect to die happy'— a memory indeed which may have consoled Mr Stephens through many hungry years in the future. 'They sat for some time over their wine,' the account goes on, 'and their reminiscences of former days, and Mr Stephens told an anecdote of the great meeting at Jones's Wood in 1866, when a poor devil who happened to wear round-toed shoes was taken for an English spy, and would have been lynched but for the prompt intervention of the police. They then held some conversation about matters political, and Mr Stephens said he was not and never had been in sympathy with half of what had been done at that time'.

The party returned from Delmonico's to the Metropolitan and Mr Stephens held a kind of levee in the large saloon, many friends recognizing him as he passed, Mr Stephens being very cordial and affable to all. The New York *Star* reporter noticed that Mr Stephens, if his beard grew with its old luxuriance down to his very waist, nevertheless looked older and even smaller than he was, 'his face shows a great deal more of the marks of time, and his hair has become more spare than it was'. The reporter found Mr Stephens leaning on the cigar show-case and chewing the end of a prime Havana between his teeth. He shook the reporter cordially by the hand and said he was very glad indeed to greet the representative of a paper which had so nobly defended the cause of his people, and added that New York reporters beat the French detective system itself: 'A man can't arrive here two hours you find him and know all about him'.

What Mr Stephens had to say about his activities in France has already been mentioned. The cross-examination, however, recorded in question and answer form went further than that:

Reporter: During the time you were away, did you set foot on any of the English possessions?
Mr Stephens: No; I could not. My friends fixed when I left here so that I could not. It was an unfortunate business all through, and done totally against my wishes. But the least I say about it the better.
Reporter: Has your return here any political significance?
Mr Stephens: None whatever. I came here to establish myself in the mercantile way. I intend going into the wine trade and settling down, abandoning politics, or at least so far as to make them my principal object.
Reporter: Do you intend joining the new Irish Confederation or any similar movement?
Mr Stephens: I intend being neither for nor against any political party, personally. I have a great many friends here who will join in nothing unless I spur them on, and these I shall certainly give an impetus to and make good and strong men of them all. But personally, I say again, nothing.

The interview ended with mutual compliments as 'an influx of friends greet Mr Stephens. And our reporter left the scene after Mr Stephens had bowed in regular Parisian style a courteous good night'.

Stephens in a letter to his wife on 17 September, from the hotel, reports exultantly that he has been discovered, interviewed, and visited ever since his arrival:

'You would marvel at the mention of some of my visitors' names. General Halpin was among the first to call on me . . . John O'Mahony throwing his arms around me and talking to me as of old, and General Millen! What do you say of our being actually *friends* again, confirmed by firm handclasps and an invitation to his house. I *wronged* Millen, sweetheart, and I am the man not only to acknowledge, but to try and make reparation for every wrong that I have ever done a human being. Millen declared with feeling and earnestness, that only a great man could act towards him as I did yesterday. Happy the mortal that wins golden opinions from his enemies!'

There was, as Stephens was too well aware, a very important group, the liberated Fenian prisoners, the 'Exiles', including Devoy, the most formidable of all Stephens's critics, with anything but golden opinions for their former Chief. Devoy was the most consistently hostile of this group; Luby and O'Donovan Rossa at heart had more affection and respect for him although they agreed with Devoy that Stephens's day as supreme leader had passed, and, moreover, he failed to see that both within the I.R.B. and the Fenian Brotherhood a movement had been in progress for years to curb a one-man leadership by an effective Supreme Council and Senate. The revised Constitution of the I.R.B. itself had been clearly framed on that basis. There was, indeed, a widespread hope that even Stephens might come to recognize this, and cease to be Stephens.

He had no illusions about the 'Exiles', and told his wife that, with the exception of Charles Underwood O'Connell, they were bitterly hostile: 'these men must have lost their wits! For it would take me but a slight effort to drag down the pillars of their temple (of Fame is it or what?)'. Yet, he wrote emphatically that he would not work with them if he could. They were doomed and would drag him down with them in the ruin of his work. There was a double-edged truth in this, indeed. The Exiles' Irish Confederation was indeed to be doomed between the clash of the rival Fenian factions, but they were to dominate the home I.R.B. and the movement in America in due course with the new-born Clan na Gael, then in progress, the real successor of the old dying Fenianism of O'Mahony and Stephens. Yet for the next decade or so, James Stephens remained blind to the reality and repeated all his mistakes.

But the spell of the Chief was still powerful, and in America and at home the hard Stephenite core was still a force. Of this

Stephens gave some most vivid evidence to his wife in a letter of 8 October 1871, describing a lecture by Thomas Clarke Luby on 18 September. O'Mahony had refused to attend because Roberts was to be present, and said sarcastically to Stephens, who had innocently bought a ticket 'not knowing the full bitterness of Mr Luby and wishing to serve him', that 'your presence would give it a success that it would otherwise not have'. The infuriated Exiles learned that Stephens intended to be present and Luby and others breathed fire and brimstone to intimidate that most friendly intention. Stephens modestly took his place at the lecture, having presented the ticket he had bought from 'Captain Costello (one of my Paris pets)'.

Stephens stole the show. 'This proved a much greater success for me that I originally calculated . . . My name passed like lightning from tongue to tongue'. Seven hundred present rose to their feet and gave a cheer to stir the dead, and stun the astonished Stephens. 'On hearing the thunders of applause Luby is said to have bounded, and, in a rage, said "By ——! This is that demon Stephens. I'll just put a stop to this." Not being aware of this, I could not imagine the wrath I saw him nursing when he appeared was meant for me. Soon as he spoke there could be no doubt about it, though he did not even mention my name. He was quite insane and denounced me in unmeasured terms, raving and writhing like one possessed. I did not move a muscle—that is under the attack; but there happened to be a drunken man by my side who could not be kept from yelling. "Stephens! Huroo! by——!, I'll shoot any man who looks crooked at him", and by the side of this genius, a *half*-drunken man, taking care of the other, and whispering and yelling: "Can't you be quiet and respect the Captain?" and "Stephens for ever!" Between these two unreasonable admirers of mine and Luby's ravings, I had a hard time of it not to laugh. But what I felt most of all, was sincere sorrow for my old friend—a good man blinded and made mad by lies. And this is how I like to look at the matter still. But he, poor man, thought he had dealt me a death-blow, spite of the cries "quite uncalled for", "bad taste", "that is bitter", "shame", etc., to be heard from all sides save the platform, where his friends were in the majority and were as dead as he was to the injury he was doing himself and the service he was rendering me.

'They were blind to the fact that I could have carried the majority of the audience with me, had I chosen. But I am not made of such stuff and am not here to divide but to unite. After the hall had been cleared, a group of three patriotic wiseacres surrounded a friend of mine, well-known for his devotion to me, and began to banter him, asking him how he felt for me. But he soon confounded them, asking them in turn, what they thought I had gone to the lecture for? "Are you sure", said he, "that the Captain did not go there to draw Mr Luby out and test the feeling of the people?" The matter did not look so pleasant to them then, and all agreed that I was "deep as hell" '.

Mr Stephens, however, agreed that if he stole the show, Mr Luby stole the press, both in America and Ireland, and played down the public expression of the feeling of the people. Yet Stephens had read Luby's latent old affection for himself rightly. He could never understand indeed that the real barrier was a profound difference on tactics and an impatience with Stephens's histrionics and self-deception. It was Luby, in fact, who finally left one of the most living portraits of Stephens in the 1890 letters to John O'Leary, and defended him against the more malignant distortions and inventions of Devoy, Denis Dowling Mulcahy and others.

On 18 October 1871, Stephens wrote to Carvallo from New York, a letter which explained the Irish-American political situation as he saw it. He emphasized his settled resolve to establish himself in commercial life, and exercise only gentle guidance and benign inspiration on the Fenian movement from a distance, until at length the Irish race at home and abroad recognized and became reconciled to the change:

'Some time before I left Brest, the British Government thought well of liberating certain political prisoners on condition that they should leave British territory. Most of these liberated prisoners have come here. They had suffered fearfully and had the sympathy of all their countrymen, and the reception given to them was almost unprecedented. This reception seems to have turned their heads; for they undertook to combine and direct all

the conflicting elements of our race here and fancied they could
dispense with my services altogether.

'I knew they were unequal to the task, but I thought they
would do more and retain power longer than has turned out,
their influence having almost certainly gone. It was on the wane
when I arrived, but my name and their manifest incapacity have
done the rest since. I say "my name" for . . . I have done
absolutely nothing here in politics beyond the reception of friends
and deputations from the various bodies. These gentlemen,
however, could not be convinced that I had not come here to
seek political position, nor, as they have it, resume my Dictatorship.
In this thought they patched up a sort of union with an unfriendly
body before I arrived and, soon after I landed attacked me as
an emissary from the enemy, scoffing at the idea of my having come
with the purpose of settling down to commerce.

'This attack was so gross and uncalled for that it shocked
public opinion and may be considered the final blow to all my
enemies on this continent.

'In truth, my friend, I am now master of the political situation,
all the vital bodies having made advances to me. You know that
this means I shall soon be master of the commercial situation
also'.

Then Stephens informs his partner that much, too, depends
on *him*, he must see that the stock is sent promptly. Stephens,
for his part, engages to secure the most promising orders (not
only from his friends, although even they must have the wine
they order *some* time, even their patience would not be
inexhaustible!) The more supplies sent, the quicker sales and
better results. All New York is thirsty for good French wines,
and astronomical figures of sales in the city generally are
quoted, beginning with the Metropolitan Hotel where Stephens
is staying. Stephens's one aim—he repeats several times—is to
establish himself and his partner firmly in the American market.
Politics for him are now a thing of the past, and his countrymen
will yet accept Stephens as a leader in American commerce,
as they at home and abroad accept him in their hearts as the
one national leader. It will take time for them to grow
accustomed to the successful merchant, Stephens. Therefore,
the sooner his enemies are confounded, the sooner and better

for the firm of Carvallo and Stephens, Bordeaux, Rheims, and New York.

Whatever sea James Stephens crossed, he remained 'the Captain' to his Old Guard, the 'Great Sir Hocus-Pocus' to his critical friends, O'Leary and Luby, and 'Old Imposition' to his enemies. What Carvallo thought of these letters with the familiar ring is not revealed, yet the torrent of egoistic self-assurance possibly cheered him. The New York office of Carvallo and Stephens received flattering and frequent notice in the press, and it was filled with crowds of visitors and friends, mainly, according to the inaccurate and somewhat malicious story of Devoy in his memoirs, old Fenians, who would do anything for the Chief except drink wine.

Yet Stephens, as Luby's description of him in the early stages of the *Irish People* suggests, had energy and executive ability at need, and was a much abler writer of business letters than of speeches or essays or manifestoes when he bent himself to the task. Colonel Arthur Lynch, who met him shortly before his death, was impressed by his appearance, especially by his head:

'I have seen such a head in capable business men holding under their control a complex system, such men as traffic managers, heads of departments and the like; I have seen such a head in a great German chemist, and in a French mathematician. Under happier auspices Stephens might have been a man of science— a well-shaped, amply rounded dome, a forehead large but not too large to disturb the harmonious proportion of cerebral activity, nor to destroy the symmetry of the compact frame and regular features: a countenance not particularly impressive, rather resembling that of a bearded German professor, the eye of an overseer, still marking the leader, and indicating what he must have been in the early days, a man of restless energy and ever busy plotting brain, prolix of detail, yet firm in carrying out a bold and well-planned scheme'.[1]

The Carvallo-Stephens experiment lasted barely twelve months, and Stephens found himself before the end in a maze of mortgages, insufficient supplies, smart practice from customers and business colleagues. John O'Leary heard from Luby in

[1]Arthur Lynch, *Ireland: Vital Hour* (London 1915), p. 175.

New York sometime in the autumn of 1872 that the business
had been sold up and he wrote to J. J. O'Kelly, then on the
staff of the New York *Herald*, for definite news. He was puzzled
as he had also heard from the *Irish Times* Paris representative
that Stephens has reappeared in the city, looking well and
prosperous.

This second tale was most certainly a false report, and a
double of Stephens must have deceived the *Irish Times* man.
On 25 October 1872, Stephens wrote to his wife from New
York, after several previous letters detailing his disappointments and cares:

> 'It would have been far better for me that this miserable place
> had been sold out long ago, as I should have found some means
> of going to France, and be less in debt than I am . . . On 30
> August, M. Boisse, Carvallo's *chef-de-bureau* arrived here. He came
> to wind up the business. Would to God I had encouraged him
> to do so.'

Eventually the wine business closed down after a further
brief struggle by Stephens to salvage the concern. How
Stephens then lived, except that he was back in the old
uncertain and penurious round, is not evident from his letters.
Debt and semi-destitution he found more irksome in New
York than Paris, although he drew sardonic parallels between
his experiences in both places to his wife. Writing to her, 26
December 1873, he mentions France nostalgically, and laments
the 'considerable liabilities incurred by that deplorable commercial enterprise'. He has just received a draft of a hundred
dollars, which were not enough to enable him to leave for
France, a course which in any case is impossible, the draft is
not even enough to repay the small debts he was compelled to
incur to live even in 'the poorest way'. 'These debts *must* be
paid to save my name here. Well, the hundred dollars were
not enough to enable me to leave. To *leave* is, of course, the one
eternal and dominant thought of all. The next is to make you
feel that there is no cause of anxiety about me. Why not send
you a telegram when I got that money? There was a terrible
struggle in my mind on this head'. Stephens continues thus:

> 'But the money-pressure on me was so severe that I had to deprive

myself of this luxury. Had I not received that money, I should certainly have been turned out into the streets, where I certainly must have died. I had to pay fifty dollars to my land-lady (a bitter, old Gorgon-eyed wretch, fifty times harder and grosser than our beauty of Reims). In other simple sums I paid out twenty-four dollars the very day I received the draft'.

Which left the tried and much pinched Stephens some twenty-six dollars, of which he finally shied at expending ten or fifteen dollars on a telegram, with the wolf's nose still in the door, so he closed his hand tightly on his dollars, hoped his wife wouldn't think him selfish, and sent many affectionate messages, one by one for each member of the Hopper household in London. These he described as 'dearer to me than I can ever be to myself'. He discusses, after some intense expressions of affection, his wife's recent illness, and continues, 'By the way, did my friend, Dr Guerant de Mussy convince you that your fears were imaginary? They have been *always* imaginary in my mind; because when you were by my side, and I trotted you about from six to fifteen hours a day, you were always all right. Darling, go on improving; and be ready to meet me, handsome and healthful as when we parted, before long . . .' Stephens then describes his Christmas Day:

'You hope I was not too badly off yesterday (Christmas Day). I had three (I might have had three hundred, the poor being ever faithful to me) invitations to dinner. But how could I have gone anywhere? I did not know how you were circumstanced at home. So I shut myself up in my room. But I was not at all "desolate", as you feared. Two or three friends (one of them the young man who is working to send me home) called in the afternoon, and remained with me till near eleven o'clock. They could never have guessed how intensely home-sick I was'.

THE darker side of Stephens's life in the 'seventies has been described by himself to his intimate correspondents, in particular in the letters written to his friend, Edward Walsh in the United States, from Paris, 19 November 1874, 7 September 1875, and in a few entries from his private diary, 8 August to 13 December 1874, published in 1910.[1]

These extracts read:

'Saturday, Aug. 8. Feeling very sick and faint on Monday afternoon, and feeling that a longer fast might break me down utterly, determined on trying to sell a book and so have some sort of food. My books are very few and I could not be sure of finding anyone to buy any of them; but on the chance of finding a purchaser, I started off about 5 or 6 p.m. Had to cross the city to the Luxembourg where I was fortunate enough to effect my sale. I bore the walk wonderfully and nobody, I flatter myself, who saw me on the way could fancy me so poor and so sick of hunger. Dined at Porret's. A good dinner, which I relished and which strengthened me considerably. Think I had coffee on the way 'home'. Be this as it may, and whether caused by the coffee or not, my stomach became very sick . . . Scene with landlord, Sergent de Ville, Commissaire de Police, etc. The rascally landlord had lost his head, and not satisfied with turning me out, had me brought before a Commissaire de Police on a charge of —I know not what. He put in no appearance himself, but sent a *garçon* and his calculation was (his wild manner proved it) that I should be sent to prison. The Commissaire told the *garçon* that

---

[1]*Dublin Xmas Magazine*, 1910, pp. 15–17, quoted in 'The Chieftain in Exile' by the editor, Thomas F. O'Sullivan. The diary had been placed at the editor's disposal by James Collins, Convent View, Drumcondra, Dublin, to whom Stephens had left his papers. Stephens's letters to Walsh cover the same ground more fully and make clear allusions and names in the diary as quoted. These have been explained in square brackets in the text.

I could not be arrested for my bill, and that all his master could do was to turn me out and keep my effects. At the same time le Commissaire was insolent to a degree with myself, and said that unless I gave a reference and found (I think) a guarantee I could be arrested *comme étranger* . . . I gave John [Hopper, his brother-in-law] as a reference, but would give no guarantee for payment beyond my word. I expected money by every post I said, and would rather go to any prison than ask money from my relatives or friends'.

Following his eviction, Stephens received an anxious letter from his wife in London, addressed to his youngest brother-in-law, Thomas Francis Hopper, who visited him regularly. Determined to keep his wife's mind at ease, he wrote her a hopeful letter. On Thursday, 13 August, he noted that he had had no food until eight that night when Tom came with twenty francs. His cousin Patrick Casey called the night before and was shocked at his position. On 9 August, 'No dinner yesterday. Went to bed hungry and ailing in various ways, not long after 9 . . . By the way, I have been suffering from deafness for a fortnight or so . . . Bad night'. Tom called on him every day bringing him help from his brother John, a few francs, food, paper, tobacco.

Stephens's letter to Walsh, on 19 November 1874, gave a detailed and moving account of his life since he returned to France that summer. It opens with the warning: 'N.B. This letter must not leave your sight. Read it or have it read for thoroughly reliable friends only, binding them on their honour to the same prudence and secrecy wherewith you are bound yourself'. It is made plain before the close that Stephens, in spite of his trials, has still had time for some Fenian activities.

After a sea voyage of some eleven days on the *Lafayette*, a slow, staunch and steady ship, he had landed in France on 24 June, and made his way to Paris to the house of his brother-in-law, John Hopper, established in business there. He was particularly touched by the devotion of his youngest brother-in-law, Thomas Francis Hopper, a youth of seventeen, whom he had not seen for nine years, 'stirred through all his being with sympathy and reverence', and who later walked across Paris every day to call on Stephens, and save him an exhausting journey and embarrassing interviews with the not always friendly Mrs John Hopper.

In his destitution, Stephens saw no virtue or aid to his leadership: 'I don't believe in your wilfully out-at-the-elbows leaders, and I could never dream of lowering the people to a ragged democracy drenched with Spartan broth. I go in for levelling up, not down'. He had landed in France with less than twenty francs, and his appearance was so shabby and down-at-heel, that John Hopper finally at their first conversation gave him twenty francs after remarking thoughtfully that he must be badly off. Stephens gently remarked to his correspondent that this showed a man of good impulses, indeed John Hopper had constantly done him little services without which in fact Stephens would have perished long before, 'but he seems to lack the will and power to be largely generous or useful'. In a word, a good lump sum of one hundred or one hundred and fifty francs at that interview rather than many small sums later.

John Hopper, by Stephens's account, had much scope for his good impulses. He had sent his father one pound a week since he lost employment a year before, 'but for which the poor old man and his family (including my wife) could not possibly have existed. His brother George was thrown out of employment at the same time as his father and for several months was in a dreadful position; then John went over to London and started George in business being his security for the necessary stock. His means are not large'.

After leaving John Hopper's house, Stephens visited his cousins, the Caseys, Andrew, James, Joseph, Patrick, and their mother, and received the warmest of welcomes. He sensed that something was seriously wrong in the household financially, and concealed his own plight. 'A subtle intimation', he wrote to Walsh, warned him to keep silent. He evidently intended to ask two of them to go to Ireland on Fenian business at their own expense, and had in an earlier letter led Walsh to expect that two at least of them could. 'True Irishmen', he terms them, 'nothing dearer to them in the world than to serve their country'. The Caseys had kept 'open house for years for people of our way of thinking'. Although they earned some £500 a year between them, he discovered they were seriously in debt, 'young men will be young men, and many a wise ripe lad is a bad manager'.

Then occurred the incident with landlord and police already quoted from his diary. He had gone back to lodge in the same hotel where he had lived before he left Paris in 1871 but it was no longer in the possession of a friend and had 'changed hands to an utter stranger and a stupid brute'. After the uproar and explosion, Stephens 'put in three months of as hard a life as during the worst time in New York'. Hunger and anxiety wore him down, his wardrobe and health were so bad that he could not avail himself of an offer of ten francs a day for an hour's work. His friends in France 'this great country', were many, 'and more than one powerful man here would gladly and even proudly be a helping friend of mine. But under such circumstances as the present I feel bound to hide my sores from all foreigners. It would not serve Ireland to have it generally known how my countrymen have treated me. So I have shrunk into myself, and so I have been able to do nothing for myself and only too little for the cause'.

Yet in spite of all, even with his papers held in captivity some time by that utter stranger and stupid brute of a landlord, with many of his letters also there detained, and unable to send home his cousins or any other messengers, Stephens managed to do something for the cause and organization. His papers were released, and he got in touch with his correspondents. Favourable reports slowly reached him from his friends in Munster, Leinster, Ulster and England which confirmed an earlier report by one Dr Barry of 'the soundness of national feeling and all earnest men' for Stephens himself. There was no news whatever from Dublin or Cork, no Stephens organization seemed to exist, and the outlook was discouraging otherwise.

In the beginning of September a young man, 'one of us', with very little news, was brought to him by one of the Caseys. He sent back a message to any sympathetic Fenian Centres to confer with him in Paris. On 2 September, two arrived and stayed in the city for a week, one a Centre, not educated or of large ideas, yet earnest and hard-working, 'a majority of such would be dangerous from their narrowness'. The two men told Stephens that only four Centres in Dublin, representing something more than 300 members of the I.R.B., had broken with the anti-Stephens Supreme Council group in March twelve months before, and later formed themselves into an independent Directory. A few points in Co. Kildare had been won for the Stephenites. 'Neither my friends nor the Supreme Council had a single working centre in Dublin or neighbourhood'. The visitors could speak for no other parts of the country. Work was going on, men were buying arms and attending their drills, although unless something were done soon, all their efforts would be vain. And Stephens gathered that he was 'expected to accomplish this something'. The opinion, though flattering, did not impress him, and he questioned the truth of the reports and the friendship of his visitors, especially one of them, the 'literary' young man rather than the earnest and hard-working Centre.

A letter from the literary young man on 11 October increased Stephens's suspicions. It warned him that there was a plot afoot to damage the 'Captain's' influence in a 'friendly' way: a begging letter about his debts and poverty issued by a writer on the *Dundalk Democrat*. Dublin, wrote the literary young Fenian, was against such publicity, and appealed to Stephens for directions. He resented it equally and yet wondered what the writer's motives were in warning him. Was it to embroil him with possible friends? A second similar move followed from a London Committee for a National Testimonial.

On Tuesday, 20 October, 7.25, Stephens wrote in his diary: 'Nothing after the tea breakfast yesterday. Dreadful night. Tom came about half-past eleven today and gave me two francs. He could stay but a short time. Was so sick and feeble I could hardly dress myself. Bought two papers and paid for one (over and above the old score of 30). Bought half a quarter of butter (6 sous), 2 eggs (6 sous), cream (1 sou) and an ounce of tea (10). Tom had previously bought 4 sous' worth of tobacco, and he took 3 sous for his fare. One sou remained with which I bought waste paper' (presumably for his diary and correspondence).

Two days later, he dictated the following letter to his cousin,

Patrick Casey, to Robert J. Grannell, Sec. of the Testimonial Committee in London:

> 50 Rue de La Rochefoucauld,
> Paris,
> Thursday Oct. 22, 1874.

Dear Sir,

It was nearly 2 o'clock this afternoon when your letter and the accompanying 'Address' were handed me. I was still in bed, suffering from a cold; but so keenly do I feel this proposed subscription—my flesh creeps at the thought of it—that I at once arose to answer your very unexpected communication. The answer must be very brief, at least this time. It is Sunday week (Oct. 11) I got the first hint of this, to me intensely painful proceeding. It needed no 'misrepresentation' whatever to make me at once send off the following 'Notice' to Dublin (whence the news had come to me). [Here Notice sent to Lucas and Dunne.]² I would indorse these words with my blood. Will the people never know me? Were Ireland free as I wish her—and though every man of our race had proclaimed me the chief instrument of her freedom, I would not accept, even from the most grateful of people, either place, pension, or as much land as would 'sod a lark'. I have not worked for recompense and shall never accept any. As to a subscription of any kind, whether public or private, it is not to be thought of by anyone sincerely calling me friend. With thanks to all single-hearted Irishmen connected with this project, but with keen regret that they should have taken a single step in it without my knowledge and consent.

> I remain, dear Sir,
> Sincerely yours,
> JAMES STEPHENS

The rebuke was accepted in good part, and finally in January 1875, Mr Stephens consented to receive an illuminated address, and nothing more, which was dispatched to Paris by a trusty messenger and quietly delivered to him. The address was 'engrossed upon one of the largest sheets of vellum procurable in London, a limited space on the bottom being left for the signatures. At the top were the mottoes, "Honour to whom honour is due", and "Thy sun shall rise again", beneath

---

²Stephens enclosed these words in square brackets. See photostat of the original, *Dublin Xmas Magazine*, 1910, p. 16.

which was an exquisitely painted allegorical scene, comprising a round tower, Celtic cross, ruined church, wolf dog, harp and stand of arms, the background consisting of a sun-illumined sea'.[3]

In another long and private letter to Walsh, 7 July 1875, Stephens recounted his continued disappointments and trials although his health had mended at the close of 1874. The most startling item is his improved relations with Colonel Roberts, who had been more friendly towards him during the last visit to America, so friendly that Stephens felt justified in applying to him for a loan of £200 to enable him to carry out his schemes as Fenian leader. Stephens built high hopes on this and was certain that Roberts would give some substantial help. Towards the end of the previous year, under pressure from his cousins the Caseys, he had agreed to live with them for a while. John Hopper, alarmed at Stephens's plight, gave him one pound a week. He found the position irksome, and finally in spite of many appeals from Patrick Casey, went off again to the precarious and independent solitude of a room of his own. On 8 January, Mrs John Hopper sent him for a New Year gift a letter in such terms that he broke with the Hoppers and refused any further aid from them.

Mrs Stephens had been seriously and indeed dangerously ill before Christmas. She urged very strongly that she must return to Paris, and Stephens agreed to let her come over from London. He received a small sum of money from a friend who had hinted several times that it was there for the asking, and sent his wife two pounds for her fare with a characteristic letter:

> Rue de Madame, 43,
> Monday, March 15, 1875.

My Dear Wife,
I could hardly believe in the money till I held it in my hand, and paid the banker. The accompanying order, too, for two pounds is bona fides and will be paid to you in sterling coin or currency of his Britannic Majesty's dominions. The fairies have nothing

---

[3]*Irishman*, 30 January 1875. Stephens's letter to the London Committee is given, *Dublin Xmas Magazine*, 1910, p. 17; also Stephens Papers where there is also his letter, 11 October, to Lucas and Dunne, in similar terms.

at all to do with it, so fear nothing and come along. God speed
you.

Write a receipt of this and tell me the route and hour you are
to start. Love to all of you.

Your own,
JAMES.

In a previous letter dated 14 March, from the new address,
Stephens informed his wife that he had taken a lodging there
the previous afternoon. Rue Madame he described as 'a good
clean street, just beside the garden of the Luxemburg. I have
reasons for coming to this neighbourhood, which I like, and
which you will like, too, I think. You must not give my address
to anybody (mind *anybody*) either here or in London or elsewhere. Of course I except those immediately around you, but
nobody at all here'.

The news of her illness had been kept from him until she
was declared out of danger, yet even then it shook him severely,
and in a letter, 29 November 1874, he had told her that her
death would have been defeat for him once and for all:
'Nothing else would make me give in'.

It was in this unsettled mood, and still blindly confident of
help from Roberts and other quarters, that he impulsively sent
his letter of consent to her return, against his better judgment.

The very next morning, 16 March, a most sympathetic, and
in Stephens's view as expressed to Edward Walsh at least, a
very sincere letter came from Colonel Roberts of such a
desolating nature that Stephens wished most fervently that he
had waited for that morning's post, in which case he would
never have agreed to his wife's coming at all. Business tightness,
the Colonel sadly intimated, prevented him from assisting Mr
Stephens in any way just then. On 20 March, Mrs Stephens
arrived, and restored amicable relations with John Hopper
and his wife. Stephens very soon had another disappointment
to face. After many interviews with a French official, described
vaguely as 'M. Starr', for an unspecified job, it ended, as with
Colonel Roberts, in many expressions of sympathy—and
nothing else. After some hard months of struggle and debt and
rent in arrears, Stephens and his wife were abruptly and
rudely evicted from their lodging on the evening of 8 June.

A laconic phrase in a letter from John O'Leary to Devoy, 13 October 1875; 'Might tell you much of Mr S. but no present need, and, besides, if any curiosity, may have all I have to say about him from Luby', characteristically concealed O'Leary's timely counterstroke. He had already told both Luby and Devoy just what he thought of the venomous 'Fenianism Photographed' recently aimed at Stephens in the *Irishman*. 'Find him', O'Leary continued, 'in his private capacity about as unlikeable as he ever was. Think, however, very differently of his capacity from what you seem to do. Think, if things were done as you all think they ought, he's still [the] man for Galway, and with all his faults, better for that purpose than all the men in Galway and out of it'.[4]

Luby's fury of 1871 against Stephens too, had long cooled and he also was in the mood to agree with O'Leary that here indeed was the man for Galway. When Edward Walsh showed him Stephens's letter of 19 November 1874, he was deeply moved. 'Mr Luby told me', wrote Walsh to Stephens, 'that it was one of the greatest mistakes of his life to have attacked you. He has felt its effects ever since . . . Having read your letter, Mr Luby said it redeemed all your former faults, and he thought more of you now than ever'.[5]

There was a very thinly concealed pleasure in Stephens's mild and mock reproach to Walsh for including Luby among the select readers of his letter, even if it provoked the outburst:

'I should like to know what Mr Luby meant, when *he* considers my faults. Doubtless I am exempt from the common failings of humanity; but my political faults, about which there has been so much babble, were either invented for vile purposes, or would be considered virtues by competent and impartial judges. I am confident no man came out of such an ordeal more justly blameless, or in every respect more justly entitled to the largest trust, esteem and affection of his countrymen'.

One passage in Stephens's letter, of 7 September 1875, to Walsh gives a poignant account of the meeting between O'Leary and himself on the night of 8 June when Stephens

[4]*Devoy's Post Bag*, Vol. I., p. 122.
[5]Quoted by Stephens in a letter, 14 March 1875, to his wife just before her return to Paris.

and his wife had walked the streets through a thunder-storm, hungry, hopeless, with only three francs between them, in search of a cheap hotel. Then, 'it occurred to me that we were not far from Mr John O'Leary's residence, and then I felt that under the circumstances, I should not shrink from borrowing of him enough to secure shelter for the night. Lest you should not be aware of it, I may here state that, when a daft and slanderous scribe began to blurt his venom at me, Mr O'Leary administered a characteristic rebuke to him and immediately afterwards called on me.

'Now, though I myself would never have stooped to notice the virulent drivel of such a creature, I cannot but feel well towards those who put the brand of calumny on all such addled sources. Apart from this, I was glad to renew relations with an old friend, who had worked with me and suffered for the cause, and if we don't always agree in politics, either in principles or policy, and though he is opposed to my leadership just now, he is a rash man who would say that, under given circumstances, Mr O'Leary would not act with me as before. I should add that unless somebody urge him on, and give him an opening as I did, there is but slight possibility of his being of much further use to his country. For he appears to me more impractical (I mean in a large way), than ever, while his self-esteem and lack of faith in the people, if not in the cause, have increased.

'But however this, he was attentive and serviceable to me from the time of his first visit till he went to the country (10 July), bringing me books and papers (of which I stood in need and some of which have been retained by the landlord), calling for my letters (which were refused) and spending many an evening with us when we could not offer him even a cup of tea; and since leaving Paris, he has written me a letter and continues to send me newspapers. His other services I am now going to particularize.

'On the night of June the 9th, it was long past eleven when we found ourselves at the door of Mr O'Leary's residence. Leaving my wife in the hall—which was "dark as Erebus"—I groped my way to the sixth storey and found him alone and reading as usual. Soon as possible, I told him how we stood and asked could he lend me a few francs. He took some money from his pocket, and picking out a ten-franc piece, held it out to me. Thinking only of my immediate need, I declined this, taking a five-franc piece

instead; and then, thanking him and bidding him good night
hurried down to my wife'.

O'Leary displayed further 'gruff kindness' which led
Stephens to tell his correspondent that O'Leary had an ardent
and tender heart hidden behind a thin disguise of aloof and
austere detachment. This meant that O'Leary had written a
lecture to Stephens on a more orderly arrangement of his life,
just as much as he knew Stephens would stand even from him;
Stephens must not seclude himself because his clothes were
shabby. He could lend Mr Stephens no more money just then
as it would upset his budget, but he presented him with a bond
worth four pounds. Finally, O'Leary arranged with his landlord
for Stephens and his wife to take over his flat when he left
Paris for Brittany that summer, and presented them with his
furniture, saying it was nothing to boast of and he had no
further use for it.

Stephens sketched the new household at 11 Rue Brochant,
Batignolles, Paris, in a letter to his sister-in-law, Mary Hopper,
Sunday, 11 July 1875:

'Jane says the last advice Mamma gave her was to get a bed, chair
and table of any kind, and have a place of our own. Well, we
have all that now, and certain other necessaries, including a good
sofa. Our bed is almost as big as "the bed of Ware", and could
accommodate half-a-dozen grown up people, having a good
spring bottom and all other requirements. We have an easy
armchair, a mahogany round table, a water filterer, a small
mahogany press, with a marble slab for the bedside, (I don't
know what you call it), a tea tray and a few kitchen utensils. So
you see we have made a beginning here, 11, Rue Brochant, where
we came yesterday afternoon. God speed us'.

In fact, both Luby and Rossa at this time, to the consterna-
tion of Devoy and the Clan na Gael chiefs, came out publicly
and strongly in favour of the restoration of Stephens as Fenian
Chief, both hoping against hope that he had learned from
experience. His name was still a power in Ireland and the
United States, and the publicity campaign of the Stephens
Memorial Committee had caused a revulsion of feeling in his
favour.

On 27 January 1876, the Convention of the Fenian Brotherhood met in New York and remained in session until 1 February. Some 77 delegates were present including General Millen, Luby, Rossa and Thomas Francis Bourke. The *Irish World* report, 12 February, stated:

'It was unanimously resolved that the Fenian system of organization is the best adapted to advance the cause of Irish independence, and a resolution favouring the return of James Stephens to his old position as chief organizer also received unanimous endorsement. Colonel John O'Mahony was re-elected Head Centre, and the new Council includes Rossa, Luby and Bourke'.

Amidst all these trials, hopes, disappointments, Stephens wrote innumerable letters, his diary, kept in touch with his admiring Old Guard in several continents, scribbled down sharp comments and drafts of letters intended for them, and read. Now he would turn to the Old Testament, again to Edmund Burke and his old friends, the French Encyclopedists' works on the evolution controversy in which he was much interested, lives of the Irish saints, histories of secret societies, a very wide range of works indeed in science and philosophy, enlivened at times by some frivolous novels and grave or gay, when he had the tobacco, with his black pipe in full blast.

Several times warnings reached him from the Old Guard that his silence was causing them grave embarrassment, and urging him to issue manifestoes and come out into the open. Even his chief lieutenant in Ireland, John Brady, wrote a strong protest to him from 58 Mulgrave Road, Kingstown, on 12 September 1875:

'Many complain of your "apathy"—especially during, and since, your run out to the States . . . a strange policy . . . Would you risk a run amongst us?'

Even when the Fenian Brotherhood, in December 1877, sent him two hundred dollars and a request that he should come out to America as soon as possible, he did not answer for a year.[6] John Lucas, one of his Dublin supporters, wrote to him on 5 June 1878, ' 'tis one of the greatest handles your enemies

[6]D'Arcy, *Fenian Movement* . . . p. 396.

have against you that there has been no communication from you nor likely to be . . . There is one thing we are at a great loss for, and that is the manifesto that you promised. It is extremely necessary that you would send it as soon as you can. The heads of departments [Fenian Centres] in the south require that Mr B[rady] should bring such a document inside of three weeks, and read it for them, and they promised if that is done, they will have the work in as forward a state as ever it was in before, even as when you were here yourself. So you see yourself the necessity of it'.

The letters of the Old Guard, apart from these appeals, were full of uncomplimentary descriptions of personalities in the other Fenian factions, of which 'Supremers', 'usurpers' and 'carpet baggers', were the mildest. In spite of all this, it is clear that peace feelers and soundings for common action took place in the 'seventies. Brady, in the letter just quoted, after a satiric description of a Fenian celebrity, 'all for the cause except a character, which was never in his stock in trade', discusses some conversations with a member of the Supreme Council of the I.R.B., John Leavy, who is anxious to secure the help of Stephens and his followers in Ireland and abroad against Butt and the Home Rulers. Leavy—(whom Brady dislikes and distrusts, with some shrewdness as he later turned out to be an embezzler, an informer and government witness against Parnell at the Special Commission)—wants to persuade Hugh Byrne, an old *Irish People* contributor, then in San Francisco, to attack Butt and his supporters in the American press, and urges Brady to ask him. Leavy appears anxious that Stephens should take no independent action 'that will upset his Company' and concerned at the growth of Butt's movement. He knows all about a recent interview between the I.R.B. representative of his S.C. group in Paris, M. W. Stackpool, and Stephens, who has once more told this very friendly and sympathetic intermediary 'that you would only work on the old terms'. Leavy and Brady were unaware that Stackpool, from time to time, urged Devoy very strongly to refrain from public attacks on Stephens.

26 *The Fenians reply to Rutherford's Attack*

In the autumn of 1877 the appearance of John Rutherford's *The Fenian Conspiracy*, described by Mr John O'Leary as the malignant and mendacious compilation of an anonymous ruffian, united the Dublin daily press and the Fenians, Stephenite and anti-Stephenite, in a common fury of denunciation. Strangely enough it survived all the attacks and, with the exception of A. M. Sullivan's *New Ireland*, became until the publication of O'Leary's, Devoy's and Denieffe's memoirs at least, one of the most frequently accepted sources for the history of the Fenian movement. The formidable and devastating Fenian replies on its publication were in due course forgotten and remained unnoticed in yellowed newspaper files and Dublin Castle's extensive collection of Fenian items.

The main bias of Rutherford's book was against James Stephens, and throughout runs the poisonous hint that Stephens was an egoist who deliberately destroyed the movement he began when he could not dominate it; and that, moreover, he made a bargain with the British Government to walk out of prison quietly and behave in future. In addition, Stephens's affiliations with the French secret societies from 1848 to 1851 provide the sub-myth of Stephens as the active and trusty agent of foreign conspiracy, who 'visited Spain occasionally, Germany now and then, Italy often, and London still more frequently'.[1]

---

[1] *The Fenian Conspiracy*, Vol. I. p. 52. A very thorough collection of the press reviews of Rutherford's book was compiled by Samuel Lee Anderson, closely connected, with his brother, Sir Robert Anderson, with the 1865 Fenian trials in the Crown Prosecutor's Department of Dublin Castle. It is now in the Anderson Papers, National Library of Ireland. For S. L. Anderson, see T. P. O'Connor, *Memoirs of an Old Parliamentarian* (London 1929), Vol. 2. p. 170. Also Sir R. Anderson, *Sidelights on the Home Rule Movement* (London 1906), *passim*.

21

An unsigned review in the *Irish Times*, possibly by William O'Donovan, in turn Paris correspondent and on the editorial staff of that newspaper, categorically denied that Stephens ever visited or in fact ever was in Spain, Germany or Italy, and denounced the theory that he was engaged as a foreign agent of continental conspiracy as a pure fabrication. The Fenian plans, he argued, were based not so much on continental plans and models as on those of Fintan Lalor. Stephens's alleged 'call' to Luby in 1853—when in fact Luby did not return from Australia until a year later, and did not meet Stephens until the autumn of 1856—the ante-dating the foundation of the I.R.B. by five years, and other inaccuracies were cited to sum up the book 'as from first to last a tissue of lies, based on a small substratum of truth'.

With unusual vigour the generally placid and non-committal *Saunders' Newsletter* attacked Rutherford as the producer of 'a work of fiction . . . wretched catchpenny . . . and, as Carlyle said of Thiers' *History of the French Revolution*, "it is instructive to those who know nothing".'[2]

The *Irishman*, in three articles from 3 November to 21 November, attacked the book in detail, and denied that Stephens had ever written a line for it; it stated that the pamphlet alleged to have been written by him, *The Future State of Ireland*, and quoted much in *The Fenian Conspiracy*, was, in fact, written by J. E. Pigot; it pointed out that Stephens's alleged pseudonym, 'Celt' was that of T. Neilson Underwood. A reference to Denis Dowling Mulcahy's biography, as given by Rutherford, produced a letter from Mulcahy on 29 November, with a list of items about him in the book, prefaced by his own comment, *not*; declaring that there were ten untruths in any twenty lines of this 'biography', without

---

[2][The character of the newspapers in question may be worth noting. The *Irish Times* was then a trenchant Unionist publication, with a remarkable reportorial staff many of whom revealed considerable insight into nationalist movements of the day. *Saunders' Newsletter* was also Unionist, but with more social and cultural interest at this point; although old-established it was now in decline and did not survive for more than a few years beyond this date. The *Irishman* was at this time edited by Richard Pigott, later the famous witness in the Parnell Commission; despite his incapacity and squalid character, Pigott possessed an unrivalled knowledge of Fenianism and was not without journalistic artistry.—O.D.E.]

including errors, and pointing out that Mr Rutherford had included the name of a Fenian who had recently died in New York, Harry Mulleda, as one of the Manchester Martyrs executed ten years before.

It was John O'Leary, however, in collaboration with Stephens himself, who made the most informed examination of *The Fenian Conspiracy* in a letter from Paris to the *Freeman's Journal*, dated 5 November 1877. He concentrated on two of Rutherford's charges, Fenian finance and the alleged Fenian Assassination Committee. Many things in early Fenian history, he stressed, were known only to Stephens, Luby and himself, 'apart from the general sketch, authentic, lengthy, though not always accurate', of John O'Mahony, published in his New York organ the *Irish People* in 1868. He added, 'Mr Stephens alone is in possession of the documents necessary for anything like an adequate treatment of the subject.'

In reply to Rutherford's stories of fabulous sums wrung from Irish-America and squandered in riotous orgies, O'Leary gave, on Stephens's authority, the figures he later quoted in his memoirs (Vol. i. pp. 135–6). From 1858 to 1864, the first six years of the organization, the money received amounted to 'a little less than £1,500; 1864 to 1866, about £28,500; during O'Leary's stay in the United States in 1866, about £2,500; in all £32,500 of which nearly £7,000 was seized by the Government. The whole amount collected by the Fenian Brotherhood in America, Canada, etc. was under $500,000, nominally £100,000 at the then rate of exchange about £75,000 or £80,000.' This total included the money already mentioned as sent to Ireland from 1858 onwards.

On the assassination accusation, O'Leary was as explicit: 'Mr Rutherford, like nearly all writers who treat of Fenianism or any other secret society, seems to revel in ridiculous stories of assassination. I cannot, of course, deny that during the long period of Fenianism there were some few cases of assassination, and that some few Fenians held (and hold) that the slaying of informers was justifiable; but I can most positively assert that up to the time of my arrest, and the cessation of my active connection with Fenianism there was no case of assassination, nor, as far as I know, any project of assassination . . . I personally denounced in the

columns of the *Irish People* assassination in all its forms . . . I also
believe that my views on this subject are fully shared by Mr
Stephens and Mr Luby'.[3]

Rutherford's book infuriated O'Leary, who waged war on
it in all his writings and at all opportunities. Stephens described
it as a 'simple tissue of calumny and misrepresentations', and
during his residence in Brussels ten years after its publication,
prepared a full reply to it which was never published. Readers
of Rutherford, however, will detect in Stephens's essay
'Fenianism—Past and Present', his answer to many of
Rutherford's assertions and innuendoes. It was for long
wrongly suspected that Rutherford was Sir Robert Anderson,
patron of Le Caron, adviser to the Home Office on Fenian
and other Irish affairs and part author of the notorious *Times*
articles on 'Parnellism and Crime'. Anderson had stated in
his *Sidelights on the Home Rule Movement* that he had used the
confidential information he gained, as a Dublin Castle and
Home Office official, as material for a history of Fenianism.
He himself specifically denied authorship and explained in an
interview published in the London *Star* in 1910 that his history
had appeared anonymously in the *Contemporary Review* in
1868–9.[4]

John O'Leary always had the self-appointed and most
unenviable job of peace intermediary between Stephens and
his former colleagues, during the several approaches made to
him during the 'seventies. A letter to Mrs Stephens on 5
September 1877, who had once again returned to London,
shows how difficult Stephens had grown in his isolation, and
the contrast between his unrestrained candour in private and
his iron self-control in public controversy under even the most

---

[3]Rutherford's myth of the Fenian Assassination Committee was based on the
evidence of the informer Corydon at the Fenian Trials. See Devoy, *Recollections* . .
p. 38 for the assassination of the alleged informer George Clarke, which led to
another verbal duel between A. M. Sullivan and Fenian organs, and to
Rutherford's fantastic story in his *Fenian Conspiracy*, Vol. 2. pp. 158–64.

[4]See *Irish Book Lover*, June 1910, No. 11. Dr Crone, the Editor discovered that
Rutherford was a West of Ireland man who worked as a journalist on the London
press in the late 'seventies and 'eighties. Dr Crone was unable to trace Rutherford
in Sligo or Galway but interviewed his widow and daughter. He also obtained
Anderson's denial of the authorship of Rutherford's book. A sketch of Rutherford's
career is given in the *Book Lover* article, [and in the biographical notes below].

virulent attack. Kickham, as it happened, was dubious of and finally hostile to Stephens's recall to leadership by the Fenian Brotherhood, and as a member of the Supreme Council of the I.R.B. in Ireland in opposition to the Stephenite body there, was circumspect about meeting him publicly during visits to Paris. He was, however, prepared to make friendly private advances, and did so diplomatically. In due course, Stephens in the 'eighties wrote solemnly and ponderously of his friend, Charles J. Kickham, the most ardent of the ardent, ready to handle the pike and rifle for Ireland at Mullinahone in '48, with a grotesquely inadequate estimate of Kickham's part in the *Irish People* where he 'served me faithfully and well by his literary contributions in prose and verse'.

The tribute in 1882 undoubtedly was sincere. There is nothing solemn and nothing ponderous in the private judgment to his wife in September 1877. She and her sister, recalls Stephens most acidly, had met Kickham who had assured them, 'through an interpreter' that is, through a friend present who communicated with him in the deaf and dumb alphabet, that the anti-Stephenite 'pack of silly lies' had left him cold, and that he was 'still the same to Stephens'. 'The gentle soul!' snorts Stephens, 'the double dealer!', 'my most effective enemy!' Kickham, it seems, two months before had come to Paris, 'vain as pitiable on the forlorn hope' of winning over the 'Doctor', that is John O'Connor, then or soon to be, Secretary of the Supreme Council I.R.B. known under many pseudonyms, including Dr Clarke and Dr Korner.

John O'Connor at the age of fifteen had begun his career in Fenianism—of which he became one of the most mysterious and active agents in Europe—by guiding Stephens and Kelly on the night of the Richmond Jail escape to their hiding place. He saved them on that occasion by his vigilance. Like John O'Leary, and unlike his brother James O'Connor he was— whatever their differences—a life-long friend of Stephens. It is clear from this September letter that all his diplomacy was extremely taxed.

'Long ago,' thunders Stephens to his wife, 'at least since you left this—the Doctor but for me would have written so strongly

to the "gentle Charles" that as gentlemen, I don't see how
they could ever [have] touched hands again'.

Kickham, in fact, was then Chairman of the Supreme
Council and on terms of perfect friendship with the Doctor
who in vain tried to bring about a reconciliation. Indeed
Kickham himself, apart from his friendly message through
Mrs Stephens and Mary Hopper, had asked Stephens to meet
him in 'his *private capacity* though he could have nothing to do
with me in his *public way*.' 'The gentle Pishogue!' exclaims
Stephens, and goes on to describe how he watched the Doctor
stretched on the sofa after he had delivered Kickham's olive
branch, and proceeded to 'punish' Kickham and the Doctor
in his own way by the emphatic caveat:

> 'The "gentle" one indeed! I have been thinking ovei Mr
> Kickham's message and everything considered, I decidedly
> decline seeing him under the circumstances. If he knew how to
> think, feel and act like a gentleman he would never have dreamed
> of sending me so boorishly insulting a message; but the Creighton
> of Mullinahone is only a half-cultured villager!'

On this refusal, the Doctor 'leaped from the sofa as if he had
received an electric shock!' Then he said, 'It is the best course'.
Kickham's friends, of course, comments Stephens, 'circulate
the story that the "gentle" creature *having come here to see me,
I would not receive him.* This exposed, feeling against the lie and
the insult is growing more and more. Even without a published
word, I crush all my enemies. I mean when they try to oppose
my actions; otherwise I would not let a——to scatter them to
"all the airs that blow" '.

There is even more bitterness, and a spice of malice in his
references to Charles G. Doran[5] of Cork whom he dubs
'Queerhead' although the identity is obvious. Although 'a

---

[5]Charles Guilfoyle Doran (1835–1909). A Wicklow man who spent most of his
life in Cork and Cobh. Then member of the Supreme Council of the I.R.B. of
which he had been secretary; involved in the '67 rising after which he escaped to
France. Associated with the Amnesty movement and the Catalpa rescue. Friend
of John Mitchel in whose famous election campaign he took part in 1875. Also
one of the pall bearers at Stephens's funeral in 1901. Clerk of Works to Cobh
Cathedral. See Dr Mark Ryan, *Fenian Memories*, pp. 97–8; *Irish Nation*, Dublin,
27 March 1909, 'Charles Guilfoyle Doran', *Devoy Post Bag; passim.; Irish Book Lover.*

patriot of a kind, he has proved false' to Stephens in the struggle between the Fenian factions in which he had the company of James Casey, scarified in passing for 'acting with my enemies'. The indictment of 'Queerhead' continues: 'You and Mary Hopper once saw him (15 August 1867) in the Rue Bildault. Then, as last year, he made promises which he never kept . . . He has a peculiar head. This character has never eaten flesh meat, drunk spirituous liquors, smoked or snuffed tobacco, played any kind of game, and professes to be what the Pagan O'Leary would call a fierce Cawtholic. Yet he professes still more to be, if possible, an enemy to the priest in politics'.

The malicious chronicle continues. John O'Connor, much tried by Doran's parade of his virtuous abstention from meat, alcohol, gaming, tobacco and snuff, had to Stephens's delight once interjected: 'Free from almost all the vices! Then you must be an awful man for the women!' 'This from the Doctor!' crows Stephens. 'I never knew him to utter anything like it before'. And the letter is rounded off with a choir of 'Irish home voices', that is quotations of compliments from his faithful Old Guard, and his confident flourish, 'I now assure you that I am master of the situation'.

Doran and Kickham had long before discussed Mr Stephens between themselves. In April 1876, Kickham had written drily to Devoy that he and his friend, Doran, were spending a holiday together in Doran's home at Queenstown. Doran had recently returned from a week in Paris where he had met John O'Leary and Stephens, 'who so far as I can make out is very like what he was when I knew him'.[6] Such outbursts as those quoted above were characteristic of Stephens throughout his career, in his days of leadership and success as in his long and painful exile in ill-health, poverty and isolation from the main currents of Irish political life. When in Stephens's last years a visitor, Colonel Arthur Lynch, reported to John O'Leary that the 'Captain's' views of other men were now expressed with urbanity and charity, he shook his head, and remarked 'When he speaks well of others, his work is done. The man is breaking up!'

Three months later, in December 1877, Stephens rejected

[6]*Devoy's Post Bag*, Vol. I. p. 163.

an even more serious overture from the Clan na Gael, through
John O'Leary, when Dr William Carroll interviewed him in
Paris and reported to Devoy that Stephens 'like the Bourbons
has "forgotten nothing and learned nothing" '.[7]

Two factors in the development of the Irish political situation
had not been correctly weighed up by Stephens: the rapid rise
of the Clan na Gael to dominance among Irish organizations in
America, combined with its alliance with the Irish Republican
Brotherhood in a joint Revolutionary Directory. Since the
death of John O'Mahony in the February of that year, the
Fenian Brotherhood had no longer an outstanding leader.
Devoy and Breslin for Clan na Gael had carried out an even
more daring rescue than their rescue of Stephens in 1865, when
the *Catalpa* carried off the Fenian military prisoners from a
penal settlement in Australia, defiantly flaunting the Stars and
Stripes at a pursuing gunboat. O'Donovan Rossa had succeeded
O'Mahony as Head Centre of the Fenian Brotherhood but
his term of office was to be brief, while even his famous
Skirmishing Fund Organization was destined to be captured
and transformed by the Clan na Gael. Parnell was a rising
political force, and Davitt on the eve of release from a prison
cell thought along lines familiar to Stephens in 1856.

There was still a spell in the name of Stephens, and the very
violence of the attacks on him is evidence of this. James
O'Connor wrote a savage protest from Dublin to Rossa after
the Fenian Brotherhood Convention invitation to him to
return. The Old Guard, on their part, in their references to
Mr James O'Connor in correspondence to the Captain, if not
as abusive, were most libellous: he had a weakness for subsi-
dising out of arms funds, ex-peelers and bankrupt anti-
Stephenites, and notorious drunkards posing as patriots.

'Let Stephens say what he pleases about his influence in Ireland.
You know the wretch is incapable of telling the truth . . . There
is not a decent man in Ireland, unless he is a known idiot, that

[7]*Devoy's Post Bag.* Vol. I. pp. 284–5, where the Carroll report and O'Leary-
Stephens letter are also given. The *Catalpa* rescue is described in the same volume.
p. 176, *passim.* Also, Devoy, *Recollections,* pp. 251–260.

belongs to his scabby little party . . . You may show this to the old villain'.[8]

The persistent battle with poverty and uncertainty continued. A letter addressed to John O'Leary by Stephens, 1 October 1878, revealed that Mrs Stephens had returned to Paris. Earlier that year, from February to April, Stephens's letters to her had been comparatively cheerful and he had forwarded several money orders. He had been teaching and mentioned the scarcity of good English teachers in Paris. His pupils, he said with pride, received from him for eighty francs instruction worth five hundred.

The October letter to O'Leary showed that hard times were with him again:

'My reason for not sending our address is, our poverty has been so great that you could not help seeing it, and then, if you offered some assistance, I could not help taking it, or perhaps resist the temptation of asking you for some, and this while fearing you had not enough for yourself, which has always been the case whenever you advanced me more than the merest trifle.

'However, I trust that in five or six weeks it will be better with my family as well as with myself, when I can ask you to come with an easy mind and a *cead mile failte*.'

In January 1879 James Stephens sailed for New York to make his last serious bid to regain supreme leadership of the Irish Revolutionary movement.

[8]The O'Connor letter is quoted at greater length, D'Arcy, pp. 396–7. The same writer, p. 399, writes, 'A reading of the many letters denouncing Stephens would lead one to believe that he was the personification of evil, unless it were kept in mind that they were written by impetuous Irishmen, who afterwards regretted their actions'. A Dublin paper is quoted as evidence that O'Connor was a pall bearer at Stephens's funeral. He was certainly present. The *Freeman's Journal*, 1 April 1901, however, names only Michael Davitt, C. G. Doran, Michael Lambert, William Brophy, James Birmingham, and William Hickey, all '67 men, as the pall bearers. The list strengthens Father D'Arcy's point, as Davitt and Doran at one time strong critics of Stephens, were later his firm friends. John Devoy, *Gaelic American*, 19 March 1910, devoted a leading article to James O'Connor's work in the Fenian and other national movements. See also, *Devoy's Post Bag*, Vol. I. pp. 55–8; Vol. 2. p. 372. Luby in his letters to John O'Leary summed up the Stephens-O'Connor dispute as one between James the Greater and James the Lesser. Having heard both men's account of the origins of the clash, Luby pronounced O'Connor to be 'decidedly and caddishly in the wrong' (Luby Papers).

ON this last visit Stephens remained in the United States little more than a year. His mission to regain the lost leadership ended in failure. He took over the leadership of the remnant of O'Mahony's Fenian Brotherhood which, in fact, with O'Mahony's death in February 1877, declined as an effective force although twenty thousand Fenian sympathisers had marched behind his coffin. Stephens, to be sure, continued to issue his characteristic manifestoes and signed himself as of old, James Stephens, Chief Organizer, Irish Republic. The Irish-American press in general was hostile to him. Patrick Ford's *Irish World* was friendly to the Clan na Gael, now in influence and membership the most powerful of all Irish-American societies, and uncompromisingly against any restoration of the Stephens one-man rule. Luby and Rossa had lost all hope that the Captain would learn from experience and consent to work with others except on his own impossible terms. They maintained a charitable silence but held aloof. John Devoy and Dr William Carroll, dominating personalities in the Clan na Gael councils, were determined to prevent Stephens from re-entering public life and carried on a remorseless campaign to discredit 'the old Ruffian'.

Stephens indeed showed still some skill in seeking support even among former enemies, including P. J. Meehan and the *Irish-American*. Rossa approached Patrick Ford and the *Irish World* with some success, until finally under Dr Carroll's urgings, Ford changed his mind and backed the Clan na Gael leaders. He declined to meet Stephens or give him publicity. The same influence prevented the presentation of addresses to Stephens in New York as 'Lawful Chieftain'. John O'Leary, then in a very conditional alliance with Devoy and Carroll so far as their national activities and some business matters in Ireland and Paris were concerned, remained a powerful neutral in this private war.

Even the forthright Dr Carroll did not shake O'Leary when he wrote to him after the battle between the Clan and Stephens had been in effect decided:

'I visited Ford's of *Irish World* on Sunday, and they promptly placed paper at my disposal; said they would publish anything I sent them, and in short left me nothing to ask in that way. If Old Imposter [Stephens] is not wiped out in it you may rely that it is because we don't think the game worth the powder . . . The funniest thing of all is the resolution sent out by young ecclesiastic D. for publication, speaking of "sincerity of Mr James Stephens's patriotism, unquestioned service to Ireland etc." When you see the young man ask him what he takes us for over here anyway. When it comes to taking into the National ranks, and puffing as a "patriot", a d—m—d old bummer of the emptiest and most disgusting species of confidence man, whose very name raises the gorge of decent people, the only thing left to be done will be the employment of some low-priced Gibbon to scribble a few lines mentioning its decline and fall—obituary it will not require. Nobody would bother themselves to read it'.[1]

This prophet had done his best to make his prophecy come true. He was convinced that Stephens, like other autocrats before him, had forgotten nothing and learned nothing. This opinion had been confirmed by his interview with him in Paris two years before when Stephens had met his overtures as Clan na Gael envoy with impossible demands and conditions, although Stephens during this visit very strongly denied that the doctor's version of the interview or of his reply was accurate.[2]

The dispute was thoroughly debated by both men before a private meeting in New York summoned by Clan na Gael where the evidence was given on oath. Among those present were J. J. Breslin who had helped to rescue Stephens from Richmond Prison in 1865, and Edward O'Meagher Condon,

[1]*Devoy's Post Bag*, Vol. I. p. 433. Carroll-O'Leary, 23 April 1879.
[2]This Paris interview with both the Carroll and Stephens versions of it is given *Devoy's Post Bag*, Vol. I. pp. 284–5.

who had been released from penal servitude some years before; only Condon's American citizenship had enabled him to escape the death sentence for his part in the Manchester rescue of Colonel Kelly and Captain Deasy in 1867. The confrontation of the Clan na Gael envoy and the Fenian leader was bitter, dramatic, intense.

Years later Devoy, for once relenting in the case of Stephens, briefly dismissed this encounter as 'an interesting but painful chapter' and forebore to enter into details. Stephens was much hampered in his defence by the legacy of his whirling speeches and promises and overstatements during 1866, and his defence of his position in 1867—which was identical with his statement, already quoted, drawn up in January 1867—and was somewhat too hastily dismissed by the conference speakers in many cases. On the Paris interview Stephens made a weaker case, even allowing for some exaggeration and bias in Dr Carroll's account. It is quite clear that Stephens had been trapped into a conference well packed beforehand with his enemies.[3]

Stephens in the end found that his mission was a failure, and that other organizations in the United States and in Ireland were now the living forces. Yet although his day, to all other eyes but his, had gone, he still held to his old arrogant assumption that he alone was the hope and guide for the Irish race at home and abroad. In Ireland the Stephenite organization dwindled into insignificance. After many months of grinding poverty, he went back to his second country, France, still the same James Stephens, to the same familiar semi-starvation, tempered by casual tuitions and casual journalism, softened at intervals by the devotion of his wife and the unswerving allegiance asserted in letter after letter from his Old Guard, small in numbers, and scattered over the face of the earth.

In June 1879, John O'Leary reached for his quill and informed Devoy and all whom it might concern the truth of the matter and just where he stood, for the benefit of Dr Carroll, the anti-Stephenites in general, and, in particular, for an unknown critic who had denounced Stephens in the New York press. Since he left prison in 1871, he wrote, he had not

[3]See, with many relevant documents quoted, the account of this conference, Dr Carroll Confronts James Stephens', *Devoy's Post Bag*, Vol. I. pp. 419–26.

acted with Stephens, nor did he think it likely that he would ever again. Then very tersely O'Leary indicated what he thought of the prevailing anti-Stephens frenzy of Devoy, Dr Carroll, J. J. O'Kelly and their press allies:

'All this is, however, in no sense to be taken as giving any expression of opinion upon the larger question of Mr Stephens's character, nor of his past conduct in Irish affairs. I am not prepared to go into that now, but I must protest against the erroneous, even ridiculously erroneous estimate formed of Mr Stephens by many people, and notably by "Lough Swilly" in *N. York World*'.[4]

In July 1881, during a visit to Paris, Henri Le Caron, cleverest and never detected British Government agent in Clan na Gael, met Stephens and seemed sincerely touched by his plight. Le Caron informed Devoy that there was much sympathy for Stephens due only to pity for 'his impoverished financial and physical condition, and not for the purposes of furthering his views of being a leader. [Patrick] E[gan] assisted the poor fellow financially to prevent him being thrown in the street when I was there'. Later in his book, *Twenty-five Years in the Secret Service*, Le Caron described his meeting with Stephens, who never suspected him, and told him the correct story of his escape. And Le Caron recalled what a 'curious being he was, he inspired feelings of the sincerest affection on the part of his immediate followers; and there were few things, that, in their regard for him, they would not seek to accomplish on his behalf'. And this most venomous hidden enemy of Fenianism, who regarded John O'Leary and Dr William Carroll as the only two men in the entire Fenian movement worthy of respectful mention, added a third at the memory of the Stephens of 1881, in his Paris garret, 'an exile broken in fortune, health, and hope, smoking his short black pipe and brooding over these days that are no more'.[5]

In the 'eighties, Stephens, however, did more than brood

---

[4] O'Leary to Devoy, 30 June 1879, *Devoy's Post Bag*, I. pp. 449–50. [O'Leary clearly wrote New York *World* in error for the *Irish World* for which 'Lough Swilly', almost certainly Dr William Carroll, was then a columnist.—O.D.E.]

[5] Le Caron to Devoy, 13 July 1881, *Devoy's Post Bag*, II. 100. Henri Le Caron, *Twenty-Five years in the Secret Service—The Recollections of a Spy* (London 1892), 163–66.

and smoke his black pipe in his Paris garret. His reminiscences of the 1848 rising were serialised in the Dublin *Irishman*, from 4 February to 10 June 1882, while from October 1883 to February 1884, his account of his 1856 tour through Ireland appeared in the Dublin *Weekly Freeman*. The last articles, according to one account, were commissioned by the editor of the *Freeman's Journal*, Edmund Dwyer Gray, who discovered him sleeping out in a Paris park. As Dwyer Gray stated in 1885 that he had never met Stephens, this story is probably untrue.

In May 1884, Stephens wrote an article, 'Ireland and the Franchise Bill', in the *Contemporary Review*. And in the same year he contributed a series of semi-autiographical articles, under the title 'A Budget of Franco-Irish News', to the Boston *Republic*. Some of the statements and items in these exposed him to some indirect criticism from John O'Leary, and some very direct invective from John Devoy in his paper, the New York *Irish Nation*, probably because of a certain animus against Parnell and his party displayed even more openly in an interview with Stephens in the New York *World*. The interview announced Stephens's plans for a new political party on anti-Parnellite lines, with 'sterner methods yet anti-dynamite'. It was hinted that Stephens had been watched by detectives after some of the London dynamite explosions the Sullivan or 'Triangle' wing of the Clan na Gael had sponsored.

Devoy insinuated that Stephens had not written the articles but that they were the work of Eugene Davis, the Cork-born Fenian poet and journalist, and life-long friend of Stephens. After this challenge, Stephens sometimes dictated official and personal letters to others, especially to his cousin, Patrick Casey. Davis was an able but erratic man, who in early life had been educated for the priesthood in the Irish College, Paris, and then spent a wandering life on the continent. He worked as a journalist in Ireland and the United States and as a freelance correspondent in Paris. He was possibly the author of the New York *World* interview which roused both Devoy and John O'Leary by its anti-Parnell bias and the sensational statements about Stephens's new party, and the conference to be held in Paris within a month when Stephens,

John O'Leary, John Savage, Sir Charles Gavan Duffy, a picturesque adventurer known as General Macadaras, among others would attend. Stephens was described as the organizer of the new party, and in touch with Irish-American circles. Parnell, he was quoted as saying, was not trusted by his own party, he was too autocratic. New leadership and a new organization were needed for the young men at home, who were either too timid or too reckless. This was also the note of the *Contemporary Review* article. Devoy and O'Leary possibly knew that such anti-Parnellite and anti-Land League personalities as Lady Florence Dixie had been in correspondence with Stephens.[6] An undated letter from her in his papers suggests he should write a candid criticism of Parnell for *Vanity Fair*.

The association of Eugene Davis and Stephens was to lead within a year to their temporary expulsion from France at the request of the British Government. Davis, with Joseph and Patrick Casey—both cousins of Stephens—were associates of the Invincible refugees, P. J. Tynan and Frank Byrne. They were also given to some convivial meetings with genuine extremists and British agents disguised as hundred per cent revolutionaries in an atmosphere of hot air, unsuspecting confidences, and some sensational journalism. Davitt dubbed these gatherings later 'a general emporium for "plots", "secrets", "revolutionary designs" and "treasonable" documents', although he admitted afterwards that his condemnation of Casey, and Davis in particular, had been overdone. Davitt has been misled because Davis and Casey had been duped by Pigott during his trip to Paris just before he planted his forgeries on the *Times*. During the Special Commission both men rounded on Pigott and gave timely aid to Davitt and Parnell. Davis was horrified at Pigott's evidence, and sent a long statement refuting Pigott's story of how he had obtained the forged Parnell letters in Paris. He directed this to his friend, Michael MacDonagh; it was published in the London *Star* in April 1889, and was generally accepted as a vindication of Davis.[7]

[6] See *Devoy's Post Bag*, Vol. 2. pp. 162–5 for John O'Leary's defence of Lady Florence Dixie against attacks by Devoy and others in the press.

[7] Statement to the author by Michael MacDonagh, 20 November 1937, in reply to pp. 274–5, *Phoenix Flame*. See also, Davitt, *Fall of Feudalism*, 434–38; Devoy, *Recollections* . . . pp. 276–77; *Devoy's Post Bag*, Vol. 2. pp. 160–62.

There is no evidence that Stephens ever attended the dangerous and convivial circles frequented by his cousins and Davis on occasion. He would certainly have made very short work of one visitor, who turned up in the 'eighties, Red Jim McDermott, very busy as *agent provocateur* during the Triangle dynamite campaign, touring London with unsuspecting dynamitards, planting documents and explosives on his dupes, landing more than one victim into penal servitude. He persuaded Davis to go on a mission to London, well primed with compromising documents, but fortunately for Davis recalled him hurriedly in a panic when a Paris Fenian learned of this, and told McDermott—already under suspicion owing to public denunciations by Davitt and O'Donovan Rossa—that if Davis were arrested, he would be shot.[8]

John O'Leary in veiled ironic terms dismissed the Stephens interview, and above all the Paris political conference report, in a letter dated 16 June 1884 to the public press. No power on earth, he declared, could bring himself and the others mentioned under the same roof for five minutes, and he alluded with asperity and contempt to the activities of unnamed Irish freelance journalists in Paris. He did not name Davis although it was evident he had no sympathy with Stephens's new political proposals.

The Devoy attack was published in his *Irish Nation*, first that on Stephens and Davis on 21 June, followed by a scathing lead-article on 28 June, following up his first onslaught on the *Contemporary Review* article on 7 June. Somewhat rashly Stephens replied indignantly and obviously truthfully that he had written all the 1882–84 articles in the Dublin *Irishman* and *Weekly Freeman* which appeared over his name. Whether in fact Davis had written the Boston *Republic* 'Franco-Irish' budget series was not made very clear. The extracts quoted from them were in Stephens's heavy and rambling style, and full of autobiographical facts, that obviously he alone could know. Yet in them and in the New York *World* interview itself there were some traces of Davis: alleged inside knowledge of terrorist circles, precise details of the Paris movements of

[8] *Weekly Irish Independent*, F. J. Allan, 'Behind Prison Bars' series: 'Red Jim McDermott'. 2 June 1894.

returned dynamitards from London (whom Stephens consistently denounced and most certainly never met on friendly terms) and chaffing of Scotland Yard detectives, in particular one Moser known as a trailer of extremists, on the prowl in Paris.

In a reply to the *Irish Nation's* onslaught Stephens very loftily referred to the days when Devoy had been an excellent 'subordinate' of his, and drew the savage, and irrelevant, retort:

'When Stephens dropped from the prison wall on John Ryan's breast, I was the "subordinate" who caught him in my arms and placed his troubled form on the ground, and I shall never forget how "he shook like a dog in a wet sack" as I dropped him and he timidly whispered "come on, come on" as the sole answer to the sturdy men who surrounded him. I began to lose faith in Mr Stephens that night and the process was completed in the next twelve months'.

Such acid pinpricks weakened the effectiveness of Devoy as a propagandist throughout his career, and every Irish leader with whom he was associated suffered from it in turn. Luby later in his letters to John O'Leary protested against this particular smear on Stephens's courage during the prison escape, and contradicted Devoy's constant insinuation that Breslin accused Stephens of cowardice during the critical moments when the escape was threatened with failure, and asked indignantly whether if, in fact, Stephens had through physical strain and excitement 'trembled', what of it? Luby went on to tell O'Leary that in his opinion that was all invention. The more serious charge made by the Roberts faction that built up the myth that Stephens had ever lived 'in luxury' in Paris, was contemptuously dismissed as 'American gossip and malice', which Luby resented all the more because he himself had shared 'the downright privation' of John O'Leary's brother Arthur and Stephens in Paris in 1860.

The activities of the Irish-American dynamitards in Great Britain spread a 'Fenian' scare throughout the country, and the picturesque inventions of the unnamed Paris journalists who angered John O'Leary rattled the French Government, and made it receptive to British Government representations.

22

On 19 February 1885, according to the *Annual Register*, 'the Dynamite Revolutionary section of the Irish Revolutionary Party issued from Paris a warning to the British Cabinet that in the event of a renewal of the Crimes Act (Ireland) they would have recourse to retaliatory measures'.

The *Annual Register* recorded for 12 March the sequel to some of Eugene Davis's journalistic and social indiscretions:

'James Stephens, formerly Fenian Head Centre, Eugene Davis, head of the Dynamite party in Europe, and two other notorious Fenians arrested by the Paris police and expelled from France'.

The London correspondent of the *Freeman's Journal*, 14 March 1885, having noted the arrests of Stephens, Davis, and of a Mr Morrissy, a native of Co. Carlow, by the French secret police, and the orders for their expulsion from France, proceeded:

'Messrs. Davis and Morrissy were stated to have been present at the dynamite convention of which a short account was given some days ago. It will be remembered that the Parisian journal *La France* published an article ridiculing the convention, which it treated as a mere *rêve de journaliste*. An Englishman named Kimberly thereupon wrote a letter stating that he had been present at the convention and had written the report in question. *La France* declined to insert it. Mr Kimberly then threatened to shoot M. Mermerx, a member of the staff of that journal, but the latter, who was also armed, set his menace at defiance. Kimberly is at present awaiting trial for this outrage.

'A letter, however, was subsequently published to which the signatures of Mr Davis and another were affixed, declaring that the meeting had been held, and that Kimberly's account of it was perfectly *bona fide*. Mr Stephens, however, it was stated, declined to have anything to do with the meeting. Mrs Stephens, who was also arrested yesterday, has since been released. The most active search is being made for a fourth person, believed to be Flannery, Secretary of the Secret Revolutionary Directory, but he is believed to have left France.

'Messrs. Stephens, Davis and Morrissy have been—after an examination before one of the officers under the command of M. Camecasse, the chief of the police force—detained prisoners at the depot, and it is believed that they will be expelled from France tomorrow.

'The *Gaulois* yesterday states that this action has been taken with a view to conciliate the British by M. Ferry. Mr Davis was a journalist by profession and had a connection with several papers'.

On 15 March the *Freeman's Journal* London correspondent declared that even the most Conservative of the Parisian journals expressed complete surprise at the action of M. Ferry in directing the expulsion of Stephens from France. And an interview with Mrs Stephens published in the *Figaro* on the day after Stephens's arrest was quoted at length. The interview was given at her house, No. 8 Rue Lebon after her release. She said that her husband had lived in Paris since 1866, and was acting as a correspondent of the *Standard*, was an occasional contributor to the *Contemporary Review*, and of several American newspapers. But the guiding purpose of the Head Centre's life—the cause of Irish Independence—he never lost sight of for one moment. He had many friends among French statesmen and journalists, and was intimate with the Marquis de Boissy and Emile Olivier, who were both very kind to him.

'My husband', added Mrs Stephens, 'never sympathized with the dynamiters, and in fact never ceased denouncing them. What he wanted was open war between England and Ireland, and he deprecated a resort to any methods but those of recognized warfare'. This disposed of the statement published by the *Pall Mall* that Stephens had proposed a basis of union between the different Irish revolutionary bodies.

As for the arrest. 'We were taking our first breakfast at eight o'clock when we heard a ringing of the bell. I opened the door to some gentleman who said he came to arrest both of us. He conducted us to the Commissary's office in the Rue Laugier. We demanded some explanation but the Commissary replied that he could not give us any until he telegraphed to the Prefecture. The only reply to the telegram was an order for my release. I went to the Prefecture where I sought again for information, which they again refused to give. My husband has no money and I don't know what he can do. If they give him up to England, I shall go in the same steamer with him, and give myself up, too'. The London *Freeman* correspondent commented that it was now clear that M. Ferry had no intention of handing over Stephens to the British, but what he had done was even more extraordinary and inexplicable.

The reaction in Ireland was swift, and sympathy with Stephens was widespread. Edmund Dwyer Gray at once launched a fund for Stephens, who, he declared had no more to do with dynamite than he had, and that the expulsion was a cruel exercise of arbitrary force. On 19 March, the *Freeman's Journal* published this appeal of its editor with extracts from a personal appeal addressed to him by Mrs Stephens: 'My husband is expelled and dying in Mons, Belgium, without one franc. I cannot go to him, having no money. Can you do any-thing for him?' Within a week the fund was over two hundred pounds, and the subscriptions continued to come in from many quarters, organizations and people. It was clear that Stephens had won his place in the memory of Ireland. Less than a month later the Ferry Government fell but the ban on Stephens remained in force for some years.

Devoy, in his *Recollections*, with possibly a vague memory of his old controversy with Stephens and Davis, denounced the second as the author of the report which led to the expulsion, 'a cruel blow to the poor old man . . . escorted to the Swiss frontier while the blackguard who wrote the fake was allowed to remain in Paris to ply his miserable trade'.[9] Davis indeed bore an indirect responsibility for the expulsion. The mention of Stephens in the report of 'the dynamite convention', even with the qualification that he had refused to attend it, and the linking of his name with the adventurer Macadaras in the announcement of the fictitious political conference, gave colour to the British representations to the French Government. This explained the bitterness of the later attacks of Davitt and Devoy on Davis and on Stephens's cousin, Patrick Casey, although these attacks certainly went too far.

Davis, in a long rambling article of over two columns in the *Freeman's Journal*, described his expulsion in the vaguest terms, and thanked the British Government for the opportunity it had given him to take up his residence in Switzerland. He paid a respectful tribute to James Stephens, and mentioned that the Head Centre had been a personal friend of Gambetta. On the pseudo-revolutionary antics which had landed Stephens in

[9] Devoy, *Recollections* . . . p. 277.

Belgium and himself in Switzerland he was discretion itself.
And day by day the Stephens fund grew, and was dispatched
to Mrs Stephens. Edmund Dwyer Gray had circumvented
Stephens's invariable repudiation of funds and testimonials.

In an interview given to an American journalist in Brussels
two years later, on 4 October 1887, Stephens showed little of
'the poor old man'. He made a dazzling impression on the
New York daily reporter, who also noted the presence of Mrs
Stephens, 'a brunette of some forty summers'. The flat was situated
in the Galerie du Parlement. Stephens's study was strewn with
books and papers, including voluminous notes for his memoirs.

'There must be a reliable and authentic history of Fenianism',
said Stephens. 'Rutherford's narrative of our movement was a
simple tissue of calumny and misrepresentation. A. M. Sullivan
and Justin McCarthy were superficial in their accounts.' The
interviewer described Stephens as an accomplished conversa-
tionalist 'with grace and gesture as when in 1866 he was the
centre of attraction under the rooftrees of Jules Sandeau and
the Marquis de Boissy'. He showed, too, a deep interest in
contemporary French literature, in English, in particular the
works of George Eliot, with, for mild distraction, the romances
of Ouida!

When he came to discuss his expulsion from France, Stephens
displayed no want of sharp words:

'Lying and libellous reports of Scotland Yard detectives
caused an infamous and diabolical injustice. M. Ferry's
Government broke up my little home in Paris, compelled me
to herd with the scum of scoundrelism in the city bridewell,
and eventually hustled me out of the country, as if tainted
with political leprosy!'

'Do you know', continued Mr Stephens with a smile as his
sense of humour cooled his anger, 'do you know that my
portrait is with those of all the notorious criminals of France in
the archives of the Paris Prefecture of Police?'

In a grimly humorous tone, he added:

'Armed guards with fixed bayonets stood behind me while
I was handcuffed and forcibly photographed!'

Becoming serious again, Stephens emphatically repudiated
all Irish terrorist activities:

'So far as I am concerned, I may state that I had nothing to do, directly or indirectly, with the so-called Irish extremists. I had on several occasions dissociated myself from their programme, and condemned their policies'.[10]

The expulsion, in fact, had done Stephens an unexpected service. The widespread and profound protests in Ireland and America and France revealed that Stephens's long silence had not after all buried him in oblivion and that he had won his place in Irish history. The bitterness of old controversies had died away. There were periodical outspoken comments in the Irish-American press that the known and prolonged hardships of Stephens, whatever the disputes over his leadership in the past and the 1867 controversy, must be ended. The fund raised by Edmund Dwyer Gray had to a large extent succeeded in this, and the response to it was more than a money tribute to Stephens.

Some years after the fall of the Ferry Government, Stephens and his wife returned quietly to Paris. Eventually through the intervention of Parnell, who approached the British Government on the matter, Stephens was allowed to return to Ireland. Only one condition was imposed by the British Government: there must be no public demonstration. So after twenty-five years of exile, Stephens and Mrs Stephens returned to Dublin on 25 September 1891, and lived in retirement in their cottage in Sutton.

On 14 November 1895, Jane Stephens died there, in her fifty-second year, of acute pneumonia. The Old Guard placed a wreath on her grave which read:

'In loving memory of the wife of Ireland's Fenian Chief from the Old Guard'.

Six years remained to the Fenian Chief himself. He died early on Friday morning, 29 March 1901, after a sudden and unexpected attack of weakness, at the house of his brother-in-law John Pain, 82 George's Avenue, Blackrock, Co. Dublin. Around his coffin was wrapped the Fenian Tricolour of Green, White and Orange, which within fifteen years became the banner of that decisive national revolt for which the dead man had plotted and dreamed so long in vain.

[10]National Library of Ireland MS. Biographical folder on James Stephens.

AND now that the story of the Fenian Chief has been told, he himself must be allowed the last word as to what he understood by Fenianism, happily preserved in his own private papers. This draft, *Fenianism—Past and Present*, which from internal evidence must have been written at the earliest in the late 'eighties, was obviously intended to be used as a magazine article. Stephens here defines what Fenianism was and is to him: the movement under his own autocratic leadership up to 1866. He repudiates most definitely the dynamite campaign. Rossa's Skirmishers and the Clan na Gael terrorists are to him merely factions. And one erasure in the MS. betrays his resentment of Parnell's ascendancy over Irish political life. In a sentence reading 'the *leader* of the Irish Parliamentary Party', he deletes the word 'leader', and substitutes 'chairman'. He ignores the significance of the New Departure, and that such brilliant Fenian leaders as Michael Davitt and J. J. O'Kelly had gone over to the Land League and Parnell, with Devoy as a most formidable ally, or that two surviving leaders of the 1858–66 Fenian phase, Luby and O'Leary, remained his personal friends but rejected very firmly any idea that Stephens could ever again become the supreme Fenian leader. Yet, in a sense, they and the hostile Kickham, remained dominated by Stephens's ideal of Fenianism.

'Twenty-five years ago', this essay begins, 'there was no such word as "Fenian" in the English language. When my friend and fellow-assistant, the late John O'Mahony, first applied the term "Fenians" to the members of the nationalist organization which he started on the American continent, and which worked hand in hand with the I.R.B. in Ireland, he borrowed it from the annalists of old who record the fact that the ancient militia

of the Kingdom of Erin were known as Fenians throughout the
length and breadth of the land. These veteran warriors lived
and flourished in this native island long before a Norman
invader set foot on its shores. Besides being the faithful and
devoted guardians of their country's honour and liberty, they
were adepts in all the military exercises of the period, and were
in themselves the very flower, the *crème de la crème* of Irish
manhood, "tall as Roman spears", broad-shouldered, muscular
and athletic. If, then, there was anything in a name, here was
one which, it was thought, should not, or could not be mis-
interpreted. Mr O'Mahony in drawing on the old Gaelic
vocabulary for a word to represent his ideas, showed a
preference for his mother tongue by doing so.[1]

'In his eyes Fenianism symbolized two principles: firstly,
that Ireland had a natural right to independence, and secondly,
that that right could be won only by an armed revolution.
The Fenians, therefore, according to him, were the men to
uphold the first of these principles in theory, and to carry out
the second to a practical and successful issue. The words
"Fenians" and "Fenianism" have since then been made to
represent organizations which John O'Mahony would not
sanction or approve of if he were alive today, and which
certainly I, for my part, could not dream of endorsing. Certain
revolutionary wings, having of late years decided on the policy
of endeavouring to intimidate English statesmen into the
concession of the Irish national demand by blowing up or
attempting to blow up certain public edifices in London and
in other parts of Great Britain, the British press unequivocally
proclaims that the policy in question is that of Fenianism. If a
man be caught carrying a black bag in which an infernal
machine is carefully stowed away, he is immediately dubbed
a Fenian, and all the newspapers refer to the circumstances as

---

[1]Stephens here ignores or forgets the dislike of many I.R.B. men for the label
Fenian, similar to the dislike of a later generation after 1916 for the term Sinn
Fein. In both cases usage imposed both words. Denieffe, p. 121, writes, 'We in
Ireland were not Fenians, as we were in existence long before this romantic name
was given to the American wing by John O'Mahony'. O'Leary Vol. 1. p. 92 note
declares, 'the word is convenient, if incorrect'. ' "Fenianism"—did I tell you I
hate the damned word?' John Boyle O'Reilly to Devoy, 11 February 1871
(*Devoy's Post Bag*, Vol. 1. p. 30).

a Fenian arrest. If the dynamiters hold a public or semi-public meeting, the journals are on the following day emblazoned with such headlines as "Fenians in Council", "Projected Fenian Explosions", and "Fenian Desperadoes". Yet to assert for a moment that Fenianism, properly so called, is responsible for the dynamite explosions that take place from time to time in England, or that Fenians, in general, are the authors of such explosions is either to speak on matters of which one is entirely ignorant, or to make a statement that one knows to be untrue. I am not assuredly disposed to go the length of saying that Irish dynamiters, or to be more correct, many of them were not Fenians in the past.

'O'Donovan Rossa, who was business manager of the official organ of the Fenians in 1865, and who was one of the most active Fenian organizers of that epoch, is today a fearless and unrelenting advocate of dynamite doctrines. Some of the men who work with him, and with others in the extreme wings of other revolutionary bodies, have been centres of the old Fenian organization of which a goodly number of the present dynamite rank and file have been members. One section, however, or a few sections do not make a springtide. To say that a proportionately fair share of dynamiters have been Fenians is to say what is unquestionably true; but to state that all Fenians, or even the majority, are dynamiters is to advance a theory which is not only essentially false, but is, on the face of it, highly and monstrously absurd. If every Fenian, morally or not, mathematically speaking, were a dynamiter, would we not have long ere now appalling proofs of such a fact? Would we not see universal destruction of public buildings carried on in England; the torch applied to city after city, and a reign of terror, before which the law would be practically powerless, predominant in the heart of London itself? If Fenianism in its welded strength and serried masses were England's real opponent in the dynamite campaign, thousands of black bags and thousands of rounds of Atlas powder and nitro-glycerine would be to the fore for every one of such commodities that has been used during the past few years; hundreds and hundreds of active men—call them criminals or honest hot-headed fanatics as you will—could be easily got to utilize these engines of destruction with dread effect at the cost, if need be, of their own lives and liberties. Instead of being a mere spasmodic upheaval of Irish hatred of England, it would be a constant, well-directed and pitiless campaign in which the aggressive party would stop at nothing, but would follow up blow by blow until it had gained its end, or confessed itself defeated.

'"To tell the whole truth and nothing but the truth" on this matter, it is only necessary to add that the dynamiters stand in the same position to the Fenians properly so-called as the Socialists or Anarchists of France do to the Radicals who acknowledge the leadership of M. Clemenceau. Jules Guéade or Citizen Felix Pyat has as little right to speak for the Extreme Left in the Palais Bourbon as Mr Patrick Ford has to put himself forward as the champion of Fenians or Fenianism'.

After that very clear condemnation of terrorism, the sincerity of which is borne out by Stephens's own conduct while undisputed leader of the movement, he turns to define Fenianism as he understood it:

'The Fenianism of the present day is identically the same as the Fenianism of the past. If it be not yet as powerful, it is not owing to any lack of faith in its principles, or to the concessions which Mr Gladstone thought opportune to make to its "intensity", but simply because since '66 it has lost that spirit of cohesion without which any political movement cannot do much in affecting the course of contemporary events. Disintegration and division scotched Fenianism very keenly indeed, although they did not kill it; for, to counterbalance in a not altogether ineffective manner the disastrous effects occasioned by the petty ambition of mushroom leaders, it had behind it the honesty, zeal, and patriotism of the rank and file the individual members of which, in the vast majority of cases, remained true to its teaching—no matter in what national camp, or under what national banner they served. Today as I shall explain further on in this paper, Fenianism is working on the same lines as of old: its strength is being gradually unified, and the same doctrines which guided it in its former days, and guide it at the present hour, will, I am confident, be never shelved or abandoned by those who will direct its destinies throughout the future.

'The Fenianism of 1864–65 was, I make bold to say, the representative of the most powerful secret and political organization that ever existed in Ireland—the United Irishmen's Society of '98 not even excepted. It had in Great Britain and Ireland, at the very lowest computation, 200,000 sworn members, banded together in the body known as the I.R.B. in various circles and under various centres, all of whom were under my directions, or, in the case of my absence in America, under the authority of my accredited lieutenants, the late Mr Charles J. Kickham, and Messrs. Thomas Clarke Luby and John O'Leary. In the United States as well as in Canada we had several hundreds of thousands more—members of the Fenian Brotherhood, properly officered and affiliated to the men at home with the avowed object of securing Irish independence by an armed upheaval of the masses in Ireland.

'In order to propagate thoroughly national ideas in the country, and rally to Fenianism the talent of the land the *Irish People* newspaper was started in Dublin in 1863, and although the journal was not financially a successful undertaking it nevertheless did much by way of crushing scandalmongers and calumniators who were very zealously inclined to blacken our characters and misrepresent our principles. The *Irish People* was a well-edited and well-written newspaper. Mr O'Leary had charge of the editorial department and was assisted by Mr Kickham who was not alone a pleasing essayist, but also a poet of no mean order, and Mr Luby who had previously contributed with success to several Irish publications. The other writers on the journal were, like the gentlemen I have named, possessed of high intellectual culture, and were facile and accomplished wielders of the pen, such as Mr J. F. O'Donnell who subsequently edited the *Tablet*, and contributed many a sparkling song and story to the pages of several English magazines; Mr T. C. Irwin, unquestionably the most fanciful or ideal poet whom Ireland has produced, next to Clarence Mangan; and Dr Robert Dwyer Joyce, who was afterwards one of the leading literary men of the Athens of America, and whose epic poem *Deirdre* was so warmly received by the press critics and by the public some years ago; while the soft sex was represented by such gifted "children of song" as the late Miss Fanny Parnell, sister of the chairman of the Irish Parliamentary Party, Miss Ellen O'Leary and others whose enthusiastic effusions served in no small way to kindle the fire of Irish nationality in quarters where it had hitherto been conspicuous by its absence'.[2]

'The moment selected for the propagation of Fenianism was, from certain points of view, a propitious one. Ireland, it was true, was in a state of general apathy when the organizers of the I.R.B. first entered on its mission. The men, however, who took it upon themselves to do in Ireland what Colonel Doheny and John O'Mahony promised to do on the American continent, were the most zealous and devoted of political apostles. Much as they have been calumniated, I can justly and fearlessly claim for them honesty and uprightness of character, sincerity in the opinions they championed, and zeal and activity in spreading these opinions wherever they directed their footsteps. In the various professions to which some of them were trained, they could easily have secured honours and wealth, but they preferred to abandon all chances of fortune rather than give up a movement which, they firmly believed, was destined to make their native land prosperous and independent. They never expected to gain, nor did they gain any material advantage themselves from their connection with Fenianism.

'When they started on the campaign—a campaign which, by the by, they inaugurated and carried on for some time without any financial assistance whatever—they foresaw the risks they were about to run in their labour of revolutionizing the country. They knew that every action of theirs, as agents of the I.R.B. meant treason felony as interpreted by the rulers of the country, and that a time would come when, in order to reach the goal, they should assume an attitude which, if they

---

[2]John O'Leary's opinion of the *Irish People* poets is an amusing contrast to Stephens's glance at them. He dismisses Fanny Parnell's verses as 'rather rhetoric than poetry, though very vigorous and sonorous rhetoric indeed'. Of another poetess 'great promise of a future that never arrived'. See O'Leary, Vol. 2. Ch. XV for a very full appreciation of the poets, most of whom Stephens ignores.

were apprehended, would suffice in a law court to convict them of high treason. They were perfectly aware that the first "crime" meant ten or twenty years or lifelong penal servitude; while the latter was punishable by death on the scaffold. The perspective, however, of imprisonment or execution troubled them as little indeed as it did their predecessors of '48 or '98. As they were the soldiers of Ireland, they were prepared, if need be, to die for Ireland. Martyrdom had its charms but none of its terrors for the founders of Fenianism.

'When after my few years of exile in Paris, consequent on the part I had taken as Smith O'Brien's *aide de camp* in the insurrectionary attempt of 1848, I returned in 1856 to Ireland to commence the struggle anew, I found the national torpor of the Irish people discouraging; but I also discovered that if they had little faith in their political regeneration by revolutionary methods, they had still less faith in constitutional agitation. Ireland, then was politically dead. She had been so cruelly and so bitterly disappointed; the hopes she cherished had been so ruthlessly blasted, and the roseate dreams that haunted her fancy and fired her hot Celtic blood turned out to be so many grinning phantasms to mock her degradation, and laugh at her despair, that she had given up the ghost, and was at last, to all intents and purposes, one of England's reconquered provinces.

'Peace reigned from Antrim to Cape Clear, and from Connemara to Dublin; but it was the "peace of Warsaw". Men shrugged their shoulders in a ghastly fashion and stared many a stupid stare when they were reminded that the green banner should be unfurled once more, and that there was hope yet for the land of their forefathers. Others, who flaunted national costumes in '48, and were free, hot-headed, enthusiastic members of Volunteer fighting clubs of that year, were as cool as cucumbers in '56, and smiled grimly and sceptically enough when they were appealed to to buckle on the armour, and enter the lists once more. What, they would say, or rather whisper, had all their previous struggles effected? O'Connell had proclaimed to them—trumpet-toned, from many a platform that Repeal was careering along the very winds of Heaven, and that fate was opening for them the portals of the Old

House in College Green. They stood in their hundreds of
thousands strong, massed in serried squares and columns
around him; they cheered him to the echo at Tara, at
Mullaghmast, in Mallow, and at scores of other monster
meetings throughout the land; he had promised them legislative independence, and assured them that such independence
could be won without the shedding of a single drop of human
blood, and they implicitly and unequivocably believed in him,
and in his power to win such a boon for them from the Lords
and Commons of Westminster. O'Connell, however, with all
this wonderful moral force behind him, failed to undo the work
of Pitt and Castlereagh. The clink of the guinea was still heard
within the precincts of College Green, and the doors of the old
Parliament House were more firmly than ever bolted to those
who could be the accredited representatives of the people.

'Then came the awful famine, swooping down pitilessly on
the island, and killing its inhabitants by thousands. The
multitudes that thronged around the tribune were melting
away at the touch of the hunger fever as snowdrifts melt before
the hot days of a long clouded sunlight; while the tribune
himself, heart-broken and desolate, had lain down to die at
Genoa. Once more, however, they were called upon to stand
up for the independence of their country. The French revolution of '48 was hailed everywhere by the democracy as a great
and glorious triumph; and the example it furnished was
followed with zeal and promptitude by other people on the
continent. The enthusiasm it kindled spread to Ireland; and
Confederation Hall in Dublin rang to the echoes of the
war trumpet. The moral or constitutional force doctrine
championed by O'Connell died with him. Thomas Francis
Meagher, the Chrysostom of Young Ireland, was kindling high
hopes in the breasts of thousands by openly proclaiming that
the hour had at last come when swords should be unsheathed,
and the long-oppressed people of Ireland should march out to
the battlefield to sweep the foreigner and the tyrant from their
shores, as the American colonists swept him from theirs, and
as the Belgians swept the Dutchman from the streets of
Louvain and the trenches of Antwerp back to their native
swamps and marshes. Other inflammatory speeches of a similar

character were delivered, not alone in Dublin but throughout the provinces; while John Mitchel was laying down plans for the coming campaign, and proclaiming the apotheosis of armed revolution with the utmost talent, and the most pungent eloquence in the pages of the *United Irishman*. Doctrines such as these, ably and enthusiastically propounded, produced their natural effect on hearts impressionable as Irishmen generally are'.

Stephens then briefly summed up the lessons of the 1848 revolt, and Smith O'Brien's defeat: physical force had failed just as O'Connell with his weapon of moral force had failed before him. Then came the betrayal of the new constitutional movement and tenant right by Sadlier, Keogh and 'the Pope's Brass Band'. This is all summed up in a summary of Irish public opinion, and the outlook of the mass of the people: 'They laughed to scorn both the polling booth and the rifle as instruments of salvation'. He claims that the I.R.B. in 1858, that is Fenianism, 'saved Irish nationality from final and irremediable destruction,' and stresses the deep despair of the people in 1856:

'They had given over the golden dreams of yore: an Irish republic with its army on land, and its navy on the broad deep, or in the impossibility of an Irish Republic, the legislative union dissolved, and an Irish senate making laws for Ireland in the Parliament House in College Green. Political theories and politics in general were at a discount. People preferred to be let alone in their various avocations, and took no interest whatever in the common zeal. Ireland had verily become, in the words of one of her former-day champions "a corpse on the dissecting table".

'If Fenianism had not arisen in 1858 and the succeeding years—not to galvanise the corpse but to put a new soul under its ribs of death, it is at least problematical if the national feeling would be so strong in Ireland as it is at the present hour. If contemporary history be written aright for the benefit of posterity I think the historian of the future will give Fenianism credit—or discredit—as the case may be, for having intervened at the proper or improper moment in the Anglo-Irish crisis, and for having saved the cause of Irish nationality from

irremediable destruction. If Fenianism had not aroused the
Irish race from its torpor, a generation would have passed
away without any uprising against English supremacy; and
the succeeding generation might possibly bury the hatchet for
ever, and accept accomplished facts. In the eyes, therefore, of
every Irish nationalist from the most inveterate Rossaite to the
merest sucking dove in the Home Rule camp, the great victory
achieved by Fenianism has been that it plucked the brand
from the burning and kept the chasm unbridged between
England on the one side and Ireland on the other. Mr
Gladstone has, in his ineffable wisdom, attributed victories of
quite another character to Fenianism; but they are insignificant
compared with what I have referred to.

'Surely but slowly did Fenianism develop itself in the land.
Often and often were its propagators discouraged and discomfited at first in their efforts to win neophytes to the new
creed. Many members of the Roman Catholic clergy denounced
it from the pulpit and in the confessional on the ground that
the I.R.B. was an oath-bound and secret society, and that all
such societies were condemned by the Church of which they
were ministers. The aristocracy and the upper mercantile
classes were too deeply imbued with ideas of loyalty to the
Crown to countenance a movement the object of which was
to sever the "golden link"; and, moreover, Fenianism was
wholly and unequivocally democratic, although the utopian
or childish theories of continental socialists did not by any
means form part and parcel of its programme. In addition to
these obstacles in our path, we had to contend with the apathy
of the farmers, and the hatred or irony of the metropolitan and
provincial press. Everything that could be devised was done
to discredit us. Journalists carped and sneered, and said that
we were far from being respectable folks. Some of us had, it
seems, patched up coats on our backs, and tattered shoes on
our feet. We were mere adventurers who were exciting the
poor to rob the rich in order that, in the confusion which would
ensue, we might be enabled to gobble up all the spoils, and fly
to some foreign clime to enjoy our *otium cum dignitate* and our
ill-acquired wealth, while our dupes lay buried in convict
cells, or were swinging from the gallows!

'A law officer of the Crown, now one of her Majesty's judges on the Irish bench, publicly asserted that one of the objects of our conspiracy was the assassination of the Roman Catholic clergy of the country, while a learned dignitary of the same Church, a bishop of one of the southern dioceses of Ireland, said that "Hell was not hot enough, or eternity long enough" for such ruffians as we were. An Irish Cardinal exhausted all the invectives of the English vocabulary in his denunciation of us; and his example was followed in quarters where we least expected it. We had with us the farmers' sons, the mechanics, the artisans, the labourers and the small shopkeepers; but the professional men, and the men of wealth either kept rigidly aloof, or were violent in their opposition to ourselves and our programme.

'In these latter days, however, I am inclined to enjoy the grim irony of fate which has in its own way scored a triumph for us Fenians of the old school.

'The whirligig of time brings around grave and startling changes indeed, and none graver and more startling than the present patronage of the Fenianism of '65 by Irish public opinion. When we see Mr John O'Leary, an ex-Fenian convict, returning after years of exile to his native land,[3] professing the same "rebellious" sentiments which he professed in the dock, cheered and acclaimed on a Dublin platform by the sub-sheriff of the city, several members of the British Parliament and members of the wealthy mercantile as well as of other classes of the community; and when at the same meeting we hear a sympathetic letter of apology read for non-attendance from an archbishop of the Church not a few of whose ministers hurled anathemas on John O'Leary's head twenty years ago, I have no other conclusion to draw save this: that the tide has unquestionably turned in our favour, and that time has vindicated our principles by proving that, while we have remained unchanged, the upper classes of Ireland have acknowledged that we were wronged, vilified and calumniated in former days; that we were not created expressly to prove the impotency of hell or eternity to punish us for our crimes; and that we were neither would-be robbers of the wealthy nor

[3]After fifteen years in Paris, c. 1884.

23

would-be assassins of the Catholic priesthood. It has, moreover,
been admitted that we crushed Ribbonism wherever it pre-
dominated—a fact which is amply proved by statistics;[4] for
during the period that Fenianism was an all-powerful factor
in the politics of the country, never was the country freer from
the strains of agrarian crime. I mention these details in present
pages, not in a spirit of vainglory, but in order to put Fenianism
in its proper light before your readers, and to show that it
could not have outlived its former foes if it had not possessed
that moral uprightness which should appeal to the best
instincts of impartial men everywhere no matter how much
they may condemn the object for the attainment of which it
was started'.

Stephens then declares that 'for obvious reasons' he cannot
discuss the reasons for the collapse of the Fenianism of '65, but
that he instead proposes to examine the Dynamite campaign
of the 'eighties objectively 'in a chronicle of facts and theories':

'Is the Dynamite policy the outcome of Fenianism, and if so,
how and why was it adopted to the abandonment of Fenianism
proper, or in other words, Fenianism of the old school? That
the Dynamite policy is the indirect creation of Fenianism, just
as the Black Hand conspiracy in Spain is that of the advanced
Republicans, or Nihilism the product of the liberal school of
Russian political thought is, I believe, a well established fact.
Every party has its *intransigents*; and a few years ago would-be

---

[4]Cf. Michael Davitt, *Fall of Feudalism*, p. 42; p. 77. 'James Stephens found the
Ribbon lodges one of the best recruiting grounds for his democratic revolutionary
brotherhood. His Fenian movement largely absorbed the younger members of
the pro-agrarian society. The landlords experienced a decade of almost
uninterrupted peace from agrarian troubles while Fenianism was educating the
peasantry and working classes of Ireland . . . The movement had one negative
virtue to them: it was not an agrarian association. This, perhaps, accounts for the
fact that from the year 1858 to that of 1870 these same landlords succeeded in
evicting close upon fifteen thousand families from homes and holdings. Two
events of far-reaching importance to the cause of land reform occurred in the
decade of greatest Fenian activity: one was the Ballycohey shooting affray, the
other, the first of Mr Gladstone's land measures, the Act of 1870'. Davitt stresses
that after the Ballycohey resistance to eviction, the number of evictions in Ireland
dropped to a lower figure over the next five years than in any similar period since
1849. The agreement between Davitt, Devoy and Parnell, which swung so many
Fenians behind the Land League from 1879, as has been seen, did not win the
support of Stephens or his old lieutenants, Kickham, Luby, Rossa and O'Leary.

dynamiters were the *intransigents* of the Fenian party; but since then the connection between both has been severed owing to the radical difference of opinion on essentially vital and important subjects that existed between them. Fenianism, properly so-called, had its programme from which no deviation could be made by men who were determined to remain loyal to its doctrines originally laid down by its founders; and that programme meant an armed revolution on Irish soil for Irish independence.

'The motives that actuated the Fenian extremists to secede from Fenianism, in abandoning its original doctrines were—so far as I could learn—two-fold. In the first place, Fenianism had become for years more of a dormant than an active organization. Owing to the rival leaderships that I have already referred to, it was split into rival camps, and had consequently lost much of its power and prestige. There were, however, in its ranks hot-headed and impatient spirits—men in whose hearts burned an unquenchable flame of hatred of England, and a fierce desire to avenge the wrongs under which their country and themselves were smarting. These men saw no immediate chance of a rising in Ireland, and gradually began to lose all hope in the success of such a rising, even if it did take place, owing to the disintegration that prevailed in the revolutionary ranks.

'In this state of things they came to the conclusion that they would remain inactive no longer. Originally, I believe, they banded themselves into skirmishing clubs, and contemplated wrecking and harassing England, without challenging her to combat on the field of battle. They would burn her mercantile shipping, destroy her navies with torpedoes, and doom her cities to desolation. One hundred thousand dollars were subscribed for these purposes in America; but, fortunately for England, there was in this case a misappropriation of funds— the money having been spent by several of the trustees in the purchase of two useless rams, and in the establishment of a newspaper the editors of which discountenanced the skirmishing idea, and advocated for the nonce moral force agitation as a panacea for the ills of Ireland.

'Were it not for this *contretemps,* the Dynamiters would be far stronger and more powerful than they are at the present time. The confidence of the subscribers was lost thanks to the conduct of the trustees in the management of the funds; and thousands of Irish-Americans refused to contribute one red cent more to the skirmishing till.[5] Just then, however, I come to the second reason that prompted the *intransigents* of the party to throw Fenianism, properly so-called, overboard—dynamite was being much talked of in the newspapers, and it was said that the Anarchists and Nihilists of the Old World had at last in their hands an instrument of destruction sufficient to destroy all the armies and navies in existence. The real force of dynamite was, of course, grossly exaggerated; it was referred to in glowing terms as the gift of science to the oppressed children of men, whereby despotism would be overthrown, and the sunshine of liberty would illumine for evermore the dwelling place of mankind! Irish extremists hailed the birth of dynamite with great and exceeding joy. "Here" they said, "is the *summum bonum* of our aspirations realized. We want to punish England as effectively and pitilessly as possible, and, lo and behold you! we are blessed with the blessings of dynamite—a power in nature far more terrible than gunpowder, and far more devastating than petroleum".

'Thereupon dynamite was patronized by some Irish-Americans in their warfare against England as the reports since of the periodical explosions in London and elsewhere

[5]Stephens here gives a very loose and tendentious account of the Dynamite campaign, and especially of the Skirmishing Fund controversy. His shafts are aimed at his enemies, Dr William Carroll and John Devoy even more than at O'Donovan Rossa. Both sides of the controversy are given, *Devoy's Post Bag*, Vol. 2. p. 60, Appendix, while Vol. 1 gives the beginning of the Skirmishing Fund campaign launched by Patrick Ford and Rossa in March 1876, and finally taken over—after a violent controversy in 1877, by Clan na Gael trustees, including Devoy and Carroll. Some of Stephens's charges here are based in the report of the hostile Spearman Committee, including the charge that Devoy started his *Irish Nation* on Skirmishing Fund money, and wrongful use of the Fund by the Clan na Gael Trustees, were repeated in the *Irish World* years later. Devoy was awarded 20,000 dollars and the charges were declared libellous. Stephens is here accepting the charges levelled by O'Donovan Rossa and his supporters against the Clan na Gael Trustees during the controversy. Rossa's case is also given in a memorandum in *Devoy's Post Bag*, Vol. 2. Devoy, Stephens, Dr Carroll, and John O'Leary, whatever their other differences, all publicly opposed and denounced Rossa's Skirmishing Campaign when he announced it, as the documents and letters given in both volumes of *Devoy's Post Bag* prove.

more than demonstrate; and for the present at least I see no immediate probability of the campaign inaugurated by O'Donovan Rossa, and carried on by him and others in the United States, drawing to anything like a speedy termination.'

This incomplete draft in the Stephens Papers—apart from some vague praise of the distinctions won by individual Fenians in Europe and the United States—ends with a prophecy of the eventual triumph of the old Fenian ideal:

'Fenianism meanwhile is girding up its loins to renew at the proper time and in the proper place the centuried fight of old. Dissensions in the ranks are gradually becoming rarer and rarer, and it is gathering to its fold enthusiastic recruits from day to day. It is not visible to the naked eye, for it does not put in an appearance on the platform or in parliament, and it is a veiled mystery to both Scotland Yard and Dublin Castle, the officials of which institutions know as little of its future plans as a Breton peasant does of the Ptolemaic system of astronomy. Though worsted in its past upheaval against English rule in Ireland, though defeated and discouraged in subsequent attempts, and torn asunder as it has been by internal discord, it has emerged from the furnace with new blood in its veins, and fresh vigour in its muscles. It has already shown the world what it can do in its own sphere, and in arenas where talent and enterprise alone can win the day'.

Postscript – Stephens and Parnell

BY OWEN DUDLEY EDWARDS

THE reader who has followed Desmond Ryan's narrative to its close will have realized, despite the vivid delineation of the subject and the clear exposition of the many facets of his life, that the author's long quest in pursuit of Stephens involved the unravelling of a myriad of mysteries. To obtain sight of the truth, Desmond Ryan had to embark on investigations as manifold and as complex as the late A. J. A. Symons encountered in his *The Quest for Corvo*. One minor aspect of the story remained hidden until after the author's death, but it became possible to document it in the light of clues left by him. It seems appropriate to include this missing piece of the jigsaw here.

After the divorce case of *O'Shea vs O'Shea and Parnell* had been concluded in the plaintiff's favour, Parnell, it will be remembered, was first re-elected chairman of the Irish parliamentary party, and then was repudiated by a majority of that party following Gladstone's statement that he could not guarantee a Home Rule settlement by a future Liberal government should Parnell retain the Irish leadership. In December 1890 the world was given the spectacle of incredibly bitter faction-fighting among Parnellite and anti-Parnellite constitutionalist politicians, as Parnell fought with all the means in his power to retain control and his opponents employed every possible tactic to destroy him. Stephens opposed constitutionalism; but he could not keep silent in face of such savage attacks on another charismatic Irish leader. Moved, it seems likely, by fellow-feeling for the embattled Parnell he wrote a letter to the

Freeman's Journal in his defence, in which these lines were included:

> 'While sincerely regretting the O'Shea incident, I look with loathing on the English pharisaical howl against the Irish Leader, and I indignantly repudiate the interference of any Englishman, not even excepting Mr Gladstone, to dictate to our people as to who should be their political leader.'

It was in the months succeeding the publication of this letter that Parnell took up the matter of Stephens's return to Ireland, and it may well have been that his motives in doing so were not totally altruistic. In his attempt to recover his command of the Irish political scene, Parnell made certain statements indicative of a bid for more extreme nationalist support than he had sought to cultivate since the 'Kilmainham Treaty' of 1882. Historians have sometimes suggested that these statements were little more than the last shots in the locker of a man at the end of his political tether. But, in fact, Parnell may have had very serious ideas of a new alliance with extreme nationalist forces in which Stephens was designed to play a role, either as activist or—more likely—as symbol.

Stephens returned to Ireland on 25 September, via London and Holyhead. The poor health of Jane Stephens forced the emancipated exiles to break their journey in both of the latter places, with the result that when the Stephenses embarked for Ireland at Holyhead their fellow-passengers included Parnell himself, travelling through from London to Dublin. But Stephens was busy nursing his wife, and Parnell invariably concealed himself from public view on board the mail-packet, and neither man knew of the proximity of the other. As he had never met Parnell, Stephens expressed natural regret at their failure to make contact when on board ship, once he had been informed of the presence of his benefactor; but by the time he knew of it he was facing reporters at Kingstown (now Dun Laoghaire) and Parnell was on the train to Dublin. Stephens probably guessed it would be his last voyage from England to Ireland; in the event, it was also Parnell's.

But Stephens was warmly greeted at Kingstown by the Parnellites, if not by Parnell. He gave a characteristic interview to *United Ireland*, the weekly Parnellite journal. His health was not bad, he declared, but he would give this interview only, for he needed rest, and Dr Kenny, the Parnellite M.P., who was in attendance, strongly endorsed this. The observant reporter learned from witnesses that the old man was in a state of considerable emotional stress. 'He was very deeply affected when the Hill of Howth, the first glimpse of Ireland he had had for twenty-six years, was sighted; and on landing at Kingstown pier he very nearly broke down.' His capacity to employ drama for emotional outlet did not desert him; he announced that it was with difficulty he had restrained himself from kneeling down to kiss the ground as he stepped ashore. One may question if the restraint was so hard to achieve: the expression of such a sentiment could not but be appropriate, but the performance of such an action could have been undignified, and Stephens was now, as ever, supremely conscious of his dignity.

His eyes flashed 'with all the fire and enthusiasm that carried him through so many trials and troubles' when it was remarked to him that his views evidently had not changed. Yet his ensuing remarks conceded more to Parnellism than he had ever done before, albeit, that he seemed grudging enough in those concessions. He had never changed his mind, he stated, 'either as to Ireland's claims to nationhood, or the road that Irishmen must travel to enforce these claims'. 'At the same time', he continued, 'I recognize the circumstance that the majority of Irishmen appear to have elected to try constitutional agitation for the present, and I see no reason why I should pursue a dog-in-the-manger policy. If this Parliamentary agitation leads up to any benefits for Ireland, I for one would be glad of it. Indeed I readily admit that some local benefits, especially connected with the land, have been won by the agitation of the past ten years.'

It would have been, in almost anyone else, far too mild an endorsement to give fuel for Parnellite hopes of future alliance with Stephens, but it was, for him, an enormous generosity. He continued in an even more strongly Parnellite vein, in the context of the constitutionalist split as distinct from the general question of constitutionalism versus revolution by violence.

'It is very clear to me', he intoned, 'that the decision in the Irish party has precipitated a crisis when the country will require to know at once what form of Home Rule or Local Government will be obtained from the British Government, and also what sacrifice of National principle would be necessary to obtain that concession.' Iron guarantees from the Liberals were precisely what Parnell insisted on. The emotional nature of the Parnellite case against the anti-Parnellites also received its meed of support from Stephens. 'Even in Parliamentary work I consider that the Irish representatives should be in no wise bound to a British party or a British leader. I will even say freely that the spirit of independent opposition as preached by Mr Parnell is in accordance with my ideas of what is called constitutionalism.' He left his audience to make the most of that forceful ambiguity. 'I have no more faith than I ever had in the promises of either British party', he declared, and, citing his letter of nine months before to the *Freeman*, 'that letter supported Mr Parnell in the present controversy, and I have in no way changed my views since it was written'.

So much for his new friends. But Stephens was not prepared to leave the scene without renewed comfort to the Old Guard. 'I have faith in the young men of Ireland, believing that they will never accept any principles except those that I followed and taught myself throughout my whole life. I know, too, that they will never accept contentedly any dictation nor even direction from British parties.' As far as Stephens was concerned, it was not a case of his becoming a Parnellite, but he was not above suggesting Parnell might have qualities of a Stephensite. He concluded by touching on the movement for amnesty of those Fenian prisoners still in British jails, most of whom were members of the dynamite faction whose theory he so strongly opposed. 'I myself will work in every way by voice and pen to forward their cause of amnesty', he vowed. The amnesty movement was one of the few remaining points of nationalist solidarity. Redmond was in the forefront of the agitation; Davitt continued to give it support; and others varied between enthusiasm and lip-service for it. Stephens declared that he would be 'astonished' to find any difference of opinion on the need to continue the movement, possibly in an

implied reference to John Dillon, whose anti-Parnellite sentiment was cooling his amnesty ardour.

Stephens and his wife returned to the house of a friend where
they resided for a time under another name. It was reported
that the old man spent his time looking constantly through the
windows at the country for which he had hungered so long.
Parnell was still unable to see him, and during those few days
contracted the chill which clung to him as he recrossed the
Irish Sea. But Dr Kenny, M.P., Patrick O'Brien, M.P., Clancy,
the under-sheriff of Dublin, and other enthusiastic Parnellites
continued to show warmth and hospitality to Stephens. A
fund was commenced to buy him a house, Kenny becoming
treasurer and O'Brien and Clancy two of the three secretaries.
Among the first of the contributions was that of Parnell himself,
who wrote to one of the secretaries in a telegram despatched
on 5 October 1891:

'REJOICED THAT A MOVEMENT IS TO BE MADE TO
PROVIDE MR STEPHENS WITH A RESTING-PLACE
DURING THE CLOSING YEARS OF HIS LIFE; HAVE SENT
MY CONTRIBUTION.'

It is very likely that these were the last lines Parnell ever
wrote, for on the next day he died at Brighton. His body was
brought back to Ireland, and buried amid scenes whose
character must have recalled the McManus funeral to
Stephens. The Fenian chief was in attendance, in the fourth
carriage behind the hearse (the first three carriages having
been reserved for clergy and relatives). His fellow-passenger
was John O'Leary. One would give much to have a record of
their conversation.

Stephens was not content with paying his tribute with the
multitude. Two weeks afterwards, on 24 October, he visited
Parnell's grave again, supported by O'Brien and Clancy. He
brought to the grave an immortelle under a glass shade and
stood holding it for some time, bare-headed and (according
to Parnellite witnesses) with tears in his eyes. 'I place this', he
said, 'on the grave of the noblest Irishman of our time', and
as he bent to lay it on the tomb, he sobbed aloud, stated the

same source. It is very probable that his Parnellite friends were still seeking to make capital from his partial support of Parnell; but the inscription on the immortelle could have been dictated by nobody but Stephens. It placed his interpretation of the priorities in no doubt whatsoever, reading, as it did:

'To the revered memory of my sincere friend, Charles Stewart Parnell, from James Stephens, Oct. 1891'.

From Stephens's viewpoint, it was the highest compliment Parnell could have been paid.

We are never likely to know whether the two men might have sought to recoup their fallen fortunes by alliance in adversity. Stephens's part would not have been excessively active—his first words on returning to Ireland were that he intended 'to take no part in politics, and to live out my remaining days in peace and quietness'—but his symbolic support would have been of great value to Parnell. The collapse of the Parnellites after their leader's death made future work with Stephens impossible. Moreover, while Parnell may have been the man to achieve the miracle of alliance with Stephens, his successor, John Redmond, certainly was not. The bid for extremist support died with Parnell. The fund for Stephens's house was revived, and ultimately produced the means to obtain the residence.

But if a final career in Irish politics was denied to Stephens by Parnell's death, the nationalist energy which Parnell had unleashed returned to the ideal of physical force, via cultural activity, and linguistic nationalism, and Gaelic athletics. As Desmond Ryan notes at the close of his book, Stephens won in the end, although he was dead when the victory was achieved. But the direction of Irish nationalism after Parnell became evident within hours of the Irish party leader's death. For whatever purposes Parnell had turned to the extremists in his last year, his doing so made it easier for his followers to gravitate to the extremists when he was gone. In the week after Parnell died, the Cork branch of the Gaelic Athletic Association met. The G.A.A. was as forceful an expression of cultural nationalism as could be found in the Ireland of the day, but it had accepted constitutional nationalism, and Parnell had held the office of Patron. Now, the Cork branch passed the inevitable resolutions of grief at his death—and symbolized the future direction of Irish nationalism by passing a motion to have the office of Patron devolve on James Stephens.[1]

Aberdeen,

November, 1967

---

[1]Material for this postscript is taken from the columns of *United Ireland*. Other newspapers of the day, such as the anti-Parnell *Freeman's Journal* and the Unionist *Irish Times*, make it clear that the prospect of a Parnell-Stephens alliance was taken very seriously.

Biographical Notes

THOMAS WILLIS or possibly Thomas Miller BEACH. *See* MAJOR HENRI LE CARON.

HENRY WARD BEECHER (1813–1887). *B.* Litchfield, Connecticut, U.S.A. *Educ.* Amherst College, Massachusetts. Son of noted evangelist Lyman Beecher and brother of anti-slavery writer Harriet Beecher Stowe, authoress of *Uncle Tom's Cabin* (1852). Preached in Indiana, and held the cure of souls in the Plymouth (Congregational) Church, Brooklyn, from 1847 until his death. His weekly audiences came to average 2,500, and many of his sermons were printed and widely circulated. An outstanding orator, and famed opponent of slavery, he sent a token number of rifles in the name of his church to the anti-slavery forces in Kansas during the undeclared civil war there in 1856, the rifles being known as 'Beecher's Bibles'. His fame as a lecturer stood firm after the Civil War, being furthered by lecture-tours. He supported current reforms, but incensed spokesmen for labour by support of the 'Gospel of Wealth', to the effect that God gave riches to the righteous and low wages were justifiable since workmen could live on bread and water. He spoke in favour of Parnell during the latter's American tour, January 1880, and subsequently moderated his anti-labour views, possibly in view of Parnell's strong labour support which protested against the Parnellite alliance with him. His reputation was somewhat tarnished by the suit brought against him by Theodore Tilton, another former abolitionist and religious writer, for adultery with Mrs Tilton (1874): the jury disagreed, and hence he was technically cleared. *D.* Brooklyn.

JAMES BUCHANAN (1791–1868). *B.* Pennsylvania. Jacksonian Democrat. Congressman, 1821–31; minister to Russia, 1832–33; Senator, 1835–45; Secretary of State under the Polk administration, 1845–49; minister to England, 1853–56. Elected 15th President of the United States, 1856. A practised machine politician, his partisan favour for the most anti-Republican elements in his party led him to a somewhat pro-Southern attitude. Industrious, capable, devious, limited, and the only lifelong bachelor to be President of the U.S. His somewhat shifty appearance was enhanced by a nervous twitch in one eye which led him to be constantly winking. Ironically, Stephens had a similar physical defect. Buchanan was succeeded by Lincoln in 1861 and retired to Lancaster, Pennsylvania, to defend his much-abused administration. *D.* 1868.

RICARD O'SULLIVAN BURKE (1838–1922). *B.* Keneagh, near Dunmanway, Co. Cork. Joined Cork Militia at age 15, and when his regiment was disbanded in 1856, he became a sailor. He travelled the Mediterranean, Japan, Peru, the Argentine, Mexico and the U.S.A. Studied French and art in Paris. Fought in Federal Army in American Civil War; demobilized as Colonel, 1865. Returned to Dublin; named as Fenian agent for arms purchase in Great Britain by Colonel Thomas J. Kelly, 1865. Unable to complete contracts because of money shortage following American split. Returned to U.S., but went back to Ireland for 1867 rising; assisted in I.R.B. reorganization after rising. Planned and supervised Manchester Rescue, shortly after which he was arrested and charged with purchase of arms for English Fenians. Unsuccessful attempt to rescue him in Clerkenwell explosion where 8 were killed and 120 maimed for life (the error being believed due to his orders smuggled from prison). Released, 1872. Returned to the U.S.A., 1874. Became prominent in Clan na Gael. Employed as clerk in U.S. War Department. Engineer in Mexican National Construction Co., and built the Laredo-Monterey-Mexico City railroad. Assistant City Engineer, Chicago; later Assistant Harbour Engineer. *D.* Chicago.

ISAAC BUTT (1813–1879). *B.* Glenfin, Co. Donegal. *Educ.* Raphoe and Trinity College, Dublin. Founder, 1833, editor, 1834–38, and contributor to *Dublin University Magazine.* Professor Political Economy, 1836–41. Opposed O'Connell in Dublin Corporation. M.P. for Harwich, 1852, for Youghal, 1852–65, for Limerick, 1871–79. Irish barrister, 1838, Irish Q.C., 1844; defense counsel for 1848 insurgents, later for Fenians, 1865–69. President, Amnesty Association to obtain release of Fenians, 1869. Leader of Home Rule parliament party, 1871–79. Opposed obstructionism of Parnell and others. *D.* Dublin.

DR WILLIAM CARROLL (1836–1926). *B.* Rathmullen, Co. Donegal. His parents, Ulster Presbyterians, brought him to Ohio at age 3. Qualified as physician. Surgeon-Major in Federal Army in American Civil War, during which he joined the Fenian Brotherhood. Settled in Philadelphia, c. 1867 after which he joined Clan na Gael. Chairman, Clan na Gael Executive, 1875-80. Vigorous revolutionist, medical adviser to Mitchel whom he accompanied on his visit to Ireland, 1874. Played part in Clan overtures to Parnell and Davitt, 1877–80, but broke with Parnell in belief the latter was only 'using' the Clan. A lifelong friend of Devoy. Strong advocate of Protection for Ireland, and influential member of economists' circle in Philadelphia advocating such ideas. *D.* Philadelphia.

ANDREW CASEY. *See* JOSEPH T. CASEY.

JOSEPH T. CASEY. *B.* Kilkenny. Cousin of Stephens. Arrested with Ricard O'Sullivan Burke and taken to Clerkenwell Prison, London, 1867; it was intended that he be rescued along with Burke in the attempt which resulted in the Clerkenwell explosion. Tried with Burke and Harry Mulleda, but acquitted after lengthy proceedings. Joined his brother Patrick in France, the latter having been involved in the rescue attempt; two other brothers made common cause with them on behalf of France whose army they all joined during the Franco-Prussian war, France having refused English efforts to obtain Patrick Casey's extradition. Three of the Caseys reported wounded during the siege of Paris, Andrew Casey suffering severely during General Ducrot's *sortie*, for which he obtained the Legion of Honour. Andrew Casey and the fourth brother, James, died some years later from the effects of their wounds, but Patrick and Joseph survived to play a fringe part in the Paris meetings of members of the Invincibles. Patrick was also on sufficiently good terms with John O'Leary early in the 1880's for the latter to employ his residence as a postal address. Davitt distrusted the Caseys, and believed, with some good grounds, that their circle included British spies; he described Joseph as 'a blatant "refugee" who lived in Paris, with a leaning towards dynamite and absinthe'. Joseph was well known to James Joyce, who met him frequently in a Paris cafe in the winter of 1903; he has been identified as the original of Kevin Egan in *Ulysses*. Patrick and Joseph Casey were both compositors, and after 1870 worked first on *Galignani's Messanger* in Paris and later on the European (Paris) edition of the New York *Herald* for several years.

PATRICK CASEY. *See* JOSEPH T. CASEY.

JOHN CAVANAGH (1825?–1862). *B.* Dublin. President of the
Fitzgerald Confederate Club, Harold's Cross, Dublin. Wounded
at Ballingarry and brought to Kilkenny, where Dr Cane looked
after him; smuggled to France, whence he sailed to U.S.A.
Became an officer in the U.S. army; served under Meagher.
Killed in the battle of Antietam.

CORYDON *the informer*. A sworn member of the I.R.B., and known
to be such by the police. He was first apprehended by them on a
very different charge, however, which seems to have been a
crime of sexual perversion. 'He begged very hard to be let off,
and not only promised disclosures, but actually gave the police
some very valuable information' about the I.R.B. Bussy, *Irish
Conspiracies*, from whom the quotations here are taken, suggests
that his prosecution was dropped partially in view of the probable
public scandal arising from his case no less than from his value
as an informer. Whatever motives of delicacy the police may have
had, Corydon was instructed by them to leave Ireland. 'Accordingly, he went over to Liverpool, and there—probably through
the deliberate design of the "G" Division of Dublin police—he got
in touch with a member of the Royal Irish Constabulary (who
was specially located at the great transatlantic shipping port
watching the movements of known Fenians and suspected
Irishmen), to whom he regularly and unreservedly informed'.
Bussy suggests that these later informations, most of which were
during the period 1867–68, were made out of simple gratitude
to the police; a more consistent, if more sordid, explanation
would be that Corydon was seeking immunity from future police
prosecution in the event of further apprehension while in the
pursuit of gratification of his peculiar sexual whims. Among
other matters he betrayed to the police the McCafferty intended
raid on Chester Castle, and the mission of Godfrey Massey, who
brought funds for the I.R.B. from the U.S. Massey afterwards
turned informer in his turn.

PAUL CARDINAL CULLEN (1803–1878). *B.* near Ballytore, Co.
Kildare. *Educ.* Carlow, and Urban College of the Propaganda,
Rome. Ordained priest, 1829; vice-rector and rector of Irish
College, Rome; and finally rector of Propaganda, 1848–9, during
Mazzini's Roman Republic. Archbishop of Armagh, 1849–52;
of Dublin, 1852–78. Opposed multi-denominational education.
Prohibited political activity by his priests, 1853, precipitating

quarrel with Charles Gavan Duffy's tenant-right movement and independent Irish party. As delegate apostolic for the foundation of an Irish Catholic University, came into conflict with its rector John Henry (later Cardinal) Newman, 1854–58. Promoted Irish Brigade for the Papacy, 1859. Opposed vigorously Fenian and all other secret movements of revolutionary character. Made cardinal-priest, 1866, being first Irishman in Sacred College. Strongly promoted the definition of papal infallibility, 1870. Presided at synod of Maynooth, 1875. *D.* Dublin.

THOMAS OSBORNE DAVIS (1814–1845). *B.* Mallow, Co. Cork. Father an English surgeon. *Educ.* Trinity College, Dublin. Joined Repeal Association, 1841. Co-founder, *Nation*, 1842, on which he was thereafter a moving influence. Wrote extensively in its columns, preaching romantic nationalism in the most sophisticated form Ireland had yet produced. Employed essays, and ballads of the type made popular by Walter Scott's imitators. *D.* unexpectedly of scarlet fever, in Dublin. His decease in early youth made him a symbol of Young Ireland, and added to the considerable influence of his writings, both in the later 1840's and thence to our own day.

MICHAEL DAVITT (1846–1906). *B.* Mayo. Evicted with his family at age 4, when they emigrated to Lancashire. Worked in cotton-mill where his right arm was torn off by the machinery, 1856. An active and militant Fenian from the age of 17. Took part in raid on Chester Castle, 1867. Made chief lieutenant to James J. O'Kelly in the dangerous work of purchasing arms and forwarding them to Ireland. Sentenced to fifteen years' imprisonment for incitement to murder, of which he was probably innocent, 1870. After grim experiences in Dartmoor, released on ticket-of-leave, 1878. Visited United States and brought Clan members, including Devoy, into land agitation. During his visit Devoy launched the 'New Departure' inaugurated co-operation between Parnell, the agrarians and the Fenians. Founded Land League of Mayo, shortly afterwards absorbed into Land League of Ireland, 1879. Returned to the U.S. to organize moral and financial support following Parnell's successful tour there, 1880. Re-arrested and ticket-of-leave revoked, 1881–82. Expelled from the Supreme Council of the I.R.B., 1880, and drifted out of the body itself. Became increasingly opposed to Parnell's scheme of peasant ownership, preferring Henry George's views, 1882. Grew increasingly involved in Socialism. Editor *Labour World*. Opposed Parnell on O'Shea divorce. M.P., 1895–1906. Author of memoir of Land League, *The Fall of Feudalism in Ireland*, and *Leaves from a Prison Diary*, which reflected his brand of social nationalism.

JOSEPH DENIEFFE. *B.* Kilkenny. *Educ.* as tailor. Emigrated to U.S.A. Returned to Ireland, 1855–56 owing to the illness of his father, and bringing also the Doheny-O'Mahony commission to Stephens, to set up revolutionary organization in Ireland. Left Ireland as Stephens's emissary to U.S.A., January 1858; returned, March 1858. On organizing tour with Stephens, and from then until after the collapse of the 1867 rising, Denieffe was in the thick of Fenian events. His book, *Recollections of the Irish Revolutionary Brotherhood* (New York, 1906) is one of the best-written documented accounts of Fenianism from 1855 to 1867. Denieffe passed the remainder of his life in the United States, where he died at an advanced age; he was associated until the end with Irish movements, the Clan na Gael among them.

JOHN DENVIR (1834–1916). *B.* Bushmills, Co. Antrim, 1834. Manager and Editor of various Liverpool newspapers including the *Catholic Times*, the *United Irishman* and the *Nationalist*. Commenced in 1870 to publish a patriotic series entitled *Denvir's Penny Library* containing Irish poetry, history and biography. It had an enormous success. His *The Irish in Britain* (1892) is a valuable though subjectively-written work, being largely concerned with Irish nationalist politics, including Fenianism and the response of the emigrant Irish in Britain. Published *Denvir's Monthly* in the early twentieth century; it contained useful Fenian memorabilia. His autobiography, *The Life Story of an Old Rebel* (1910) has a utility far beyond its somewhat narrow theme. *D.* Wimbledon.

JOHN DEVOY (1842–1928). *B.* at Kill near Naas, Co. Kildare. Joined the Fenian organization in 1861, and the same year against Stephens's strongest appeals insisted on going to France and joining the Foreign Legion. Spent a year in Algeria, returning to Ireland in 1862. A Centre of the I.R.B. in Naas, 1862–65. Won fame as Fenian organizer in the British Army, October 1865–February 1866. Selected and headed party which helped Stephens escape from Richmond, but himself arrested three months later. Pleaded 'Guilty' at trial on the instructions of Edward Duffy, Stephens's acting deputy, as plan had been mooted to rescue him for participation in forthcoming rising. Plan failed, and Devoy sentenced to fifteen years' penal servitude. Released and went to U.S.A., 1871. A major figure in Irish-

American nationalism thereafter. One of the organizers of the *Catalpa* rescue of former Fenians in the British Army imprisoned in Australia, 1875. Accepted land agitation and alliance with Parnell and Davitt, throwing American support and finance behind them, 1878–82. Played key part in building up the Clan na Gael in place of the moribund and fragmented Fenian Brotherhood. Worked on various newspapers, including his own *Irish Nation* (1881–85) and *Gaelic American* (1903–27). Lost influence through opposition of the Sullivan wing of the Clan in Chicago, but recovered it when Sullivan—and very nearly the Clan too—was ruined by the Cronin murder, 1889. After the Parnell split, Devoy and the remnant of his support returned to physical force, and he played an inspirational part in bringing about the 1916 insurrection. He also supervised links with the German government, 1914–16, rather less successfully, and attempted to influence American opinion against Britain, less successfully still. In his final years he fell under the influence of Judge Daniel F. Cohalan. In 1929 his body was brought back to Ireland and buried with full honours in Glasnevin cemetery.

JOHN BLAKE DILLON (1814–1866). *B.* Ballaghadereen, Co. Mayo. *Educ.* Maynooth (in an abortive ambition for the priesthood) and Trinity College, Dublin. Called to the Irish Bar, 1842, and practised. Founded *Nation* with Davis and Gavan Duffy but only contributed occasionally after 1844. Supported Young Ireland in split with O'Connell. Called Rotunda meeting of 13 January 1847, to launch Irish Confederation. Engaged in 1848 rising in belief that honour left him no other course. Escaped to U.S.A. afterwards. Went into practice at New York bar with Richard O'Gorman. Advocated a federal republic for Britain and Ireland, 1849. Returned to Ireland, 1855, becoming Alderman in Dublin Corporation. Elected M.P. for Tipperary, 1865. Supported ultra-moderate National Association in 1860's, as did Paul Cardinal Cullen. Advocated pro-clerical policy and opposed Fenianism. *D.* suddenly at Killiney, Co. Dublin. His son John was afterwards one of Parnell's more capable and extreme lieutenants.

MICHAEL DOHENY (1805–1862). *B.* near Fethard, Co. Tipperary. *Educ.* Dublin and London, commencing 1826. Called to the Bar, Middle Temple, 1838. Contributor to the *Nation*. Assisted in preparations for 1848 rising. Escaped to France and thence to U.S.A. Trained military company of recruits in New York for service in Irish cause, 1849, company afterwards incorporated in New York State Militia, of whose 75th Regiment he was made

Colonel. Said to have wished to make McManus funeral the signal for insurrection. Died suddenly on his return to New York. His *Felon's Track* is a thrilling account of escape after '48 and still preserves a high reputation. He was one of the very few Young Irelanders to speak and write in the Irish language.

CHARLES GUILFOYLE DORAN (1835–1909). A Wicklowman. Clerk of Works to Cobh Cathedral. Member of the Supreme Council of the I.R.B. Joined Fenian movement after 1867 and became Secretary of the Supreme Council. Took an active part in John Mitchel's election campaign in Tipperary in 1875 as a speaker. Acted as link between Fenians and constitutionalists before the Devoy-Parnell connection, and was said to have received an understanding from Isaac Butt that the Fenians tolerate his movement on the understanding that if he failed to win within three years, he would retire and leave the field open to the physical force men. That time limit expired in 1876. Doran, who stated that he had Butt's own signature to the undertaking, was extremely angry that the chief significance of the years, from a Fenian standpoint, had lain in the loss of several members to the Home Rulers. Opposed the Land League and the Devoy alliance with Parnell. Acted as anonymous spokesman for revolutionary sentiment critical of that alliance, and used for the purpose by the New York *Herald's* Irish representative. See footnote 5, p.300.

CHARLES GAVAN DUFFY (1816–1903). *B*. Monaghan. Founded *The Nation*, a romantic nationalist weekly, in 1842, with Thomas Davis and John Blake Dillon. Associated with Daniel O'Connell in his repeal movement and sentenced with him for conspiracy, 1844, sentence afterwards quashed. Duffy and other 'Young Irelanders', as the *Nation* group called themselves, broke with O'Connell in 1846. Arrested in July 1848, but the indictment of treason felony against him failed. Re-established *The Nation* (suppressed during his imprisonment), 1849. Worked thereafter with tenant-right movement and effort to set up Irish party in Westminster independent of British parties. Emigrated to Australia, 1855. Prime Minister of Victoria, 1871; knighted, 1873. Returned to Ireland, 1875. Involved marginally in Irish politics thereafter as conservative nationalist. *D*. Nice. His son George was a signatory to the Anglo-Irish Treaty of 1921 under which the Irish Free State was established. Duffy wrote many autobiographical accounts of the Irish nationalist movements he had known, notably *Young Ireland* and *My Life in Two Hemispheres*.

P. W. DUNNE. Fenian and associate of John O'Mahony, described
by John Devoy as one of the best of the Senate wing leaders,
'big-hearted, forceful and impetuous'. Lived in Illinois, moving
between Peoria, Chicago and other towns. He accompanied the
Fenian envoy, Patrick J. Meehan, to Ireland in 1865; the note
of introduction and a draft of 500 pounds sterling, both intended
for Stephens, fell into the hands of the British authorities. The
documents were used against the Fenian prisoners arrested in
1865, and it was believed that their loss had led to the Government swoop on the organization and the *Irish People*. The documents however in themselves, were not very important with the
exception of the draft. Dunne did his best to heal the split in the
Fenian organization in 1866, with a proposal that the leaders of
the Roberts and O'Mahony wings should resign, and that
Stephens should be the leader of a re-united organization. Dunne
seems to have had close links with Tipperary Fenianism, and
supported efforts to obtain public subscriptions in aid of Charles
J. Kickham, T. P. O'Connor of Laffana and other Tipperary
Fenians. He gave vague support to the alliance of Davitt and
Devoy in 1878, but some evidence exists that he hoped to maintain it on a more doctrinaire basis than it actually held to. His
relations with Devoy improved as his hostility to Alexander
Sullivan of Chicago increased; he maintained some form of
alliance with John Finerty, the pro-dynamite journalist and
Congressman, during the '80's, and supported Devoy, Rossa and
others in the campaign against Sullivan which culminated in
the Cronin murder and Sullivan's overthrow. In later years he
became involved in unsuccessful efforts to publish memoirs by
Fenian associates of his, on which topic he was still corresponding
with Devoy in 1914.

PATRICK FORD (1834–1913). *B.* Galway. Brought to Boston at
age of 7. Learned printing and journalism in the office of the
Liberator, organ of the abolitionist William Lloyd Garrison.
Served in American Civil War. Founded *Irish World*, 1870;
conducted it until his death. Collected and sent to Ireland half
a million dollars for various national movements. An active and
doctrinaire reformer and spokesman for American labour as well
as for Irish freedom. Insisted on Irish social as well as political
questions being agitated. His paper enjoyed wide circulation,
employed sensationalist techniques before their general adoption
in the newspaper world, and debated all aspects of social reform.
Maintained close relations with Fenians, won an Irish and Irish-

American audience for Henry George's theories of abolition of
land ownership in its existent form, advocated everything from
universal humanitarianism to the use of dynamite against
England, supported Parnell, 1879–82, 1886–90, opposed him
otherwise. Of highly moral if querulously expressed ideals.
Became rather more conservative towards the end of his life.
D. Brooklyn. His brother, Augustine, was also heavily involved
in Fenian activities. On Patrick Ford's death his nephew Robert
took over the paper, 1913–20. Under his control it followed
Patrick's final policy in backing John Redmond until the latter's
support for the British war effort in 1914, after which the *Irish
World* returned to a more uncompromising position.

HORACE GREELEY (1811–1872). *B*. New Hampshire. *Educ*.
largely on a Vermont country newspaper. Founded and edited
the *New Yorker* (1834–41), a critical journal; founded daily New
York *Tribune*, 1841, which had reached one-fifth of a million in
circulation by 1860 and was the most influential American daily,
in the Republican party, for most of the latter half of the nineteenth century. In politics Greeley commenced as a Whig, but
possessed much of the Utopianism of American reformers,
including advocacy of labourers' and farmers' rights, opposition
to slavery, land for those without it, and Fourierism. Karl Marx
was for some time his London correspondent. He criticized
Lincoln during the war for apparent laxness on the question of
emancipating the slaves, and elicited a famous reply placing the
preservation of the Union foremost among the Presidential
objectives. He counted himself as a Radical Republican, but
opposed political corruption and advocated personal, though not
political, clemency to prominent Confederates; drifting into
hostility towards the Grant regime he became the candidate of
the ill-assorted 'Liberal Republican' faction in 1872, in the
presidential election in which Grant won a second term. Greeley
had been pushed into the candidacy by his ambitious second-in-
command, Whitelaw Reid, and after the election discovered that
the latter had no intention of relinquishing the *Tribune* editorial
chair to its former occupant. Broken by this realization, Greeley
died insane three weeks after the election; his death being tanta-
mount to murder and accomplished by the presidential election
must surely rank as one of the strangest in history. He was a warm
friend to Ireland, and shared with many Irish-American nationalists a zealous advocacy of economic protectionism for the
United States, against English efforts to exploit the American

market. Despite the universality of his liberalism, Greeley was shrewd enough as an editor and greatly raised the prestige and political influence of newspaper editors in the U.S.A.

ARCHBISHOP JOHN JOSEPH HUGHES (1797–1864). *B.* Ireland. Emigrated to the U.S.A., 1817. Ordained priest, 1826. Vigorous advocate for separate and adequate parochial schools for all American Catholics. Archbishop of New York, 1850. Many contacts abroad won him international recognition as spokesman for American Catholicism. His intransigence led to political breaches with New York Whig leaders, initially on the public school issue; his confidence in the Democrats also contributed to his criticism of their opponents, whether anti-Catholic, Whig, or anti-slavery. Played an influential part in dictating Catholic hierarchical malevolent neutrality towards the anti-slavery movement. Discouraged lay expression of opinion on Catholic affairs; took a broad interpretation as to what constituted such affairs. Lincoln employed him as agent abroad for the Union cause during the war, particularly in appealing to Catholic countries.

COLONEL THOMAS J. KELLY. Considering the position held by this man in the Fenian movement, and the influence he exercised on its history, it is amazing how little is known about him. He was sent to Ireland in 1865 to estimate the degree of preparedness existing in the movement, and returned to New York in April 1866. He became Deputy to Stephens in May 1866, and brought about Stephens's downfall later in the year. He made his way to England on 12 January 1867, and was moving regularly between English and Irish centres of Fenianism when his career was checked by an almost chance arrest in Manchester. On 18 September 1867, Captain Timothy Deasy and himself were rescued from a police van by Fenian action; police-sergeant Brett was unintentionally killed and a number of men were arrested of whom three—Allen, Larkin and O'Brien (henceforth known as the Manchester Martyrs)—were hanged. Kelly and Deasy were smuggled out of the country. Kelly returned to the U.S.A. and was later mixed up in efforts to exploit Canadian discontent. He seems to have been on the fringe of Louis Riel's rebellion.

JOHN KENYON (1812–1869). *B.* Limerick. *Educ.* locally and at Maynooth. Ordained priest, 1836. Appointed curate, Templederry, Co. Tipperary, 1842, where he remained until his death, having ultimately been made parish priest. Wrote poetry and letters to *The Nation*. President of the Confederate Club, Temple-derry. Supported Young Ireland in breach with O'Connell. In that connection he defended physical force, 1846, and slavery, 1847, in opposition to O'Connellite denunciations of both. Wrote for *United Irishman*, 1848. Briefly suspended from his parish by his bishop (Kennedy of Killaloe) for violent language at insurgent meeting, but reinstated on withdrawal of sentiments accredited to him, June 1848. Maintained close friendship with Mitchel and John Martin, and visited Paris with Mitchel, 1866. Played little part in public life after 1848. *D*. Templederry.

CHARLES J. KICKHAM (1828–1882). *B*. Mullinahone, Co. Tipperary. Largely deaf and nearly blind as result of the explosion of a powder flask which damaged his sight and hearing when he was 13 years old. One of the chief writers on the *Irish People* and one of the most prominent men in the first Fenian movement, after Stephens and O'Mahony. Sentenced to fourteen years' penal servitude, 1866. Released under partial amnesty of March, 1869, when in ill-health. Chairman of the Supreme Council of the I.R.B. and, according to Devoy, 'the unchallenged leader' of the reorganized movement. Author of many stories, sketches, and ballads, and several highly realistic novels of Tipperary life of which *Knocknagow*, the most famous, still maintains a deservedly high reputation. An effective orator and chairman of meetings in spite of his physical handicaps. Wore an ear trumpet, could read only when he held the book or paper within a few inches of his eyes and for many years carried on conversation by means of the deaf and dumb alphabet. Aware though he was of the significance of the land question to the Irish peasantry—'I am only sorry to say that they would go to hell for it', he told Parnell, thus strengthening the latter's resolve to take up the issue— Kickham rigidly opposed its introduction into the Fenian pro-gramme and also denounced co-operation with the constitution-alists. *D*. in Blackrock, Co. Dublin. Devoy called him 'the finest intellect in the Fenian movement, either in Ireland or in America'.

JAMES FINTAN LALOR (1807–1849). *B*. Tennakill, Abbeyleix. Father an O'Connellite M.P. *Educ*. Carlow Lay College. Lived for some time in France. A hunchback and asthmatic. Com-menced correspondence with Young Irelanders, 1847, differing from them in his insistence on the primacy of the land question. Influenced Mitchel, Devin Reilly and Doheny in this direction; met with suspicion elsewhere. Held that all title in land derived from the whole community. Sought to rouse the tenant-farmers by meeting, September 1847. Failed. After Mitchel's arrest edited *Irish Felon* with John Martin, June-July 1848. Imprisoned for some months under suspension of Habeas Corpus Act. Worked unsuccessfully to revive insurrection, 1849. Lalor produced the first sophisticated agitation of the land question as part of the Irish nationalist agenda, and was to have a profound influence on later advocates of social as well as political agitation and action, including Michael Davitt, Henry George, Patrick Pearse, James Connolly, and possibly Parnell.

SIR THOMAS AISKEW LARCOM (1801–1879). *Educ.* Royal Military Academy, Woolwich. Worked on ordnance survey England and Wales, 1824–26, Ireland, 1826–46. Modernized Irish Official cartography. Assisted reform work of his friend, under-secretary Thomas Drummond. Census commissioner, 1841, systematizing Irish census, with influence on future English census-taking. Commissioner of public works during the famine, 1846–49. Deputy chairman, Board of Works, 1850. Under-secretary for Ireland, 1853–68. Sought to follow Drummond's example in removing abuses. Increased intelligence effectiveness, seeking image of ubiquity of government power. K.C.B., 1860. After retirement, collected vast body of information on Ireland during his administration, which he left to learned societies, chiefly in Ireland.

MAJOR HENRI LE CARON (1841–1894). *B.* Colchester, Essex, as Thomas Beach, middle name 'Willis' or possibly 'Miller'. Ran away from home to London, 1857, and thence to Paris. Travelled to U.S.A. and enlisted in Northern army in Civil War as Henri Le Caron, 1861. Served with distinction; drawn into Fenian groups whose confidence he won. Reported initial discoveries to father who informed the British government, after which Le Caron became a salaried secret British agent. Assisted in preparations for second Fenian raid on Canada, 1870, and contributed to its destruction by his information to British and Canadian authorities. Settled near Chicago. Joined Clan na Gael and became intimate with its leaders, 1876. Acted as liaison between Devoy and the Clan, and Parnell, Patrick Egan, John O'Leary and others, during a visit to Europe, 1881. Practised as doctor, attending Michael Davitt among others. Consistently informed British authorities of all Clan activities within his knowledge. Made his final exit from U.S.A., 1888. Disclosed his true identity in witness-box when he appeared for *The Times* at the Parnell

Commission, 1889. Settled in England under governmental protective custody. Wrote impressive autobiography *Twenty-Five Years in the Secret Service. D.* London.

WILLIAM MACKEY LOMASNEY (1841–1884). *B.* Cincinnati, Ohio, of Irish-born parents. Father a Fenian. Lomasney returned to Ireland to take part in the expected rising of 1865. Arrested in Cork and permitted to leave the country together with John McCafferty. Returned, 1867, and took a leading part in the capture of Ballyknockane Constabulary barracks. When the insurgents were pressing the police to surrender, Father Neville arrived and asked Lomasney to guarantee the safety of the police if they surrendered. He replied: 'Here is my revolver, let the contents of it be put through me if one of them be injured.' After the collapse of the rising, Lomasney became famous for his raids for arms on Cork gunshops and coastguard stations, with which he plagued the British authorities for nearly twelve months after. On 7 February 1868, he was captured in Cork, acquitted on a murder charge and sentenced to twelve years' penal servitude for treason felony. Released under the amnesty of 1871, returned to the U.S., settled in Detroit as proprietor of book and stationery store. Active Clan na Gael worker in the American Land League. Made several visits to Ireland in a simple but complete disguise achieved by shaving off his beard. Took up dynamite activism. It was apparently on his third dynamite mission that he attempted to blow up London Bridge by boat with two others. All three were blown to fragments in the explosion. No bodies were ever found.

THOMAS CLARKE LUBY (1822–1901). *B.* Dublin. Joined Repeal Association in his twenties. Much influenced by *The Nation.* Assisted Lalor in his efforts to revive insurrection, 1849. One of the chief writers on the Fenian *Irish People.* Sentenced to twenty years' imprisonment, 1865. Lived briefly in Belgium after release, 1871. On his arrival in the U.S.A., threw himself into the work of the Irish Confederation. Went on several lecturing tours with Thomas Francis Bourke. Later joined Clan na Gael and was one of the Trustees of the Skirmishing Fund. John O'Leary's *Recollections of Fenians and Fenianism* is largely based on Luby's own reminiscences of Fenianism.

CAPTAIN JOHN MCCAFFERTY (1838– ?). *B.* Sandusky, Ohio, U.S.A., of Irish parents. Fought with Morgan's guerrillas on the Confederate side in American Civil War. Arrested in

Dungarvan in 1865 as he landed. Both he and Captain William Mackey Lomasney, as aliens, were liberated on condition they left the country. McCafferty returned to England, 1866, when Stephens again announced an insurrection as imminent. Organized the raid on Chester Castle, 11 February 1867, which was betrayed by Corydon. Arrested on the collier *New Draper* in Dublin Bay, 23 February, sentenced to death, commuted to life imprisonment. Released and shipped to America from London, June 1871. Attempted to persuade the Fenians to kidnap the Prince of Wales (afterwards Edward VII) and hold him captive on a sailing vessel as hostage until the British Government agreed to release the remaining Fenian prisoners, including Davitt and Condon. He is said to have visited Liverpool in connection with this scheme, which he took very seriously, even to drawing up a memorandum of the Prince's favourite amusements as it was intended to treat him with every consideration. The Clan na Gael Executive and the Supreme Council of the I.R.B. severally turned the proposal down. McCafferty was described as one of the most desperate—although also the coolest—man in the Fenian movement. Later became involved in the Invincibles, and held control for some time as the dread leader, 'No. 1'. The counterclaims of P. J. P. Tynan to have been 'No. 1' at the critical time were the pretentions of a fraud. It would seem that the Cavendish-Burke murders took place during McCafferty's leadership. He was in Paris in 1884, and was quoted in the *Irishman* as saying: 'Terrorism is the lawful weapon of the weak against the strong.' (8 March 1884).

JAMES ('Red Jim') McDERMOTT. *B.* Dublin. Believed to be illegitimate son of lawyer named O'Brien. In Irish Papal Brigade under Major Myles O'Reilly, 1859. Claimed to have fought at Castelfidardo and to have been made K.S.S. by Pius IX. Entered Fenian ranks in Ireland; visited New York and won perpetual confidence of John O'Mahony, who sent him back to Dublin as confidential secretary, 1865, at which date he probably entered British secret service. Betrayed O'Mahony's Campo Bello expedition. *Agent provocateur* in Ireland, 1883. Betrayed dynamite schemes. *Times* witness in Parnell Commission, according to Davitt, but his role as perpetrator of designs in which he later betrayed his confederates prevented his being called.

THOMAS D'ARCY McGEE (1825–1868). *B.* Carlingford, Co. Louth. *Educ.* Wexford. Emigrated to U.S.A., 1842, where he became an agitator in Boston for the repeal of the Anglo-Irish

Union. Returned to Ireland, 1845; leader-writer for *The Nation*. Supported Young Ireland in split with O'Connell, 1846, and assisted in preparation for 1848 rising. Went to Scotland to win recruits, but fled back to U.S.A. following governmental decision to arrest him. Founded various Irish-American newspapers, growing increasingly pro-clerical and anti-revolutionary. Settled in Canada, 1857, becoming active in Montreal politics. Election to Dominion Parliament, 1867; appointed Minister for Agriculture. Denounced Fenians and their invasion of Canada. Shot dead in Ottawa, apparently by a Fenian supporter. Author of various pro-nationalist and pro-Catholic poems and histories of Irish and American events.

TERENCE BELLEW MCMANUS (1823–1860). *B.* Co. Fermanagh. Member of Repeal Association '82 Club, 1844. Supported Young Ireland against O'Connell. With Smith O'Brien at Ballingarry, 1848. Arrested on board America-bound vessel at Cork. Tried and sentenced to death, sentence commuted to transportation for life. In Van Dieman's Land, 1849–52, whence he escaped with Meagher to San Francisco. Failed as shipping agent. *D.* there in poverty. His funeral was to prove of greater significance than his life.

JOHN MARTIN (1812–1875). *B.* Lougherne, near Newry, Co. Down. *Educ.* Trinity College, Dublin. Visited U.S. and Canada, 1839–40. Joined Repeal Association, 1844. Identified with Young Ireland. Started the *Irish Felon* in succession to Mitchel's *United Irishman*, 1848. Arrested, July, and found guilty of treason-felony, August; transported to Tasmania, 1849, on ten-year sentence; released with Smith O'Brien, 1854. Permitted to return to Ireland, 1856, and settled there once more, 1858. Maintained links with Mitchel, whom he met again in Paris, 1859. Founded the National League together with The O'Donoghue; but the League collapsed under Fenian attack a few years after its inauguration in 1864. Opposed to Fenians, but assisted in Manchester Martyrs' funeral procession as graveside orator, 1867. Visited Mitchel in U.S., 1869–70; lionized in the U.S., where he lectured to obtain funds for the dependents of the Manchester Martyrs. Founder-member of Home Government Association, 1870; elected M.P. for Meath, 1871, as Home Ruler; re-elected, 1874. Vigorously supported Mitchel's claim to take his seat, 1875. Contracted bronchitis at Mitchel's funeral and died nine days later in Mitchel's old home at Dromolane, near Newry. In the ensuing by-election his seat was retained by the Home Rulers, whose candidate was C. S. Parnell.

THOMAS FRANCIS MEAGHER (1825–1867). *B.* Waterford. Father a supporter of O'Connell, and M.P. Young Meagher became identified with Young Ireland. Deeply engaged in 1848 rising; sentenced to death for high treason, sentence commuted to transportation to Tasmania. Escaped to the U.S.A., 1852. Associated with Mitchel in anti-clerical and anti-abolitionist journalism, but supported Union cause in American Civil War. His regiment cut to pieces at Fredericksburg, 1862, in an engagement which historians believe did much to raise the status of Irish-Americans in American eyes. Gazetted brigadier-general, 1862. Nominated Secretary of Montana territory after war, and territorial Governor, 1866. Drowned in Missouri in fall from steamer. His speech of 28 July 1846, defending the use of physical force against Daniel O'Connell's insistence on constitutionalism, made the most dramatic moment in the events immediately preceding O'Connell's breach with Young Ireland, and also won him the name 'Meagher of the Sword'.

GENERAL F. F. MILLEN. According to John O'Mahony (letter in the *Irish People*, 11 February 1871), Millen got in touch with him in 1860 when an officer in the Mexican army, and was active in New York from 1865 onwards. Sent to Ireland, he was made President of the Irish Military Council by Stephens, 1865. Ordered back to America by Stephens when the news reached him in jail that Millen had been selected to act as his deputy. Rejoined Mexican army as Brigadier-General of Artillery but retired, 1866. Became Executive Secretary, Fenian Brotherhood, under O'Mahony, also C.O., Legion of St Patrick. Still regarding himself as chief military officer I.R.B., sent about 500 rifles to the London section of the Fenians, conditional on their supporting O'Mahony, 1870. Their leader, James J. O'Kelly, became friendly with Millen following O'Kelly's arrival in New York, 1871, and brought him to the Cuban insurrection on behalf of the New York *Herald*. Millen was one of the Clan na Gael delegation of five who visited the Russian Minister in Washington, M. Shiskin, to seek the aid of Russia for Ireland, 1876. Devoy later criticitized the Clan Executive for having appointed Millen to this delegation. Millen also sought to exploit British difficulties in Afghanistan in the Fenian interest, 1877, and later in the same year was drumming up recruits for an insurrection in Ireland to take place in the event of an Anglo-

Russian war. Foiled by the Congress of Berlin, 1878, he next sought to inflame border disputes between British Honduras and Mexico, and the next year volunteered to travel to South Africa to stir up trouble among the Boers. Visited Ireland, 1879, and toured the I.R.B., observing its weakness; he was in the capacity of military envoy of the Clan. His ensuing recommendations involved suggestions that the eventual Irish insurrection should include risings in India and Australia. His mission was evidently resented by the I.R.B., Davitt and Devoy. Millen was defended by Alexander Sullivan of Chicago, John O'Leary and Dr Carroll, and threatened public proceedings against Devoy in view of the latter's attacks, 1882. He was involved in an abortive effort to create a dynamite outrage during Queen Victoria's jubilee, 1887. 'An Adventurer' (Devoy); 'An honourable and brave man and a good Irishman' (John O'Leary).

JOHN MITCHEL (1815–1875). *B.* near Dungiven, Co. Derry. Son of dissident Presbyterian minister. *Educ.* Newry, Co. Down and Trinity College, Dublin. Practised as solicitor, Banbridge, Co. Down, 1840–45. Joined Repeal Association, 1843. Joined staff of *The Nation* on Davis's death, 1845. Supported Young Ireland in split with O'Connell, 1846. Formed friendly acquaintance with Thomas Carlyle. Left *The Nation* in quest of more vigorously anti-governmental policy and founded the *United Irishman*, 1847–48. Arrested and sentenced to transportation, May, 1848. Wrote impressive *Jail Journal* (published 1854) while serving sentence in Bermuda and Tasmania. Escaped to U.S.A., 1853. Founder and editor of *Citizen*, New York, 1854–55, opposing anti-Catholicism, the temporal rule of the Papacy, British government of Ireland, and defending Negro slavery. Settled in Tennessee, 1855. Founded and edited *Southern Citizen*, 1857–59, on same lines. Transferred to Washington, D.C., 1859. Went to Paris, 1860, with hopes of Irish benefit from a putative English embroilment in French-Austrian conflict. Returned to New York, 1862. Withdrew behind Confederate lines, supported the South, by ambulance work and writing. Briefly imprisoned on conclusion of war, 1865. Joined Fenians on release and went to Paris to act as financial agent for the movement. Disillusioned by Fenian inefficiency, resigned in June, 1866. Returned to New York where he founded and edited *Irish Citizen*, 1867–72. Returned to Ireland, 1874, and again in February, 1875, having agreed to be nominated as M.P. for Co. Tipperary with the proviso he would not take his seat. Elected unopposed, unseated as convicted felon, re-elected by 4–1 majority. *D*. Newry, some days after re-election. Second only to Davis among the Young Irelanders as an ideological influence on subsequent nationalist generations.

BISHOP DAVID MORIARTY (1814–1877). *B*. Derryvrin, Kilcarah, Co. Kerry. *Educ*. Boulogne and Maynooth. Vice-rector and professor of sacred scripture in Irish College, Paris, 1839–45 (on his ordination). Rector, Foreign Missionary College of All Hallows, Drumcondra, Dublin, 1845–54. Appointed coadjutor bishop of Kerry, 1854; appointed bishop of Kerry, 1856. Became famous for his pronouncements on public questions. Denounced Fenianism, and sought to exert his political influence against the Home Rule party, which severely discomfited him by its success in his diocese during the election of 1874. Opposed the move to define papal infallibility at the 1st Vatican Council, 1870, on the ground that it was not opportune so to do, but accepted the decision once it had been promulgated.

DENIS DOWLING MULCAHY (1833–1900). Of Tipperary background. Member of *Irish People* staff. Arrested in 1865 raid and sentenced to ten years' penal servitude. Practised as a medical man in the United States for many years after his release in *c*. 1871. Discovered John O'Mahony starving and neglected in a New York tenement some months before his death. Mulcahy was one of those who accompanied O'Mahony's remains to Ireland. This later led to a lawsuit between him and the Trustees of the Skirmishing Fund, and subsequent bitter personal enmity between him and the Devoy group. *D*. Newark, N.J.

WILLIAM SMITH O'BRIEN (1803–1864). *B*. Dromoland, Co. Clare. Son of baronet, brother became Baron Inchiquin. Took middle name 'Smith' from maternal uncle whose estate at Cahirmoyle, Co. Limerick, he inherited. *Educ*. Harrow and Trinity College, Dublin. M.P. for Ennis, 1828–48. Not openly for Repeal of the Union before 1843. Associated thereafter with Young Ireland. Led an Irish delegation to Paris, March 1848. Sentenced to be hanged, drawn and quartered, October 1848, for his part in the '48 rising, sentence commuted to transportation for life to Tasmania. Pardoned in 1854, on condition of his not returning to the United Kingdom; settled in Brussels. Release made unconditional, 1856, and on 8 July of that year he returned to Ireland. Took little active part in Irish politics thereafter. Visited U.S.A., 1859, where he publicly opposed slavery. Advocated neutrality for the Irish-Americans in the American Civil War. Visited Poland, 1863. *D.* at Bangor, Wales.

CHARLES UNDERWOOD O'CONNELL (? –1902). *B.* Offaly. Emigrated to U.S.A. Served in American Civil War. Arrested when he landed in Cobh in 1865 with papers entrusted to him by Stephens dealing with the organization of Fenianism in the United States Army. Sentenced to ten years' penal servitude, part of which he spent in Portland and Millbank with Devoy. Released following amnesty agitation, 1870, and travelled to U.S.A. with Devoy and Rossa, 1871. Opposed Devoy's alliance with Parnell. *D.* New York.

FRANK HUGH O'DONNELL (1848–1916). *B.* Co. Donegal. *Educ.* Queen's College, Galway. Elected M.P. for Galway city, 1874, but unseated on grounds of clerical intimidation having been employed on his behalf. M.P. for Dungarvan, 1877–83. Despite his extreme 'ultramontane' clericalism and support for Tory imperialism at this time, O'Donnell quickly became noted as one of the most implacable of the obstructionists in Butt's Home Rule party. Social conservatism and extreme egotism prevented his maintaining close links with Parnell as the land agitation got under way. The Devoy group showed some interest in him as a possible ally alternative to Parnell in 1877, but found he did not improve on acquaintance. His individualism and enthusiasm for a variety of crusades won him the nickname 'Crank Hugh O'Donnell' (inevitably, from Tim Healy). His personal jealousy of Parnell increased, and his self-adulation made it impossible for him to accept the discipline of the new party under the iron control of Parnell, whom he later termed 'my runaway errand-boy'. His libel action against Walter, proprietor of *The Times*, for alleged references to himself in the 'Parnellism and Crime' articles (which included the Pigott forgeries), was unsuccessful and enabled the Unionist government to set up the Special Commission to investigate the Parnell movement; the absurdity of O'Donnell's action led to suspicion, possibly unjust, that he undertook the action to injure Parnell. Ultimately became a violent critic of clerical influence in Irish education. His *History of the Irish Parliamentary Party*, 2 Vols. (1910), is detailed and useful on the period 1873–80, but is poor on the later phases. Of it Conor Cruise O'Brien has written that it 'contains shrewd comments, but is marred by extreme bitterness . . . and an egoism which leads the writer to magnify the importance of events with which he himself was connected and to distort his own role'.

O'Donnell was a fine speaker with an incredible store of knowledge on a multiplicity of subjects. *D*. London.

DIARMUID (*Anglicised as* JEREMIAH) O'DONOVAN ROSSA (1831–1915). *B*. Roscarbery, Co. Cork. Spoke only Irish in early life. Learnt English at school and was taught to read and write Irish by his father. Apprenticed as grocer, later opened his own store. Organized 'Phoenix Society' in Skibbereen. Arrested with others on charges arising out of it, December 1858. Released, July 1859. His business in ruins, visited America, and returned to Ireland in 1863 to act as business manager of the *Irish People*. Became one of the most energetic organizers of Fenianism. Was believed by Devoy to have sworn in more members than any other ten men in Ireland. Travelled through England, Ireland and Scotland, and again visited America. Put on trial in 1865, dismissed his counsel and conducted his own defence. His address to the jury lasted eight hours during which he read through a great part of the *Irish People* file, selecting in particular those articles which denounced Judge Keogh, who tried him, as a political renegade. Sentenced by Keogh to penal servitude for life. His fight against his prison treatment—told later in his own *Prison Life*—attracted international attention. Was elected M.P. for Tipperary in 1869 as a demonstration in favour of the Amnesty movement. The story of how he had been handcuffed for 35 days aroused world-wide reactions and forced Gladstone to release the Fenian prisoners. After release travelled to U.S.A. in 1871, where he engaged in the hotel business and started his own paper, the *United Irishman*. In 1877 he was Head Centre of the Fenian Brotherhood from which position he later resigned. For the next years he advocated a policy of terrorism in England, claiming credit for ineffectual gunpowder explosions. His organization and convention of the 'United Irishmen' in 1880 led to an open break with Devoy and expulsion from Clan na Gael. Strongly opposed alliance with Parnell and the constitutionalists. Wounded, 1885, when a demented Englishwoman tried to shoot him. Was on the worst of terms with most of his fellow Fenians for the rest of his life, but was reconciled with Devoy shortly before his death, at Staten Island, New York. Buried in Glasnevin, Dublin, in 1915, amid scenes reminiscent of the McManus funeral; many of those prominent on the occasion played a major part in the next year's insurrection.

EDMUND O'DONOVAN (1844–1883). Son of the Gaelic scholar John O'Donovan. Fenian, linguist, war correspondent. Served

25

in French Foreign Legion, 1870–1. Described Carlist rising, 1873, Russo-Turkish war, 1877. Wrote *The Merv Oasis*—his adventures in Central Asia, 1882. Supposed to have perished with Hicks Pasha in Soudan, 1883.

RICHARD O'GORMAN (1826–1895). *B*. Dublin. Father an insurgent in 1798 insurrection and later supporter of O'Connell. *Educ*. Trinity College, Dublin. Joined Irish Confederation and assisted in drive for 1848 insurrection. Sought to raise Limerick in support of Smith O'Brien, with some indications of possible success which were dashed on the news of Ballingarry. Escaped to U.S.A. Called to New York bar. Practised in partnership with John Blake Dillon. Counsel to New York Corporation after 1869; judge of the Superior Court of New York until his death. O'Gorman represented the 'lace curtain' element in Irish-American nationalism, and was extremely critical of later movements whose American support possessed more of a prole-tarian cast. Associated with Tammany Hall—in whose interest he made a brief, abortive effort to win political capital from the arrival of Devoy and Rossa in the U.S.A. after their release. Otherwise his relations with the Fenians were extremely bad, and he allowed his name to be used against Parnell when the latter toured the U.S.A. for the Land League in 1880. Kept himself in the Irish-American public eye by St Patrick's Day orations. *D*. New York.

JAMES J. O'KELLY (1845–1916). *B*. Dublin. Joined the Fenian organization, 1860, and became a member of the Supreme Council towards the end of 1867. Elected Captain of the London Irish Volunteers, 1862, and soon afterwards went to Paris and joined the Foreign Legion. Served in Mexico, taking part in several battles during Napoleon III's Mexican adventure, 1864. Devoy sent him a letter which reached him six months later, to inform him that Stephens had announced an insurrection for 1865. O'Kelly left the Foreign Legion, and, after many exciting adventures, reached London on the eve of the 1867 rising, which he opposed on the grounds that the insurgents were insufficiently armed. Helped reorganize I.R.B. after collapse of rising; acted as London correspondent of the *Irishman*. Went to Paris shortly after outbreak of the Franco-Prussian war; appointed Colonel in the French army with authority to recruit for an Irish brigade which he offered to organize, having convinced the French military authorities he had been captured by Mexican guerrillas and hence was unable to fulfil his duties in the Legion—which was true, except the capture had taken place after his desertion. Sailed to New York after surrender of Paris, joining New York *Herald* in which he rose rapidly to special correspondent during the Spanish-Cuban war, 1873, in which he was arrested and courtmartialled as a spy by the Spaniards. On parole in Spain, but revoked his parole and fled to Gibraltar, which he concluded could be captured by Spaniards with Irish-American Fenian support. The Spaniards declined such an arrangement, 1877. O'Kelly abandoned his successful profession as journalist in the U.S. to settle in England, after which following I.R.B. refusal to assume activist attitude, he turned to Parnell, whose closest political friend he later became. Elected M.P. for North Roscommon, a position he held with one short interval until his death. Despite his resignation from the I.R.B. and acceptance of his seat in the Commons, he retained good relations with many Fenians until he followed Redmond and the Irish party in supporting the British war effort, 1914.

JOHN O'LEARY (1830–1907). *B.* Tipperary town. Son of a prosperous merchant, who left him a small private income. *Educ.* Carlow, Trinity College, Dublin, and Queen's College, Galway, which left him with the foible that only college-educated men could be revolutionary leaders, much to the amusement of his Fenian colleagues. Took part in Lalor's attempt to revive an insurrection, 1849. Declined to continue studies for the Bar when he discovered an oath of allegiance was necessary. Released by Stephens and his successors from the obligation of taking the Fenian oath. Named with Luby and Kickham by Stephens to the Executive of Three with power to act in Stephens's absence in America. Editor of the *Irish People*. Sentenced to twenty years' penal servitude, 1865, on which occasion he preserved a demeanour of persistent refusal either to be intimidated or to lose his dignity. Released in 1871, following Amnesty Agitation. Went to Belgium, and later Paris. He was a close friend of John O'Mahony and always a critical admirer of Stephens. Acted as financial agent of the movement in Paris. Visited U.S.A. in 1859, 1872 and 1880—the first time at Stephens's request to assist O'Mahony and act as a link between the home and American-Fenian bodies, and the last time as envoy of the I.R.B. Returned to Ireland when his sentence expired in 1885, settled in Dublin and became president of the Young Ireland Society, devoting himself to national, industrial and literary activities. Strongly opposed to the Land League and the Irish Parliamentary Party, although he had a liking for Parnell. Denounced dynamite campaigns, assassination, agitation of social questions by nationalists, compromise with constitutionalism. His idealism is said to have inspired Yeats's literary generation.

JOHN O'MAHONY (1816?–1877). *B.* Clonkilla, near Mitchelstown, Co. Cork. *Educ.* Cork and Trinity College, Dublin. Organized some 2,000 men in his own district in Tipperary during the 1848 rising, but was prevented from utilizing them before its collapse. Fled to Paris, where he remained with Stephens until 1852. Emigrated thence to New York, where he remained until his death. Head Centre of the Fenian Brotherhood in America from its foundation in 1858. The previous year he had translated Keating's History of Ireland in a version long famous for its Gaelic scholarship. During the American Civil War, O'Mahony organized a regiment of Fenians, the Ninety-Ninth, of the New York National Guard, and was appointed honorary Colonel. Devoy summed up O'Mahony as a dreamer and not a good judge of men, although he knew the Irish Question theoretically better than any Irishman of his day. His evil genius was the notorious spy, 'Red Jim' MacDermott, whom he insisted on trusting after his exposure. His last days were spent in poverty and Denis Dowling Mulcahy found him dying in a fireless New York garret. His body was brought back to Ireland and buried in a great public funeral. 'I believe', wrote Kickham to Devoy of O'Mahony on 29 April 1876, 'no Irishman had a better claim to the name of patriot than he has'.

JOHN BOYLE O'REILLY (1844–1890). *B.* Dowth Castle, Co. Meath. Worked as journalist in England. Enlisted in 10th Hussars at Dundalk, 1863. Although he was already a Fenian, his motive for enlisting was pure love of soldiering. In October 1865, was asked by John Devoy to win over the hundred Irishmen in his regiment to Fenianism, and by the following February had won over 80 men, at which point he was arrested, courtmartialled, sentenced to death (sentence commuted to 20 years' penal servitude). After 3 attempts at escape from prison, was transported to Western Australia, 1868; escaped to U.S.A., 1869. Joined Boston *Pilot*, 1870, where his first assignment was as war correspondent to the second Fenian raid on Canada, June 1870, which he sharply criticized in his dispatches. Editor and proprietor, *Pilot*, 1876. Played minor part in Boston Democratic politics, and obtained celebrity as poet. Ceased membership of the Fenian organization, 1870, but retained interest. Devoy

states he was trusted and consulted by the leaders of the Clan na
Gael on every important issue from the rescue of Fenian military
prisoners in 1876 and throughout the years of the 'New Departure', and support for Parnell and the Land League. *D.*
Boston, from an accidental overdose of chloral.

JOHN AUGUSTUS O'SHEA (1839–1905). Irish writer and journalist. Worked for the London *Standard* and various other journals.
Achieved close links with Mitchel, Stephens and others. His
Leaves from the Life of a Special Correspondent contains intimate
portraits of several of them. Visited U.S.A. briefly in 1884, but
was severely shaken by the contrast between the gentlemanly
nature of London journalism and the exacting toil required in
the American branch of the profession.

CHARLES STEWART PARNELL (1846–1891). *B.* Avondale, Co.
Wicklow. M.P. for Meath, 1875–80, for Cork, 1880–91. Obstruc-
tionist in House of Commons, 1876–80. Won support for such
Fenians as favoured alliance with constitutionalists. Supported
Davitt's land agitation; President, National Land League of
Ireland, 1879–82, and of its more conservative successor, the
National League. Obtained widespread support in visit to U.S.A.,
Jan.–Mar. 1880, his tour being organized by Devoy among
others. Chairman, Home Rule parliamentary party, 1880–90.
Imprisoned, 1881–2. Forced British government to adopt remedial
legislation on land ownership, 1881, 1882, 1886, 1890. Brought
down Liberal and Tory governments, 1885, 1886. Achieved
alliance with Liberals, and assurance of Home Rule legislation
when they returned to power after their initial defeat on the
issue, 1886. Almost ruined *The Times* in forged letters scandal
and enquiry, 1887–90. Found guilty as co-respondent in *O'Shea
vs O'Shea & Parnell*, 1889–90; his continued leadership opposed
by Gladstone and thereafter by party majority; fought to his
death to retain leadership. *D.* Brighton.

RICHARD PIGOTT (1828–1889). Origins obscure. Journalist and
proprietor of the *Irishman*, the *Flag of Ireland* and the *Shamrock*.
Assisted O'Donovan Rossa during his imprisonment, lent money
to Mrs O'Donovan Rossa to travel to the U.S.A. in 1867 and
published in the *Irishman* letters from Rossa exposing his ill-
treatment. Published letters from Rossa attacking A. M. Sullivan
which led to libel actions. Seems to have appropriated Fenian
or allied funds entrusted to him at various times. Attacked
apparent deviations from pure Fenianism, including the link

between Davitt, Devoy and Parnell, 1878–82. Sold his papers to Parnell. Subsequently engaged in selling his 'disclosures' on Fenian-Parnellite conspiracy to Unionist and landlord publicists, such as Houston, Bagenal, Figgis the publisher, etc., most of whom he swindled. Dabbled in pornography, endeavoured to extract money from Parnell's sympathizers and enemies by all means, blackmail included. Forged letters implicating Parnell in the Phoenix Park murders which he sold to *The Times* (via Irish Unionist agents). Admitted having done so after he collapsed under cross-examination in the subsequent Special Commission on 'Parnellism and Crime'. Fled to Madrid, where he committed suicide just before being arrested. His efforts to raise money seem to have been based on a desire to keep his sons at the Jesuit school, Clongowes Wood College, where they were being educated.

THOMAS DEVIN REILLY (1824–1854). *B.* Monaghan town. Settled, Dublin, 1836; *educ.* there. Student but not graduate of Trinity College, Dublin. Joined *The Nation*, 1845. His second article for it was review of Blanc's *Dix Ans* (*The Nation*, 27 December 1845, 17 January 1846) which won him recognition. Backed Young Ireland in split with O'Connell; left *The Nation* with Mitchel to write for the latter's *United Irishman*. Arrested, May 1848; allowed bail and escaped to U.S.A. after assisting John Martin on *Irish Felon*. Worked with the pro-labour Boston *Protective Union*, 1850; wrote highly successful articles on international affairs for *American Review*, 1851–52, and *Democratic Review*. Edited Washington *Union*, 1853; appointed to Land Office by President Franklin Pierce. *D.* Washington.

WILLIAM FRANCIS ROANTREE (1829?–1918). *B.* Leixlip, Co. Kildare. Served in the American Navy and saw service with General Walker in Nicaragua before he returned to Ireland in 1861. His Leixlip I.R.B. circle was one of the largest in Ireland and consisted of 2,000 men. Stephens appointed him to organize Fenianism in the British Army after Pagan O'Leary's arrest in 1864. Roantree was arrested in September 1865, and sentenced to ten years' penal servitude. Released under the amnesty of 1871, went to U.S. and finally settled in Philadelphia where he became traveller to a wholesaler's firm. In Clan na Gael in the later 1870's; befriended by Dr William Carroll. His economic circumstances appear to have worsened towards the end of the

1880's. Returned to Ireland about 1900 and was employed by the Dublin Corporation. *D*. Dublin.

COLONEL WILLIAM R. ROBERTS. An associate of John O'Mahony, by profession 'a successful dry goods merchant who was vain and shallow but showy' (Devoy, *Recollections*, p. 268). In the conflict of the American wing of Fenianism against O'Mahony, he became the rallying-point of opposition. The change of the Fenian Constitution on 16 October 1865, in Philadelphia, reduced O'Mahony's formerly autocratic power as Head Centre to subjection to a two-thirds majority of the newly-created Senate in the case of any disputed measure. The chairman or president of the Senate, Roberts, became *ex officio* vice-president of the Brotherhood, and could, if occasion arose, take the place of the Head Centre or President. Soon afterwards, O'Mahony and the Senate clashed on his proposal to issue bonds to finance a rising in Ireland, then thought imminent. When O'Mahony heard of the arrest of Stephens, he issued the bonds on his own responsibility, whereupon the Senate deposed him and elected Roberts to his place. O'Mahony retained control of the funds and the Fenian headquarters in New York, the Moffat Mansion; but the Senate managed to seize the Fenian arsenal, and thereby proceeded with their new tactical plan. Its members felt an invasion of Canada was more effective and practicable than a rising in Ireland. The failure of the first Fenian raid on Canada in June 1866, discredited the Roberts faction. The following year a small number of Fenians from both wings came together in the organization known as the Clan na Gael or United Brotherhood. Colonel Roberts himself eventually retired into private life.

ROSSA—*see* O'DONOVAN ROSSA

JOHN RUTHERFORD (1829–1889). *B*. Galway. Emigrated to Liverpool, where he married in 1862. Settled in London, 1864. Worked on the *Pall Mall Gazette* and the *Cornhill Magazine*. His first volume was a study of The Troubadours, dealing with their loves, lyrics and social influence (published 1873). May have received some assistance from Sir Robert Anderson of the Home Office with his *Fenian Conspiracy;* at one point Anderson was credited with being the real author of the book but he denied this. After concluding his volumes on the Fenians he went on to journalism on London lower-class life, one of the products of which was *Sketches from Shady Places* (1879), which he issued under the pseudonym Thor Fredur (anagram of Rutherford). His only other work on Fenianism appeared in the *Whitehall Review,* 29 Nov. 1879: 'Passages in the career of a Fenian Conspirator'. Information on his life was obtained from his widow by the London *Star* in 1910.

JOHN SAVAGE (1828–1888). *B.* Dublin. Joined the revolutionary movement in 1848 when studying art there. Issued an inflammatory journal *The Patriot* in April; it was at once seized and suppressed. Wrote nationalist poems for Mitchel's *United Irishman* and Kevin Izod O'Doherty's *Irish Tribune*. Helped to found *Irish Felon*. Aided John O'Mahony in guerrilla attempts after collapse of Ballingarry. Escaped to New York, November 1848; won position within a week as proof reader on Greeley's New York *Tribune*. Associated with Mitchel's *Citizen,* 1854, and the same year married Louise, daughter of the sea captain Samuel Chester Reid who has been credited with designing the present form of the American flag. Savage was principal leader writer on Washington *States Journal,* 1857. His writings include '*98 and '48* (1856) and *Fenian Heroes and Martyrs* (1868). Wrote sketches of likely Presidential candidates, *Our Leading Representative Men* (1860), one of which he later worked into a *Life* of Andrew Johnson, who afterwards proposed him, without success, for the post of U.S. Consul at Leeds. Refused offers from leading Confederates to join their ranks, joined the 69th regiment, and was captain in General Corcoran's staff throughout the Civil War. An energetic Fenian organizer in the U.S., through which he travelled widely. A popular speaker. Succeeded John O'Mahony for a time in the leadership of the Fenian Brotherhood, sometimes known as the O'Mahony-Savage wing. Honorary LL.D. (Fordham), 1879. *D.* Laurelside, near Spraigueville, Pennsylvania.

ALEXANDER MARTIN SULLIVAN (1830–1884). *B.* Bantry, Co. Cork. Clerk on relief works during famine, 1846–47. Joined Confederate Club, giving enthusiastic non-violent support to Smith O'Brien in 1848. Journalist, Dublin and Liverpool, 1853–55. Assistant editor, *Nation,* 1855; editor and sole proprietor, 1858. Opposed Fenianism, but briefly imprisoned in 1868 for editorial attack on the execution of the 'Manchester Martyrs', Allen, Larkin and O'Brien. Founder member of Home Rule movement. M.P. for Louth, 1874–81; for Meath, 1881–84. Called to Irish bar, 1876, 'special call' to English bar, 1877, following which he resided in England. Supported Parnell on obstruction but was permitted to stand for Meath unpledged to support him as leader, 1880. Relinquished control of *Nation* to his brother Timothy, 1876. Resigned seat for reasons of health, 1881. *D.* Dublin. His *The Story of Ireland* (1870) was a standard nationalistic popular history in its day; his *New Ireland* (1877) is still of value to historians as a vivid, impressionistic account of the Ireland he knew. Not to be confused with Alexander Sullivan of Chicago, who had no connection with him.

TIMOTHY DANIEL SULLIVAN (1827–1914). *B.* Bantry, Co. Cork. Brother of A. M. Sullivan, with whom he worked on *The Nation* which ultimately came under his control. His connections with Fenianism were apparently closer than those of his brother, and Dublin Castle believed him to have been 'an active agent in 1864–65'. Whatever the truth in this, his subsequent place in Fenian history exists as a writer of patriotic ballads of which the most famous was 'God save Ireland', written on the trial of the Manchester Martyrs, and subsequently for many years regarded as the Irish national anthem although it never obtained official recognition as such after Ireland won her independence. Associated with Parnell, Sullivan won election to Parliament in 1880 and was one of the very few M.P.s of senior rank in Parnell's party to be paid a salary by it. Naturally conservative, he was one of the most prominent of Parnell's lieutenants in early years. He was generally regarded as a clericalist, but it might be more true to say that personal beliefs led him to take up attitudes of the same kind as were held by supporters of Parnell among the clergy. He was one of the very few party members to repudiate Parnell immediately after the divorce and not merely subsequent to Gladstone's intervention. He was M.P. for Westmeath, Dublin and Donegal at various times, and became Lord Mayor of Dublin. His *Recollections of Troubled Times in Irish Politics* (1905) is of moderate value; as literature, it lacks the distinction and persuasive power of his brother's writing. Wrote a *History of Bantry* (1908). *Speeches from the Dock* (1867) edited by A. M. Sullivan and himself became one of the most famous and most widely-disseminated volumes of Irish patriotic literature. *D.* Dublin.

WILLIAM STEUART TRENCH (1808–1872). Nephew of first Lord Ashtown. *Educ.* Trinity College, Dublin. Gold medallist, Royal Agricultural Society. Land Agent on the Shirley estates, Co. Monaghan, 1843–45; on the Lansdowne estates, Co. Kerry, 1849–67; on the estates of Lord Bath in Co. Monaghan, 1851–68. Published his *Realities of Irish Life* in the latter year. A keen and observant witness, a writer of distinction, and a commentator of insight as well as vivid descriptive powers, he combined a resolute front on business matters with a capacity to be aware of suffering in an objective fashion. He did not, however, permit his consciousness of peasant poverty to lessen his zeal for the exaction of rent. He had some sense of the need for public works and rural improvements, and played a part in their furtherance.

JOHN WODEHOUSE, *first Earl of* KIMBERLEY (1826–1902). *B.* Norfolk, England. *Educ.* Eton and Oxford. Succeeded grandfather as Baron Wodehouse. Followed family tradition of Whig politics, serving in Aberdeen and Palmerston administrations. Lord Lieutenant of Ireland, 1864–66, where he was noted for his vigour in dealing with Fenianism. Created Earl of Kimberley, 1866. Lord privy seal, 1868–70; colonial secretary, 1870–74 (when the South African city was named after him), and 1880–82; secretary of State for India, 1882–85, 1886; and 1892–94, all under Gladstone. Foreign secretary under Rosebery, 1894–95. One of the very few peers who had held cabinet office under Gladstone to support him on Home Rule. *D.* London.

INDEX

denotes entry in biographical notes